I'd do it again...

I'd do it again...

The Journey of a Medical Missionary in Central Africa

MARGERY BENEDICT

Printed in Canada
by
Guardian BOOKS

PERMISSIONS

Although the information presented in this book is historical fact as remembered by Margery Benedict, a few of the character names have been changed.

All Scripture quotations in this book, except those noted otherwise, are from the King James Version.

National Library of Canada Cataloguing in Publication

Benedict, Margery, 1924-

   I'd do it again : the journey of a medical missionary in central Africa / Margery Benedict.

ISBN 1-55306-527-1.--ISBN 1-55306-529-8 (LSI ed.)

   1. Benedict, Margery, 1924- 2. Missionaries, Medical—Africa, Central—Biography. 3. Missionaries, Medical—United States—Biography. I. Title.

R722.32.B45A3 2002   266'.02373067   C2002-905411-7

First printing November 2002
Second printing April 2003

Guardian Books is an imprint of *Essence Publishing*. For more information, contact: 20 Hanna Court, Belleville, Ontario, Canada K8P 5J2.
Phone: 1-800-238-6376. Fax: (613) 962-3055.
E-mail: publishing@essencegroup.com
Internet: www.essencegroup.com

ACKNOWLEDGMENTS

Many thanks to:
The team who lovingly critiqued, edited and proofread my attempts at writing this book.

Peggy Love - administrative assistant at the Union
Gospel Mission in Seattle, Washington

Jean Scott - retired missionary from Village Missions,
based in Dallas, Oregon

Rose Reynoldson - retired professor from Seattle
Pacific University

Paul Benedict - my brother, retired teacher from
Ferndale High School in Washington, and
short term missionary

Janice E. Manual - freelance editor in Arizona who
completed the line edit

Anna Herrman - retired teacher, partner in their family
farm, and trustee of Western Baptist College

To Aleta Widows, who willingly typed all the many versions of the manuscript and who provided such encouragement when I did not think the book would be interesting to others. Aleta's uplifting emails were posted above my desk as an inspiration to "keep going" until the end.

And to the inmates who attended the Sunday Chapel services at Monroe State Prison who prayed for me and encouraged me when at times my dizziness kept me from working on this project.

DEDICATION

This effort is dedicated to my parents, John and Margie Beck Benedict
who taught me to love God
and
to all their descendants

Mother wanted to be a missionary to Africa, but with her marriage
and nine children this was not possible. The Lord led my parents to raise
their family so that some of us would become missionaries of the
Good News of Christ Jesus.

To Robin Herrman who started me on the journey of writing my
autobiography, who found the typists, the graphic artist, and the printer,
assembled the final version of the manuscript and continually
encouraged me that it could be done.

To all who prayed and gave so that it would be possible for me to serve
under Baptist Mid-Missions between 1950 and 1995.

CONTENTS

FOREWORD

Anyone who has dined with Margery Benedict leaves the table hungry only for more of her fascinating stories describing the 45 years spent ministering to the African people. This book is a collection of those stories, wonderfully told in her own unique style.

During her years in Africa, Margery wrote over one-thousand letters "back home" to her parents. Her recollections were refreshed by reviewing these letters and the hundreds of photographs taken during her years of service. She also drew from the events described in many of her *prayer letters* sent three to four times per year to her supporters in the United States.

So what does it take to be a successful missionary to a foreign country, where many of the basic things that you and I take for granted have never been heard of? Inside this book you will find out. Margery's *can-do* attitude, often found in successful people, is combined with the humbleness of a servant. Her adaptability is recognizable not only in her stories of Africa, but also through the use of her ministry skills in Seattle, Washington.

After returning from Africa, Margery lived for several years in Seattle. I marvel at her versatility—from Central African Republic with slow going rutted roads, few vehicles, and a pace of life marked by years, not seconds—to Capital Hill in Seattle with crowded streets, competitive parking, eight-lane freeways, and a frantic pace to match. Everywhere she goes, she finds a way to serve her Lord.

"As the Scriptures tell us, 'Anyone who believes in him will not be disappointed.' Jew and Gentile are the same in this respect. They all have the same Lord, who generously gives his riches to all who ask for them. For 'Anyone who calls on the name of the Lord will be saved.'

But how can they call on him to save them unless they believe in him? And how can they believe in him if they have never heard about him? And how can they hear about him unless someone tells them? And how will anyone go and tell them without being sent? That is what the Scriptures mean when they say,

'How beautiful are the feet of those who bring good news!"
Romans 10:11-15, NLT

— Robin Herrman

Through Margery's Eyes

I stood on Sibut hill one day and gazed upon a scene
Spread out before me like a painting on a picture screen;
'Twas beautiful beyond compare and took my breath away,
As I saw the panorama at my feet that bright day.

Birds, trees, grass, flowers, butterflies—colors of every shade,
And farther on the brown grass roofs lined up as on parade;
Little black dots moving around, and though so far away;
I guessed that I'd see some of them at the clinic that day.

And as I looked there came to me the mem'ry of my Lord
And He, too, stood upon a hill, and there His love outpoured.
"O Lord," I prayed, "Help me to love these sheep who've gone astray
Just as Thou didst Jerusalem there on that hill that day.

"May they see Thee in my life and my love for them
That eagerness to follow Thee from this contact will stem;
And then at last all the redeemed before Thy throne shall stand,
May there be many precious souls gathered from this great land."

—Helen Metzler

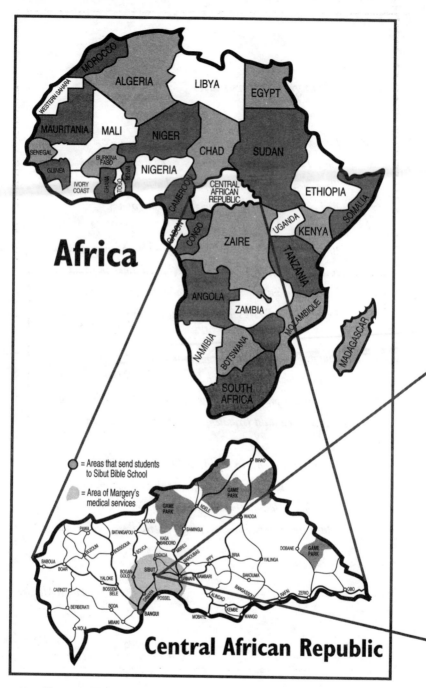

Africa

MOROCCO
WESTERN SAHARA
ALGERIA
LIBYA
EGYPT
MAURITANIA
MALI
NIGER
CHAD
SUDAN
SENEGAL
BURKINA FASO
GUINEA
IVORY COAST
GHANA
TOGO
BENIN
NIGERIA
CAMEROON
CENTRAL AFRICAN REPUBLIC
ETHIOPIA
SOMALIA
GABON
CONGO
ZAIRE
UGANDA
KENYA
TANZANIA
ANGOLA
ZAMBIA
MOZAMBIQUE
MADAGASCAR
NAMIBIA
BOTSWANA
SOUTH AFRICA

⬤ = Areas that send students to Sibut Bible School

⬤ = Area of Margery's medical services

BIRAO
GAME PARK
GAME PARK
NDELE
WADDA
KABO
BAMINGUI
PAWA
BATANGAFOU
KAGA BANDORO
BOSSSOUM
BOUCA
NDERES
DOBANE
GAME PARK
BOZOUM
DEKOA
MARGUBAS
IPPY
BRIA
YALINGA
BABOUA
BOAR
BOGAN-GOLD
SIBUT
GRIMARI
BAMBARI
BAKOUMA
YALOKE
BANGASSOU
CARNOT
BOSSEM-BELE
DAMARA
POSSEL
ALINDAO
RAFAI
ZERIO
OBO
BERBERATI
BODA
KEMBE
BANGUI
MOBAYE
WANGO
NOLA
MBAIKI

Central African Republic

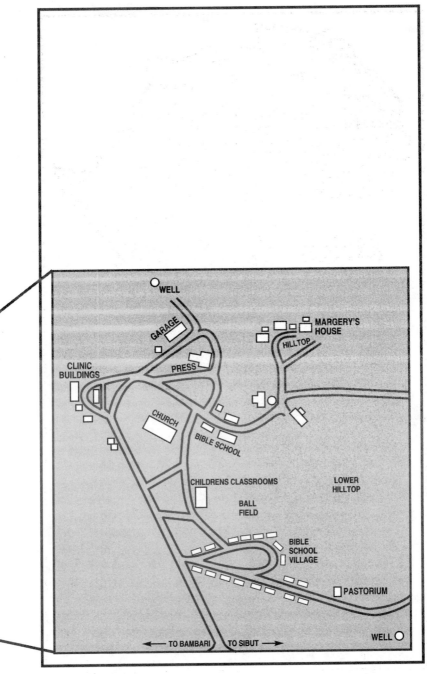

Part One

Focusing On The Goal

1 - Emergency at Bedtime

The lights in the house flickered. This was the signal from the African who was responsible for turning off the generator at the bottom of the hill. It meant we had five more minutes of electricity. The generator was shut off at 9 p.m. each night. If we wanted to keep working, we quickly lit our lamps. If not, we checked to see that flashlights were within reach, crawled under our mosquito netting, said our prayers, and settled down for the night.

Just as I was thinking how nice my bed would feel, an African on my veranda loudly cleared his throat. When Africans didn't have wooden doors to knock on, clearing the throat was the customary way to announce their presence.

I called out, "Who is there?"

"*A yeke mbi* [It is I]."

In those early years Africans seldom gave their names because among their own people everyone knew each other's voices. It was our policy that when someone came to my door for help at night, he had to be accompanied by our night guard. But on this evening the rule had been ignored. "Mademoiselle, the chief of our village, Ngueregaza, is very ill."

I opened my door to a teenage boy who was breathing heavily. He had thrown down his bike at the bottom of the hill and run pell-mell up to my house — not even taking time to speak to our guard. I asked, "Where is your village, and what is the matter with your chief?"

"Seven kilometers away, " he replied. "The chief's stomach is all swollen. We think he has been poisoned. He is in much pain." I asked him to be more specific, but all he would say was, "Come quickly. Come quickly." I would have been on the go nearly constantly if I had responded to every nighttime request. If the case permitted, I would send medicine with the messenger and pick up the patient the following morning, but this particular evening I decided to go see the chief myself.

By this time the generator had been turned off. As I went outside, I could see a lamp burning in the bedroom of the Eugene Rosenau house up the hill. I walked the fifty yards up to their house and called to Ernestine. She poked her head out of the window and asked, "What's the matter?" I explained the situation and asked her to go with me. This was unusual, but I was so glad I did. We got into my 1954 half-ton Chevy truck, picked up the boy and his bike at the bottom of the hill, and off we went.

When we arrived at the village, we didn't have to ask where Chief Ngueregaza lived; it looked like the whole village was there in his front yard. When Ernie and I got to his door, we could see that only some of the villagers were in the yard; the rest were filling the house, making it impossible for us to enter. I asked them to make a path for us to get to the chief's bed in the opposite corner. At first they wouldn't move for fear of being out of position to see what was going on. The chief moaned loudly from across the room. *Just what am I going to find?* I wondered as I elbowed my way through the crowd.

At first I couldn't get the chief to talk. I asked him where he was hurting, but he just kept moaning loudly. Finally I spoke to him sternly, "How can I help you if I do not know what and where your illness is?"

He looked at me with agony and said, "My tooth, my tooth."

I would be lying if I said I wasn't upset. If the boy hadn't lied to me, I could have given him some aspirin and a sedative for his chief and I would now be sleeping. But we were here now, so I decided to take the chief and his wife to the clinic. The Africans started to lift the chief to carry him to the pickup, but I said, "He can walk. There is nothing wrong with his legs." So the chief calmly walked to the back of the truck and got in. I talked with the people and explained that their chief had a toothache and that it wasn't a life-or-death matter. Then we climbed into the truck, said goodnight, and began the four-mile trip back to the mission station.

Just as I turned into the mission road, we saw two women—one standing waving her lantern and the other crouching on the ground. I stopped the truck to investigate. I recognized the woman crouching down as one of my expectant mothers. The moans she uttered indicated her time to give birth was very near. Ernie and I quickly lifted her to the front seat, and I pressed down hard on the gas pedal for the quarter-mile trip to the clinic. We carried the woman into the clinic and put her on the table. How thankful I was for Ernie's efficient helping hands, for the baby was born in a matter of minutes.

After the mother and baby were settled in a room in the back of the dispensary, Ernie and I walked out to the veranda. Only then did I remember the chief! He and his wife were sitting quietly on one of the benches waiting for me. I gave him some aspirin, a sedative, and a bed and told him I would see him in the morning. What a night!

The next morning, with better light in the dental room, I could see that the tooth needed to be extracted, which I did. Later, when talking to the chief, I found out he did not know Christ, which did not surprise me. To give us time to talk with him further about his soul, I kept him at the clinic an additional day. One of my staff presented the plan of salvation to him, and he accepted Christ as his Savior.

I had heard about Chief Ngueregaza's village, as well as the village next to it, ever since I arrived in Africa in the early 1950s. They wanted nothing to do with the Gospel. They loved their sin. Their practice of witchcraft led to lives lived in fear. Drinking and the accompanying lifestyle only promoted immorality. Our Bible School students had gone there to start a village Bible class but to no avail. In the latter part of my first term, before getting a pickup truck, I went to the village a few times on my bike to tell Bible stories with a picture roll, but the road was so hilly that I soon had to give it up. You can imagine my joy when Chief Ngueregaza became a Christian!

A few years later, after my second furlough, as I was hauling rock in my pickup for a construction project, I passed Chief Ngueregaza's village and saw people gathered under a tree for a meeting. I stopped, and the village leader came to greet me.

"What kind of meeting are you having here?" I asked.

"A prayer meeting," he replied. My heart rejoiced as I remembered the day when Chief Ngueregaza believed. He had been truly born again, and many came to know Christ as a result.

A church was soon organized there, and an average of 150 people attended on Sunday mornings. Pierre, one of my favorite students in the Bible School, became the pastor there in 1994. Pierre's wife, Theresa, was a former patient who the Lord gave me the privilege of leading to Him years ago. Was it worth missing sleep on that night so many years ago? Yes, a thousand times yes! We never know the worth of a soul and what the Lord can bring from a new life in Christ.

How did a missionary nurse come to be in the middle of Africa? It all started before I was born.

2 - From the Days of My Youth

In 1920, an eighteen-year-old nursing student knelt in prayer and saw a vision so real that she remembered the details for the rest of her life.

In the vision Christ came down and took her up with Him. Then they passed over Central Africa. The girl noticed that blood was flowing from

Jesus' hands and feet. His expression was one of sorrow. Jesus said, "My blood was shed for these people also. I want you to be one to come tell them the story of redemption." The next thing the girl knew she was on her knees in her room. The girl said, "Lord, I'll go. I dedicate my life to You to go to Africa."

My mother, Margie Beck never forgot the vision the Lord had given her, even though she wouldn't fulfill it herself. World War I had thrown the world into turmoil. At the youth group of Fourth Baptist Church in St. Louis, Missouri, Margie met a godly young soldier, and they fell in love. When the war was over, the two were married.

John Benedict felt called into the ministry, so he and Margie moved to Liberty, Missouri, to receive Bible training at William Jewell College. They had two children, first John, and then Margery. Margie quit her college studies to care for her children.

Six months after Margery's birth, both children contracted whooping cough. One day, as the young mother was giving her sick baby girl a bath, she smelled smoke. The house was on fire! She quickly took the children to the next door neighbor and asked, "Please dry my baby and dress her." Once her children were safe, Margie then returned to her house and fought valiantly against the flames. Her efforts were to no avail, however, and the house was destroyed.

The author's mother, Margie Beck, age 19, while attending nurses training in St. Louis, MO.

Exhausted, the young mother returned to her children—only to find that her sick baby was still naked and exposed. The neighbor lady had been so interested in the fire that she failed to take care of the baby as she had been asked. The little girl developed pneumonia on top of the whooping cough.

With their baby near death, the young parents and their friends prayed earnestly that her life would be saved. The Lord answered, and Margery Benedict was spared for the work God had for her life. You see it was in the daughter, rather than in the mother, that the vision of telling Africans of God's love was fulfilled. The following is that daughter's story of how God used this girl from a very poor family to tell Africans of God's redeeming grace through Jesus Christ.

The Narrow Path

When Dad finished at William Jewell College, we moved to Kansas City, Missouri, so he could enter Central Baptist Seminary. Dad worked his way through seminary, so he took a long time to graduate. During that time three more children—David, Paul, and Esther—were born.

Those were the years of the Great Depression and money was scarce. Once, just before Christmas, my family had nothing more than potatoes to eat. There would be no gifts. I remember hearing my parents discussing what to do. All the money they had left was the tithe from the salary Dad had for that week.

Dad asked, "Should we use the tithe for food and gifts for the children?"

No, they determined they couldn't use the Lord's money for themselves. They could, however, trust the Lord to provide. They went to their knees and presented the problem to the Lord and asked for His help. After they rose from their prayers, there was a knock at the door. Two men were there, their arms laden with groceries, oranges, candy, and presents for Christmas. They were from a church some distance away. We did not know how they knew our family was in need. But God answers prayer and honors His word in Matthew 6:33, "Seek ye first the kingdom of God, and His righteousness; and all these things shall be added unto you."

One evening, at a meeting in our church, my brother John and I gave our hearts to the Lord. We were now a part of God's family.

Our family was faithful in going to church. The Sunday School gave out pins for perfect yearly attendance, and I always got one; but one summer Sunday I came close to not earning that pin. In the summertime we went barefooted during the week and only wore shoes on Sundays. One Sunday I couldn't find one of my shoes. I didn't know what to do but decided to wait until opening exercises for the primary

John Benedict, the author's father, at his graduation from Central Baptist Seminary.

department were over and then slip into our smaller room for the lesson. Once inside I tried to hide my feet under the chair so no one would notice my bare feet. During the closing prayer I slipped out of the room and ran home. But I received my pin!

After Dad graduated from seminary, he was called to pastor a church in Dade County, on the edge of the Ozarks, in southern Missouri. With five children during the Depression, Mother's call to be a missionary to Central Africa had to be laid aside. My parents rented an old farm about five miles from Greenfield, and we lived there for about four months. We had lots of fun digging up Indian arrowheads, learning to swim in the large creek on the property, and exploring the beautiful woods.

We also had added chores to do because there was no electricity. My folks took the laundry for the seven of us down to the creek. They built a fire to heat the wash water, and all the clothes were scrubbed on a washboard. Then my parents threw the clothes into the creek, and John and I rinsed them. We couldn't play while we did this work, for if we didn't catch the clothes, the current would run away with them.

In late September we moved to town, into a two-story house with electricity. There we could use our washing machine!

When I was a freshman the school had just built their first gymnasium. Since no one except John and I had previously played basketball, we were on the varsity teams. I was in my glory. I was so thankful for our women's coach, who took me under her wing and helped me in so many ways.

That summer I got pinkeye and Mother put Argyrol drops in my eyes. One day she asked me to go get the drops. I didn't look at the label carefully and brought a bottle the same size and color. Mom took it for granted it was the correct medicine and didn't read the label either. She ended up putting iodine in my eye. I screamed in pain. Mom said, "Run to the doctor's office." I wanted to change my dress, but she told me to go immediately. I did, and he washed my eye out with water.

I remembered that treatment years later, in Africa, when a spitting cobra found the target for its venom in the eye of one of my patients. I washed the eye with water for several minutes, and the patient recovered.

Mother became pregnant again. This discouraged her, for the family had no money for a doctor or to buy baby clothes. When mother was praying, the Lord gave her the assurance that He would take care of all of those things. So Daniel was born.

When Daniel was six months old, he became very ill. My brother Paul was ill at the same time. Mother didn't go to the doctor immediately because we couldn't afford to, but she finally had to when Daniel became more lethargic. The doctor diagnosed the baby's illness as diphtheria. None of us had the vaccinations that all babies nowadays receive. For Danny it was too late. That evening he quietly passed away and was buried in an unmarked grave. The nurses came and diagnosed Paul's illness also as diphtheria. We were all immunized and, with the exception of my father, put under quarantine. In time Paul made a good recovery.

One Sunday evening, when I was twelve, I went by myself to a little Baptist church nearby. The pastor spoke on dedicating our lives to Christ for service. I knew God was speaking to me. Mother had often spoken to me about her call to Africa and of her sadness that she couldn't go. She also had told me that she and my father had given me to the Lord for missionary work before I was born. But that evening I knew it wasn't just what my parents wanted; I knew it was God putting His hand on my shoulder and saying, *I want you for My service in Africa.*

The congregation was singing,

> *I'll go where you want me to go, dear Lord,*
> *O'er mountain, or plain, or sea;*
> *I'll say what you want me to say, dear Lord,*
> *I'll be what you want me to be.*

> —Mary Brown

I knew I had to fulfill the command in Matthew 28:19-20, verses that I had memorized: "Go ye therefore, and teach all nations, baptizing them in the name of the Father, and of the Son, and of the Holy Ghost: teaching them to observe all things whatsoever I have commanded you: and, lo, I am with you always, even unto the end of the world."

I stepped out of the pew, went forward, and dedicated my life for missionary work in Africa. I never once doubted this call from the Lord, and from that time on it was my goal in life. And just as King David's desire to build a temple for the Jews was fulfilled in his son Solomon, so my mother's vision for central Africa was fulfilled in me.

About a year later another child, Judith, was born. Then, since my dad suffered from asthma and the weed pollens in Missouri made it worse, the doctors advised him to move away. Dad had quit the ministry and was earning $1.00 a day. He heard how jobs were available in southeastern Oregon, so my folks decided moving there was the right thing to do.

Imagine an old Pontiac filled with six children plus pots and pans, and with three mattresses on the roof, a washing machine tied on the back, and pulling an old trailer. We looked like hillbillies as we drove from Missouri to

Oregon. We stopped to camp out at night in old deserted barns, under trees, or wherever we could find a free place.

Only once did we stay in a rented cabin. That evening the sky was black with clouds. It was getting dark fast, and a strong wind had come up. We knew it was going to pour. Mom kept praying out loud, "Lord, keep back the rain until we find a place out of the rain," and, "Lord, help us." We didn't have anything to cover our mattresses with and couldn't afford to do without them. Soon we came to a small town where there were cabins with carports beside them! Dad had just driven under a carport when the rain burst in a tremendous fury. But we were safe and dry, thanks to God's protecting care.

On a hot Memorial Day in 1940 we arrived in Nyssa, Oregon. There on the banks of the Snake River my parents counted their money—$2.35. What could they do with that amount of money? They didn't know anyone in Oregon.

Since prayer was always a part of our daily existence, we presented this problem to the Lord. Then Dad walked into town. There someone told him about a migrant camp three miles the other side of Nyssa on the old Oregon Trail. At the camp we were able to rent two large board-floor tents, where we lived until November. Then we were able to rent a house in town.

Dad, Mother, John, and I worked in the beet and lettuce fields all that summer and the next. In addition, Dad was soon preaching in an American Sunday School Union church in the area.

My brother John graduated from high school in 1941 and that fall went to Seattle to work at Boeing. He made this his career, except for the two years he was in the Navy during the war. In April 1942 my brother Stephen was born, and then there were seven children. I attended my last two years of high school in Nyssa, finishing in 1942. It was then that God took me out of Nyssa and started me on a path that eventually led to Africa.

3 - War Days

World War II had been going on for six months when I graduated from high school in 1942. I wanted to continue my schooling, but I had no way to finance it. I never talked it over with my parents because I knew we existed day by day on the little my father made going door to door selling Raleigh household products.

At each house my dad left a Christian tract because he wanted to be a witness for Christ. Half of the population in our little town of Nyssa was

Mormon, and this caused problems for my father. The Mormon bishop in town didn't want his people being taught about the Bible by anyone other than Mormons, so he instructed his congregation not to buy anything from my father.

In July, when I was seventeen, a government worker came to town and explained how I could go to school in Pendleton, Oregon, and learn a skill that would qualify me for a war job. I jumped at the opportunity, for I knew I wouldn't get anywhere in a career if I stayed in Nyssa. I moved to Pendleton, and under a government-sponsored program called the National Youth Organization, studied radio in a class of twenty-five.

After three months of study and practical work, the director told eight of us girls he was going to take us to Boardman, Oregon, to be interviewed to work in the Ordnance Depot. This was a military installation midway between Boardman and Hermiston. We were taken to the electrical department, and the foreman gave us a tour of the main building, showing us huge machines. After the tour our director told us we had to take the job. We were discouraged as we rode back to Pendleton. None of us wanted to work with those huge machines, especially since we had studied radio.

All eight of us returned to Ordnance but fortunately were spared having to work with those machines. One girl with clerical experience was put in the office. The rest of us worked out of a small electrical shack among more than a thousand cement igloos where ammunition was stored. The igloos were round, half-underground buildings without electricity. Our job was to supply light for the ammunition crews by setting up a light pole near the door of each igloo. A huge 1000-watt bulb was attached to each pole.

There were no cellular phones then, so the foreman would come to our shack and give us the number of the igloo where we were to take a generator in one of our 3/4-ton trucks. The work at the depot was carried on around the clock. Our shift assignment would change every two weeks. At our shack we had two crews, with one girl and one man assigned for each truck. If we were on the evening shift, we had the responsibility of starting a huge generator that illuminated the area by the railroad track. I often heard crews singing a World War II song, "Praise the Lord, and Pass the Ammunition," as they rolled the ammo into the boxcars going to the Pacific theater of war.

I liked all our crewmembers. Our supervisor was thirty-five-year-old Ruth Carter, whose husband, Cecil, along with Red Williams, serviced the generators. We all remained special friends the rest of our lives.

It was a year of learning responsibility. Except for one midnight shift during a blizzard, I enjoyed working there. On that particular night the two men didn't show up, and it was just another girl, Norma, and I, and Norma didn't drive. I still have a partially numb toe from the frostbite I received that unforgettable night.

On another night I had an interesting experience while driving alone back to our shack headquarters. I was following a semi when suddenly a couple of 2,000-pound bombs fell out of the back of the larger truck. I did some dodging and stepped on the gas, trying to catch up with it, but the driver was going too fast. I could just imagine the look on his face when he arrived at his destination minus the bombs and received a reprimand. I only hoped a shipment would not be delayed.

All of us girls lived in Hermiston, and my roommate Charmian and I attended the Baptist church. I spent a lot of my free time with the youth group, and they all knew I wanted to be a missionary. Luc, a soldier, also attended. I had dated a few fellows in Pendleton and Hermiston, but I spent more time with Luc than with anyone else. However, Luc and I both realized that our lives were on different paths. I was called to be a missionary in Africa, and Luc was bound to the military for the duration of the war, so we parted friends. I knew I had to put my missionary calling first in my life. I never was serious with a man again.

After I left the Ordnance Depot and entered nursing school in Portland, I started to really grow in my Christian faith. I began to be especially burdened for those who worked with me at the Ordnance Depot. I wasn't sure if any of them knew the Lord. I kept in close contact with Ruth and Cecil Carter, and they visited me in Portland. I tried to tell them about Christ, but they didn't see their need of Him. They were churchgoers and good people and could not understand that they needed to repent before God. But the Bible says, "All have sinned, and come short of the glory of the Lord" (Romans 3:23).

Each time I came home from Africa on furlough, I visited them. I prayed faithfully for their salvation each week. I kept a prayer list, and I always tried to pray for an unsaved friend each day of the week. Twenty years later they wrote to me in Africa to let me know the joyful news that they had accepted Jesus Christ as their Savior. On my next furlough I went to see them. I told them I always prayed for them on Tuesdays. When Cecil introduced me to their church friends, he would say with a twinkle in his eye, "This is our missionary friend who prayed for us on Tuesdays."

Another person whose soul I was concerned about was Red, the man who serviced the generators with Cecil. One evening during my second furlough, Red took me to the bus depot after a visit with him and his wife. I asked him, "Red, when are you going to make your peace with God? Your wife and daughter have been praying for years for you to become a Christian."

He was quiet for a few moments and then replied, "I know I need to. I will." Soon after that he did accept Christ, and a change was evident in his life when I talked with him during my next furlough.

Christ does make a change in people's lives. "If any man be in Christ, he is a new creature: old things are passed away; behold, all things are become new" (2 Corinthians 5:17).

It takes an average of seven presentations of the Gospel before a person accepts Christ as Savior, and I learned through the years not to give up hope when praying for the Holy Spirit to work in the life of an unsaved person.

4 - Preparing to Serve

At the end of July 1943 I decided it was time I left Hermiston, Oregon, to further my education. I thought I could be helpful to the Africans as a nurse, by taking care of the ill. One day I approached my pastor's wife and asked, "Do you know of a nursing school I could go to?"

She replied, "I had surgery at Emanuel Lutheran Hospital in Portland, and the nurses were very nice. Why don't you try there?"

I sent off an inquiry. I was very naïve; I should have been planning months before. A return letter arrived saying, "I'm sorry, our fall class starts August 2, and the class is full. If you would like, we can send you an application for the next class that starts in February."

I prayed, *Lord, you can work this out. If you want me to enter now, please show me what to do.* I sent the school a telegram saying, "If a vacancy opens up, I can come immediately." Then I wrote for an application. I quit my job and went home to visit my parents.

Soon a telegram from the nursing school arrived, saying, "There is a vacancy. Come." A Seventh Day Adventist student had quit the nursing program when she realized that she would be expected to attend classes on Saturday. In this manner the Lord answered my prayer and opened up a vacancy.

I arrived at Emanuel on August 9, just one week after classes started, and began the three-year program. There were fifty-seven in our class, and we all lived at the hospital. It provided our room, board, and uniforms. There was an entrance fee of $250, but that was returned to us when we joined the Cadet Nurses Corps, a government-sponsored agency. Then the Corps gave us $15 a month, with the requirement that, if the war were still on when we graduated, we would join the Army Nurses Corps.

We could choose our roommates after six months. Ruth Ann Lowe and I teamed up. Both of us were Christians, growing in our faith. The Christian Nurses Fellowship meetings on Friday nights were especially beneficial to our spiritual growth.

One day Ruth Ann came to our room after working in surgery and said, "Benny, I sure blew it today."

"What happened?" I asked.

"I was assisting Dr. Steinburg in surgery. During the long surgery he stretched his tightened leg muscles by kicking the metal waste bucket. I looked up and asked him, 'Did you ever hear the saying about old man Mo kicking the bucket?' There was such silence in the room, until the intern couldn't keep back his laughter. Then everyone started laughing. Benny, I really did forget Dr. Steinburg's first name is Moses. I wonder what evaluation I'll get now?"

But no report was made of it in her evaluation. Later she did get one reprimand—for humming a hymn while carrying a bedpan down the hall. This was not considered professional.

In our classes I sat next to a very intelligent girl, Donna. She never needed to take notes—she learned by listening. One evening she came staggering into our dormitory, drunk. Another girl, Marjorie, and I tried to sober her up before the housemother made rounds.

In the morning Donna said to me, "All I can remember of last night was the shocked expression on your face."

From that time on, I prayed for Donna's salvation. My prayers were answered about ten years later. Donna became a real student of the Bible and visited the Holy Land three times. In later years I visited her while I was on furlough. I loved hearing her talk about the Lord. In spite of being very ill later in life, she was always praising and thanking the Lord.

During this time I received a letter from my mother saying that I had a new brother, Philip. (Mother never informed any of us when she was pregnant.) Upon hearing this news, I thought, *No, not another baby!* But the Lord knew how much Phil would be needed in my parents' lives. Later I realized anew that each child God gives is for a special purpose. Phil was always near with a helping hand, even after his marriage and having a family of four children. Phil and his family lived next to our parents and helped care for them until the Lord took them home.

Dad passed away in 1979 at the age of eighty-three and Mother nine months later at the age of seventy-eight. Soon after, Phil and his family went to Quito, Ecuador, for a two-year mission trip. He was one of the electricians in the construction of a mission hospital. His wife, Linda, taught in the school for the missionary children. Phil worked for two years with Missionary Tech, a Texas missionary board, and has since then worked with Indian missions in Oklahoma.

During my last year at Emanuel, Mary Jane, an attractive, vibrant girl, entered the school program. She attended our nurse's Christian fellowship. It didn't take me long to know she had a deep, sincere love for Jesus. One day I told her I would be going to some Bible school because I wanted to go to Africa and needed Bible training. She told me she had recently graduated from Simpson Bible Institute in Seattle. Since Mary Jane was such a dedicated, lovable Christian, I thought, *If that school produces young people like her, that is where I am going.* I didn't realize until I was in the school that it was affiliated with the Christian and Missionary Alliance rather than a Baptist association. That didn't matter to me; I had peace that I was where the Lord wanted me.

Three years to the day after entering Emanuel Hospital Nursing School I received my Registered Nurse degree. There is never an August 9 that rolls around when I don't think of that day in 1943 when the Lord performed a miracle so I could enter nursing school.

Three weeks after graduation I was on a Greyhound bus heading for Seattle, Washington, to enter Simpson Bible Institute. On the bus I sat next to a Christian girl who used to live in Seattle. When she found out that I was a Baptist, she recommended her former church, Tabernacle Baptist. I went there my first Sunday in Seattle and knew this was the church for me. Two weeks later I became a member. I could only attend Tabernacle Baptist Church once in a while during my years at the Bible Institute because the school assigned me to teach a junior girls' Sunday School class and play the piano for the morning service at the White Center housing project in south Seattle.

Tabernacle Baptist was so large and I was there so infrequently that I knew very few people. The only person in the church I really got to know was Ilene Douglas. She was the head lab technician at

Graduation from nurses training, August 9th, 1946.

Maynard Hospital, where I worked two evenings a week for the three years I was at Simpson, thus paying for my schooling.

My brother John lived in Seattle. He was with the Navy during the war, but at the end of the war he came back to work again at Boeing Airplane Company. How terrific it was when I found out he was living with his in-laws just a mile from my school. Mrs. Littlejohn, his mother-in-law, loved the Lord dearly. She made me feel very welcome in their home and the Littlejohns are still my friends to this day. She and her five children became a second family to me. John and his wife Jerry had two children, John and Becky. How privileged I was.

I planned to spend my second summer in Seattle with Dorothy Kopper, a good friend from school. We were both headed for Africa. Dorothy was going to teach me how to cook and sew. My domestic plans, however, never materialized.

After church one May Sunday morning at the end of my second year, I boarded the number ten Capitol Hill bus with many of the church people. I found myself standing next to a lady from the church, and as we talked, she made the statement, "They need another girl counselor at Lake Sammamish Bible Camp."

I had heard of the camp, Sambica, through some students at school who had worked there the summer before. It was located on Lake Sammamish near Redmond, Washington, in a beautiful setting among evergreen trees. Dr. Annis and Ruby Jepson were the directors.

Margery with friends Betty Johnson and Donna Wilson in 1948.

As the churchwoman finished her sentence, the Holy Spirit spoke to me. *You are going to be that counselor.* I never knew the leading of the Lord so quickly in all of my life. The next day I went to Miss Yeager, the school cook who also cooked at camp during the summer, and asked her a couple of questions about the camp. Her face lit up with joy as she answered my questions. And later that week Ruby Jepson called me and said, "We need another girl counselor at Sambica, and you have been recommended to us. Would you be interested?"

Would I? I knew it was of the Lord. Words can't begin to explain what the three summers I spent at this camp meant to me. "Aunt Ruby," who ran the camp, had trained in Europe to be an opera singer but left that profession to invest her life in boys and girls. Ruby Jepson was the godliest woman I ever met. Her life touched thousands of counselors, campers, and others who heard her sing and give her testimony. The songs she wrote, her godly life, and her complete dependence on the Lord in every situation were always a testimony. I learned that if we abide in Christ, we have the privilege of living the victorious life.

Pauline Driver, an experienced counselor, was my partner for the first week. I was so glad she was the one I was with as we supervised a dorm of twenty high school girls. Both of us taught a lesson a day, and that week the lessons were on Satan. We became depressed and nothing seemed to go right.

On Wednesday Pauline said to me, "I believe the depression we are experiencing is of Satan. He is not happy that we are exposing his tactics of using discouragement, neglect of prayer, and failure to read the Word to lead Christians to a defeated walk with Christ."

I agreed. We went down on our knees and prayed that the Lord would defeat the darts that Satan was throwing at us. Soon there was a different attitude among us, and we knew that the Lord had answered our prayer. I learned an invaluable lesson that week for my teaching years in Africa. When teaching lessons on Satan, you should be prayerfully prepared for an all-out attack from this enemy.

One week at camp we had an overflow of eight- and nine-year-old girls, so they were housed in the tabernacle building. I became one of the two counselors for that group. I was awakened one night by a little voice calling me from across the room saying, "Teacher there is a horse in here." Immediately I went over to her and found the *horse* to be the neighbor's Great Dane. The dog was standing right over her. I was surprised that she wasn't screaming. I took the dog out and locked the door, which had been left open.

Daily we saw answers to prayer at the camp. Hundreds of campers came to Christ, and many other decisions were made to live righteously for Him. What joy! Those summers at camp were a blessed training ground for my service in Africa.

During my last semester in school I went to the Navigators headquarters in Seattle to learn their method of becoming a disciple of Christ. The ideas and lessons I received were the most valuable Bible training of my life. Their topical system for Scripture memorization was such a blessing to me. I not only memorized the ninety-six verses in English, but later I also learned them in French and Sango. In Africa the learning of these verses was included in the curriculum in many of my classes. They had meant so much to me; I wanted others to know also the joy and growth in their Christian life from memorizing the Word of God.

5 - The Lord Who Calls Is Faithful

I had no idea how to select a mission board, so I made it a matter of much prayer. During my last year of school someone had mentioned Baptist Mid-Missions, an independent Baptist mission board with headquarters in Cleveland, Ohio.

After graduation from Simpson Bible Institute I sent my application there. On the blank for country of intended service, I just put Africa because I did not know which countries in Africa the mission had ministries in. Meanwhile the mission board wrote to Tabernacle Baptist Church for a letter of recommendation.

Years later, I learned what happened when the church received the request for a recommendation. The missions committee met and determined they couldn't recommend me because nobody knew who I was. Our church had over 500 people at that time, and I was just one rather quiet girl among about one hundred college-age students. In addition, I had the Sunday morning school assignment, teaching and playing the piano at the housing project. It was no wonder that no one knew me.

Later that evening Pastor Johnson happened to mention at the dinner table that someone named Margery Benedict from Tabernacle Baptist Church had applied to Baptist Mid-Missions but that no one on the missions committee knew who she was. At that his nine-year-old daughter, Judy, piped up and said, "I know her. She was my counselor at Lake Sammamish Bible Camp."

Her father asked her several more questions and then later met with the missions committee again. The committee determined they ought to call Dr. Annis and Ruby Jepson, the directors of the camp, and if they offered a good recommendation, the missions committee would pass that on to Baptist Mid-Missions. The word was good, and Baptist Mid-Missions invited me to come to their February 1950 conference, to be interviewed by the general council, the governing board of the mission.

It was a cold, wintry day when I left my family in Nyssa, Oregon, and boarded a Trailways bus for Cleveland. After three snowy days and nights on the bus I finally arrived, only to find myself sitting wearily in the

Cleveland bus depot wondering if anyone could be more stupid than I was: I had forgotten to bring my arrival instructions. All I could remember of the information was that the conference was to begin the next day.

I called the mission office several times, but of course no one was there because it was 7 p.m. I also called the home of the mission secretary with whom I had corresponded, a Mr. Fetzer, but no one answered there either. Then it dawned on me, This was a Wednesday evening, and he was probably in a prayer meeting at some church. I prayed silently, *Lord, what shall I do?*

The answer came, *Call the office again.* I did, and a man's voice answered, "Baptist Mid-Missions, Ed Morrel speaking." I told him who I was, and he gave me the name of the church where I was to go. Then he said, "This is certainly unusual. I just came into the office for a minute to find a paper that I needed." My response to him was, "I know why you came into the office. The Lord was answering my prayer."

I took a taxi to the church and arrived just as the prayer meeting was concluding. Someone introduced me to the lady with whom I was to stay during the conference. Her first remark was, "I wasn't expecting to see you until tomorrow."

My heart sank. I was ready to drop from fatigue and longed for nothing more than to stretch out in a bed. Immediately that dear lady realized the impact of her words, and she quickly said, "I'm sorry how that must have sounded. It's okay, you can come home with me now."

Under my breath I said, "Thank you, Lord."

At this conference there were more than thirty candidates waiting to be interviewed. Next morning I was amazed to see many of them busily studying their Bibles and quizzing each other. I wondered, "Should I be doing this, too?" I didn't have any idea what the interview would be like. Once I got into the interview I was thankful that I had learned the Bible verses in the Navigator Topical Memory System. In answer to many of their questions I simply quoted verses that I had learned.

Upon my acceptance, the board suggested I go to French Equatorial Africa in central Africa. The field council for that country had voted to start a hospital at the mission station at Ippy. Two doctors had been accepted earlier for that work, and nurses would be needed. I was thankful that another nurse, Nancy, had also been accepted for the same country. Neither of us wanted to travel to Africa alone, so we prayed that we would be able to leave the United States together.

At the conference I also learned that Baptist Mid-Missions was a faith mission board, and thus we were expected to look to the Lord to raise our support.

Among the many denominations, there are different methods of sending money to missionaries. In some, churches budget a particular sum each year for missions. This money is sent to the denominational mission board, and the board distributes the money to the various missionaries they have sent out. A congregation may, according to their interest in missions, learn about the overall program and even have missionaries visit and tell about their work, but it is not necessary for the missionaries to go directly to churches to raise support. As a result, fewer local churches have direct contact with missionaries.

In other denominations, including our Baptist association, local churches directly support individual missionaries serving in what we call faith missions, which may be carried out under any of various mission boards. After missionaries are accepted by their faith mission boards, they arrange appointments to speak at local churches. There they explain the ministry to which the Lord has called them, describing the country and the work they will do there. Then the churches' missionary committees decide which missionaries each of them will support. The missionaries also have many individuals who help them. In either case, the relationship between local church people and the missionary is a direct commitment.

The belief behind the faith mission system is that this approach strengthens the trust missionaries have in their Lord when they pray that the amount needed will come in, and that the people will get to know their missionaries as they take a personal interest in them, and pray for their needs. Also, the young people in the church are able to hear missionaries speak and are challenged to give their lives to the Lord for missionary service. There is by far more money given to missions and more missionaries going out per capita in churches where the faith principal is carried out.

My heart was overflowing with thankfulness to the Lord as I took the return bus to Nyssa. This time I was an appointee for the mission field instead of just a candidate. How my family rejoiced at the good news!

After a month at home I had my first deputation meeting near Portland. There I gave my testimony and shared with the people how I felt God was calling me to serve Him in French Equatorial Africa.

From there I went to Seattle and stayed once again with my wonderful friend Ilene, the head lab technician at Maynard Hospital. The head pathologist gave her permission to teach me some lab work. This was of the Lord, as I learned how to use a microscope and do simple analysis of blood and urine. This knowledge would prove to be valuable for my work in Africa.

After two months at the hospital and working in the lab, I still had no meetings lined up where I could speak in Baptist churches. Two efforts to solicit help in this area had proved fruitless. Discouraged, I returned to Nyssa and spent most of the summer there.

My folks welcomed me home and joined me in prayer as I sought the Lord's next step. I remember so vividly the day I went down on my knees and prayed, "Lord, I know you have called me to go to Africa. But I don't know how I am going to get the money I need. I have asked people for help in vain. Now I am going to ask only You. If you want me there, You are going to have to undertake for me."

The Lord sweetly reminded me of a verse that I had learned: "Faithful is he that calleth you, who also will do it" (1 Thessalonians 5:24).

A wonderful peace filled my soul. I knew without a doubt that the Lord would provide for me!

Soon I received an invitation to speak at Baptist Temple in Boise, Idaho. A man who heard me speak that evening felt led by the Lord to give me the small inheritance of $250 that he had recently received. I later used that money for my train fare to New York City and the boat passage to France.

The Lord had a lesson He wanted me to learn right from the start of my ministry as a missionary: I would have no sufficiency of my own, but His sufficiency would always be available, whether financial, physical or spiritual.

In September I received a letter from Pastor Johnson in Seattle. He wanted

Margery's first sponsors, Pastor Forrest and Mary Johnson of Tabernacle Baptist Church in Seattle, Washington.

me to take care of his four children for a month while he and his wife went back east to attend a conference and to visit her relatives. He also wanted his congregation to get to know me. I accepted the invitation and hoped that my limited domestic skills might be sufficient for four children. I arrived at the Johnson home on Capitol Hill in Seattle and was in for a surprise.

"I have changed my mind," said Pastor Johnson. I am not going now. I want to go to a conference in Europe later on, and I can't leave the church twice. However, my wife is still going to visit her family for a month."

What terrible news for me! I was too ashamed to tell him that I couldn't cook. The Lord knew I wouldn't have accepted his offer if I had known that I would have to cook for the pastor too. Thus began the longest month of my life. One Sunday morning Pastor Johnson wanted to emphasize a point in his message. He said, "I do not want any of you to be thinking of your Sunday dinner; please listen to what I have to say." At that moment I had been thinking of Sunday dinner—his Sunday dinner—because I had never cooked a roast before!

Pastor Johnson had a burden for lost souls. Sometimes he would weep during his message, pleading for people to surrender their lives to the Lord so they would be ready if the Lord should call them to go to the mission field. No wonder that in his twenty-five years of ministry as pastor of Tabernacle Baptist Church more than forty people went to serve the Lord on the foreign fields of the world and about that same number went into full-time ministries in the United States.

Finally it was the night for Mrs. Johnson to return home. I wanted everything to be just right for her homecoming. Erma Swanson, a church member who lived just across the street, rescued me by telling me how to cook a luscious chicken dinner. The friendship the Lord forged between Erma and me during that month lasted throughout my years on the mission field. Time and time again Erma was a great help to me.

After dinner that evening I walked over to the church building to pray. I needed the Lord to show me the next step I was to take. After spending some time there, I had peace that the Lord would show me what to do. As I entered the house, I saw Pastor and his wife still sitting in the living room. They called me into the room and said, "Margery, we want you to consider our home your home until you leave to go to the mission field."

I was stunned. My first thought was Isaiah 65:24, which reads, "Before they call, I will answer." Mrs. Johnson took me under her wing, and she and her husband started the ball rolling to get me to the mission field. She asked, "Where is the list of the things the mission gave you that you will need to take to Africa?" As she looked over the list, she remarked, "The women of the church will give you a shower, and you will have all the things you will need."

And they did! In two months I had $100 of monthly support from the church and individuals. I only lacked $40. One day Polly and Weldon Gwinn (who themselves had already pledged $30 a month to me) were visiting the Johnsons. Polly's brother and her Canadian sister-in-law were also there. I came in the front door and intended to go upstairs to change into my uniform for work. Pastor called me into the living room and said, "I want you to meet this couple." After greeting them, I said, "Would you excuse me please? I need to get ready for work." When I came downstairs, I was called into the living room for a second time. Pastor Johnson declared, "This Canadian couple will take on the rest of your support." What a miracle of God! The Lord is faithful!

I did not go back to Nyssa again but wrote to my praying family about the good news. On a cold and snowy December 7, 1950, I left the Johnson home, bound for New York City. Pastor Johnson said he wanted me to remember snow when I got to Africa, so he playfully pelted me with snowballs as I got into the car. I had come to love Pastor and Mrs. Johnson and their four children, Jan, Judy, Dan, and Kathy. In one of the letters I received from Mrs. Johnson when I was in France, she told me Danny had just asked her, "Does Margery have any family but ours?"

By this time I had many friends at Tabernacle Baptist Church, and many of them showed up at the train station to bid me goodbye. As they were singing, "God will take care of you," the conductor took my arm and said, "So will I. It is time to get aboard."

I stopped off at Cleveland, where Nancy lived. The Lord had supplied for her also, and she was ready to leave. I went to the home office of Baptist Mid-Missions and visited with Arthur Fetzer, our mission secretary. He looked very ill, but he wanted to talk. I kept thinking, *I wish you would go to bed before you collapse.* All of the missionaries at that time can verify with me what a caring and concerned man Mr. Fetzer was to us all.

I was pleasantly surprised that another nurse, Ruth Nephew, also from Cleveland, was going with us. The three of us boarded the train for New York. We had a busy and exciting day in New York City. In the evening we walked down to the harbor to see the Queen Mary, the ship that was to take us to France. Nancy said, "That's a big ship!" I thoughtlessly added, "So was the Titanic when it sank." We had a good laugh and then headed back to the place where we were staying the night. Tomorrow we would set sail for France—and beyond, to Africa!

6 - Delightful Days in France

A nurse who had already served a term in French Equatorial Africa with Baptist Mid-Missions came over from New Jersey to see us off. We didn't know her, but she knew how much it would mean to us to have someone there to say goodbye and wish us Godspeed. As our ship, the Queen Mary, left the port of New York and sailed past the Statue of Liberty, we were filled with emotion. As the statue faded from view, we realized that one chapter of our lives was closing. The unknown was before us. But we were confident the Lord would be with us even to the end of the world.

When we had sailed about an hour out of New York, I received a telegram from my home church letting me know they were thinking of and praying for me. It was a thoughtful gesture and very comforting to me.

Our time aboard ship was uneventful. Four of us shared a stuffy cabin — the three missionary nurses and one lady who did not speak much English. The rocking of the ship made Ruth and me dizzy enough that we didn't enjoy our five days on the high seas. On Sunday we were able to leave our tourist-class section and go up to the chapel in first-class to hear Billy Graham. That was the highlight of our trip! Our ship landed in Cherbourg, France. From there we took the "boat train" to Paris.

A Baptist Mid-Missions missionary, Dan Feryance, met our train in Paris on December 21, 1950. Dan and his wife Ida had served with Mid-Missions in Czechoslovakia until the Communists had forced them out in 1949. Dan took Nancy and me to a boarding house within walking distance of our language school, Alliance Francaise, where students from all over the world were learning the French language. Ruth was taken to a French home in a suburb of Paris.

It didn't take me long to realize that Nancy had a brilliant mind. She had graduated from nursing and Bible school with almost perfect marks. She learned the French grammar quickly but was very hesitant to speak French. I had previously studied French for two years, and I would try and speak it, even if my grammar wasn't correct. We soon made friends with other American language students.

About two weeks into my time in France, I developed little red pimples all over my body that itched like mad. What could it be? The more I scratched, the more they itched. An American girl who lived close to us came to visit one day and laughed after examining me. "Those are flea bites," she exclaimed.

Oh no, I thought, I had scabies (the seven-year itch) once in the States, and I had been in France only two weeks and had fleas! *I bet when I arrive in Africa I'll catch every skin disease there is.* (By the grace of God, I didn't.)

One evening Nancy and I were joking around in our room when suddenly she stopped and said, "I used to act silly like this before I came down with a migraine headache. I hope they aren't coming back. I haven't had one for ten years."

Alas, before the hour had gone by she was lying down moaning with a migraine. I finally had to give her a narcotic injection before she had any relief. Later in March she had to be admitted to a hospital because her headaches had become so severe that I had nothing to give her. I always took responsibility for Nancy's care, even when we no longer lived in the same boarding house.

Once when Nancy was having a bad migraine, she agreed to have a couple of our missionaries come and pray especially for her headaches. Many had been praying for her but not in a special prayer time like I wanted to have. I asked two of our missionaries who lived close by to come and pray for her healing. The Bible says in James to call the elders of the church when a believer is ill. But when it came time for the prayer meeting, one of our missionaries backed out and the other was not able to make it. One of them sent his neighbor, a Pentecostal missionary, instead. This man brought another missionary with him. So instead of two Baptist missionaries we had two Pentecostals. I was glad to welcome them. The three of us knelt near Nancy's bed and started to pray. As the second man prayed, Nancy sat up in bed and exclaimed, "Margery, my headache is gone!" How we rejoiced and thanked the Lord for answered prayer!

Word got around quickly among all the missionaries about Nancy's healing, and they rejoiced with us. About two weeks later, Nancy and I went to a monthly missionary meeting we had on Sunday afternoons. This group included language students from several different mission boards. One of the ladies said joyfully to Nancy, "Isn't it great how the Lord healed you?" Nancy shrugged her shoulders and murmured something.

Oh no, I thought, *If Nancy doesn't give the glory to the Lord, I'm afraid for her.*

A few weeks later, she came down with another terrible headache. Our doctors agreed that Nancy would be unable to go to Africa and would have to return to the United States. Nancy didn't want anyone to see her off at the train in Paris, but I couldn't let her go alone. I accompanied her to the train that would take her to the coast. She appeared calm, but I knew that underneath her heart must have been breaking. Now I think her headaches came mostly because of stress. After being in the top of her class in the

United States, she was unable to make the adjustment necessary to learn a foreign language and culture.

After three months in the boarding house, I moved into a French home that kept two boarders. The French lady who managed the home was very stern and only changed the sheets once in six weeks. But it was worth the adjustment in order to have more opportunity to practice my French. Guillemete, a university student from eastern France, lived in the room next to mine. We became good friends, and it wasn't long before she was asking many questions about missions and my faith. We talked often, for she had many questions. I spoke of the relationship we could have with Christ. She was especially interested in the Rapture, as she had never heard that Jesus was coming back some day to take all believers—those who had died and those who are still alive—to Heaven.

When she left for her summer vacation, she asked me, "Have you ever prayed for someone to become a Christian and they did?"

"Many times," I answered.

"Would you pray for me that I might have faith to believe?" she asked.

I put my arm around her and said, "I have been praying, Guillemete. And I will continue to do so."

Across the street from where I lived was Luxembourg Park, one of the many beautiful parks of Paris. One day I went to the park and sat down next to a girl reading an English newspaper. We started talking, and I learned she was French and her name was Jeannette. She was majoring in English at a university in Paris. She was Roman Catholic and had spent three years in a convent in China.

Jeannette was eager to learn English and I was eager to learn French, so a friendship was born. I wanted an opportunity to talk to her about Christ. She was interested in learning what the Bible said about salvation, so we spent much time together reading the Word of God. One Friday I invited her to attend a Navigator Bible study. That night Jeannette went with me, and Dave Roher, our leader, was surely led by the Spirit. The words he shared spoke to Jeannette's heart. Later that night in her hotel room, I had the joy of leading her to Christ.

In August 1951 I moved again, this time to the home of a Jewish-Christian family named Guedj. When Guillemete came back to the university, I wasn't at my old address. She thought that I must have already gone on to Africa. Two days before I was to leave for Africa I went back to my old address in hopes of finding Guillemete. She was there. She excitedly shared her news: while she was home on vacation, she had believed in the Lord Jesus Christ as her Savior. I was thrilled.

The Guedj family lived an hour's train ride from Paris, in the small town of Sannois. There were four children, ages twenty-one, twenty, eighteen, and nine. It didn't take me long to learn to love them and their wonderful Christian mother. The father, however, was very self-centered and harsh.

Monique, the nine-year-old, was my special little friend. Occasionally after school I would walk with her to the dairy to buy milk. On the way home one day, I asked her if she knew Jesus.

"I don't, but I want to," she said, "but my parents say I am too young to believe.

"No, you aren't," I countered. "I was your age when I became a Christian. Please come to my room when we get home and I will talk with you about it." Monique did come, and she understood perfectly that she was a sinner in need of a Savior. Sweetly she accepted the Lord. Then she ran down the stairs, yelling to her mother, "I'm a Christian. I know Jesus now."

I could hardly believe my ears when I heard her precious Christian mother saying, "You can't understand. You have to wait until you are older."

At that time in France that was the thinking of most French Christians. Consequently they rarely had Sunday Schools, and the French children were neglected. In later years that attitude changed and the French children began to be reached for Christ.

For three months in the fall of 1951 I had the wonderful privilege of attending a parasitology course in medical school in Paris for three hours each afternoon. On the first day I was surprised when I looked over at the next table to see our missionary doctors with their microscope in front of them. They, however, were even more surprised to see a nurse in the class with them. A Swedish missionary had obtained permission for his wife and me to audit the class. This was of the Lord, for the course was invaluable when I started a medical work from scratch in Sibut.

One day Dr. Jon Rouch, one of our Mid-Missions doctors, said to me, "I know where we can buy some surplus army equipment. Would you be interested in having me place an order for you?"

I didn't know then what kind of medical work I would be doing, but I bought a field operating table, a dental case, a couple of metal folding tables, and a stretcher. Dr. Rouch took care of seeing that these items were shipped with his things to French Equatorial Africa. The money was well spent, for this equipment, bought in 1951, was still being used into the next century—some fifty years later.

Thirteen months had gone by since I arrived in France, and it was time for Ruth and me to leave for Africa. I had failed my French exam, but since I was not to be a teacher in Africa, I was not required to pass it before leaving for the field. In a way I didn't want to leave France. I loved the French people and would have been happy to stay there. But my calling was to Africa.

A month before I was to leave France, I thought to myself, *I wish I weren't a nurse. I would just like to work with the youth and have a teaching ministry.* For a couple of weeks I struggled with this idea. Then one day I read Romans 12. I came to verse eight and read there that one of the gifts of the Spirit was to "show mercy, with cheerfulness." The Lord said to me, *Margery, what is nursing but showing mercy? If you can do that cheerfully, this is your gift.* It was settled in my mind, and I was at peace! Many times years later, when I would scold an old man for spitting tobacco juice on the newly whitewashed wall of the sick ward or get angry when I saw patients throwing their garbage out the sick room window, that verse would come to mind. The Holy Spirit would remind me, *Margery, with cheerfulness.* In His time, two years later the Lord did give me a teaching ministry in addition to the nursing.

There were many people at the train station to see Ruth Nephew and me off on February 2, 1952. I realized anew the many friends we Christians have and the bond of love that unites us. At the airport we remembered Art Fetzer's admonition, "Don't forget to take your malaria pills just before you leave for Africa." Each of us took two bitter tablets as protection against the bite of a female anopheles mosquito. Bitter anti-malaria pills were taken for all our years in Africa, and even then we weren't exempt from the disease.

As Ruth and I were getting on the plane bound for Africa, I wondered what Nancy was doing and wished she could have been with us.

As we flew over the Sahara Desert, we saw one of the most beautiful sunsets ever! It lasted so long it was like a benediction. I recognized anew what an awesome Creator we have.

Africa here we come!

Part Two

My First Term

W hile in France in December 1951, Ruth Nephew and I received letters from Ferd Rosenau, the president of our mission in French Equatorial Africa, where we were to be assigned as missionaries. Ruth was going to Koumra, in the province of Tchad, to learn the Sango language and work with another nurse, Jessica Minns. I would go to Sibut, in the province of Oubangui-Chari where I would be starting a new medical clinic.

French Equatorial Africa was a French colony when I arrived in 1952— made up of four provinces: Tchad, Oubangui-Chari, Gabon, and Middle Congo. The country received its independence in 1960, and the four provinces became four separate countries. Baptist Mid-Missions (BMM) served in two of these provinces, later countries: Tchad, which became the nation we more commonly know as Chad; and Oubangui-Chari, which became the country of Central African Republic (CAR). This latter country is the size of the state of Texas, with about three million people, making it as sparsely populated as the states of North and South Dakota. Baptist Mid-Missions ministered to the central part, or about half of its area.

There were several stops before I landed at my final destination of Bangui, the capitol of the province Oubangui-Chari. We had our evening meal in Tripoli, and after a night on the plane we landed in the early morning in desolate, hot, dry Fort Lamy, the capitol of the province of Tchad. At Archambault, Tchad, Ruth deplaned and was met by the missionaries who lived there and by Jessica Minns and Bessie Falls, who came to escort her the seventy-five miles to Koumra.

One hour later, as the plane was descending over Bangui, I looked down and saw some people hurriedly leaving a house and going toward a parked car. I thought, *Could that be the missionaries coming to meet me?* It was. They had heard the sound of the plane and were driving the mile to the landing field to meet it.

I hardly had time to meet Ted Wimer of Bangui, and Bruce and Wilma Rosenau and their small daughter, Judy, from Sibut, when Ted said to me, "Put on your helmet." In those days all the missionaries wore safari type hard hats to prevent the sunrays from beating down on their heads, thus preventing sunstroke. Far more important to me were my sunglasses —and later the photo-gray lenses—to prevent the sun from glaring into my sensitive eyes.

What I remember most from our short drive to the mission were the large flowering acacia and flame trees. February is the middle of the dry season, and these beautiful trees make a delightful change of scenery from the brown, dry grass and bushes.

It was good meeting my future co-workers. Bruce and Wilma were a good-looking couple my age, in their first term as missionaries. We would work together many years. Of that time, most was joyful, some was difficult, and once we experienced great sadness, but always we found harmony and love together. Bruce was the third of five sons whose parents were Ferd and Ina Rosenau, pioneer missionaries to the area some thirty years earlier. Bruce had attended grade school in Africa but went to high school in the States.

As we were eating our noon meal, I got a terrible headache and my body and mind fell into turmoil. I hadn't a clue what was happening to me, but felt like I was losing my mind. Finally I said to Mrs. Wimer, "May I go lie down for a while? I don't feel well."

"Yes, of course," she replied. "You do look quite pale." I was so glad she didn't ask more questions but just escorted me into a bedroom.

There I could see the mosquito netting folded up over the top of the bed. At night it would be tucked under the mattress. I knew the netting was a necessity. It was one of the things on my missionary list that the church women had made for me.

As I was lying on the bed, I thought, *I've only been in Africa one hour, and already I'm ill. Is this what Africa is going to do to me?* I cried out in desperation, "Oh, Lord, help me." Later that evening I felt a little better but still had a throbbing headache. I found out later, by trial and error, that the malaria pills I had taken before leaving France caused the headache and accompanying symptoms. After I switched to a different anti-malaria drug, there were no more allergic reactions.

Next morning, the hundred-mile, four-hour trip to Sibut with Bruce and Wilma was uneventful. Bruce saw a leopard in the bushes by the side of the road, but by the time I looked, it was gone. As their car went over the bumps and ruts, Bruce and Wilma told me about Sibut and some of its history.

The mission was originally named Mid-Africa Mission because of its location midway between North and South Africa and between East and West Africa. A missionary to the Belgian Congo (later known as Zaire and now the Democratic Republic of Congo) named Mr. Haas had recognized the need for missions work in neighboring French Equatorial Africa. He recruited the first five missionaries for French Equatorial Africa and brought them to Sibut in 1921. Ina and Ferd Rosenau were in that first group. The Grace Brethren started their mission the same year and our two missions were the first Protestant ones in French Equatorial Africa. Later our home mission office in the States started sending missionaries to several countries of the world. They asked us to change our name to theirs, Baptist Mid-Missions, which now has 1,200 missionaries worldwide.

The Rosenaus' first son, Eugene, was born shortly after their arrival in 1921—the first white baby to be born at Sibut. The birth took place in a grass hut on top of the hill, attended only by Ferd. Eugene grew up and later came back to Sibut as a missionary, along with his wife, Ernestine (Ernie). They were on their first furlough when I arrived.

The area on the way to Sibut was mostly dry grass and bush country interspersed with woods. The first fires set by the Africans during dry season (from November to May) had burned some bush and grass. As we passed the small villages, where I could see the people in front of their mud-brick and grass houses, I kept thinking, *Lord, can I really learn to love these people? Their culture is so different from mine.* As I came to know them it didn't take long to develop a great love and respect for the people I had come to serve.

As we came into Sibut from the south, Wilma said, "Margery, look over on your right. You can see the hill where our mission station is located." At that first gaze, I would never have dreamed I would spend most of my life walking up and down that hill. The missionary houses were at the top, and the ministry buildings were down below. We went through the town of Sibut and turned east to go the two miles to our turnoff road, which in turn ran a quarter-mile to our hilltop.

On the mission road we passed by the Bible School village, where the students lived in mud-brick and grass houses. Then, leaving the three blocks of level ground where the student village stood, we started up the hill. To

The Rosenau family, with Florence Almen and Margery in the early 50's.

the right was a wide path lined on both sides with tall mango trees, which had been planted soon after the arrival of Ferd and Ina in 1921. Among the trees stood the children's class building and, 200 yards further, the thatched-roof brick church. As we rounded the corner before going up the steepest part of the hill, I was happy to see a beautiful flowering acacia tree. Palm trees with branches swaying in the breeze lined the rutted road. The missionaries had planted a species of grass that stayed a beautiful green through most of the dry season. How beautiful it was. My emotions were high. I kept thinking, *I'm really here! Here in Africa! Thank you Lord.*

As we reached the hilltop, I was awed by the spectacular view of the surrounding area. You could see for miles. I remember a missionary from the desert area of northern Tchad who visited Sibut years later during the rainy season. She spent many spare minutes outside, letting her gaze take in the vast countryside. When I inquired what she was doing, she said, "I'm soaking up this wonderful scenery to take back to my home in Tchad. Our place is sand and desert. We see very little green."

Over the years I too spent many hours outside in the early morning freshness, having devotions or eating breakfast on the veranda overlooking the vast countryside. One of the other houses faced the opposite direction as my house and had not only the distant view, but also a view of the Bible School village a couple of blocks down the hill, the children's classrooms over to the far right of the village, and the large soccer field between them. Later, in the 1990's, when I lived alone in that house, I enjoyed watching

Coming in on the mission road with the mission hill in the distance.

large birds flying back and forth in the valley below. There was a current of air that made it fun for them to soar on the air stream. As I watched this scene, I often thought of the day when Christ shall descend from heaven with a shout, with the voice of the archangel and the trumpet of God, and we will soar up to heaven to live with Him forever.

But back to my arrival. What a welcome I received! Instead of just Ferd and Ina Rosenau meeting me, there were six visiting missionaries from our mission and the Brethren mission. The Sango language committee was meeting (which they did four or five times a year) to work on their translation of the Old Testament into Sango. The New Testament was finished in 1934, and the French Equatorial Africa Christians were anxiously waiting for the day when the complete Bible would be theirs to read. It was 1967 before the completed Bible was printed.

I stayed with Bruce and Wilma for three months while studying Sango. Before I arrived, I had no idea what kind of houses the missionaries lived in. The Rosenau home was a seven-room brick structure with an aluminum roof and a covered veranda. Inside, it had cement floors, wood ceilings in part of the house, and homemade furniture.

I was quickly introduced to the Sibut stinkbugs. They inhabit all the houses on the hilltop by the tens of thousands and are a terrible nuisance. I was thankful for the mosquito net over my bed that night and every night so I could be rid of them for a while. Thankfully, they didn't bite, but if one happened to creep or fly into our food without our knowing it, we discovered it the second we chewed down on it. It was crunchy and ill tasting.

My bedroom didn't have a ceiling, and that first night I was awakened two times by a sound like a gun going off. Each time I quickly sat up in bed and wondered what was happening, but everything was quiet, so I settled back down. The next morning I asked Wilma, "What was the shot I heard a couple of times during the night?"

A smile quickly spread across her face as she replied, "They were green mangoes dropping off the trees onto the aluminum roof." Two months later, when I ate my first mango, I thought it tasted like turpentine, so I didn't try any more that season. Later I realized I had eaten it before it was completely ripe.

During the following years, I ate my share of mangoes. Wilma made mango sauce out of the green ones, and it tasted very good but needed lots of sugar to be edible. Mango sauce added much to the menu during the dry season, when fruits and vegetables were scarce.

The first church service I attended was on the mission station where Pokamandja was the pastor. The church building was brick, with a grass roof and an uneven brick floor. It was packed with 650 people. When Mr. Rosenau introduced me to the people, I spoke briefly, telling them how happy I was to be with them and how I had been looking forward to being a missionary in Africa since I was twelve years old.

The first song we sang was "I Will Praise Him." Even now, whenever I sing that song, my thoughts go back to my first Sunday in my new land. That day my heart was overflowing as I realized that hundreds of voices were praising the Lord. As I looked over the congregation and saw many of them singing without a songbook, I realized that they knew the hymns from memory. The realization came over me that one does not need to be in a beautiful church building, sitting in padded pews and singing to the accompaniment of a piano and organ, to be worshipping the Lord.

After the service many people surrounded me to shake my hand and say, "*balao mingui* [many greetings]." I soon learned that when one greets you with the word *balao*, you respond with *merci* (thank you). A warm feeling came over me, as I knew without a shadow of doubt I was welcomed.

One day it was especially hot, and Bruce remarked, "It could be 120 degrees out." I couldn't believe it was that hot, so Bruce said, "Take the thermometer outside and see." I did, and it went up to 110 and then broke. He was right.

Soon after I arrived, there was an event in my life that I will never forget. It was difficult for Wilma to get her daughter Judy to take malaria medicine. In fun I said to Judy, "Look, Judy, it is easy to take a pill," and I threw my quinine pill into my mouth—and it caught in my windpipe. I could scarcely breathe. I began wheezing and turned blue. The Heimlich maneuver was not known then, so Bruce and Wilma pounded my back. I knew I might die. Fortunately the pounding finally dislodged the pill. What a glorious feeling—I could breathe! The Lord knew my life wasn't finished yet.

Everyone called Ina Rosenau "Madame", the French word for "Mrs.," so I followed suit. She was my language teacher and taught me from her bed because of an infection in her legs, which caused them to be swollen, red, and ulcerated. At that time there were no Sango lesson books to study from, so in the daily hour we had together, I took notes and studied the language with her. Madame talked about her experiences in Africa for forty minutes and only taught me Sango for twenty minutes. I became frustrated. Her experiences were interesting, but I was anxious to learn the language at a faster pace. How good it was to go with Wilma to the children's classes, which helped me a lot.

Sango is not a difficult language. The vocabulary is limited, and the grammar is not complicated. The tonal quality is what makes the spoken language difficult. For example, in John 3:17 it says, "For God sent not his Son into the world to condemn the world, but that the world through him might be saved." In Sango the word for "sent" is "to." "To" can also mean, "to cook," depending on the tone of the voice. I often wonder if, when I quoted that famous verse, I had the wrong tone for "to" and actually said, "God cooked His Son."

The first national pastor I met, besides the mission church pastor, was Sana. As Bruce and Wilma introduced me to him, I was struck by the joy expressed on his smiling face as he put out his hand to say, "*Balao*." Then he said, "We have been praying for years for a nurse to come, and I am so thankful you have arrived." That sentence thrilled my soul.

I thought Sana was in his twenties, but Bruce informed me that he was in his late thirties. To me the Africans never looked their age. Also, I never dreamed then how I would later enjoy his last child, Joshua, in my classes. His melodious voice was a great addition to the bass section of the choir.

There was no medical work at the mission in Sibut, not even a building. I would be starting from scratch. The missionary men were going to make a temporary building so I could start sometime in the near future. I already felt the load of responsibility that some day would be mine. Thankfully, only the Lord knew what lay ahead of me.

8 - Louvrou Veronique

I feel like I am on sacred ground as I write about Louvrou Veronique. The Lord took an uneducated, heathen woman and transformed her into one of His most precious jewels.

One day, when we knew she would soon be coming from her village 400 miles away to help me in the medical ministry, Madame told me her story.

"A soldier, Sergeant Ajepandngo went to Louvrou's village in the district of Mobaye and saw this attractive seventeen-year-old teenager. A few weeks later, after negotiations, she became his fourth wife. He took her and her orphaned niece 500 miles to Sibut, where he was stationed in the military.

"Louvrou first heard the Word of God from the wives of two soldiers who were also stationed at Sibut. The good news of salvation was music to her ears, and she soon believed in the Lord. There was no question about her conversion because from the first she had an insatiable longing to know more about Christ. She never missed walking the two and a half miles to the mission church for the Sunday morning services and always stayed for the reading classes.

"In those days there were no reading primers in the Sango language, but hundreds of people learned to read from the book of John. Each learner had a stick and pointed to the word the leader said and repeated the word. And so it went, line after line in the same chapter.

"It wasn't long before Louvrou was reading fluently. She witnessed to her husband and the other wives but to no avail. The first wife told her husband that if he changed and left the idols and spirits, she would work witchcraft on him.

"Some of the soldiers in the camp didn't want Sergeant Ajepandngo to be in charge of their unit, so they worked witchcraft on him, and he later died of a strangulated hernia. The unbelievers claimed it was the witchcraft that killed him. There was much witchcraft in those days; even today in some areas it is still prevalent."

Louvrou Veronique was Margery's main mid-wife and also tended skin sores.

Throughout Louvrou's time at Sibut she maintained an excellent testimony. The missionaries were impressed with her growing knowledge of the Scriptures, as well as her love and zeal for the Lord. Madame Rosenau liked to use her in the women's work, and she soon learned to give a Gospel message. In fact, in later years at the dispensary, when it was her turn to give the message to those waiting, she would speak more than the ten minutes that we allowed for the message. I would say to myself, Louvrou, don't you know we have lots of work to do and we need to get started? But she was so filled with Jesus, she just had to proclaim Him.

About two years after her

husband died Louvrou came to Madame and said, "I am going home to my village."

Madame asked her, "Why do you want to go back there? Everyone here loves you, and you are learning so much about God's Word."

"My family is without Christ, and I want to tell them about Him. Also, I want my niece to find a husband among our tribe there."

In a way Madame was very sorry to see her go, but she answered Louvrou, "We will miss you here, but I am so glad you have a concern for your family's salvation. We will be praying for you."

One day soon after her conversation with Madame, Louvrou and her niece, Alissa, boarded an old rickety bus to go home. After two days of rough riding they arrived back home. She found out that her father had died while she was at Sibut, but her mother and siblings were still living. Louvrou soon started having classes for the women and children. Many believed, including her family.

There was an African Catholic lay worker named Selekon who had a small thatched chapel in the village, and a small group of people worshiped there. After a while Selekon had enough of seeing many people gathering under the trees near Louvrou's house and listening to her teaching. He came to her and said, "Who gave you permission to have classes in this village? It is my job to teach the people about God."

Louvrou looked him straight in the eye and said, "The Lord Jesus said in His Word that believers should tell others about Him, and I am only obeying His command."

He replied, "What does a woman like you know about the Bible? I don't have one, and it isn't necessary because I have a booklet that tells me what to teach about God. If you continue, I'll send for the French Catholic priest in Mobaye, and he will come and stop you."

Louvrou finished their conversation by saying, "The people here are hungry for the truth as it is proclaimed in the Bible, and I will continue to tell them about Jesus."

Many of the village men worked at a large coffee plantation close by the village. Many of these men attended Louvrou's classes and some of them believed, and the classes became larger as more people believed.

After Selekon threatened Louvrou one more time, he did send for the French priest. He came and had a talk with Louvrou, ending with these words" "If you don't stop your classes, we will return and burn your house down because what you are doing is not right." Of course, these words didn't deter her; she went on with the work for the Lord.

But as the date drew near for the priest to return, some of the people said to Louvrou, "We will hide your belongings and the benches in the woods, and at least they won't be burned."

She replied, "We will continue to ask the Lord to protect everything and the house. We have been praying about this; let us have the faith to believe that the Lord will answer our prayers."

One of the frequent storms that comes up quickly at the start of the rainy season blew in with such ferocity that the chapel in the village was blown down. Selekon appealed to the people to rebuild, but they refused. By this time there were about eighty believers.

The priest came again, and Louvrou met him with dignity, confidence, and a quiet and humble spirit. The priest met her in anger and said, "We have heard that you are continuing to teach the Bible. You have been warned about what the consequences would be for disobeying my words. Your house and benches will now be burned."

Calmly Louvrou replied, "I am only doing what Jesus has asked me to do. Many people here have burned their idols and witchcraft medicine, and they do not live in fear of them anymore because Jesus has changed their lives. If you burn my house and the benches, you will be fighting against God."

The words must have pierced his heart, for he turned abruptly and said to the Africans that came with him, "Let us go." They got into their truck and left. This was another lesson to the Africans as to how the Lord answers prayer.

Louvrou knew that the group of believers should have an African pastor, so she sent word to the closest missionary group, the Elim mission station in Mobaye, asking to have one sent to them. The Swiss missionary and an African pastor who came to check out the village were surprised to find so many believers. An African pastor did come to stay in their village, and they built a chapel so they wouldn't have to worship out under the trees. The African thatched chapels do not have any rooms attached, so the children and youth have their classes under the trees nearby.

After the arrival of the pastor, Louvrou received a letter from Madame Rosenau in Sibut. She wrote that a nurse would be coming to Sibut to start a medical ministry and she would need helpers. "Would you like to come back to Sibut and help her?" Madame asked.

Louvrou knew that this is what she wanted to do. She asked someone in the village to write a letter for her to Madame telling her that she would come.

Florence Almen

Florence Almen and I were the only single missionary ladies living at Sibut. She was away on furlough when I arrived in Sibut and had returned while I was away at Crampel. I couldn't help wondering what the lady that I was going to live with was like. When I first arrived at Sibut, Madame had told me some things about her.

She was Swedish-American and had had many adversities in her life, but she never let difficulties get her down. At first the six-room brick house that was her home (which was also to be mine) had a thatched roof. During one of the annual wildfires, the wind blew a burning bird's nest onto the roof, quickly setting it ablaze. After she lost the roof on her house, she lived in the storeroom, a small building behind the house, until the house roof was replaced with tile.

She first arrived in 1937 and returned to the States on furlough in 1940. After a year and a half, in the spring of 1941, she set out on her return trip to Africa. She sailed from New York on the Zam Zam, an Egyptian ship bound for Capetown, South Africa. It carried 202 passengers, including 120 missionaries and their children. Two days before its scheduled arrival date of April 19, the Zam Zam was torpedoed, and within only ten minutes it was listing.

A second German ship rescued survivors from the sea, and for over a month they were prisoners of war. During that time life was very difficult for them. Women and children were crowded into any spare cabins and the hold, while the men had to sleep on deck. The German ship did not carry sufficient supplies for feeding 200 extra people, so little food was

Florence Almen did the cooking in our house.

available to the captives. The children were fed first, and the adults just had to go hungry most of the time.

Finally the Germans took them to Lisbon, Portugal being a neutral country, from where the missionaries were able eventually to get back to New York.

After a few months of recuperation from their ordeal, she, along with two missionary couples, started back to Africa. While crossing the Atlantic Ocean on the way to France, their ship was part of a convoy due to the threat of German attack. In France, they boarded a freighter that was bound for Matadi, a town on the west coast of Africa. From there they found ground travel to French Equatorial Africa.

While on furlough ten years later, she had an eye removed due to cancer and had a prosthesis put in. When she returned to Africa, God in His wisdom brought us to live together, which we did until Florence returned to the United States in 1979 to fight abdominal cancer

Both of us had adjustments to make. In our first meeting she brought up two things that made me want to shout "hallelujah." First, she remarked, "I have cooked for many years, and if you don't mind, I'll keep on doing that." I was delighted only to have to help her. She had two African helpers: Demele, who was trained to do the cooking, and Oumar, who did everything else.

Second, she brought out a fifty-gallon drum of bandages from Johnson & Johnson, in Chicago, her hometown. The company had given them to her for use in Africa. I was amazed! I knew I would need bandages and had been praying for some. I had even written letters home concerning them. Now they were here, three months before I needed them! My heart was filled with praise to our Almighty God. Why is it that we are sometimes amazed when the Lord answers our prayers?

Florence loved to entertain and frequently had co-workers over. I was privileged to help at those times. Her main ministry was with the children, but she was also an excellent teacher in our Bible School. She had paid and volunteer staff in her children's classes, where the children learned to read, write, sew, color, memorize scripture, and most importantly, have Bible lessons.

In earlier years most of the children didn't go to the government schools, so the mission classes were very important in their lives. These classes were held in a large building down the hill that we always referred to as "the children's class building," even though other classes were held there also. She taught at our school in the mornings. Then, a couple of afternoons each week, she walked to a village close by to teach the children. In later years, when she couldn't see very well, a ten-year-old girl, Sylvia, held her hand and walked with her as a guide.

The more I got to know Florence, the more I appreciated her love for the Lord and for the African people.

One day a high government official, a minister from Bangui, came to see Bruce. As he and Bruce were talking on the veranda, he looked down the hill and saw the children's class building. He smiled and remarked, "I learned to read in that building under Mademoiselle Almen. I hoed weeds around the building for four days to earn a New Testament."

In a letter to her family and friends at home in the States, Florence told what it was like to conduct classes in this building.

Sibut, May 26, 1964
Dear Friends,

Life still continues to be interesting—even in Africa! Company and more company! Every car on the place has been worked on—and worked on strenuously as Bob Vaughn helped Gene during the family's stay here. Are we ever thankful for SUCH help! Time and strength go into motors on cars, pump, and light plant. — Then there's sickness, and more sickness! Maybe it's a flu bug, but IF it is, how did it ever slip by me? But I may be speaking too soon! Natives and whites alike have been "hit". — Then there are UPS and DOWNS in children's classes, and we really HAD IT one day last week. I shall have to take the rest of the letter to tell you about it.

In the classroom there are no mothers some days, but THIS DAY there were two. I could hear and feel that all wasn't going well, so I finally went in the TINY TOTS room. A child had vomited all over the floor and toys, and was crying HARD. When I asked the mothers why they didn't help the child, one answered me, "nothing is wrong!" I said, "Come here and see." If black faces could be red, theirs were. I try to make them realize we do not have them there just to visit together, BUT that it is really WORK to care for 30 little ones.

Then, when they were marching out, a snake fell from the roof right into the midst of the girls! Did they EVER scream! The boys had gone on out, and the screaming so excited Sibuti, Louvrou's dog, that he bit a boy in the seat. The boy came in bleeding, so I told him to go quickly to the clinic.

To add to the confusion, while I was giving out the

handwork two girls got into a fight. My, how they went at it, like savages, right in the class building. When words didn't stop them, I picked up a twig that was on the floor and whacked them on the shoulders and arms with it. It worked. Because one had started to bite the other, I took both of them by the hand to hold them apart and tried to shame them by asking them what they thought they were. Animals? As they calmed down, and because they were both Christians, I asked if they thought Jesus was happy to see them act like that. They shook hands, but only God knows what was in their hearts. A little brother had gone for the mother of one of the girls, so she arrived to wreak vengeance also, but I told her the classroom was my domain. Oh, it happens every once in a while!—Oh yes, Kaila killed the snake while I held on to our dog, Smoky.

Later, I found out that a French reading book and a pair of scissors was missing. THAT is never supposed to happen, but with all the excitement it did. In three years that was only the second pair of scissors missing. That isn't a bad record, especially for boys and girls who do not have scissors in their homes. BUT they know that if the scissors, crayons, or books disappear, there won't be any more, so we really had to have cooperation on that. Once a ball point pen was missing after writing class. The next day a boy told me he had seen someone with one of our blue and yellow pens. I sent a staff person to retrieve it. With the excuse it was taken "by mistake," it was given back. I do thank the Lord that we did not have more stealing in class. True, the TINY TOTS tried to take a toy every once in a while, and if they didn't succeed, they would just take the stuffing out!

Isn't that all interesting? All in the Lord's work, and yes a part in the training of the teacher and the boys and girls. Is it worthwhile? YES, a thousand times, YES. So many have come to know Jesus and have learned to read the Word in children's classes through all the years He has given me here. I still say they are the "love" the Lord has given me. Sometimes they are quite naughty, or maybe very stupid, or trying, but IF there were NO KIDS, I doubt that I'd be here either. So I thank Him for MY

KIDS. They make me draw nigh to Him!

Now this letter is lengthy, and you've heard about MY KIDS. All the other classes keep going, too, you know: teenage boys and teenage girls, a college group, women's work, Bible School, the Press, the clinic, the village work, and the churches here. The work goes on in the other towns and in the bush of the Sibut area. All need your prayer help in these trying days. The Bookstore papers haven't come through yet. This IS Africa. But we trust we can soon tell you it is being used for His glory in getting literature out to the people.

With much love, because of His love for us, and many thanks for your letters,

Florence

The Rosenaus

For most of my years in Africa there was at least one Rosenau couple at Sibut. This family was an encouragement and inspiration to all of us privileged to serve with Baptist Mid-Missions in Africa.

As children, all the Rosenau boys learned a lot of practical knowledge from their father, Ferd, as he worked on various projects around the station. Ferd Rosenau was always teaching as he worked. Even in later years, when Dr. Fisher came to Sibut and needed to have his truck repaired, I heard Ferd say, "I don't mind helping you, but you come with me to the garage. You need to know what is under the hood of your truck. You won't always have someone with you when you need help."

Ferd was a hard worker. When Madame would say, "Ferd, slow down, take a siesta," he always had his answer ready, "I will, some day when I can put my feet in the cool, clean river of The River of Life in our heavenly home." He did just that in 1959, in the arms of his son Bruce at the Bangui Hospital. He lived long enough to see the Sango Bible in the last stages of preparation before being sent to the printer. He had been the director of the language committee and had worked on translating the Old Testament for almost fourteen years.

Two of Ferd's sons, Eugene and Bruce, returned to Central African Republic as missionaries. As adults, his sons' knowledge enabled them to be builders, mechanics, electricians, linguists, botanists, teachers, and preachers. What a terrific combination, using all that knowledge on the mission field to reach the lost for Christ.

Above all, they learned to trust in the Lord and follow the faith as their parents had. They would not give up when difficult circumstances came. Bruce was aware of how the Lord had helped his parents in their grief over the loss of a six-month-old son. The Lord also helped Bruce and his wife through a similar loss when their two-year-old Carol died of malaria after only seven hours of illness. Both sons also learned how to give, for their parents gave everything they had to their ministry. And if they didn't have the money for a needed project, their faith-believing prayers brought it in.

The brothers both married women as supportive as their own mother was in the home and in the ministry. Eugene met Ernestine (Ernie) while they were working in the kitchen at Bryan University in Tennessee. He couldn't have picked a more loving, gracious, hospitable woman, or one who was more right for his temperament. Bruce met Wilma at the same school, and she had qualities similar to those of her sister-in-law. Her great expertise was sewing, with music following as a close second. Both women were good teachers, and they were like sisters to me.

The Rosenau men also had leadership abilities. Ferd, Bruce, and Eugene's son Vernon served at different times as president of our Missionaries' Field Council. I am thankful the Lord gave me four families of Rosenaus to be my co-workers. Since we were a large station, with many different ministries —Bible School, printing, garage, medical clinic, the care of forty churches and their pastors, and a large missionary staff to oversee—it was a challenge to trust God to work on behalf of our African people. Many other missionaries came to work with us at different times.

A few months after I arrived in Africa, Eugene, Ernestine, and their three children, Anna Kay, Douglas, and Vernon, returned to Africa from furlough while I was at Crampel. They were able to bring back an old hand-fed press with them. Sibut didn't have a building for it, so with much prayer, ingenuity, and work, they put the press on the second floor of the big house where the elder Rosenaus lived. Years later they built a large building downhill that had a print shop and a scripture book house, which had a national ministry.

Eugene amazed us with his photographic memory and could converse on any subject he had read or heard about. One day, when several of us were having a meal together, his son Doug asked his father something about the cobra snake. I sat there spellbound as Eugene gave a lengthy lecture on it as if he was quoting from an encyclopedia. It was an education to listen to him.

Right after their arrival they invited me to go with them on a trip to the mission station at Ippy. I hadn't opened up the clinic yet, so I was glad for the opportunity. The part of that six-hour, hot, dusty trip that I remember best was three-year-old Vernon standing by the knees of his mother in the front seat, singing with gusto over and over again:

> *To the East, to the West, to the North and the South,*
> *We must go, we must go, with the Gospel of Light.*

I never dreamed as I sat in the back seat listening to little Vernon sing that someday he would come back to Sibut as a third-generation missionary, to proclaim the Gospel of Light.

Eugene and Ernestine Rosenau's youngest son, Vernon, returned to Africa as a missionary in August 1977. Coming with him was his wife, Jan, a niece of his Aunt Wilma. I worked with them until I left the field in 1994. Many are the memories of the months when the three of us were the only missionaries on Sibut station. It was almost like the time Florence and I, along with Bruce and Wilma, were the only ones on the station for almost a year. Vernon was a leader, a good mechanic, and a teacher, while Jan was a good homemaker and had the job of home-schooling their three children.

In the early '70s most missionaries wanted to home-school their children rather than send them off to the missionary school in Crampel. Thus there weren't enough children to keep the school open for the children of the parents who preferred the regular school. Also, there were fewer missionaries on the field.

Vernon and Jan were on the field until December 1999, when they felt they should not go back as missionaries. As Vernon stood on the veranda of one of the missionary houses overlooking the mission village, his mind went over the past, back to the time when his grandparents came to the field in 1921. He felt that if he stayed on, the Africans wouldn't mature in leadership. So, with much sorrow in their hearts but with perfect peace, they left. He then became field administrator in the mission office in Cleveland for our missionaries in Africa and Europe.

Lynn and Margo Muhr

Many missionaries worked at Sibut over the years. Some are only briefly mentioned in the following chapters because it would take too long to tell about them all at any length. However, I would like to mention one more couple, Lynn and Margo Muhr.

Lynn and Margo and their daughters, Leanne and Jennifer, came to the field in 1972. Lynn was a printer, mechanic, and teacher, and Margo was a teacher. At daybreak one Sunday morning when they had only been at Sibut for five months, I stood under their bedroom window and called, "Lynn, Lynn, are you awake?"

It took time for him to get out of bed, come to the window, and ask, "Is something wrong?"

I replied, "A man passed away last night, and I need to get his body and his family home. I have to teach my Sunday School class, and I can't go and get back in time. Would you take my truck and take them home?"

"Yes, I would be glad to."

Lynn asked his African printer, Kilas, to go with him. It was always good to take an African with us when we traveled.

When Lynn and Kilas came to a village about eight miles out, a soldier was standing beside the road waving for them to stop. Since Lynn was still a little shy about speaking Sango, he said to Kilas, "You do the talking." Kilas asked the soldier what he wanted, but in his mind he knew the soldier needed a ride.

The soldier replied, "I need to go to Grimari. Would you take me as far as you are going?"

Kilas replied, "We have a body in the truck that we are taking to his village, but you can ride that far." The soldier's facial expression quickly changed to fear. He saluted and said, "Go ahead. Bon voyage."

On Lynn and Kilas's return trip they arrived at the church at Nguerko just as Sunday School was starting, so they stopped for worship. The pastor was preaching in his other church, so a deacon was in charge.

When Sunday School and all the church preliminaries were finished, the deacon announced with joy, "We are so happy that a missionary could be with us today. He will be giving us God's word now." The deacon hadn't asked Lynn first. Whenever a missionary was present, the Africans always wanted them to preach.

Lynn was dumfounded! As yet he had not acquired enough courage to preach a sermon in Sango. Each Sunday he would go to a church with either Bruce or Eugene, and they would do the speaking. As he arose from his chair and slowly made his way to the small wooden pulpit, he sent an SOS prayer to God for His help. He spoke for ten or fifteen minutes. I'll always remember it took someone's death to start Lynn preaching. After that experience he and Margo, along with their daughters, went out most Sundays to preach in one of our forty churches.

We constantly had patients coming to the clinic from all over our district. After their treatment and purchases of food they seldom had enough money to pay the fare home on one of their dilapidated, run-down busses. The missionary men knew when I asked the question, "Where are you going to preach this Sunday?" that I wanted them to take people home from the clinic. They never refused if they were going in the direction our clients needed to go. I am so grateful for the missionary men on Sibut station who helped me with their trucks by serving as ambulance, bus, or hearse chauffeurs. Many times I couldn't do those chores because of other pressing duties, or it was a night call, and I didn't travel long distances at night, especially in the later years. The men considered this a ministry to the African people. Galatians 6:10 says, "As we have therefore opportunity, let us do good unto all men, especially unto them who are of the household of faith."

10 - Learning From Others

After three months at Sibut I went a hundred miles north to Crampel (later renamed Kaga-Bondoro) to work with Ruth Bartow in order to learn more about tropical medicine. Ruth was the nurse who had come to see us off when we left for France. Now she was filling in for a nurse who was home on furlough. When the person for whom she was substituting returned, Ruth would return to her work at Kyabe, Tchad. The missionary children's school, having forty children, was at Crampel, and they needed a nurse in case of an emergency.

I loved the 4:00 p.m. daily prayer meetings the missionaries held in a small, one-room thatched building. They would pray for the ministries of the station, which included the Bible School and the forty graduates who were now pastors of churches in their large area.

Ruth was a dear, and I followed her around like a puppy, ready to learn what I could. After only a month Ruth left me in charge, as she had to go back to her station in Tchad to restock the supply of medicine for Crampel. By noon the first day I was so discouraged I could have quit. I couldn't understand what the patients were saying. When I did understand, I wasn't sure what to do for their illnesses, and when I felt pretty sure I gave the right medicine, I kept thinking, *Did I do the right thing?*

At noon, when I went to the house where I was staying, carrying a load of medical books under my arm, I was at my wit's end. After lunch I went down on my knees in my room and poured out my heart to the Lord, saying, "Lord, I can't do this without a doctor." Again the Lord brought to mind the wonderful verse He had given me in Nyssa, Oregon, two years earlier: "Faithful is he that calleth you, who also will do it" (1 Thessalonians 5:24). I said, "Thank you, Lord, for reminding me again of Your faithfulness, and forgive me for doubting. I know I can't do this work by myself, but You can do it through me." In this I had peace.

Later after Ruth came back, it was vacation time for the missionary school. The missionary school teacher, Catherine Ayers, my hostess Bertha Manuel, and the African children's worker took me to the large village of Mbres. They worked there with the pastor, teaching women and children. I loved their ministry; even living in a hut with a dirt floor didn't matter.

But the outhouse! It was dark when I first went out there. I shone my flashlight down the hole and saw hundreds of fat six-inch worms, each with at least twenty-five legs, crawling all over each other. I learned later they were called millipedes. I ran pell-mell out of there. Catherine said, "Don't get disturbed; they are way down, and they won't bother you. If you are going to do 'road work,' you will have to get used to all different kinds of outhouses."

One evening after a busy day, while sitting around talking, I asked Catherine something that had been going through my mind. "Don't you ever worry that something will happen to your truck when you go this far away from the mission?"

Her answer gave me the courage to trust God likewise. She said, "Margery, before I brought a truck to Africa, I prayed that the Lord would keep it from breaking down whenever I go out like this. And you know what? It never has."

Profoundly affected, I said, "If the Lord can do it for you, He can do it for me." From then on I started asking the Lord to provide a truck for me to use in the medical ministry and to take to the villages to teach. The men on Sibut station knew mechanics and took good care of my vehicles. Over the years I traveled thousands of miles in three different trucks and a car, and I had only one breakdown—about twenty miles from Sibut. A missionary came out to rescue me.

One day a small, thin lady with a sweet smile came to me. She said, "My name is Louvrou, and Madame Rosenau sent me to be with Mademoiselle Benedict." Knowing her history, I was anxious to meet her, and I immediately loved her. I showed her how to take care of the sores and skin ulcers that are prevalent everywhere in Africa. She helped me very much in pronouncing and learning more Sango.

One day soon after her arrival she said to me, "My stomach has been hurting me for a long time. Can you help me?"

I replied, "Of course I will. Please bring me a small sample of your stool, and I will examine it under the microscope." (The class I took at the medical school in Paris on parasitology was certainly being profitable!)

We examined the stool sample, then drew a blood sample. To my amazement we found the eggs of four different parasites and microfilaria in her blood. No wonder she was having tummy aches, with roundworm, hookworm, tapeworm, bilharziasis, and filaria inhabiting her body. This was the largest number of parasites I ever found in one person.

When we left Crampel to go to Koumra, she went back to Sibut to wait for me. She gradually regained her health and strength. As we worked together, I taught her hygiene, and I never remember treating her again for intestinal parasites.

After three months at Crampel, I received word from Sibut that the missionaries had not had time to build the temporary clinic building. It was decided I should go to Koumra and learn more under Jessica Minns. I was fortunate in the fact that there was a missionary couple going to Tchad at that time, so I was able to go with them. The missionaries hardly ever traveled on the rickety African busses or trucks, for those vehicles were always breaking down.

I remember once, years later, when I had to go by African truck from Crampel to Sibut. Two trucks were going, but how could I decide which one to take, and how would I know if the drivers had been drinking? I went up close to shake each chauffeur's hand. I almost put my face next to theirs in order to smell if they had alcohol on their breath. One of them had, so you know which truck I chose! Even so, it took eight hours to go the hundred miles to Sibut.

Staff helper Yakete showing the tapeworm that came from the child beside him.

It was so good to see Ruth Nephew again at Koumra and compare experiences of our first six months in Africa. She laughed as she told me how she once greeted an African by saying "sweet potatoes" instead of saying "hello." The words were similar, *babalo* and *balao*. *Balao* not only means "hello" but can also mean "good morning," "good afternoon," or "good night."

I enjoyed working with Jessica. She was a capable nurse and had a sense of humor that rubbed off on anyone near her. She could make us all laugh with her descriptions of experiences of every day life, whether with the Frontier Nursing Service in Kentucky or in Africa. But one day she wasn't laughing. Three patients had died. That was a tough day to get through. The clinic saw 100 to 200 patients a day, besides having a thriving maternity ward. She had taken her midwifery training in Hyden, Kentucky, and I entertained the thought that maybe I could go there when I came home on furlough.

I will never forget one experience I had at Koumra. A pregnant African woman was on her way to the clinic, but before she could make it, her baby was born alongside the road in a small pile of sand. The baby was covered with vernix, a cheese-like substance that newborns have. But this little one had by far more vernix than any newborn I had ever seen, and the sand was really embedded in it. It took me over an hour to clean the baby, and I wondered while I worked if I would rub her skin off in the process.

After spending a profitable month at Kourma, I went back to Sibut when a ride became available.

11 - Back on the Hilltop

When I returned to Sibut from Crampel, I was not yet able to start my medical work. The temporary building that Eugene and his father were building for the clinic was not finished. They were adding three rooms to the Bible School for the clinic. The work had been progressing slowly, as the men were also supervising the last of the building of the Grimari church, an out-station sixty miles from Sibut. If that church project were not done within the agreed upon time, the property would have to be returned to the government.

Florence Almen had returned from furlough while I was in Crampel and so I spent my mornings with Florence in her children's classes. In the afternoons I spent time typing the first draft of Mr. Rosenau's translation of the books of Ezra and Psalms. These books were to be edited at the next language committee meeting. Meanwhile the new missionaries who had finished their French studies were coming to Sibut for three months of language study with Madame. I enjoyed having them around because we had good times together.

Our annual missionary conference met at Crampel in November 1952. At that time it was two weeks long, though in later years it lasted only one week. That year twenty-three new missionaries arrived to join the ranks, including three doctors and six nurses. We then had ninety-five missionaries, the most on the field at any time in our history. (From 1952 to 2000 the ranks dwindled to nine.)

I was amazed that all the ladies wore long stockings on Sunday. After ten months of being stockingless, I didn't relish wearing them again, especially in the heat. So I broke the tradition, and no one said a word. In fact, comfort won out over tradition, and the other new recruits soon followed suit.

The theme of the conference was love. I had been having a spiritual battle about an attitude that had been bothering me for a quite some time. I knew I had to change and had been earnestly praying for the Lord's guidance. At daybreak one morning I again went into the prayer hut to take my burden to the Lord. Soon a veteran missionary, Mrs. Nimmo, came in and knelt down beside me and said, "I feel that you need someone to pray with you about a burden you are carrying. Would you like me to help you?"

"Please," I replied. "I don't want to tell you about it, but I need victory about something."

She seemed to understand and starting praying. After her prayer, such a wonderful peace overwhelmed my soul that is hard to describe. The Lord worked a miracle! I knew He was undertaking for me. Praise the Lord for prayer partners, especially those whose Spirit-filled lives are an inspiration to others, like dear Mrs. Nimmo.

The big day arrived! December 1952 saw the opening of the clinic. My equipment from France and the medicines I ordered from the States had arrived. The African carpenter had finished making enamel-top tables, a cabinet with wheels, and shelves for the pharmacy room. The cabinet was made so it could be wheeled outside each day. There Louvrou could take care of sores while being in the fresh air. Mr. Rosenau was quite creative in seeing that the cabinet was made properly.

Classes were held for my two helpers, Levi and Louvrou, to teach them the routine of the clinic. Levi was a senior in our Bible School, chosen for his ready smile and willingness to work. That first morning we had our Bible reading and prayer together, a procedure we followed throughout the years. Our mission pastor, Pokamandja, gave a short message to thirty patients waiting outside under the mango trees. In the following months we all took turns giving the morning talk about Jesus.

That first day I began to see again the frightening implications of a nursing career in Africa without the assistance of a doctor. I found comfort that the Lord promises wisdom to those who lack it. Now I was seeing what it really meant to be a "missionary on her own." How I prayed that I would be a good one.

Two weeks after we opened, we had forty-five patients a day. The most serious case was a man who received a bad leg burn because of an epileptic seizure that caused him to fall into a fire. I would have been scared to death if someone at home had asked me to undertake treating an injury like that. If it weren't for the Lord, I wouldn't have had the courage to help him.

To prevent infection, I gave him a week's treatment with a sulfa drug and was careful to use sterile techniques in changing his daily Vaseline dressings. Over the next month he returned every other day to have his dressings changed. The burned area healed up nicely, and he became a walking billboard for the work we were doing.

Two of our first converts in the medical ministry were teenagers. Right away I had a longing to have a Bible class for them, but I didn't feel ready just yet. I wasn't fluent enough to teach a Bible class without a lot of study,

Margery with dispensary helpers Michel Demijou (left), Louvrou Veronique and Levi Besioni at the microscope.

and I knew the clinic work would take up most of my time. I encouraged them to attend our local church and hoped they would be discipled. I was better prepared in my second term, and I began teaching a class for the youth, who were so hungry for the Word.

The first weeks and months treating patients was on-the-job training, and I began to see what was needed to make running the clinic easier. As each day passed, I realized anew how much better I could help the sick if I had a half-ton truck. Florence and I prayed in earnest for one. We remembered the Lord's words in John 16:24: "Ask, and ye shall receive, that your joy may be full." We needed a vehicle that could be used as an ambulance and a hearse, and to transport us out to the villages for evangelistic work.

12 - Experiences in 1953

My First African Conference

A couple of months before the opening of the clinic, as Florence and I were sitting at the dinner table, I remarked, "I wish the clinic would be finished so I could start my medical work."

She answered, "You wouldn't want a smallpox epidemic to break out, would you?" It was just a passing statement, but a couple of months later it became a reality.

Each year in March the African churches had a Bible conference on the mission station. Three months after I opened the clinic, it was time for the conference. At first we thought we weren't going to have it because smallpox was developing in the Wawa area. Soon our hearts were saddened to learn that Pastor Demagaza of the Gbabete church, just ten miles from Wawa, his wife and his mother had all three died of smallpox. His nine-year-old girl was also infected, but she lived.

In spite of the epidemic, the Africans and missionaries decided to proceed with the conference. The men went hunting and found enough wild game to feed 300 people. Eugene and his father took their trucks and made several trips to pick up pastors and their families from miles out so they could be there. Dr. Cullen, our newest doctor in Ippy, came to examine all of our students and the pastors and their families. I was so thankful that my microscope had arrived from the States so we could do lab exams.

I had one wonderful surprise. The Saturday before the conference started on Monday, Ruth Nephew came to spend her vacation with me. She never got to rest on that vacation. She worked with me from morning into the night. I can't imagine what I would have done without her. The Lord knew I needed her.

Ruth was an extremely organized nurse. She worked at several of our clinics when the primary nurse was on furlough, then later became the permanent nurse at Bangassou. Dr. Rouch once mentioned that Ruth's clinic was the most organized of all our clinics.

On Tuesday morning Zeneba, a pastor's wife with seven children, the youngest only two months old, came to see me. I knew her because she had been at the clinic a month before with a very infected hand and had had to have one finger amputated. She said, "Mademoiselle, would you come down to the village and see my husband? He is too ill to climb the hill to the clinic."

"What are his symptoms?" I asked her.

"His body is very hot, and he hurts all over," she answered.

I left my other work, and we walked single file down the rocky, steep, narrow path to the house where Pastor Punio was staying. He had a temperature of 105 degrees, so I temporarily treated him for malaria. Ruth and I watched him closely for two days. Each day he became more lethargic and his temperature rose higher.

On the third day small pimples covered his body. "Oh, no," I cried within myself and to Ruth, "not another pastor with smallpox."

Ruth and I quickly set up an isolation unit in a one-room brick house at the end of the student village. We sent word for Eugene to announce to the conference attendees not to go near the brick house and to please pray for Pastor Punio. I don't know exactly what he said in his flawless Sango, but it was sufficient for them to heed his warning. Zeneba told me then that Punio had gone to visit Pastor Demagaza at Gbabete before his death and had been exposed to the disease. Africans are a very compassionate people, especially the Christians, visiting and helping the sick.

The pimples on Punio's body turned into pustules, and his temperature went up to 107 degrees. His body was so full of pustules that a person couldn't put a finger anywhere on his body without touching one, and maggots started feeding on them. He mumbled, "I want to go be with Jesus." His prayers were answered.

I couldn't let the people have a wake or take time to build a casket for him. He was wrapped in a mat and carried to the burial ground. I had a very real sense of the reality of two of God's promises: "To be absent from the body is to be with Christ" (2 Corinthians 5:8), and "Precious in the sight of the Lord is the death of his saints" (Psalm 116:15), which also brought much comfort to my heart. The Lord knew how much I needed those scriptures. This was the first death in my ministry, and it was one of our pastors. I could almost visualize Punio being ushered into heaven and being welcomed by the One whom he had faithfully proclaimed. What a hope we believers have! My heart ached for Zeneba, though, with her family of seven children, and I was amazed at her serenity through it all. What a testimony she was to everyone!

We were all praying, "Lord, don't let this disease spread." But Stephen, the two-year-old son of a deacon in Punio's church, came down with it. He had been exposed before he came to the conference. He recovered, but the disease left pockmark scars on his face. All the other people at the conference said they had been vaccinated. Even so, I ordered enough vaccine from France to vaccinate approximately 150 Africans living in our village.

One other episode of that conference stands out in my memory. I was at home when someone ran up the hill and yelled some frightful news to me. "Come quickly to the clinic. A teenage girl is writhing on the ground in excruciating pain." I hurried as quickly as I could. As I came to the top of the steep path that led down to the clinic, I could hear her distress. When I was about ten feet from her, a woman came with a basin and put it under the girl's face. She vomited enough food to have fed several people. I was relieved to know she wasn't dying. I didn't admonish her not to eat that much again. I thought she had learned her lesson.

Along with smallpox, we treated whooping cough cases. Nearly everyone had at least one parasite and ever so many other things. During her "vacation time" Ruth kept busy extracting teeth that had been given no care. By the time the villagers came to our clinic with their tooth problems, we had no choice but to extract the offending teeth.

Madame wrote several of the hymns in our book *Bia ti Sepala* (Songs of Praise). She was an excellent song leader, and when her health permitted, she taught a new hymn each year at the conference. She got enthusiastic singing from our African Christians, who loved her songs.

I couldn't attend the conference that year or the following one, as there were too many patients to take care of. I tried to let the staff go to one meeting a day. They needed the spiritual fellowship. I would have liked to hear the pastor's testimonies, but that had to wait until later years, when I

Ruth Nephew after just pulling a pastors tooth. Levi is holding the basin.

went to a district conference. At the second conference Levi told me about a testimony Pastor Kabalegue gave. I will always remember it.

Kabalegue was moving to a new village not far from where he used to live. Just before he moved into his new house, Madugu, an unbeliever, and one of the men from the village put all kinds of witchcraft paraphernalia around and in the new house. He bragged to the unbelievers in his village that the pastor was going to die. A week went by, and the pastor was still alive. One day soon after this, Madugu and people from his village were walking to their gardens. A buffalo rushed out of the tall grass, headed straight for Madugu. and killed him. None of the other people were harmed. For days the people talked about this incident among themselves, and they said, "This must be of God." As a result many of the people in the village believed and burned their witchcraft materials. The Lord turned evil into good.

The Fetzers' Visit

In July of 1953 it was so good to have the Fetzers and the Balyos visit our mission field. Arthur Fetzer was the home secretary who took care of much of our business, and Rev. John Balyo was on our mission council. When Mrs. Fetzer visited the clinic and saw so many people with skin ulcers, she remarked, "One has to be 'called' out here or they will never be happy doing this work." What she said was true. I was called, and I was content.

The main thing I remember about Mr. Fetzer's visit was the short speech he gave in Bangui to about 3,000 people sitting under mango trees. There was not yet a church building on the mission property. Just as Mr. Fetzer started to speak, he grabbed his right pant leg, and then he grabbed the left one, then the right one again. He interrupted his talk with, "I do not know what is the matter with me." We missionaries were also sitting under the mango trees and had an idea what was troubling him. Some mango ants had gone up his sock, and when they found bare skin, they decided to have their dinner. Their bite stings. Because of these ants, the Africans very seldom climb mango trees to pick the delicious fruit. Instead they throw small rocks or use long bamboo sticks tied together, with a small, open cloth bag attached to the end.

I know I should be able to remember Mr. Fetzer's short greeting, but his "ant dance" antics are all that I can recall. I am so glad that the Lord gave us all a sense of humor.

Ingo's Mother

Believing in God shows on our face, and it brings joy! We saw it on Ingo's mother's face when she was born into the Lord's family. She had come to the clinic several times before because her baby, Ingo (which means "salt") was ill with malaria.

One morning I asked her if she was a believer, and she replied, "No, but I am seeking The Way." As I was talking, a man who had believed two weeks earlier put his words with mine and said, "If you believe, you will find peace." It gave me a thrill as I saw this young Christian encouraging her to believe. I asked Louvrou to continue to more fully explain the plan of salvation to this woman. God gave understanding and the joy of the Lord shone on her face.

Shortly after that Ingo's mother came into the clinic with a new believer friend and her baby. One look at the friend's one-month-old baby boy and I knew he wasn't going to live long. I made a diagnosis of bronchial pneumonia and thought each breath was going to be his last. I told the mother that even with medicine, it would only be the Lord that could save him. I told the two new Christian mothers I felt it would be to the glory of God to heal this little one, so we prayed for the Lord to undertake. I treated the pneumonia, and they stayed until the clinic closed. I did not want to see her return to their village, but there was nothing else I could do. I had no place to keep them. The next morning the mother returned, and one glance at the baby told us the Lord had answered our prayer!

Many times I saw the Lord heal sick bodies when it seemed hopeless. And yet many times I saw them pass on. We always did what we could and left the outcome to the Lord.

Changing the Rule

What is the worth of a human soul? That thought struck me quite forcibly when I was trying to explain to Yassabada that I would not repeat her injections for bilharziasis, a parasite. I had made a policy at the clinic that treatments would not be repeated if patients weren't faithful in following instructions completely to the end. There were just too many who followed instructions only when it was convenient, not realizing that a treatment had to be finished in order for them to get well.

As I was talking to Yassabada, I felt compelled to give her another opportunity. I knew she was not saved. Louvrou had witnessed to her many times, but she had no desire to repent of her sins. The Bible says there is not anything in this world that can be exchanged for the human soul, and here I was almost sending her away because of a two-dollar treatment.

During her second series of shots, Louvrou had the joy of leading Yassabada to the Lord. The next Sunday she gave her testimony to the deacons, and they enrolled her in the new convert's class. It was a lesson for me to relearn—not to be so busy that I fail to heed the voice of the Holy Spirit in my daily walk with Him.

An Epidemic

For two months in the latter part of the year, an epidemic of mouth infections, especially among the children, was troubling. Blood flowed out of their gums, dribbling down on their clothes. It had a horrible odor. It took a messy treatment, with penicillin shots in their bottoms and gentian violet on their gums. Gentian violet is a stain which, if it got on their clothing, could not be washed out. Thankfully, if they came twice daily for three days of treatments and did what we said when they went home to their villages, the infection could be stopped. One of the children who came to me with it was Stephen, the one who had survived smallpox that spring. His memory served him well. He screamed when he saw me, but I gave him a couple of lumps of sugar and won him over before I treated him.

Chief Sanjo

Sanjo was an old chief who didn't seem to have much personality and was a man of few words. He came from the village of Wawa, about thirty-five miles from Sibut. For a month he received injections three times weekly for the bilharziasis parasite, all the while listening to the daily Gospel message.

Wawa and the parasite bilharziasis seemed to go together. The parasite lives in water and enters the human body by mouth or skin. Most of the creeks and wells in Wawa (and many surrounding places) were contaminated with it. The majority of the people who came to our clinic from Wawa had this parasite. It was often a killer because it caused dysentery (a disease of the intestines), cirrhosis of the liver, or brain damage.

In the '60s and '70s there was a drug, Ambilar, that was 70 percent effective, but oh, the horrible reactions. The patient was supposed to take food with the drug, which was to be taken three times daily for seven days. Many times no food was available, and the reaction could cause the patient to go crazy. I don't think the memory will ever fade from my mind of one night when I was called to the clinic ward because two patients had gone berserk. I had to give them strong tranquilizer injections before they quieted down. Out of the many that had reactions from the drug, only one person suffered permanent damage. I felt badly about this. One time I had to give this drug to Eugene, and I was on pins and needles until he finished his treatment without any reactions.

What a marvelous day it was in 1985 when a new drug was discovered that could replace Ambilar. This new drug could be given by mouth for two days instead of by many painful injections—and produced NO reactions.

This parasite (and others) was the reason I always took my own drinking water when I went to the villages to stay. When I bathed in their water, I always dried myself quickly before the parasite could penetrate my skin, just in case it was in the water.

On the last day of Sanjo's injections, Levi, my helper, told him, "You can go back to your village now." Imagine our surprise when he showed up again the following day. Levi asked him, "Why are you still here? Your treatment is finished."

"I don't want to go back to my village until I know this Jesus you have talked about. I want to repent of my sins."

Levi took time to talk to him about Jesus. "Do you realize that you are a sinner?"

"Yes, my sins are weighing heavy on my heart. I am a very wicked man. There is a pastor in my village, and I have tried many times to prevent people from going to his church to learn about God. I wanted the people in our village to worship the spirit of the water, Guerengou. After listening to the words that you have told us each morning about Jesus who loves us, I know that my life isn't a happy one and my way of life leads to death."

"Do you realize that this Jesus we have been telling you about is the Son of the true God who came to this world to die on the cross to save sinners?"

"Yes, I know now. He has been knocking at my heart, and I want to have a heart change."

After talking to him a little more, Levi led him in the prayer of salvation. How we all rejoiced that Sanjo had made the greatest decision of his life.

A few months later I saw Pastor Ndekamali of the Wawa church. Pastor said, "Chief Sanjo, who came to you for medicine, is really a changed man. Thank you for your words that spoke to him about his sinful life."

"If God could change Sanjo's life, He can change anyone," I replied

Pastor continued, "Sanjo is very faithful to worship with the believers. He burned his charm pieces of wood, rock, feathers, and animal teeth. He is always urging the people in his village to come to church and find the peace that he found."

Chief Sanjo, who we wondered about, was a man God loved. Now he was letting his life shine for his Savior. When I think of him, I think of the verse in Ephesians 5:8: "For you were once darkness, but now you are light in the Lord. Walk as children of light" (NKJV).

13 - Experiences in 1954

Second Thoughts

Pierre came to our clinic, and after a lab exam we diagnosed him as having amoebic dysentery. We gave him two days' worth of pills for his illness. We didn't give pills for the complete treatment in those earlier days; some had the idea that if a few pills helped, several taken at one time would get them well more quickly. When they did that, I had to pump out their stomachs to save their lives. I never enjoyed the procedure.

When Pierre didn't show up for two days, I became anxious about him. I asked Marie, one of our students, if she would walk with me the half-mile to his village. She gladly agreed. When we walked into his yard, we saw him lying on a grass mat under a shade tree. When his wife saw us, she hurried to greet us with a handshake and then went to get chairs for us. As we sat down beside Pierre's mat, I said to him, "I became worried about you when you didn't return for your medicine."

"My strength is gone," he responded. "I can barely walk. I knew if I tried to go to your clinic, I would fall by the wayside."

"I'm so sorry," I answered. "How I wish I had a place to keep you, but I don't. And I don't have a vehicle to take you to the government hospital. Can two of your relatives or friends come to the clinic and get our stretcher to carry you to the town hospital?"

Thoughtfully he replied, "I think we can find enough people to do that."

Marie and I shook hands with Pierre and his wife and walked to the road. All of a sudden I stopped. I felt led by the Lord to go back and talk to him about his soul. I didn't know if he was a Christian or not.

"I have to go back and talk with Pierre," I told Marie.

He had a surprised look on his face as he saw us by his side again. "Pierre," I said, "you live close to the mission, and I'm sure you have heard about Jesus, the Son of God that believers talk about. I don't know anything about you except that you are very ill. But do you know Jesus? Have you believed in Him?"

Pierre's face was very grave as he replied, "Yes, I have heard about Jesus, and I always said I would believe some day. I have put it off too long, but I am ready to believe right now."

And he was. I was very touched to hear his prayer as he received the Lord, and at the end he said, "Thank you, Lord, that I am sick, because through it, I have found Jesus." Then he feebly reached up his hand again to shake our hands and said, "Thank you, thank you for coming." I knew his conversion was real. We will know the rest of his story, whether he got well or not, when we meet him in glory. I don't remember now.

The White Man

I arranged for a native pastor and his wife to go to our mission hospital because they both needed hernia operations.

His uncle, who was chief of their village, tried his best to discourage them from going. "Don't you know the white man just wants an opportunity to kill you?

But his nephew didn't believe him, and he and his wife went to our Ippy hospital. Upon their return I bicycled out to their village to see how they were doing and to become better acquainted. They had both had their surgeries and were very pleased about how kind everyone was and how quickly they had recovered. I learned that they had never met before their marriage. She was the widow of a Crampel pastor, and others thought she would make a good match for one of their students who needed a wife. It seemed like a good marriage. Interestingly, the chief must have changed his mind about the white man because the next week he sent me a gift of three eggs.

A Leopard and a Dog

Bruce and Wilma had a large dog whose name was Buck. He usually stayed inside at night, sleeping on their cement floor. For some reason, one night he slept outside on the veranda. About midnight Bruce heard a bark, then silence. When Bruce ran outside, he could not find Buck. After

The leopard that killed Bruces dog, Buck.

repeatedly calling in vain for Buck, he reasoned that a leopard took off with him.

The next morning Bruce and a couple of Africans searched in the tall grass and found the partly eaten body of his dog. Everyone felt terrible about the loss. Since they didn't want a leopard roaming around, one of the Africans said, "Why don't you ask Gamaguido [one of the two big hunters in the area] to come and build a gun trap where the dog is? The leopard will surely come back tonight to finish eating his prey."

Gamaguido came and made the trap. Just before midnight the gun went off. Sure enough, the next morning there was the dead leopard. I was thinking, *I'm glad I don't have to make many night trips to see sick ones at the clinic or village with leopards prowling around.*

A Night Call

A few nights after the leopard incident I was called down to the village. To claim I wasn't scared would be a lie!

One of our women students had just had a convulsion and was in a coma. She had been complaining of a headache for a couple of days. I prayed for wisdom as I walked with her husband down the winding road then onto the steep, rocky, narrow path to the village. Most of the villagers were milling around outside the house, anxious about their fellow student. I examined her and found that she had a very high temperature. This was the most serious case I had seen among our student body.

I walked back up to the clinic to prepare three injections for her, one being quinine for malaria. I gave her the injections and told the family I would be back in a couple of hours to check on her. (How I wish I'd had my three-wheel Honda motorcycle in those days!) Again I walked alone down to the village, asking the Lord to protect me along the way and to give me wisdom in continuing her care. I was pleased when on my return I heard her husband's words: "She woke up and talked a little and then went back to sleep."

I breathed a sigh of relief, and all I could say was "Thank you, Lord, thank you."

Her temperature had gone down to 102, and a week later she was back in class.

The Ax Missed the Log

One day, when I thought my day's work was finished, I was immediately called back to the clinic. Two miles out in the brush a man had cut his foot with an ax. He left a trail of blood all the way to the clinic, and blood filled the bottom of a pan before I was able to stop the hemorrhage. How he ever lived was beyond me. Even his bone was split. (I saw my need then to be trained to give blood transfusions and later learned the skill at Ippy.) I sewed up the wound and was astonished that it didn't become infected. Not having anything to immobilize the leg, I had to ask our doctors in Ippy to send me some plaster of Paris so I could put a cast on his foot. So plaster of Paris was then added to my list of supplies to have on hand. Another lesson was learned.

Rainy and Dry Seasons

In March and April, the last part of our dry season, our usual number of patients was 175 per day. One day we had 220, and that made a long, long day! I had hired another worker, Michel. With the coming of the rains to start the new season, our patient load could be reduced to 120-140 per day.

My heart was warmed one day when one of our most faithful Christian women remarked, "Mademoiselle, we are seeing a lot of backsliders coming to church these days. I know it is a result of the medical ministry you have here." Many of them lived near the crossroads of our mission, and as they became ill, their feet once more found their way to the mission station. Here they heard the Word of God preached each morning, and it spoke once more to their hearts, for many were longing for the peace they once knew in Christ.

We were seeing many come to the Lord. One day we all rejoiced when four were saved. A little later I remembered how sad I was when I realized there hadn't been a conversion for two weeks. Over the years hundreds came to Christ, and many who had been saved and were not walking with the Lord came back to Him. If they were near one of our out-station churches, we sent a note with them for the pastor or deacons, telling them what had happened. That way they could receive follow-up care and counseling and be encouraged in their faith.

I could hardly contain myself when I was asked to teach a one-hour-a-week personal evangelism class to the women in our Bible School at Sibut. I knew that some day I would be helping in the school, but I wasn't expecting it so soon. In one of the first assignments given to the women, I said, "I want each of you to talk each week to at least one person about their soul. At class time you will give testimonies of your witnessing". The first time one of the women told us about leading another to the Lord, there was much clapping and rejoicing.

I always attended church on our mission station. The church was usually packed with 800 inside and some mothers with babies and toddlers sitting on the outside, depending on whether it was the dry or rainy season. In those days many of the babies didn't have diapers on, so leaves would be used in cleanup. A few mothers with babies would sit inside with a child beside her. It wasn't unusual for the mother to send a small child outside. In a few minutes the child would walk down the aisle with several leaves in his hand. No one thought anything about it. That was their way of life. That changed when mothers became better prepared to take care of their little ones.

During the six months of dry season, from December to May, there were more people in church. But during the rainy season, many Africans built tiny grass houses near their gardens and stayed there for a week or so. These were sometimes eight to ten miles or more out in the bush. One Sunday when the attendance was more than usual, a deacon handed me the statistics. There were 950 for the church service. Fifty people had come to give their salvation testimonies to the deacons so they could enter the new converts' class. In that class there were 215 people. Later, two more churches were started, one on either side of town. That made it a lot easier for those who walked so far to go to church.

If Two of You...

It became increasingly apparent that we must have a sick-ward building because so many of our clinic patients needed hospitalization. One of our students, Raymond Pouniguinza, was very ill, having a 104-degree temperature. There was no way he could walk down the uneven rocky path to his house, so a stretcher in my consultation room at the clinic became his bed.

I went home that evening with a very sorrowful heart. As I was praying for a sick ward, the Lord brought to mind Matthew 18:19: *"If two of you shall agree on earth as touching any thing that they shall ask, it shall be done for them of my Father which is in heaven."* I thought, *Lord, when we pray in the mornings, our group includes Levi, Louvrou, Andre, Michel and myself. That makes five of us.* We had been praying about this need before, but I knew we should be more definite in our prayers.

The next morning I was eager to go to work to share my thoughts with my helpers. I said, "Let us be more specific and ask the Lord for money to build a sick ward before the end of 1954."

I could see Levi's face light up. His faith was growing, and with enthusiasm he said, "Why don't we also include the salvation of Canton Chief Adrissi in our prayers, that he would be converted before the end of this year?"

I was thrilled to hear Levi say this and quickly replied, "An excellent idea. Do the rest of you agree?"

They nodded their heads in agreement and onto our knees we went. Adrissi was called canton chief because he was the chief over all the chiefs in our district. He had been coming to the dispensary for treatment, and he always came in time for the Gospel message. He would listen intently but would not make a decision to believe in Christ. So together that morning we claimed his salvation by faith.

Three months later, when I was home on furlough, studying in Kentucky, I received a letter from my supporters, Polly and Weldon Gwinn, saying, "The Lord has blessed our construction business, and we have some extra money we want to give to the Lord. Could you use it?"

Wow! Could we use it? You bet we could! That was God's answer to our prayer for the building of our sick ward. Oh, how I rejoiced!

And what happened with Adrissi? When I returned to Africa after my furlough, Levi told me the rest of the story. In November of 1954 Chief Adrissi became very ill and was carried to the town hospital. When the Catholic priest heard the canton chief was seriously ill, he came and wanted to administer the last rites.

Adrissi refused and said to him, "I know how to get ready to die. I have heard the way many times, but I was too stubborn to believe. I want the pastor of the mission on the hill to come to me."

One of Adrissi's relatives walked to our mission and asked Pastor Sesse to go to the hospital and talk with the chief. When Pastor Sesse came, Adrissi prayed the prayer of repentance and trusted in Christ's atonement on the cross for his salvation. He told Pastor, "Now I am ready to meet God." He died a short time later. God had again answered our prayer.

When I heard the story about Adrissi, I thought, *How gracious the Lord was to give him time to believe. We never know when our time is coming. "Now is the day of salvation"* 2 Corinthians 6:2. People who say the Christian life is dull don't begin to realize the promises we have in Christ and the joy of seeing the God of the universe answer our prayers.

Our First Truck

Florence had written home to her family that we needed a truck. Her family was always very supportive of her ministry in Africa. This time it was her sister Helen who got the ball rolling. Unbeknown to me, she wrote to my church saying, "Margery and Florence could have a more profitable ministry if they had a truck. If Florence's family could come up with half of the money for a one-half-ton pickup truck, could you, as a church, pay the other half?" Florence's family came up with $1,800, and my church paid the same amount. You can imagine my delight when I heard that a truck for us was on its way to Africa. This would be the first of three different trucks that I would use during my years in Africa.

But how was the truck going to get from the coastal city of Douala, Cameroon, to Sibut? The Lord has ways of solving our problems. There were two single ladies who had to fly to Douala; Marian Lankin to see a dentist and Clara Crumb to see a doctor. They gladly agreed to drive our truck back to Sibut. What a thrill it was a couple of weeks after their departure to see them drive into our yard with the green 1954 Chevy half-ton pickup truck!

We were thankful to hear of the Lord's protection over them during the 1,000-mile trip inland. Marian was a nurse who was to take my place while I went home on furlough, so she had the work of teaching Florence to drive. In all of our years of sharing this pickup, Florence and I never had any difficulty between us.

14 - My Would-Be Replacement

It was decided at our mission conference that Ruth Carlson, a nurse who was temporarily at Koumra, was to take my place at Sibut when I went to the States for my first furlough. Eugene and Ernie traveled to Koumra to get her.

Shortly after her arrival, Ruth, Florence, Bertha (a guest), and I were eating supper in our dining room. As usual, Chubby, Florence's dog, was lying by her chair. Suddenly he started barking and kept it up, so we couldn't hear ourselves talking. I thought to myself, *That's enough of that.* I opened the dining room door and said "Out!" He hesitated, so I again said, "Out," and he unwillingly went. No sooner had I shut the door behind me than it flew open and Chubby jumped back inside. At the same moment a leopard leaped across the three steps outside our dining room to the other side. He just missed Chubby by seconds.

Florence yelled for Oumar to go get Bruce and tell him a leopard was outside our dining-room door. She didn't stop to think that he might have been too scared to go out. But he obeyed her, went out the back door, and soon Bruce was there yelling, "Let me in!" He came in with his loaded gun, asking us a couple of questions before going to our small living room window, tearing out the screen, and shining his extra-bright flashlight out the window. Soon he said, "The leopard is hiding in the circle of bushes out in front."

He shot at least five times, until Oumar said, "He has to be dead by now."

Bruce said, "Don't go out and see. Wait until morning." The next morning we found the dead leopard with five bullets in him. The skin couldn't be saved because the holes had ruined the hide. After that I respected Chubby's barking. I am sure that if he could have spoken to me that night, he would have said, "Why did you make me go out like that?"

A few days after Ruth's arrival I heard a weak voice coming from the bathroom. "Margery, Margery, come. I need help." I ran to the bathroom and found Ruth having an intestinal hemorrhage. She was sitting on the stool with her head leaning over the sink. Blood was everywhere. I was very frightened. I asked Florence to go tell Bruce and Wilma what had happened and to prepare to go to Bangui to take Ruth and me. Her pulse was weak, and I feared for her life.

The three-hour trip to the government hospital seemed endless. Once we arrived, the doctor took a short history and then began giving orders. Ruth received two blood transfusions.

The word spread quickly to the African churches that a missionary was in the hospital and seriously ill. Prayers immediately went up on her behalf. Two African deacons came to the hospital. I can still see them kneeling by Ruth's bed praying for her healing. That made a great impression on me, and I realized anew that the love of Christ knows no boundaries, race, or color in His body.

That evening Ruth again passed blood, this time dark, digested blood that had not been expelled earlier. I called the nurse. I could not feel her pulse, and Ruth went in and out of consciousness. I knew she was close to leaving this world for her heavenly home. The nurses gave her several injections, and finally I felt a faint pulse. The next day she said, "I saw a glowing, beautiful figure at knee level by the side of my bed. I knew I was close to departing. I wasn't disturbed or anxious because the Lord was giving me such a great experience of peace."

She was diagnosed with a bleeding ulcer and had to stay in the hospital for two weeks. After she was released, she stayed with Effie Peck, a missionary in Bangui, for a month to regain her strength, and then she went home to the States for six months. When she returned to French Equatorial Africa, she worked at our hospital in Ippy. Once again she had the same medical crisis and was sent home for surgery. The surgery took care of her problem, and in time she continued her work in Africa as a missionary nurse.

Ruth had another experience of great peace later, when she was working at Koumra. In Southern Tchad there was an uprising among some of the unsaved people called the Social and Cultural Revolution. The Satan worshippers were taking the young men to the woods for their cultural and circumcision rites; they were also trying to force the young Christian men to deny their faith. Anyone who opposed this teaching would be killed, including the youth. Seventeen pastors and other Christians were killed. Some were buried alive. Bibles and songbooks were burned.

One day a witch doctor who was part of the revolution and his group of men were passing by the road near Ruth's house. She took some photographs from a location where they couldn't see her. She started trembling with fear when she realized what she had done and what the consequences would be if they knew it. Then all of a sudden her trembling stopped and a great calm came over her. She realized that no matter what might happen, underneath were the everlasting arms of her Lord.

15 - First Furlough

Part of our mission plan required that we return to the States for furlough each fifth year. It was kind of like a working vacation. I used this time to update my medical training, visit my family, get medical checkups and purchase needed supplies for the next four years. I also would visit my supporting churches to bring them up to date on the work in Africa.

Ilene Douglas

Some years I would work in summer youth camps as a counselor.

Going home on my first furlough was the most exciting of my nine furloughs. Faithful friends at church had sent me a new suit, hat, and gloves, and I thought I looked spiffy. It was so exciting to stop off in France to see my wonderful French family, the Guedjs. I loved them dearly, and Mrs. Guedj was one of my most faithful prayer warriors. We talked nonstop, sharing experiences. Andre, the son, was leaving soon for Canada to learn to be a pilot.

I also had a lunch with other friends. As we were having our meal together, we talked about reigning with Christ. Without thinking I said, "I don't want to reign; that is too much responsibility." We all had a good laugh.

In New York my friend from Seattle, Ilene Douglas, was there to meet me. She had a longer wait than expected because our plane circled for an hour, waiting for permission to land. Once I was finally off the plane, we gave each other a good hug and started toward the baggage claim.

Suddenly we heard someone calling, "Ilene, Margery." Who would be calling our names? It turned out to be Georgia Harris, a member of our home church who had just flown in from Germany, where she had been teaching military school children for the past year.

Ilene was so excited about telling me the plans she had for us. Pastor Johnson, from our Seattle church, had arranged for us to go to Detroit and pick up a new car destined for National Car Rental in Seattle and we drove it cross-country in six days, with all expenses paid. What a wonderful relaxing trip we had. Ilene was always a restful person to be with. I don't know why I was privileged to have such a friend. She prepared and sent out my prayer letters until 1990, when it became too much for her.

I was only in Seattle with the Johnson family a short time. My parents had moved to Boise, Idaho, so my plans were to visit them there before traveling to Kentucky to attend the midwife school. I did have time to buy a couple of dresses, though, but when I tried them on for Mrs. Johnson to see, she said, "Margery, neither one does a thing for you."

"But I went to many stores to find these."

"Did you go to Frederick and Nelson?"

"No, that store is too expensive."

"Tomorrow I have to go downtown, and if you want, I can help you. You take the dresses back in the morning and get a refund, and I will meet you at 11 a.m. in front of Frederick and Nelson's.

"Okay," I agreed.

True to her word we met on time, and she excitedly said, "We don't have to go to the store. I just saw the perfect dress for you in the window of a little boutique on the corner where my husband let me out." And the dress she saw fit perfectly; it was the "right" dress. Blessed be those people that help missionaries who come home on furlough to get adjusted to a life that they haven't been a part of for many years.

It was great to see my parents and my siblings, Judy, Stephen, and Philip. I could stay only a couple of weeks before I had to go to Kentucky to start my midwife training. I had read the school brochure, and they said to come with a pair of riding boots, so I bought a pair of very decorative cowboy boots.

The Frontier Nursing Service

On the way to Kentucky I stopped in St. Louis to speak at a banquet arranged by my mother's one-time Sunday School class at the Fourth Baptist Church. They were proud that a daughter of one of their former members had gone to the mission field. It was so good to have my grandmother, two aunts, and Uncle Clyde there as well.

The Frontier Nursing Service served an impoverished area in the hills of Kentucky. When I arrived, five classmates and the dean of our school, Miss Rayson, a teacher from England, greeted me.

When the other students saw my boots, they really laughed. "Those boots won't go with the riding uniform that we wear when we go out to visit in the area homes, whether by horseback or by Jeep. But don't worry, the attic is filled with boots other nurses have long since discarded."

The school gave a six-month course to only six nurses at a time. They wanted all the students to have their quota of delivering at least thirty babies in order to graduate. Those deliveries had to include both home and hospital deliveries. All of us exceeded our quotas.

Frontier Nursing Service at Hyden, Kentucky where Margery took her midwifery training on her first furlough. Shown here with one of the babies and the baby's mother, Betty.

During our course we were asked not to talk to the people about three things, politics, religion and moonshine, but I did take opportunities to talk about the Lord.

October was beautiful in Kentucky; the colored leaves were spectacular everywhere we went. But soon autumn changed to winter.

I especially remember two of the winter home deliveries that my supervisor and I attended. Both were in very poor homes, as many of them were.

The first was at Betty's. She was an eighteen year-old whose house was spotless. She was having her third baby in the middle of a cold night. The bed was in the living room, across from the fireplace, and it was so cold we could see our breath. Miss Rayson whispered to me, "For this delivery don't take off your jacket. Just scrub and put on gloves and an apron." I really felt sorry for Betty and the baby that would soon be born in such a cold environment. The delivery went well and a healthy baby was born. Later, as we made our post-delivery call on them, I realized that Betty couldn't have had more dignity and graciousness if she had lived in a fancy home. I guess you know by this time that she made an impression on me and I realized anew not to judge people by their worldly possessions.

The second memorable delivery was on another snowy winter night. It was only seven miles from the school, but it took us one and a half hours to get there. The truck that the father-to-be drove got stuck in the ice when he was trying to ford a creek, and it had to be left there. He had to walk to a house and find someone to bring him the rest of the way to call us. My supervisor and I started out in our Jeep. At one place we thought we would slip off the icy embankment. Then we had to ford a creek. The ice had only partly broken up, but we made it. We were nearly exhausted by the time we reached our destination. The mother delivered a few hours after our arrival.

The ice in the creek had refrozen before we started home. We forded the creek with our Jeep in reverse gear, as we were afraid the ice would ruin the fan belt. We would go a foot or so, break up the ice, then go forward, until with great relief we made it across the creek. We learned later it took three men four hours to get the new father's truck out of the ice. My, what a night! And what a change from Africa!

One Friday the daughter of the Queen of England's personal physician visited the Frontier Nursing Service, and she wanted to visit in the district. My supervisor asked me to take her with me when I went back in the hills to visit a new mother. I really gave the lady a ride on one of the rocky creek beds, and she took pictures, saying, "The people in England would never believe this could be possible in the States if I just told them about it. They will have to see the pictures." And guess what? I received an invitation to stay with her if I ever travel to England.

Each of us six students had to spend three weeks with a nurse and a nurse-midwife in one of their six house clinics, each of which was in a different area of the mountains. One of my most memorable days with the Service was at the Beechfork House Clinic. To make a postpartum visit to a new mother and baby, my midwife supervisor and I had to go on horseback up a rocky, dry creek bed with frost-covered tree branches spreading majestically over the creek, which was coming down from the snow covered mountains. What a beautiful day!

Another day a supervisor and I went to another house clinic to see patients. My supervisor pointed to the house across the street along the creek and said, "The people who live there keep poisonous snakes that a church near here uses when they have their revival meetings. They test their faith by handling the snakes." I thought, *If they only knew that the Word of God says in Romans 10:17, "Faith cometh by hearing, and hearing by the word of God."*

Three of us were taking the midwife course to be able to use the knowledge on the mission field. One was a Lutheran girl who was engaged to marry a fellow who had one term as a missionary in India. Shortly after we started our studies, she came to my room and said, "I haven't had any Bible training. Could you help me?" She couldn't quote one Bible verse by memory. So during our time there, it was my privilege to help her learn how to have Bible study on her own.

My six-month training was a relaxing time. I didn't have the responsibility of making final decisions; my teachers and the doctor did that. At the end of April I received my Certified Midwife Diploma and was on my way back to Boise. My cowboy boots were a perfect fit for my little brother, Phil.

Dollars from Heaven

When I came to the States, I knew that our clinic building in Africa was only temporary. It wasn't large enough, and the medical center, with its outhouses and ward buildings, had to be on level ground, away from the other ministry buildings. We knew the ward building would be built first and placed in an ideal location.

I had mentioned this need in a regular prayer letter. One day at home in Boise, I received a letter from Seattle. In it was a note saying, "This money is for your new clinic building," and enclosed was what I thought was a $100 bill.

I called out to mother, "Look, I just received a $100 bill in an unregistered letter." My dear mother looked at it and exclaimed, "That isn't a $100 bill; it is a $1,000 one! Who is it from?"

It was from a woman that I didn't even know, a Mrs. White from Seattle. Later I learned she was a seventy-year-old widow in West Seattle who had a small orchard beside her house. She called it "God's orchard." She picked and sold the fruit herself, and the proceeds went to someone in the Lord's work. I was the recipient that year. I received one more gift from her after I returned to Africa. She sent two $100 bills in another letter. At that time I had a bill for two tons of cement, amounting to $200. It was just the right amount, and it came at the right time! Isn't the Lord good? He knew the time and the amount I needed.

That year on furlough I got my second supporting church, which was the First Baptist Church in the small town of Kuna, Idaho. Little did I know then what the people in that church would mean to me.

Each time I came home, another church and different people took on more of my support, so I never lacked nor had to mention finances. If people asked me what I needed, I told them, and the Lord never let me down. Oh, the Lord is good; He is the Almighty One.

More Surprises

Another surprise came one day in Seattle when I was called into one of the offices of Maynard Hospital, where I had worked for a few weeks. A man said, "We have an operating table and a surgical overhead light we would like to give you to take back to Africa. Do you want it?"

It didn't take more than a few seconds to say, "Yes, thank you!" But as I left the hospital, my thinking gears were again in motion, *How in the world am I going to get these things crated and sent to Africa?*

When I told Pastor Johnson and his wife from my church in Seattle the good news of the equipment Maynard Hospital had given to me, he lost no time in phoning a group called Missionary Purchasing and Packing. Al Undi answered and Pastor explained why he was calling. At the mention of my name, Al said, "I know Margery. We attended Simpson Bible Institute at the same time, and for a few months we were on the King County Jail team together." He was glad to help, and Pastor informed him that some of the men from Tabernacle Baptist Church would also help. Al and his wife, Olive, became some of my dearest friends. Never again did I have to wonder how I would ship my baggage to Africa.

Special Times in Washington

The highlight of that summer was counseling at Camp Gilead, our church camp in Carnation, Washington. Walking with the Lord is never dull, and as we give out to others, we are blessed, sometimes with joy unspeakable and full of glory. That is how I felt when for a few weeks I had a group of young people around me night and day.

Return to Africa

In October 1955 I visited my parents for the last time before I left to go back to Africa. My sister, Esther, also came home before leaving for the first time as a missionary to Mexico. Because she was ten years younger than I was, we hadn't spent much time together as adults. The Lord was good to let us have that time together with our parents.

It was time to return to Central African Republic and so I sailed on the ship United States to France. There I visited my French family again in Paris, then flew to Rome and then non-stop to Lamy, Tchad. I hadn't learned yet how to dress in layers, which is necessary when going from a cold country to a hot one. I had on a beautiful, long-sleeved gray wool suit.

At the airport, which they were in the process of building, I went to the restroom and shut the door behind me and it locked. It was a small room, and with my wool suit on, I was hot, hot, hot. The door didn't have a handle, so there was no way I could get out. I just waited in misery, knowing that one of the missionaries with whom I was traveling would soon miss me. Effie Peck did, and what a relief it was when I heard her voice saying, "Margery, are you there?"

"I am," I replied, "and I'm roasting. I can't get out. Would you please open the door?"

After a couple of seconds she spoke again, "There is no handle on this side of the door either. I'll go ask the French attendant if he has a key to the door." He didn't, but he managed to open it with a screwdriver. When I stepped out, he was standing with another Frenchman a few feet away. I could see from the smirk on their faces that they were wondering what kind of prey they had caught this time.

We then had a one-hour wait while a truckload of fresh meat was packed into the plane. We could smell it all the way to Sarh, our next stop. At Sarh we had to wait another hour while two more truckloads of meat were loaded for Bangui. Yes, I was back in Africa.

Bruce and Wilma Rosenau met me in Bangui to take me back to Sibut. I was glad to see them again. It took us four hours to go from Bangui to Sibut because we stopped to say hello to some of our pastors along the way. As we came down the hill on the main road approaching the turnoff to our mission, the people were lined up on both sides of the road yelling and waving. It was the same along our mission road and as we arrived at the mission village crossroads. I was overwhelmed by everyone's welcome. There was no doubt I was loved. I silently prayed, "Thank you Lord, I am home. This is where I belong."

Part Three

A Day in the Life of a Missionary

16 - A Day in the Life of a Missionary

I have often been asked about everyday life on the mission field. I can begin to explain that simply by telling you about one extraordinary day.

On October 23, 1968, the day started at 5:15 a.m., when I had my quiet time with Jesus. At 6:35 I went to Eugene and Ernie's house to run off two stencils on their mimeograph machine and ended up doing four. I returned home at 7:15 and ate an American breakfast alone—cream of wheat. Florence and Polly had already eaten. There was only one piece of bread, and our houseboy Antoine came out looking sheepish because he had burned it to charcoal.

Later he baked more fresh bread. There was no bakery nearby, so each household baked its own supply. It was often difficult to keep up with the demand.

At 7:30 I went to my Bible School class. It usually met at 6:30 on Wednesdays, but Lee Einfeldt had requested the early hour this day, so we traded times. I gave the papers I had mimeographed—a summary of their final exam in child evangelism—to the men.

At 8:30 I went further down the hill to the clinic. The sky was a beautiful purple, and I knew it wouldn't be long before a downpour began. By the time I arrived at the clinic, my helpers had the seven hospital patients all taken care of. They had already had a prayer time, and Louvrou, my female nurse, had preached the message, and they now were starting to treat the waiting clinic patients.

The storm arrived. As a result about 150 people who had been out on the veranda crowded into the dispensary, creating mass confusion. There was loud talking because of the rain beating down on the aluminum roof. Babies were crying. It was so dark we could hardly see and so crowded that one had to look twice to see where to put their feet. Every time I wanted to get to the medicine supply cupboard, people had to get up from their benches to let me pass by. We couldn't let that precious water go to waste, so we had buckets, pans, and filters under the eaves catching the rain. As the containers filled up they were carried into the dispensary and emptied into our water barrels. The print shop staff, who had the power plant on for printing, switched on our lights when we sent them an SOS.

We always took the sick babies' temperatures the first thing, and that day two thermometers were broken. (You see where some of the money goes?) That made three broken ones in a week. It didn't pay to get upset. I did say to one of the mothers today that all she had to do while sitting there was to keep that thermometer in place and why did she have to let it slip to the floor. How many times I was reminded of those words in I Corinthians 13:4, "Love is patient and kind" (NLT). I prayed many times the Lord would make this more of a reality in my life—real Calvary love.

In the afternoon, after enjoying a siesta, I gave an accordion lesson to a very talented African teacher. He used my accordion as I hardly played it any more. I then had a class for teenage girls. I was glad to see two new girls in attendance.

The class ran five minutes into our church prayer meeting time, which started at 5:00 p.m. That evening a young patient I had helped many times was prepared to accept the Lord. My helper, Joseph, counseled with him and his wife while I prayed in my office. What a wonderful job Joseph did, as the Lord directed him to the right scriptures. How we and the angels also rejoiced over two more sinners that had come home. Praise His Name!

Afterward I went back to the clinic to work on teeth, routine for a Wednesday night. I arrived back at the house at 8:00 p.m., saw Melba, a missionary lady who had an infected ear, and ate supper.

By 8:30 my bed looked very inviting. Yes, we were often in bed at that hour, but the lights did not go out until 9:30. We had one couple who were in bed by 8:00 most evenings. This is a little different from the American way of life.

Living so close to the Equator, the sun rises and sets very close to 6 o'clock each morning and evening. This remains fairly constant throughout the entire year varying only a half hour or so as the seasons change. The lack of electricity caused us to adjust our lives to the rising and setting sun.

Being in Africa rather than the United States also made some differences in what we did for recreation. What I missed most at first was participating in sports. There was no way we could do anything on our hilltop, and it was too hot if we could. When the airfield was built on the backside of our hill, sometimes Ernie, Eugene, and I would go down at dawn to walk.

I liked to do that, but I found that on the days we walked, if I didn't have my devotional time with the Lord at that time of day, it was haphazardly done. So I had to choose, and without a doubt, it was to be my time with the Lord. That part of my life was most important. I knew from the Word that Jesus said, "Without me ye can do nothing" (John 15:5), and I needed His help to let my life shine for Him.

When I was in school in Portland, Oregon, I heard Dawson Trotman (the man who started the Navigator organization) speak, and I will never forget what he said: "A daily quiet time with the Lord is a necessity for spiritual growth."

I had heard words like that before, but that time it made a real impression on me. I didn't always do it while in nursing school, but it was daily when I was in school in Seattle, and it was always a part of my life in France and Africa. I always set aside the early morning, for it set the focus for the whole day. The Psalmist said, "In the morning, O Lord, you hear my voice; in the morning I lay my requests before you and wait in expectation" (Psalm 5:3, NIV). It is a great way to start the day, letting the Lord speak to you through His Word, then in prayer lifting praise, thanksgiving, and requests to God, and then eagerly watching God go to work. For it is not I but Christ who dwells within me.

These times with Jesus gave me strength and helped to make everyday living worthwhile. A verse of the song "Day by Day" expresses my thoughts:

Everyday the Lord Himself is near me,
With a special mercy for each hour;
All my cares He fain would bear and cheer me,
He whose name is Counselor and Power,
The protection of His child and treasure
Is a charge that on Himself He laid;
As thy days, thy strength shall be in measure,
This the pledge to me He made.

—Carolina (Lina) Sandell Berg

Sometimes in the evening Ernie, Madame, and I played *Scrabble* , and almost everyone was a reader. The *Newsweek* magazines that came by air from France got passed around on the station. We also used our short-wave radios to listen to the news on the BBC. I knew more of what was going on in the world while I was in Africa than I did when I was in the States on furlough.

I never dreamed of the enjoyment and comfort I would find in music tapes. Two of my favorites were tapes that Larry Bauman and a friend of his made for me. Sometimes Larry would say a few words between the numbers, just as if he were talking to me. The first time I heard the song "Until Then" was on one of those tapes. It became my theme song.

Once, when I was home on furlough, friends of mine sang a duet in church. Their singing was so beautiful that I asked them to make a tape of their singing. To my great disappointment, however, they sent me a tape of professional Christian singers. I appreciated what they did, but I just wanted to hear their singing, not the great artists.

Very few missionaries there ever took vacations because there was no place to go to get out of the tropics and to get away from our responsibilities for a short time. In all my years spent in Africa, I had just three vacations, two of them unexpected. Once in the early '70s I accompanied a sick, elderly missionary lady to Dr. Brison's home in Florida. My sister, Judy, lived there, so I took two weeks to visit her and my brother, Steve, in Tennessee. When I went back to Africa, I felt renewed and full of energy. Another time my friend Erma Swanson Sowers took me to Israel as her guest. What a difference it made to be out of the tropics for two and a half weeks, visiting Egypt, Cyprus, Israel, Greece, and Rome.

I know vacations are important, but I always felt just a little bit guilty when I took one. However, remembering how rejuvenated I was when I came back from the unexpected trip to the States and the trip with Erma, in 1987 I asked June Stone if she would be interested in having a midterm break in Europe. She was. One of the Bixby families that worked in Europe was back home in the States on vacation, so we stayed at their house in France for eight days. Another of the Bixby brothers lived close by. He and his family had worked as Baptist Mid-Missions missionaries in Sibut for a term, and then also in Bangui. They had since moved to France. It was fun to see them again and they treated us royally. We really enjoyed the church people we met there, especially the youth. They were on fire for the Lord and many were getting saved. We not only were refreshed physically but spiritually as well. We ended our European stay by taking a train to Holland, to spend four days with two missionary families, John and Anna Kay (Rosenau) Haskill and Kathy and Boyd Griffith.

We missionaries always celebrated Christmas among ourselves and also with the Africans. As long as Florence was on the field, our missionary co-workers came to our house for Christmas Eve. She always made a delicious meal. After the meal we would give our houseboy his present, and while he was doing the dishes, we would go to other missionary houses to distribute presents.

After the gift exchange and a lot of talk, we piled into the back of a truck and went to different villages where African Christians would be celebrating Christmas in their cell groups. When we arrived, we greeted them and sang a song in Sango and then "We Wish You a Merry Christmas" in English. They didn't understand it, but it had a catchy tune. It was a fun time.

With hardly any sleep the night before, the Africans gathered in the churches at 9:00 a.m. for their three-hour Christmas program. There were special musical numbers and quoting of the Christmas story from either Luke or Matthew. As the program would go on and on, heads would begin to nod or the people would begin to lean on one another's shoulders. Later the African deacons decided that the Christmas Eve celebration was to be stopped at midnight.

On Christmas Day, if I didn't go to out-station churches, I would attend a nearby church. I always gave my clinic workers their new shirts the day before so they could have something new to wear for Christmas. While home on furlough I would go to sales and buy thirty or more shirts to provide the workers in the clinic and in the house with gifts for the four years on the field. I remember once I had the happy fortune to buy several shirts for only one dollar each. I didn't have to worry about the sizes or kinds; my helpers came in all sizes. It was always so enjoyable to be able to give.

Along with many joyous experiences, the years brought difficult times as well, of course. You will read about some in this book. In addition, conditions were not always easy to tolerate. One time the pastor of a church that helped to support the Rosenau families made a trip out to visit us in Central African Republic. He asked, "When you missionaries come home to the States and speak in the churches, why don't you tell how it really is concerning the difficulties and hardships?"

I pondered that for a while. We did, of course, sometimes tell our friends about our bugs, the heat, and the long hours of work that everyone has to do to keep a station going. Central African Republic is not considered a "garden spot" of the world. The American government gives its embassy personnel in Bangui extra money, for it is considered a hardship post. That is because there is excessive heat, only a couple of restaurants, neither of them fancy, no places of entertainment such as the cinema or theaters, and at times a troublesome government. The American embassy personnel do have the nicest homes in Bangui, though, and some of them have swimming pools. We missionaries wouldn't consider having a swimming pool a hardship post. I was glad that Polly Strong always had friends among the embassy personnel who let her use their pools. She needed exercise to help her keep in good health.

As I continued to think about the pastor's question, I knew that I didn't want people to think that I was complaining about the difficulties we experienced. Two verses that helped me throughout the years were from Philippians: "I have learned to be content whatever the circumstances" (4:11, NIV) and "I can do everything through him that gives me strength" (4:13, NIV).

I would be lying if I said I never complained. But how wonderful are those verses in Psalms: "If the Lord delights in a man's way, he makes his steps firm; though he stumble, he will not fall, for the Lord upholds him with his hand" (37:23-24, NIV).

Also, I knew that if I complained a lot about circumstances, it might scare away some young people who wanted to go to the Central African Republic. I knew that if the Lord called them and they went, they would find Him sufficient. I realized what a privilege we had to work there, too. The countries are few in the world where the gospel is received so well, and it was a joy to serve. That is what Jesus, the Son of God, did when He was on this earth.

17 - Where We Lived and Worked

Before leaving for Africa the first time, I had never spoken to a missionary from French Equatorial Africa, much less seen any pictures of the ministry, so when I arrived in Bangui, I was pleasantly surprised to see, for Africa, three nice houses. They had cement floors and aluminum or tile roofs, but only one of them had a ceiling at that time. The Sibut station had houses of a similar style. In the early days, well before I arrived, the missionaries lived in houses with dirt floors, adobe walls, and thatched roofs.

The first permanent house on the Sibut station was built in 1934—a large one on the very top of the hill. One room upstairs was large enough for the first missionary children's school and continued to be so used until they constructed the schoolhouse at Crampel.

When I arrived in Africa there were no inside toilets. The first at the mission was installed in 1954 in the house where Florence and I lived. No more outhouse trips. Florence's uncle, who was a plumber, had given her the necessary equipment when she returned from furlough two years earlier. The men finally found the time to install it. For showers we used a bucket with small holes punched out in the middle. It hung on a pulley rope so it could be raised to the height needed. A small rope was attached to the shower plug. When we wanted the water to flow, we pulled the rope. We were thankful for even this crude equipment. Most of the time we took our shower in the evening.

Once I called to Florence, "I don't think I'll take a shower this evening, it is too chilly."

She called back, "What's the temperature?"

I looked at the thermometer and said, " Seventy-five degrees." I took my shower.

At the time of my arrival at Sibut, something was wrong with the mission water pump, and parts to repair equipment like that couldn't be bought in Africa. Our missionary men had to spend a lot of time hauling barrels of water by truck from a well down the hill. In addition, two cisterns were made to catch rainwater. These ended up leaking all the time, so each house had a wooden frame built that held a large metal reservoir on top.

When they installed the first pump and water system, one of the nationals said to Ferd Rosenau, "There is no way that water can go uphill, " but Ferd assured him it would be possible.

During the first twenty-five years, all our drinking water was boiled and filtered due to the bacteria and parasites. When we obtained a better filter from Switzerland, we no longer needed to boil the water. The filters had to be cleaned often, though, or they would become so dirty the water couldn't flow through them.

Generators transported from the States supplied electricity. For years the men spent hours repairing them. Blessed was the day in the seventies when our station voted to buy a 22,000-watt generator. We knew the generator and transport would be very expensive, but by faith we all prayed and gave for this very needed project. One of the things I appreciated about Ferd, Eugene, Bruce and their wives was that they never faltered when it came to buying something really needed for the ministry. What money they had, they gave freely, even if it wasn't in their mission account. They let the need be known among their churches and trusted the Lord to provide the money, and the Lord answered; we got our generator.

The day came when electric washing machines became a part of our lives.

Aerial view of the Sibut Mission among mango trees planted by early missionaries.

We all had the same morning for washing clothes. Our washboards were no more. When the new generator arrived, there was enough wattage to keep the printing press going as well as our houses, our classrooms, and the clinic. Jeannot had electricity for doing his dental work; the lab could operate the microscope light, and the clinic could have light on cloudy days. In addition, there was a wonderful bonus: our student houses could have lights at night. Oh, happy day, there was wattage for all!

We usually didn't use the generator much during the day if the printing press wasn't running, unless it was our washing morning. At night it ran for four hours. Diesel fuel was expensive. We divided the expenses between the press and the missionary station fund.

The kitchen in our house wasn't very attractive. It had old, different-sized cupboards, and some of the doors didn't completely shut. I didn't think too much about it; this was Africa. When I returned to Africa in 1984 from furlough, I was happily surprised to see a new kitchen. Lynn and Margo Muhr, with the help of students, had redone it by painting the walls, installing new cupboards, and putting linoleum on the cement floor. I really appreciated their love and the time and effort they put into making my kitchen more convenient and attractive.

Kerosene refrigerators are used on all the mission stations except for Bangui, which has electricity. The kerosene refrigerators never get as cold as the electric ones and have many more idiosyncrasies. In fact, it seems that each individual refrigerator had to be treated a little differently. Many times in the hot dry season we would make a thermos of ice cold water and set it by the fridge so the door wouldn't have to be opened every time we wanted a cool drink. In Chad, the dry season is even more severe, so the missionaries would often put a damp quilt over the refrigerator to help retain the cold.

The kerosene reservoirs are at the bottom of the refrigerators and have to be filled approximately once every five days. Each missionary household has a fifty-gallon drum and two jerry cans of kerosene in their storerooms. The suction of the kerosene is started by mouth from one of the jerry cans perched up on a high stool. After the tank is full, the wick has to be trimmed and the burner and glass chimney replaced just right to produce a blue flame. An orange flame will not make the fridge cold. Sometimes our patience was tested trying to get that blue flame.

Once I tried several times to get that blue flame going in our fridge, but it just wouldn't come. I don't know how many matches I used to re-light the wick. Finally I let it go until the next morning, even though the fridge was losing its coldness. Early the next day I sent a note by Antoine, our houseboy, to Bruce. The men were always willing to help, but they had so much to do that I hated to bother them.

Bruce came right over and sat down on the low stool to find the problem. For over fifteen minutes he tried in vain to produce the blue flame. Then from the kitchen I heard a booming voice: "Margery! There is gasoline in the tank!"

Those words stuck terror through my being.

Bruce continued, "The Lord still has work for you; it is only the mercy of the Lord that the refrigerator didn't explode."

I knew his words were true and that they applied to him as well. I don't know how many matches he also lit before making the discovery. But how did we get gasoline in the refrigerator instead of kerosene?

My thoughts went to the African who had filled the refrigerator reservoir. I had an elderly nurse friend from a village near Bangui visiting me for several days. She had her African chauffeur/houseboy, Gokara, with her. She asked me several times to give him some work to do. Finally I replied that he could fill the refrigerator reservoir. I asked my houseboy to take him to the storeroom, show him how to fill the jerry can from the kerosene drum, and then fill the reservoir in the fridge. Gokara filled the jerry can from the wrong drum. As the wrong fuel was put in the reservoir, there must have been just enough kerosene left to create a mixture that was not quite as explosive as gasoline. We are so thankful that the Lord kept even the gasoline fumes from exploding! God had planned twenty more years for me to serve in Africa and thirteen more for Bruce.

During my last term, I lived for a time in the Muhr house while they

The brick house that was Margery's home.

were on furlough. My refrigerator was left in my former house for Alice to use, so I had to become accustomed to a different refrigerator.

One day I walked into the kitchen after my siesta to be met by a strong kerosene smell. There was kerosene all over the floor—the reservoir had sprung a leak. I opened the bottom door, took out the tank to inspect it, and found a dark, thick, mucky substance on the bottom. It had accumulated contaminants from years of putting fuel into it without cleaning it.

After cleaning up the mess and scraping the corrosion from the reservoir, I discovered not one but ten holes that had developed from the effect of the contaminants. What was I to do now? I was sure that Doug Murtoff, our mechanic, would be working in the garage that Saturday afternoon. He almost lived there, working as he did on so many projects. I found someone to take the tank down to the garage, and sure enough, there was Doug working away. He was able to repair the tank by soldering the holes, and in a couple of hours he had it back to do its work in the fridge.

Before I went to Africa, I thought I would be suffering continually from the heat for everyone 'knows' that Africa is hot, but that isn't always so. The Central African Republic is located on the equator, so there are months when it is very hot, but there are some mornings in the rainy season and a couple of weeks in late December and early January, in the dry season, that it is chilly. A few times I wore a flannel shirt until 8:00 a.m. Occasionally in January it gets down to 67 degrees overnight.

I felt sorry for our people who didn't have sweaters or blankets. I remember one time during this cold season when a pastor asked me to come out to his place and haul bricks from his house and church to a new location nearby. The contour of the road was being changed, so the moving had to be done. I agreed to help, and so I went out late one morning and worked until dark. A small grass hut was built for me and another one built for the pastor and his family. Before retiring for the night, I went over to say good night to the family. The five children were already lying on mats placed on the floor. They had nothing but a cloth to cover them, but the pastor did have a blanket to cover himself and his wife. I had brought a blanket for myself, but it wasn't enough to keep me warm, and I spent a miserable, chilly night. I thought of the children next door with almost nothing and how uncomfortable they must have been. We have so much here in America.

My flannel shirt lasted for twenty years, but it was time to get another one, so on furlough that was on my agenda. A friend from one of the Boise churches knew I needed one and told me not to buy one just yet. Her husband had received a good flannel shirt for Christmas two years earlier but had never worn it, so she asked me to come over and try it on. I wondered about her giving her husband's gifts away, but she said her husband would never miss it. The fit was perfect.

The first time I wore the shirt back in Africa was on a drizzly Sunday morning when a student and I went out to a village class. A blind man sat close by shivering in the open portion of a broken down hut. He had only a torn old shirt and some ragged old shorts to wear. I immediately took off my shirt and gave it to him. He hugged it and lifted his blind eyes to me and said, "Thank you, thank you."

The next Sunday, at the end of our meeting in the village, the blind man, led by a young boy with a stick, came slowly over to me with a chicken clutched in his hand. It was his gift for me. I thought, *How could I take this precious gift from someone who has nothing?*

I whispered to the student with me, "Do I have to take it?"

He quietly replied, "Yes, Mademoiselle, you do. You would insult him if you didn't." It was one of the hardest gifts to accept that I ever received.

After giving my new shirt away, I just continued to wear my old one until I went to the States for good.

The cool weather didn't stay around, however. There were other times when the heat was almost unbearable. One such time was just before I came home for my first furlough. We didn't have a ceiling in our house, and the heat from the dry season sun on the tile roof that day made sleeping almost impossible. I wanted to take a cot outside to see if there was a little breeze, but I knew I couldn't because of the leopards roaming about. Then I had a brilliant idea—or so I thought. I would sleep on the small, flat roof of the veranda outside my bedroom door. I got Florence's stepladder, grabbed my medical bag and a cot mattress, and climbed up. I hadn't realized there was a full moon, and in spite of the small breeze, I couldn't really sleep under

Blind man with his gift to me of a chicken.

that brilliant light. It was almost like day. After midnight, one of the nearby pastors arrived with a sick toddler and called, "*Mademoiselle, a yeke?*"

Was he surprised when he looked up to see where my voice came from as I said, "Yes, I'm here." I explained why I was on the roof and asked what was wrong with Kembi, his little boy. I opened my medicine bag, and as he climbed up a couple of the rungs of the ladder, I reached down to give him the needed medication.

Just at dawn the next morning, I tried to get down, but I couldn't quite reach the ladder comfortably without sliding part way down. What was I to do?

Just then Madame's voice came from the big house up the hill, "Ferd, you gotta come and see this." The 'this' was me trying to get down.

Ferd came to the window and saw my predicament, got dressed, and came over to help me. He brought my pickup over next to the veranda so I could slip down onto the top of the cab. Needless to say, he enjoyed helping, finding it difficult to keep from laughing.

You can be sure that I never tried that again. I never did quite figure out why Madame was up at dawn, looking out the window down at my house, but I was glad she had been.

By the way, that little toddler whose father came to see me that night fully recovered and is now a pastor himself. He worked for me in the clinic for two years after graduating from our school.

18 - Fires

During the months of January and February, all the grass in the countryside would be burned off by the Africans. Therefore, in December, students always made a ten-foot fire path, cutting the tall grass that surrounded our 124-acre mission station.

From our hilltop at night we could see fires burning, sometimes in several different directions. When there was a fire burning a large area, we missionaries would sit on our veranda and watch the spectacular scene. Sometimes there would be three or four rows of flames leaping to twenty feet or more. At those times we always hoped the Africans had made a large fire path around their manioc gardens. (This was one garden that grew all year around.)

But sometimes fire would jump the fire path and burn up the hill. I have vivid memories of one time this happened and we had to fight the fire with buckets of water and beating the flames with palm branches. Another time, when the language committee was at Sibut, we all ran out in the middle of the night and fought fire until we were exhausted. One noonday my African house helper and I fought fire by the side of my house. We couldn't leave it to go call for help. Finally he said, "Mademoiselle, you can't do it any more. Your face is so red, and your strength is gone." It was only the Lord that kept me from having heat exhaustion.

Fires can spread so quickly when there is a strong wind. For a few years the Africans who worked for us built their houses almost a block from the student village, where there was some level ground. This was a precarious place to have their home (due to fires), but they all enjoyed living close to their work, and there was a strong camaraderie among them.

One day at noon during the dry season, in over one-hundred-degree weather, we had a spectacular fire. The flames were leaping high as they came up the hill towards the station. Worst of all, the fire was roaring fast toward our workers' and students' villages; their houses only had grass roofs, and they hadn't burned around their houses yet. We knew that nothing could keep the villages from going up in flames.

Nothing, that is, except the Lord. We prayed, and they prayed. We saw the wind change as the students lit the grass around the village for a backfire, and the flames were sent in the opposite direction. It was nothing but a miracle before our eyes. Needless to say there was great rejoicing and thankfulness to the Lord who does hear and answer prayer. We fought the fire from the hilltop and were also able to save our fruit trees.

Many years before, the Lord had kept fire from burning the Ferd Rosenau house soon after their arrival in Sibut in 1921. There were leopard-men that didn't want the missionaries there because the hilltop was previously used for their human sacrifices. Attempts were made on the Rosenau lives. I quote from Madame Rosenau's booklet, *God in Some of My Valley Days:*

> Not long after that they made another attempt on my life, when they saw my husband walk to town. They set a grass fire about two miles from our house, with no house or gardens between. The wind was blowing very hard in our direction. The grass was ten to fifteen feet high, and we had cleared very little around our house. We had cut a path for one person to walk out to the main road.
>
> My little houseboy came to me and said, "Madame, we have to run, or we'll get burned up. That fire is coming like a wild animal."
>
> I said, "Where shall we run? We can't make it to the main road, for on the path we surely would get burned

up, with the grass so high on either side, all around."

We lived on a high hill. The fire came up all around us.

I said, "We have only One to look to, and that One is God."

So I placed the baby (Eugene) just inside the door and stood outside and looked up to Him who was able. The grass roof was drier than the grass that was growing. I had seen houses touched with a match go down in ten minutes. It was certainly our extremity, but His opportunity. It was like we were in a huge furnace, with flames going up all around us, higher than the trees. I saw one big bunch of burning grass light on that roof one right after another and each one went right out. Ferd was on the road on the way home but was unable to reach us. What a testimony to all around, when they saw our house standing there on that hill in plain view, with ashes all over everywhere. They had to admit that our God had power that they knew nothing of.

19 - All God's Little Creatures

Every mission station has its own kind of live creatures that like to inhabit the missionary houses. At Sibut it was stinkbugs, stink mice (the shrew), stink ants, and indelible bugs. All stations have scorpions and snakes, and there isn't a missionary who doesn't have their own stories about them.

One day I was making my bed and found I had been sleeping with a scorpion. Another time during our weekly prayer meeting, when it was my turn to pray, I heard something drop beside me. I opened my eyes to behold a scorpion close to my knees. I quickly stopped praying and said, "I can't continue, for a scorpion has just fallen from the ceiling by me." It had to be killed before our prayer time could continue with safety.

It wasn't until I had been on the mission field for thirty-seven years that a scorpion or a centipede whipped its tail up over my sandal and stung me on the instep. Oh, how it hurt! Loie, a nurse who often lived with me, quickly injected my instep with a local anesthetic, but it didn't do a thing to ease the pain. I couldn't walk and had to crawl to go to the bathroom. Then she went down to the clinic and got an injection of Demerol, which did dull the pain. Now I knew why my sting patients cried and almost screamed with pain that sometimes lasted for two days.

There were also the indelible bugs. Once in the '60s, just before Bruce and Wilma went home one furlough, Bruce said to Florence and me, "When we come back from furlough, we are going to bring back metal frames for glass windows for our house. Do you want us to bring some for your house also?" Up to this time we had wooden shutters.

"Yes, yes." It didn't take a lot of thinking to answer in the positive. It would be wonderful to have the new kind of windows, not only to have more light on a rainy day but because of the bugs. Bugs! Bugs! Bugs! Not by the dozen, not by the hundreds, but by the tens of thousands. One morning I swept my bedroom floor ten times. I had sprayed the bugs, and they kept falling and falling and falling.

At that time the "bugs of the month" were the kind we had nicknamed "indelible bugs." Eugene said they were like the Japanese beetle. They were one-fourth of an inch long, and we called them indelible because if one was mashed, it left an un-removable, greasy, yellowish stain. More than once, as I removed a five carbon letter from my typewriter (no copiers in those days), I saw with disgust the greasy stain of a bug that had got mashed as he hid behind the roller. These bugs came out of the cracks in our board ceilings, the wooden shutters, and around our doors.

A veteran missionary couple, Bob and Vera Vaughn, came to work at Sibut for a couple of years. A few months after they were here, Vera said to us, "Before, when I visited you at Sibut, I thought the missionaries were careless in their housekeeping because of all the bugs I saw. But now, after sweeping up this quarter of a pail of bugs, I understand."

The windows arrived when Bruce and Wilma returned, and Bruce supervised the making of new doors. What a blessing to have fewer bugs in our house.

And then there were the stinkbugs! One day in my first term it was so hot that thousands of stink bugs that had hidden in our tile roof couldn't stand the heat and came down onto our rafters. (At that time we didn't have a ceiling in our house.) I put a stool on top of my desk

Nurse Loie Knight

and took a long, homemade broom and knocked some of them down. It was a mad scramble getting quickly to the floor to try to sweep them up as they scampered every which way. After I swept them up, I would put them in a tin can with kerosene in the bottom, then go back to the top of my desk and do it all over again.

We were thankful for our African house help that periodically did a thorough house cleaning. They would clean out the stinkbugs that had hidden behind books, between canned goods, and anywhere and everywhere. One thing we were thankful for: stinkbugs didn't bite—that is, unless one accidentally squished one against the body.

The month of November is the height of the stink bug season. It is also our annual missionary conference time. Whenever we had the conference at Sibut, the missionaries always knew that when they left, they would carry some stinkbugs home in their suitcases.

On my first furlough, I was staying with my friend Ilene in Seattle, Washington. We were sitting in her living room when my eyes spotted a familiar creature crawling up her drapes. I suddenly exclaimed, "Do you see what I see?"

"What? Where?"

"Going up your drape is a stink bug. I thought before I left Africa I was so thorough in examining everything when I packed."

But the stink of the bugs is mild when compared with that of stink mice. Early in my time at Sibut, they kept coming into my room at night. I could hear them playing around under my bed. Their toenails clicked across the linoleum floor, and they let off a horrible smell, something like a skunk.

Loie Knight removing the stink bugs from our dining room wall.

Nightly we'd have a contest to see if I could find my flashlight and my glasses and slip out from underneath my mosquito net to catch one before it slid under my closed door and disappeared into another part of the house or outdoors to safety. During my first term I did manage to send two of them to "animal heaven."

My first experience with a snake was late one afternoon in the dispensary. I realized anew the protecting hand of the Lord. It was getting dark and difficult to see. I saw that one of the shelves of the skin ulcer cabinet seemed to have more things on it than usual. As I began to straighten the items on the shelf, I wondered what some of that extra bulk was. To find out, I put my hand on it—a very foolish thing to do. I quickly realized what it was as I felt a curled-up four-foot snake taking his afternoon nap. I quickly went to the door and yelled "*ngbo, ngbo*" to a couple of our students who were cleaning the yard nearby. After the students had killed it, they said, "Mademoiselle, do you realize this is a very poisonous snake and if it bites a person, they can die in ten minutes?" They said, "*Merci na Nzapa, Merci na Nzapa* (Thank the Lord, thank the Lord)."

One evening at dusk I was standing near the edge of our retaining wall. Oumar, one of our house helpers, said to me, "Mademoiselle, don't stand near the rocks. At this time of the evening snakes come out from under them." I always appreciated his advice.

I was working in my house one day when I heard a familiar voice from the veranda calling, "*Mademoiselle, a yeke?*" It was Michel, a former nurse helper of mine who now lived in Bangui. As I got to the door, Michel yelled at me, "Don't come out." I instantly knew there must be a snake. He said, "Throw something out to kill a snake." The only thing handy was a curtain rod. It wasn't durable, but in Michel's hands it did the trick in killing the green mamba snake draped over the top of my front screen door. I thought how easily that snake could have jumped down on me if I had gone out that door. My heart was overwhelmed with gratitude to the Lord that He enabled Michel to be there at that time.

There are two kinds of mambas, the black and the green. The young of the black variety are green. The color of the green mamba is a very beautiful shade of lime green. That doesn't mean I wanted to see this variety just to admire its color! Both snakes are thin and swift, measuring four to eight feet long. Both can jump several yards. They are as deadly as vipers and cobra, all of which are feared in our area.

During our annual missionary conference, I left the dining room at the big house early one noontime to go to my house. As I arrived at the edge of the small veranda going into my bedroom, I noticed a green mamba just sliding underneath my screen door.

I called to two missionaries, Doug and Charles, as they walked out of the dining room. "A green mamba has just entered my house!"

They came quickly, looked for some sticks, and went into my house.

I was praying outside. "Lord, keep them safe, and let them find it."

Only minutes later they came out smiling, with the dead mamba dangling over one of the sticks. The snake had entered the bathroom; the easiest place in the house to find it, for it had only one cupboard.

Another time I was quietly reading in a chair on the veranda near a three-foot wall overlooking the countryside. I saw movement to my right. I turned my head ever so slowly and discovered it to be a four-foot green mamba gracefully standing upright, making a dancing movement, coming into the entrance-way of the veranda. It danced to the left, slithered around the corner by the side of the house, and headed toward the front door. It then dropped down on its belly and tried to go under the screen door. Thankfully the door was tightly closed. By this time I was slowly and very quietly exiting the veranda in the direction that the mamba had entered. The snake stood upright again and continued to the north side veranda wall and then jumped over it, going off into the grass. I had never seen anything like it before and never desired it to be repeated. I was barely breathing but cool as a cucumber. Now I gave a sigh of relief, and once again my heart was filled with thanks to the Lord for his protection.

One Friday morning, when I arrived at the clinic, Andre greeted me with the news that a snake had tried to strike him and had wiggled under the door into the pharmacy. For a few seconds I didn't know what to do. I always had to get medications out of the pharmacy. The snake could be anywhere on the shelves. I thought to myself, *I prayed this morning for the Lord to take care of me, and He can truly do it.* I was careful where I put my hands when I took medications off the shelf. Thankfully there was no sign of the snake.

There are many tales that could be told about cobras. Once one wrapped itself around a leg of our dining room table. Another time one entered our chicken coop and swallowed the eggs right out from underneath a setting hen. Bruce shot the snake, cut it open, and put the eggs back under the hen!

The most unforgettable snake story happened when I was rounding a curve going up the Sibut hill on my three-wheeled Honda. On the left near the ditch was a seven-foot cobra lying in an S position. Upon hearing the loud motor of my Honda, a yard of its body rose up. He quickly puffed out his head and was in the position to strike. There was nothing I could do but say the short prayer, "Lord, help me." With my heart pounding, I put on speed and roared on to the top of the hill. I was safe. I was so thankful that out of all the snakebites we treated, we only had one death, even though the Central African Republic is known for having the greatest number of different kinds of poisonous snakes in the world.

Snake vaccine was expensive. In 1975 a vial that would take care of venom from three different poisonous snakes cost $30, and the kind that could take care of ten different kinds cost $65. Sometimes it was puzzling to know what to do when someone came in with snakebite. Did a poisonous snake bite this person? If so, was it a bite that the $30 vaccine would take care of or would it require the $65 vaccine? We could only tell by a victim's vital signs when they arrived at the clinic if a deadly snake had bitten them. But we really had very few people bitten in comparison to the number of snakes roaming around.

Sometimes I went months without seeing a snake. Missionaries take precautions, and we do not live in fear. We have confidence in the One who called us. The Lord protects us from dangers seen and unseen. How wonderful to know we are in His care. I love that verse in I Peter, "casting all your care upon him; for he careth for you" (5:7).

20 - Food, Supplies, and Getting Around

Boiled rice with ground peanuts mixed with milk was the main breakfast menu for years. Sometimes we were able to get oatmeal in one of the two small Bangui supermarkets.

Our main meal was at noon, except on Sundays, when we took turns in the evening sharing the meal with everyone. We were fortunate at Sibut, for we could buy beef most of the time. Spinach, small tomatoes, lima beans, and corn were about the only vegetables raised by the Africans that could be purchased in the market.

The Africans wait until corn is hard before they harvest it. They thought it odd when we ate it soft. Once an African asked me, "Don't the white people have strong teeth?"

We used rice and sweet manioc instead of potatoes until the early nineties, when they learned to grow some fairly good potatoes in the northwest part of our country. Before then, we could buy potatoes in the supermarket in Bangui, but they came from France by air and were just too expensive. The Africans at Ippy raised a very small potato about the size of a quarter. Sometimes we bought and canned them for future use.

Once while I was on furlough in the States, some friends and I helped a Christian farmer harvest part of his potato crop that was to be given to the mission church he attended. The potatoes were then sent to the village mission headquarters to be distributed as needed. They only picked up the larger potatoes and left the smaller ones on the ground. As an African would say, "*be ti mbi asso mbi mingui*" (my heart hurt much) to see all those smaller ones the size of lemons left behind. I thought of all those tiny potatoes grown in Ippy. I proceeded to put all the potatoes I could fit in the palm of my hand into my sack. I was told to leave them behind, but I couldn't bear to see them go to waste, so when they weren't looking I picked them up anyway. It is hard for one who has seen so much poverty to watch as so much food is wasted.

Every mission station, including ours, had a garden. In the early years we received our seeds from the States. I recall Anna Herrman from Connell, Washington faithfully sending me garden seeds each year. She would plan many months in advance to make sure that the seeds arrived on time. Later, we were able to purchase our seeds in Bangui. The produce would be divided among the various households, depending on the number of people in each, and everyone canned produce not eaten right away, for use during the dry season. I was fortunate to have house help who could do the canning, as I didn't have time to do it myself. In addition to our garden produce, we often bought delicious pineapple on the Bangui Road to Sibut, and all of us canned that. One Sunday I found about ten of my pineapples ripe for canning—their aroma was filling the house—so I spent all afternoon canning them, with juice running down my arms and onto the floor.

One of the Rosenaus always brought out Iowa seed corn. We looked forward to sinking our teeth into those delicious yellow ears. Once during corn season we had guests, and a missionary couple from Kaga-Bondoro ate nothing but corn. The husband ate nine ears.

It didn't take long after the arrival of Ferd and Ina Rosenau in 1921, for them to start planting fruit trees, so by the time I arrived we were blessed with grapefruit, orange, lemon, avocado, guava, papaya, and mango trees. One avocado tree had some avocados seven inches in length. During my first term, I took a slide picture of one of them beside an African egg that was half the size of an American egg. Not one person in the audiences during my presentations could guess what the avocado was.

I remember going into a store right after my arrival home on that first furlough and seeing large eggs. I asked the clerk, "Are those duck eggs?" In my mind I can still see the expression on his face; I knew he was wondering if that lady was in her right mind.

Eggs were hard to come by. We received a few as gifts, and occasionally we were able to buy one or two. During my last ten years in Africa, there was a Canadian agriculture aid program in Sibut. Their purpose was to help the Africans raise better food, including chickens. You can't imagine how happy we were to be able to buy eggs by the dozen and to know they were fresh.

The main butcher at the market place was an Arab Muslim named Oumar. When he came to the clinic, we often took care of him first because we knew he had work to do. My helpers often witnessed to him about Jesus. He would be polite and listen, but we didn't know his heart, and many times it seemed he let the words go in one ear and out the other.

The Muslim religion limits the number of wives a man can have to four at any one time. This does not, however, limit how many wives they may have had in the past and divorced. In a divorce, the father always keeps the children. A couple of times Oumar didn't take Arab women for wives, and once he took one of our Christian girls. It really upset me to think that her father and relatives would choose money over the Christian way of life for her.

The meat market in town had three long, dirty, smelly tables covered with flies, each belonging to a different butcher. I preferred going to Oumar because he would wait on me as soon as he spotted me among the crowd clamoring to purchase meat. The butchers just chopped chunks of meat off the beef they had. Oumar always gave me fairly good meat and didn't cheat me by holding his finger on the scale or by using false weights. Even so, out of any five kilos of meat, at least one kilo would only be fit to be used for dog food.

Lumiere girls giving me a gift of eggs.

Another Arab butcher sold meat at a different market in the afternoon. Often, after my Thursday afternoon class downtown, I would go over to that market to buy meat. It seemed that each time I bought a kilo of meat the amount I received would be smaller and smaller. A couple of times I said to him, "I know that isn't a kilo of meat."

"Oh, yes it is, Mademoiselle, yes it is," he would reply. Finally, after several times of this, I brought a kilo box of cube sugar and took it with me to the meat table. When the butcher put a small amount of meat on the scale and declared that it was a kilo, I quickly took off the weight and replaced it with the kilo of sugar. Yes, indeed, he had been cheating everyone. Needless to say, after that he didn't like to see me coming.

The Arabs own most of the stores. Their shops are usually very small one-room buildings stocked with sugar, oil, macaroni, colorful lengths of women's fabrics, matches, lanterns, sardines, and other simple things.

Some of the Arab merchants sell used clothing from the United States. The clothing comes pressed in hundred-pound bales covered in burlap. They never know what kind of clothing is in them. Each bundle will have only one kind of clothes, such as men's pants or shirts or girls' dresses. The merchants put the clothing on large pieces of plastic in front of their houses, making it easier for the people to rummage through. Most of the Africans wear these used clothes from America; it would be difficult for parents to clothe their families if this source were not available. It is interesting to see the tee shirts with all kinds of American slogans on them, which the Africans could not understand. One year I had to smile when I saw a group of high school boys wearing wide-brimmed, pastel colored bridesmaid hats

The meat market.

to shield themselves from the sun.

Most of our groceries were bought in Bangui. When we shopped there, we usually bought enough to last two or three months.

In the market places we had to learn to bargain. When buying groceries, I usually paid the original price mentioned, but when it came to buying souvenirs, that was different. One time I looked at a few things an Arab was selling on a sidewalk corner. I asked the price of some articles. Of course it was outrageous, so I just walked away. He called after me and said, "Aren't you going to have fun with me so we can come to a reasonable price?" Before that I hated haggling. I was embarrassed to try and get a lower price; the sellers have so little. But I had to learn that if I stepped outside of the bargaining system, shopping would become impossible. The vendors would mob you trying to make some fast money. After that any short-term missionary who took me along with them to shop would say that I had learned to haggle over prices.

Our mail arrived up country about once a week, and in Bangui twice a week, when the planes arrived from France. When the French were in charge, second-class mail came through from the States in one or two months. After French Equatorial Africa gained its independence from France in 1960 it gradually took longer and longer, until finally the mail was not coming at all. One time I received a letter with a notice that a subscription to some garden magazine had expired and needed to be renewed. I was dumfounded! I didn't know I was supposed to have received it because not one copy had ever arrived.

In 1974, when I was on furlough, I went to a Christian bookstore in

The market in Sibut.

Boise, Idaho that was going out of business and selling books at a reduced price. I had a heyday going through the store, picking up some choice books. When I went to the post office to mail four packages of the books to Africa, the clerk there casually mentioned that they should arrive in about six weeks. I replied, "It will take at least six months." Naively, he told me that the law stated that when something is mailed, it would arrive anywhere in the world within six weeks. I knew it would be useless to say anything more. One package did arrive in six months; the second in two years, with mildew on the books, but I never received the other two. After that I told people not to send anything to me by regular mail.

The local post office at Sibut was unreliable, but we were fortunate in that missionaries were coming and going from other stations and they would take our mail on to Bangui. Each mission station had color-coded mail bags, so all mail coming and going from that particular station would be placed in the respective bag. That way lost mail was minimized. When we knew that someone was going to Bangui, we tried to get all our letters written so that they could be transported safely to their destinations. Sometimes, when the mail was secured and ready to go, Ruth Slocum, who was at our station for a short time, would come running out waving a short piece of paper and say, "Wait a minute! I just need to add a P. S. on this letter," or something similar. We enjoyed teasing her, saying her last name matched one of her characteristics, slow-come. In all other areas, though, she was a very efficient lady.

Our missionaries always brought out a lot of baggage. It was less expensive to buy things in America than to buy anything in Africa. Besides, most of our provisions couldn't be bought in Africa anyway. In the late '70s we brought our things out in ship containers or with us by plane. We could ship seventy pounds for $110 when we were flying.

One time we had a full container sent to us. The person in charge was given specific instructions as to how it was to be sent, but he thought he had found a better way. Instead of sending it to Douala, Cameroon, to come in by truck, he sent it to the country of Congo (not Zaire), to come by boat up the Ubangui River. Unfortunately, that year the rains were scarce and no large boats could come up the river, so the container sat in a port city for fifteen months. It was tempting for workers there to find out what was in it. They broke it open and stole what they wanted. They set fire to the inside so as to make it look like spontaneous combustion. Then to top it off, someone threw water on the fire. You can imagine what the contents looked like. Two of my accordions were stolen and two were destroyed, but I did manage to receive one in good shape.

Once Bruce needed an important part from America to fix his truck. He gave specific instructions to a friend as to how to send it by air, but the friend believed he had arranged a better route—or so he thought—and it stayed in North Africa somewhere, with no plane coming our way. I can still hear Bruce saying in an exasperated voice, "Why, oh, why didn't he follow my directions? Didn't he know that I knew the best way to send it?" In Africa, the most direct route is usually not the best route.

It was a happy day at our annual missionary conference when we voted to buy radios in order to communicate between the stations. Talking to one another helped us to bond more closely. It also enabled us to know when a missionary would be coming, so we could prepare for them or go out to look for them if they didn't arrive as expected. And we could talk to our doctor at Ippy for medical advice. More than once our radios saved a life.

Late one evening John, my head African nurse, and I diagnosed a woman student from Ippy as having a ruptured ectopic pregnancy. Only immediate surgery could save her life, so we called to Ippy by radio to make arrangements for her. Vernon Rosenau was available for transportation. I'll let him tell about that trip to the hospital with my main clinic nurse helping:

> John Saboyambo and I left the mission station at Sibut around midnight for the trip to Bambari with the student wife who needed to be transported to the hospital at Ippy. We would take her the 200 miles to Bambari, and then Jim Johnson from Ippy would meet us there and take her the rest of the way. It was the rainy season and the roads were full of mud puddles, with the red clay turning into a quagmire. Of course, this night it was raining and continued to rain throughout the night. I remember at one point driving into a large mud puddle and having the muddy water come up over the hood of the jeep and on over the top of the vehicle. I drove with the four-wheel drive engaged for the complete trip because of the terrible slippery mud. At one point, John was trying to change the IV drip, but because the road was so bumpy, we had to stop to complete the change.
>
> I will always remember John as a man of compassion. He was suffering for the woman who was being bounced about so terribly on the bad roads, but when I tried to slow down, he insisted that I keep pushing on or we would lose the patient.

Another complication, which made the trip even more difficult, was the road rain barriers. These were put in place to stop vehicles from traveling while the laterite roads were so saturated with rain. Large trucks would cut enormous ruts into the road surface, so they were restricted from travel until twelve hours after a heavy rain. Of course, every barrier was down in place that night, which meant that we had to go through the villages trying to find out where the agent for the barrier was so that we could wake him to come unlock and open the barrier. It is not fun slipping around in red mud in the middle of the night and of course, the agent never lived close to the barrier.

Many times we wondered if the patient was going to survive, and it was only the Lord's intervention that allowed us to arrive in Bambari in time to transfer her to Jim Johnson's vehicle and on for a successful surgical operation.

21 - African Helping Hands

Christian male employees were a part of every day life of the missionaries in the Central African Republic. To find those who were honest, with a real desire to help and work as unto the Lord, was a real treasure. Some fellows spent their lives working in the missionary homes. We didn't employ women for this type of work (except Patsy) because the African women had the time consuming and important responsibility of their homes and gardens. The men worked in their gardens as well when their other work was finished. I can still picture entire families coming home together in the evening from their gardens with firewood, basins of water on their heads, and the machetes and short hoes in their hands.

When I first arrived on the field, Florence had employed Demele, an older man who had worked several years for her. She had a lot of confidence in Demele's ability to do many things—he was her right hand man. He baked our bread, delicious cinnamon rolls, cakes, and pies, and also cooked regular meals.

One time at midnight a year after my arrival, I heard Demele's familiar voice outside my door saying, "*Mademoiselle, a yeke* [Is Mademoiselle there]?" When I opened the door, he had one of his small children in his arms. I noticed he didn't come too close to me because he held out the boy away from him, so I could examine the little one. After I knew his illness, I fixed a teaspoon of medication and asked Demele to come closer, to hold his little son tightly so I could give him the needed medication. When he came closer, I realized why he had tried to keep his distance. His breath stank of foul liquor.

I asked him, "How come you are drinking now?"

He said that he didn't drink; it was only *doumba* (fermented honey). Neither Florence nor I had known he had a drinking problem, but everyone in his village knew it. They thought we knew, so we were never told.

The next morning I told Florence about Demele's night visit.

She said to me, "It can't be true."

When she asked him about it, he said the same thing to her, that it was just fermented honey. She chose not to pursue it further and let the matter rest.

Later a guest observed that on baking days Demele always brought a sweater to work, and when he went home, it was always thrown over his shoulder. With a little detective work we discovered that he always baked an extra loaf for himself and then hid it in his sweater. With much sorrow Florence finally had to let him go. I'm sure she must have wept many tears in private, as I did in later years when I had to let someone go whom I liked and depended on at the clinic. Stealing was a great temptation for our house employees because they had so little compared to us.

We had many employees that were a joy to have working for us. I remember once, after Florence retired, when I had to employ a new house-boy and had asked people at home to make this a matter of prayer. My clinic and class ministry depended on adequate house help. Michel had worked several years as a cook for Ernie and was well trained. One day Michel brought his cousin Nozo Louis to see me for an interview. Nozo's facial features were different from any other African I knew; his eyes were slanted like the Asians'.

I liked Nozo immediately. I told Michel I didn't have time to teach Nozo to make bread but if he would teach him the essentials in cooking, I would hire him. He agreed. Nozo became a great person to have around. He was so willing to please and had a ready smile for everyone.

I have never forgotten the day when Nozo and I were painting one of our bedrooms, preparing it for Judy Stanton, a short-term nurse. He was up on an old stepladder painting when the ladder buckled underneath him. He fell, but he held that can of paint upright in his hands. I don't know how he did it, but he didn't spill a drop. He had such an astonished expression on his face at the miracle, that I just had to laugh, and he joined in. After a good spell of laughter we went back to work.

Several years later I had a vacancy at the clinic, and he asked me if he could work there. I reluctantly agreed; then he in turn brought Nicholas, a fellow of nineteen, to be interviewed. Nicholas was hired, and Nozo had the job of teaching Nicholas what Michel had taught him. It took a lot of effort for Nozo to learn the work of the clinic, but he became a good helper. Nicholas is now a pastor.

Once I had gone to Tchad for a leadership conference, to teach their churchwomen the program of the girls' youth organization formed by four different mission groups. I took John and Georgette with me. Georgette went to help me teach, and her husband, John, went to learn anything he could at their hospital. With both John and me gone, the clinic had to be closed except for our students, people with sores, and those on a series of injections. I gave this responsibility to Etienne, one of our workers.

When we returned, I learned Etienne had missed some days of work, and I asked him about it. "Etienne, why did you go off and leave the work I gave you to do?"

"But, Mademoiselle, I only went to Bangui for three days. Then I came back and worked until now." He was the only employee I ever fired for not taking responsibility.

In the thirty-nine years I employed helpers only two people were fired for stealing. Today it is difficult for missionaries to fire an employee. In such cases the accused person goes to a local African court and an African judge generally rules in favor of the African. The fines given by judges are outrageous. Recently our hospital in Ippy had to fire a head nurse for stealing money and medicines. In spite of evidence that proved him guilty, the judge ruled in favor of the nurse, and the hospital finally had to pay him 7,000 United States dollars.

Over the years many people worked in our clinic. After my first furlough many more ill ones came to us for help. We had to have four full-time workers. Months later we needed more than that. Many of our Bible School students worked part-time at the clinic, and some of them stayed on for a couple of years after graduation. I was especially grateful for Kembi and Philip because they were real soul winners who did their work well. Later they became pastors.

My main employees were Bible School graduates. I not only wanted medical employees but also those who had a concern for souls. They needed to know the Word of God in order to give a Gospel message, to lead someone to Christ, and to know how to counsel. Many times when I talked to someone about their soul and knew they were interested, I would call one of the workers. They knew their people better than I did. I also wanted them to experience the joy of helping someone find salvation.

I spent hours instructing the new employees because they very seldom had any previous medical knowledge. We couldn't hire graduate nurses from the government school because we couldn't afford to pay the required salaries. Their first requirement was to spend a couple of months learning about all the different areas of the medical ministry. After that they usually concentrated on one type of work. This cross-training provided backup if another worker became ill or was overwhelmed with his or her own work.

So many people wanted work; it was difficult sometimes to know whom to hire and train. Once when I had an opening for an assistant helper, I had three choices. I knew the men well, because they had been in my classes from fifth grade through high school. They were all equally qualified, and I could not choose one over another, so I did something entirely different. I wrote each name on a slip of paper and then prayed, "Lord, in Bible times they frequently cast lots. Please help me to pick just the right one." I closed my eyes and selected one. It was Yologaza, and I hired him. He was a good choice and worked with me for many years.

I was so thankful my helpers in Sibut worked together in harmony. One day I realized they were from four different tribes (five including me). I rejoiced at how well they liked each other. Isn't that the way it should be in the body of Christ? Christ said in John 13:35, "By this shall all men know that ye are my disciples, if ye have love one to another."

I usually had one main nurse and 3-5 assistants to help with the clinic work. In addition to my loving, dependable Louvrou, who worked for me for thirty-three years, there were four "right-hand" nurses who labored alongside me over the years:

Levi Besioni

After graduating from Bible School, Levi and his family continued to live in our mission village, though in a different area from the students. In addition to his own family, he had four orphan siblings to raise.

I enjoyed working with him and with others. We had some precious times together on our knees talking to the Lord. Besides the many hours I spent teaching him nursing, he went to Ippy for a month so Knute Orton could train him to stain and read microscope slides. After a few years he did the patient consultations. The responsibility he shouldered allowed me to do more class and camp work.

I want to share this condensed message, "Where Is Your Heart?" that Levi preached one morning at the clinic. The English translation is as follows:

You can always tell where people put their hearts. If someone fixed food for you and you were hungry, your heart would be where the food is. You trust the person who fixed it and therefore you would eat it. When someone is good to you and helps you in times of need, you trust that person.

There is Someone who has done a lot for you, more than anyone in the whole world. But many of you have not yet set your hearts to trust that person. That person is the Lord Jesus. The Word of God says in Isaiah 26:4, "Trust ye in the Lord for ever," and verse 3 says, "Thou wilt keep him in perfect peace, whose mind is stayed on thee: because he trusteth in thee."

Formerly your ancestors put their hearts to fight; they killed one another with spears. That is the work of darkness. But with the coming of the missionary, that is finished. We didn't know peace. And you won't know peace until you have trusted the Lord. You know whether or not you have trusted the Lord if you have put away your sins. If you are still sinning, you haven't put your heart to know God.

You people come here for medicine, and expect the medicine to do some good for your sick bodies. But do you know you have a greater sickness, a sickness of your soul? If you want peace, put your heart to know God, whose Son, the Lord Jesus, died on the cross for your sins. If you don't know Christ, and if you don't accept Him now as your Savior, then you can't tell God on Judgment Day that you didn't hear about Him.

You are hearing right now. So won't you trust the Lord while you still have time? We aren't to stay long in this world. The Bible says our lives are like a vapor that appears for a time and then vanishes. If you trust the Lord today you will have peace.

One day after he had worked for me for fifteen years, he came to me and said he wanted to quit. His wife wanted to go to Bangui and live there. I knew that with his medical knowledge, he could make more money for his family living in the capital. Oh, how I wept. He left a huge gap that was hard to fill.

Andre Komesse

Andre graduated in the same class as Levi. He and another graduate went to Ippy to take a medical training program at our hospital there. I don't know what happened, but two years later they both became very bitter and came back to Sibut. Andre thought I wouldn't have anything to do with him because he left his training at Ippy. He learned otherwise. We talked on several occasions over the next few months, and I could see his attitude changing and the bitterness leaving him. I hired him, and he worked with us until his death in 1970. He was always a great help in my medical work.

One day a drunken school inspector came in when I was working in the treatment room. Agitated, he put his hand on my arm. Andre noticed it from the other room. Quickly and quietly he came to us and stood between the inspector and me. I had the warmest feeling in my heart, knowing that Andre was watching out for me.

When I was home on furlough in 1970, Andre was about forty years of age. One of my missionary co-workers wrote that he was very ill and the doctors in Bangui had diagnosed liver cancer. I immediately wrote Andre a letter. My helper, John, who nursed him during his last days, sent a letter that Andre wrote to me. Translated into English, it partly read:

> I know I am going to die, but I have peace in my heart. Since I started to work with you, I had much joy. If there was any disagreement in our work together, you didn't harbor it in your heart. I do have sadness in leaving my wife and six children, for I know I can't help them when I am gone. But I know that when they become ill, you will take care of them.

He then asked pardon for a couple of trivial things and forgiveness for anything he said or did that wasn't right. He wanted to face eternity with a clear conscience. He continued writing:

> You know Oumar is working with Mademoiselle Marian at Kaga-Bondoro, and when he visited me, he told me that he would return to Sibut and work for you if you wanted him to.

That last line especially touched me, for he knew his going would leave me without adequate help. He concluded his letter:

I can't walk now; I am bedridden. My words are finished. Please greet you and your family in the name of Jesus. Thank you.

[Signed] Andre

Oumar Judd

Oumar was a sixteen-year-old fellow who was working in our house when I arrived in Africa as a new missionary. I once asked him, "Oumar, would the Africans think more of the missionaries if we lived like they do, in mud-brick houses with dirt floors?"

Immediately he answered, "No, they wouldn't. They want to come up to your standard of living, not have you go down to theirs."

That made me feel much better. In later years Oumar built a six-room, cement-block house for his family. It was so good to see it could be done.

Oumar went through our Bible School, but he didn't feel called to the ministry. Marion, the nurse at Kaga-Bondoro, asked him to work for her, and she trained him. He was with her for ten years.

After I returned from furlough in 1970, Oumar worked for me for several years. He was a very good helper. He was a mature, dignified man. Unfortunately I had to let him go in the mid-80's. In 1990, Alice, the nurse who took my place, hired him back, and he worked with her until he passed away with AIDS. Oumar meant a lot to me, and at the end of his illness I went several times to *douti na lo* (an African expression that means "to sit with few words spoken"). One Christmas, before his death, each of his six children drew a colored flower for me. I still keep those drawings with me.

Oumar Judd

Louvrou

The story of Louvrou's early life has already been written. She worked with me longer than any of my helpers, from

1952 to 1980. She was very faithful, never complaining, and always telling people about Jesus. I often wrote home of her and spoke frequently about her when I was on furlough. Some of my close friends felt they also knew her. The churchwomen in Connell, Washington made many dresses for my helpers' wives, and there were always special ones for Louvrou.

Once in the '60s she became very ill for two weeks. I had her stay in my guestroom, so I could have the pleasure of taking care of her, for I loved her dearly. It was such help when her niece Alissa came to care for her the last three years of her life.

Louvrou was older than I was (the older Africans do not know their ages), and in 1980 I felt the medical ministry was becoming too much for her, so I encouraged her to retire from the medical work. In our mission village she was a very Godly influence on the young women who attended our Bible School. She was like a mother and counselor to them, and they would often visit and help her with the heavier tasks. Their children would gather around her for a story. As long as she had strength, she walked to the children's class building to help take care of the toddlers, and often she brought bread to satisfy any child who was hungry.

Even though her strength was waning, she took a hoe and made a small rice garden in back of her house. The new rice sprouts coming out of the ground made delicious food for the birds. To prevent this, African children are in their gardens by daybreak pounding an old metal pot, shaking a can partly filled with rocks, yelling or doing everything possible to chase the birds away.

One evening Louvrou gave this testimony at our Wednesday prayer meeting: "I don't have anyone to chase the birds away from my rice garden, and I don't have the strength to do it myself. So I asked the Lord to do it, and He answered my prayer." Her faith in Jesus never wavered throughout her life.

In September 1994, when I was almost seventy years old, I left Sibut, my home for forty-four years, to go to the States for good. There were so many people coming to my door to tell me good-bye, I didn't have time to go to the village to see Louvrou. As I got into the Muhr's truck to leave, I said to them, "I've got to say my last good-bye to Louvrou."

As we drove through our village to Louvrou's house, the village people started following the truck. I just waved to them, for I had already told them good-bye many times. As I went into Louvrou's house, she slowly raised her arthritic body from the bed and tottered towards me. I hurriedly grabbed her, or she would have fallen. With tears streaming down her face, she said, "What am I going to do without you?"

I answered, "I've left money, so you will be taken care of."

She quickly replied, "I didn't mean money."

I knew what was in her heart, for our friendship meant much to both of us. A month later she went to meet her Lord, whom she loved and served so faithfully. What a wonderful hope I have to know that some day we can continue our friendship!

John Saboyambo

Everybody had a special love for John Saboyambo and his wife, Georgette. Both came from Godly, hard-working parents. John worked for me part-time all through his Bible School years. After graduating he came to work full time.

One day before he was married, he came to my house and handed me a half-sheet of paper with two names written on it. He said, "I know you work with teenage girls. Please tell me which of the two girls named on the paper would make the better wife for me."

I read the names and replied, "Neither one, John."

He looked at me in astonishment and asked, "But who would you suggest?" A few moments went by as I silently sent up an SOS to the Lord for help. I then wrote down the names of two girls I knew very well. He didn't make a

choice right then but took the paper home to think and to pray about. I was satisfied with the girl he chose, Georgette, as she had helped me in a couple of girls' camps and was a very capable and reliable girl. Her face radiated the joy of living, for she had a deep relationship with Christ. I knew she would make a good wife for John.

Years later, after they had four children, he appeared at my door. I thought he wanted to consult me about a patient. With a kind of shy grin that only John could give, he said, "I want to thank you for suggesting Georgette to me." Those words warmed my heart.

John Saboyambo

After John had worked full-time for me three years, he said something one day that saddened me. "I want to go to Ippy and go through the medical training program."

I didn't want him to go, for many reasons. First, because I needed his help. Although he would receive some wonderful training, I also knew the Baptist Mid-Missions doctors at Ippy teach the trainees how to do major surgery, enabling them to help and even operate in emergency situations. I knew how talented he was and in all likelihood, the doctors would want him to stay in Ippy. But most of all, some graduates of our medical training program had left the mission to take positions in government hospitals as surgeons, making a lot more money. Those hospitals sought our graduates because they were well trained. I didn't want John to be tempted in this way. The mission, of course, could only afford to train medical workers who were going to continue in the rural mission clinics and the mission hospital.

When John saw tears in my eyes, he said, "Don't cry, Mademoiselle I just want to learn more and come back to help you in your old age." At that remark I couldn't help but grin.

Months later a large crowd gathered when I took my truck to John's house to load his family and belongings for the seven-hour trip to Ippy.

Many tears were falling. You would have thought it was a funeral procession. Everyone loved John and Georgette, and no one wanted either of them to leave. Earlier that day at the clinic I found Oumar sobbing, and I asked him, "What is troubling you?"

He answered, "I've never had a friend like John. I'm going to miss him." We all would.

It took John ten years to go through the five-year program. John didn't lack intelligence, but our doctor was in the United States almost the same amount of time he was on the field. Thus John didn't receive the classes he needed in the first five years. Meanwhile

Georgette Saboyambo

Georgette learned to be a midwife and became the head matron.

John and Georgette did come back, in spite of the Ippy doctors wanting them to stay and work there. This capable medical worker helped me tremendously "in my old age," until I left the medical work at age 65. He did the things I couldn't do anymore. With him working in the clinic, I was able to spend many hours in the teaching ministry. Words can't express what this couple meant to me. After I left the clinic, they both worked for Alice when she took over the medical work during my last term.

There are no missionaries at Sibut now, but the clinic is still functioning. Director John Saboyambo and his helpers (Georgette being one of them) are taking care of the ill. I recently received a letter from both of them that I treasure:

> There is a great desire of us in the CAR to see you. But we can't hear you speak or see you. We go to the different places where you worked, the choir, the clinic, among the churches, the young people, teaching in the Bible School and we can't find you.

John and his family are now living in the house where I lived for so many years. I hope they are taking time to sit on the veranda in the early morning or in the evening to enjoy the wonderful view I appreciated so much.

22 - Our Pharmacy

When I first went to Africa, I had no idea that I would start a medical work from scratch, so I didn't take any supplies with me, but I did have a year to get started. I put in an order to Art Fetzer, our mission secretary and a pharmacist in Cleveland, Ohio. He was able to acquire the medicine for us very reasonably, so I had supplies on the shelves when I opened the clinic in December of 1952.

At first I didn't charge for any medicines, but when Dr. Rouch, from our Ippy hospital, realized what I was doing, he suggested I at least charge for venereal disease medications. I followed his advice. Later, when so many more patients were coming to us, I charged ten cents for a medical card that was good for twenty consultations. Later the price became twenty-five cents. Also, I only charged the patients the same price for the medicines that I had paid for them. This allowed us to continue to fund our pharmacy.

Later a wholesale pharmaceutical company started a business in Bangui, but even buying medicine from them was expensive.

In the early sixties Dr. Rouch heard of the Missionary Assistant Program (MAP), an organization near Chicago to which drug companies donated for overseas missions. I was soon ordering from them, not only for my clinic but for the other clinics as well. We received some real "goodies". One crate that I will never forget was filled with 100,000 Band-Aids. What fun I had distributing those to the clinics and missionaries and to our pastors.

Mr. Young came to the Central African Republic looking for useful projects that he could support. I talked to him about building a pharmacy depot that would support the hospital and our four clinics. I told him I would like to do it but didn't have the building or the time to manage it. Later Dr. Charles Rhodes, from our Ippy hospital, had the same idea, so the depot was established there at Ippy. Mr. Young supplied the money for the building and the first shipment of medicine. The main responsibility for the management of the depot was put into June Stone's capable hands.

When June and I came home for our furlough in 1964, my friend Ilene met us at the airport in Chicago. Since Chicago was close to the headquarters of MAP, I asked Ilene to drive June and me there. The personnel gave us a warm welcome, and the director took us out to lunch. He wanted to discuss the best way the organization could help. I suggested that if a company could come and dig wells, that would be the best gift our country could have. After our lunch we were taken into their storeroom and told, "There is not a sufficient amount of medicine and supplies of the same kind to put them in the quarterly bulletins, but we would like for you to

Margery in the clinic pharmacy.

help yourselves to anything you want." For four hours June and I had a great time taking many of the treasures from the shelves.

Later Great Britain, Germany, and the Netherlands had large pharmaceutical companies that sold medicine for less than wholesale to aid projects in third world countries. This was a breakthrough for us. At first I had the medicine come by post, but there was much stealing and it took three or more months to receive it. Once I received a box from France with nothing but paper inside, though it was supposed to contain 10,000 malaria pills. That was a great blow. After that I had the products sent by air. The cost for transportation was equal to the cost of the medicines, but at least they came without being stolen and the pharmacy shelves began to fill up. Now there was even a back-up supply in the storeroom. This always gave me great satisfaction. I really hated to tell patients that we were all out of the medicine that could help cure their illnesses.

My friend Al Undi was one of the first directors of Medicines for Missions at King's Garden in Seattle. (King's Garden eventually became CRISTA, and Medicine for Missions became World Concern.) I was one of the first to go there and help myself to their supplies. At first I could go and select what I needed and they would then pack the medicines away in fifty-gallon drums, lined with beautiful quilts that were made for us. But later they did the choosing. World Concern received many of their supplies as samples from doctors' offices, pharmacies, drug companies, etc. Volunteers spent hours tearing apart the samples and putting them into bottles. It gave me much pleasure to thank the volunteers of World Concern and tell them how wonderful it was to be on the receiving end of their hard work in preparing the medications for shipment.

A problem developed at the clinic in 1987. The town hospital rarely had medicines, and if they did, only a selected few patients received them. The people had to buy their medicine from a small pharmacy, paying a high price. Later the pharmacy went out of business, and the people came to me to fill their prescriptions. I sold the medicine to them at cost. So many came, it took much of my time selling medicine and didn't allow adequate time to take care of those who came to us for medical help. After a couple of months, I realized what I was doing—selling medicine without a license or authority. I had to stop. Happily, the small pharmacy came back into business again.

"Tetracycline, tetracycline, ten francs a pill" was the cry I frequently heard when I went down to the market. A boy about twelve years old, with a bag of tetracycline that was bought in Zaire, was going through the market place selling the pills. I was very disturbed to see people buying four pills, maybe for a cold. And anyone could go into pharmacies in the Central African Republic and buy antibiotics without a prescription. This way of doing things was a real sore spot for me, for I knew they wouldn't take the antibiotics correctly and their bodies would soon build up immunity against them.

Once when I was a delegate from our mission to a government medical meeting in Bangui, I brought up the subject of people being able to buy antibiotics at will. The moderator, who was the minister of health, replied, "We know it isn't right, but there is nothing we can do about it." Again I realized I was in Africa and not in the United States.

Today, to save on airfreight and to cut down on thievery, all the missions in the Central African Republic coordinate their ordering of pharmaceutical supplies. These supplies come in containers to Bangui, where each mission can claim what belongs to them. This is a great solution to many of the problems we had in the past.

Part Four

Medical Memories

After returning from my first furlough I walked into the pharmacy and was so disappointed to find the shelves almost empty. Orders were immediately placed to three different drug companies for medicine. It took three months before they arrived and we were able to open the clinic once again.

Meanwhile, I started a Bible class for teenage boys. This was the beginning of my work with the youth at Sibut. Before I went home for my next furlough in 1959, I was so encouraged and happy when three of my students enrolled in our Bible School.

One had been a Jehovah's Witness, but he found Jesus to be his Savior. We had agreed among my helpers at the clinic to pray for him until he really gave himself over to the Lord in complete surrender. It was a thrill to see him in school in answer to our prayers.

I also helped teach in our Bible School, and that always made me happy. When we acquired our truck, Florence and I were able to go with the students and conduct Bible classes in villages where there wasn't a nearby church.

Ferd Rosenau had just started construction of the new ward building. It was being placed down the hill, on the other side of the road away from any other buildings. My heart hurt to see Mr. Rosenau down on the acreage, working away with a couple of Africans in the hot tropical sun, with his long-sleeved shirt soaked with perspiration. Most of the time he didn't take siestas, and he wasn't young any more.

He had wanted to have the building finished by the time I returned from furlough, but it takes so much time to build anything in Africa. If you think it should take six months, it would probably take eighteen. The two African masons worked so slowly, but considering how hot it was and how many times they probably came to work without eating, it wasn't surprising how little was accomplished. It was too bad that in those days they didn't have the short-term mission trips when qualified men go to different countries to construct buildings. That would have allowed the missionaries to use more of their time on things others couldn't do.

The day came when the ward building was finished. It had three rooms, each containing two beds. It didn't look like much yet because it hadn't been whitewashed, but what a relief to have a place to hospitalize patients.

I could now put on my nurse's uniform again and start work. Once more I could have morning devotions with my helpers before the clinic opened. Each day we read the Word and prayed for the Lord's help and for our ill patients.

Right after our reopening, I had my first tetanus case, an eight-day-old baby. She had been born in the village and probably got the infection from whatever instrument they used to cut the cord. I was really scared, but after a little research and with prayer I proceeded to treat her. She survived.

And then, I will never forget John, whom the missionaries in Bangui sent to us. In the letter they said he was a very sincere Christian believer but was now mentally off much of the time. He roamed the villages, sleeping in the woods at night, and never made a garden or lived with his family. The missionaries had hope that I could do something for him. I was stunned. I knew almost nothing about psychiatry. But John had so much hope expressed in his face that my helpers and I desperately prayed that God would give us wisdom in treating him. We did what we do with most people who come to us, examine them for parasites. We found filaria in his blood and treated him for it. Oh, our joy knew no bounds when John soon became a normal person again. He went back to Bangui, lived with his family, made a garden, and happily told others about Jesus and what great things He could do.

It was a day of rejoicing when my baggage finally arrived from the United States. I needed the medical books I had purchased while I was home. There were volumes on diagnosis, tropical medicine, minor surgery, and advanced obstetrics, all subjects not taught to nursing students. Throughout the years I spent countless hours studying and poring over them because I desperately needed this knowledge to help my precious African friends. I also found my Merck Manual to be a very useful resource.

I was longing for the day when the new clinic building would be built in

Before landscaping.

front of the ward building. Since Baptist Mid-Missions had five other clinics and a hospital, I could draw from the experience of the other nurses. Four of us nurses got together and planned the layout. I had about $1500 to start the project. I brought out some green Plexiglas windows and metal cupboards that had to be assembled. I had no doubt in my mind that the Lord would supply the finances for the building, and He did. When a bill came in, it was paid. I remember once a bill came in for $200 for two tons of cement. When the weekly mail arrived there was a letter with two $100 bills in it. I never went into debt.

It took almost three years for the clinic building to be constructed. Many Africans wanted to help move my clinic equipment to the new building when the day arrived on April 25, 1958. It had six rooms: a small office, examining room, pharmacy, laboratory, treatment, and a large consultation room. A special place was fixed at the end of the veranda for treating sores and skin ulcers.

We planted two flame trees between the clinic and the road. One of them grew to be graceful and majestic, while the roots of the other must have been rockbound, for the tree was small and always had a sickly look to it. We also planted several mango trees for their shade and fruit. What a blessing they were.

It was wonderful to have the large veranda where people could sit out of the hot sun and the rain. It was also convenient to have people in one place when we gave the Gospel message each morning.

We had three outbreaks of the flu. The first was the Asian flu of 1957. One day we treated 500 ill ones, but most of the time it was around 350.

After landscaping.

For many, the flu developed into pneumonia. We had a few deaths. I told our sick Bible students to stay at their homes. I went through the village giving out lemons (we ran out of Vitamin C pills), aspirin, and quinine and encouraging them to drink a lot of water.

When I came to the house of a student named Ziba, he was really having a coughing spell. I said to him, "Stop it." The French word for stop is the same, but I had used the English pronunciation. When he could get his breath, he had a quick reply: "Mademoiselle, I have no brakes."

Ziba had two boys about six or seven years of age that looked like twins. They had full cheeks, and with their sweet smiles they were so loveable. More than once I knelt down beside them to give them a hug. A month before, one of them had walked up the hill to our house when Florence and I were having our noon meal. Florence went to the dining room door in response to a quiet knock. She was very surprised to see him, and when she asked what he wanted, he looked up at her with his sweet smile and said, "I want to believe in Jesus." So another one of Florence's children came into the fold.

He was one of the many that contracted the flu, then developed pneumonia, and much to our sorrow, he died. Earlier he had been ill with parasites, which left him weak, but he had been getting better after being treated and fortified with vitamins.

At last the flu subsided, and we were back to our more usual 180 patients per day.

The second flu epidemic hit Sibut with a bang in October of 1975. One man walked six miles with a temperature of 104 degrees, arrived at the clinic,

People waited on the clinic veranda for their turn to be treated.

and collapsed. During the height of the flu epidemic we again reached 500 patients. Oumar and I were running an ambulance service. I didn't begin to have enough beds, even though we now had fourteen more than we did in 1957 to take care of the ones who developed pneumonia. The floor was filled with the ill. We no sooner got one from the floor to a bed than I was called to go get another pneumonia patient.

Thankfully, in about three weeks the patient load diminished to 250 daily, then gradually back to our normal 150-200. I thanked the Lord that my helpers and I remained in good health. I remarked to one of our Christians, "I wonder when my turn is coming."

He quickly replied, "Mademoiselle, haven't we been praying that God would keep you well so you can take care of all of us?"

At the end of the flu outbreak, I went to get someone on the main road. When a patient came in to us by a truck or one of the rickety busses, their driver always left them at the mission crossroads. This time the ill one was a thirteen-year-old girl, just skin and bones. I did a quick hemoglobin check by pulling down her eyelid. The conjunctiva was white instead of the normal red. I wondered how she was still alive. One of my first thoughts was, *Why did they bring this girl on the brink of death to me now?* We were all so tired from the flu epidemic. The Holy Spirit quickly rebuked me for such a thought. I remembered a Bible verse that says, *"In every thing give thanks"* (1 Thessalonians 5:18). Then I thanked the Lord for bringing us this girl, who had been having bloody dysentery for seven months, who had tried the hospital in Bangui for three months, and who had then gone home, where they used native medicine on her for another three or four months.

I will always remember what the girl's mother said to me: "We know the Lord is with all of you here." I learned later they were two-month-old Christians. We prayed; oh, how we prayed. "Lord, you will just have to show You are able. How can I get her well when doctors in Bangui failed to do so?" And miracles of miracles, she was soon better. She became hungry as a bear, and the continual bloody stools were a thing of the past. I had only one treatment left of a drug that would take care of two parasites at one time, and she had been the one to receive that treatment. We all thanked the Lord. He was with all of us.

Over the years we had epidemics of mumps, whooping cough, meningitis, polio, chicken pox, and measles. Once measles and whooping cough appeared about the same time. That was more than a rough time. I remember three epidemics of measles.

When the people got measles, they also had diarrhea and became very dehydrated, especially the babies. Some of their little bodies were so dry I could lift up the skin on their tummies and it would just stay up. We lost some of them, and that was always heartbreaking. By the time of the second outbreak I had learned about keeping electrolyte balance in the human body. I always kept hundreds of packages of re-hydration powder on hand, to be mixed with water. Each person with measles now received a packet with instructions on how to use it, thus replacing their lost fluids. Out of fifty babies we lost only three.

I remember a time when we had one family with measles in our village. In my next class with the wives, I gave a ten-minute talk on how measles could be spread. The Africans are a very sympathetic people, and if they know of a sick person, they will go to visit them. I pleaded with our students' wives, "Please, not one of you go to the house where there is someone with measles. Do not eat any of their food, and do not even shake their hand." They understood. Then we had prayer that the Lord would keep the rest of the village families free from measles. The Lord granted our request. Hallelujah!

When the third measles epidemic came along, my nurse helpers and I made a bold request of the Lord, "Do not let one baby who comes to us die." We had fifty-two cases. There were some close calls, but we prayed and worked, and the Lord answered. Not one died!

When I taught hygiene to the students, I gave them a simple formula of baking soda, salt, sugar, and orange juice for making up their own solution of re-hydration fluid when needed.

During this time we became acquainted with the nicest Swiss missionary couple and their two adorable daughters. Their mission station was between two of ours, so they had to pass through Sibut when going to the capital. Charles was from the German part of Switzerland, and his wife, Margaret, was from the French part. When we spoke to Charles, we spoke English, and we used French to speak to them together. But the children knew neither French nor English because they spoke German in their home, so we spoke to them in our African language, Sango.

24 - Midwives, Mothers, and Babies

It was time for Madame Dipounia to have her sixth baby. Her pastor-husband said to me, "I do hope we have a girl this time. All of our children are boys." I agreed it would be nice if they had a girl, but it was not to be. Another little boy made his appearance into the world, and they thanked the Lord that he was a perfect baby.

Six weeks later Pastor Sesse and his wife came in to have their fifth child. They had already chosen the name Andre. This was very unusual for their culture. With four girls already, they wanted this baby to be a boy. We were all waiting for Andre to be born. When the pastor saw the baby, he exclaimed with sadness in his voice, "It didn't come out Andre, it came out Andrea!" Louvrou cleaned and dressed little Andrea in a layette made by dear women in America for such a time as this. Mother and baby were settled for the night.

Later I was outside talking to Pastor Sesse before I went back up the hill. I said to him with the straightest of faces, "I know how disappointed you are that you didn't have a boy. When Pastor Dipounia was here, he was disappointed

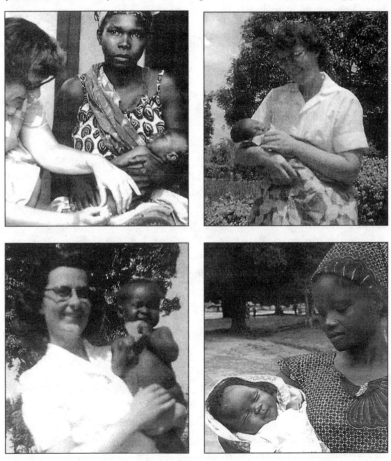

Just a few of the approximately 200 babies Margery helped bring into this world.

that they didn't have a girl. I have a solution for you. Why don't you just trade babies? Then they would have their girl, and you would have your boy." He looked at me with a strange expression on his face and replied, "But, Mademoiselle, we do not do that in our culture."

I smiled at him and said, "We don't do that in our culture either. I was just joking with you." Then he got a grin on his face, for he understood my humor. We said goodnight, and he went to be with his family.

When I returned to Africa in 1955, after my first furlough, I was enthusiastic about practicing my midwife skills. Unfortunately that had to be put on hold until the clinic building could be built. The expectant mothers in our mission village usually went to the town hospital for their maternity care. They would have their babies at home, and then, carrying their babies, they would walk two miles to the hospital in order to get the baby's birth certificate. I was appalled at this. I finally said to the women, "I will take you to town to have your babies. But if you continue to have them in the village, I will refuse to take you, and you will not receive a baby layette." That statement turned the tide. I never did understand why they didn't want their babies delivered in a place where they could have help if there were complications.

During this waiting period I had maternity classes with Louvrou and Kaila, another widow woman who lived on the mission property. Neither could write, but they could read typewritten notes. Sometimes the male nurse aides would attend. We knew that some day I might not arrive in time for a delivery, and they would have to do it. As it turned out, this did happen occasionally.

When I was in training in Kentucky, I never delivered twins. Unbelievable as it may seem, out of the first twelve deliveries in Africa, there were three sets of twins. Years later, after her prenatal exam, I told a mother I had felt two heads. "You are going to have twins." I thought she would surely say, "Oh no, that would be too much." She already had three children under the age of five, and she had been taking care of a six-year-old boy. Imagine my surprise when she calmly replied, "If God so wills." I could hardly believe my ears, and I was always amazed to see how well she managed her family, with five children under the age of five.

I started out delivering babies on the operating table that was given to me by the Maynard Hospital in Seattle. One day Dr. Rouch from our Ippy hospital came by our clinic. When he saw the nice operating table I was using for deliveries, he exclaimed, "I am doing surgeries on a delivery table, and we have two of them. Why don't we make a trade?" So we did. I was happy to have a table that was several inches wider for deliveries, and Dr.

Rouch was happy with his narrower table for surgeries.

Pauline Yamete, a pastor's wife who lived seventy miles down the Bangui road, came to my clinic, bringing along her beloved sister to attend her. Her husband was unable to make the journey. I had delivered her second child, David, two years earlier, and she had had no trouble with that earlier birth. With this labor, pregnancy complications arose when it was time for her to deliver. It was 8 p.m., and I knew she needed a Caesarean section. I took her to the town hospital, explained the situation to the African midwife, and told her she needed to call the doctor immediately.

In those early days we had French doctors who would come to the Sibut government hospital for two years at a time, but they had little surgical training. I thought everything would go well for Pauline, but when I returned to the hospital at 5 a.m. the next morning, I discovered the doctor hadn't done anything for her. I was appalled! I drove the two-hour trip to her village to get her husband.

When Pastor Yamete and I arrived at the hospital, the doctor was just coming out of the delivery room, and he said to me, "I am glad you are here. Pauline has a ruptured uterus, you have to take her to Bangui immediately." I wasn't surprised, for a woman can't have two to three minute contractions for nine hours and have nothing happen. I wanted to ask him why he hadn't done a Caesarean, but I knew it wouldn't do any good now. He had failed her.

I went back to the mission and explained the situation to my co-workers. One of our visiting missionaries, who was there for a language conference, loaned me his station wagon, and Eugene offered to drive so I could sit in the back and monitor Pauline. Fifteen miles out of town Pauline was having frequent and shallow breathing with a very fast pulse. Quietly she said to me, "Margery, I'm so thirsty, so thirsty." And then she quietly slipped away into eternity. Her husband began to sob, and my heart and eyes were weeping also. This death didn't need to happen, but we just have to leave some things in the Lord's hands, even if it seems so senseless.

As we returned and drove into the mission road, the students gathered around the car, and soon all of them began to cry. Eugene asked our students to dig the grave while he and a student made the casket. (We always made a casket for any family members of our pastors or our student body.) There is a cemetery close by where only Christians are buried. We know that on the day of the rapture, when Jesus returns to take believers home to glory, all the graves in that cemetery will be empty.

A few years later, European Catholic nurse-midwives came to Sibut to work in the government hospital maternity ward. I knew if I took a mother there in need of more help than I could give her, she would receive their undivided attention.

The first midwife was a very quiet, sweet woman named Sister Marie, and we became friends. Soon we were talking about the Lord, and I learned that she didn't own a Bible but would like to have one. At that time the Sisters were not allowed to have Bibles, and she cherished the one I gave her. She kept it in her office at the hospital and read it in secret.

Once when a French midwife came to my house to say good-bye before leaving for France on her vacation, I said to her, "I'll see you when you come back unless the Lord comes back first, and then I'll be gone." With a bewildered expression on her face she asked me, "Is Jesus coming back?" I then had the joy of explaining the glorious hope we have in Christ that He will be returning. I was saddened that she didn't know this wonderful doctrine of the Bible. As she left, I gave her a book, *The Late Great Planet Earth*, by Hal Lindsey, and she said she would read it.

In 1965 the French government only sent doctors to the Bangui government hospital. An African, Mamadou, became the director of the Sibut hospital. He wasn't a doctor, but he learned how to do surgery and many other things from a well-trained French doctor. We could always talk things over, and he took my word seriously. He saved many lives with his surgical skills. It was a sad day when he was killed in a road accident while riding his moped. Soon they started a medical school in Bangui, and after that we always had a doctor. But none of them were as capable as Mamadou, and I longed to have someone close by again who could do surgery.

Until 1970 I not only delivered the babies for our student wives but also for the women who lived close to our mission. Gradually I realized I was taking on more work than I could handle and had to set priorities. I was into our youth ministry, government-release-time classes in their schools, and teaching in our Bible School. It wasn't right to put so much maternity responsibility on Louvrou and Kaila. For a while we had the maternity clinic only for our student wives. But as Louvrou became older, night work became too much for me. I finally quit maternity altogether and took the pregnant mothers downtown for their deliveries. It was a hard decision to make, and the women weren't too happy. But each baby continued to receive a baby layette.

I do want to pay tribute to the many ladies in America that spent money and hours of their time making hundreds of layettes for our African babies. It was such a comfort and joy to be able to wrap a newborn baby in a new clean layette.

The last and largest baby we had was Billy, the third and last child of

Vernon and Jan Rosenau. After the birth I handed the baby to Vernon to weigh, and he said, "Eleven pounds, thirteen ounces." I said, "That can't be possible. Weigh him again." I heard the same response, "Eleven pounds, thirteen ounces."

Billy uttered the last cry of a newborn baby in the delivery room, and it was fitting it should come from a fourth-generation Rosenau. After that the room waited silently for the occasional times that the Ippy doctors came to perform surgery.

After I retired from the medical work in 1990, another nurse took over, and the room was used for dentistry. Knute Orton, the last of the missionaries at Kaga-Bondoro, was transferring to Bangui to work, and he brought some of his dental equipment to Sibut. Jeannot, our African dentist, could benefit from another dental chair, and Knute could make trips to Sibut to do dentistry, a work he enjoyed so much.

25 - Be Thankful for Healthy Skin

Pasteur Daboumrou appeared at my door one day with a concerned look on his face. I invited him to sit in one of our veranda chairs and asked, "What can I do for you?"

"Mademoiselle, every child in my village has skin ulcers, and I want to help them. Would you give me some *yolo* [medicine] and bandages to help them?"

Very rarely would an African have any medicine to put on a cut, much less a Band-Aid or a bandage. When the tropical ulcer germ finds a break in the skin, there can be a round skin ulcer within a week. The stench of an ulcer is unbearable but not as bad as the pain. Unfortunately everything grows well in tropical climates, including disease.

I replied, "But Pasteur, these skin ulcers need penicillin injections. Is there anyone in your village who can give them?"

"Oh yes," he answered, "there is a fellow that knows first aid, but he doesn't have a thing to work with. I know would be glad to do it." I prepared a small box of three different kinds of topical medicine to use in the different stages of healing, three vials of multiple doses of penicillin, and a large can of bandages. I went over the instructions a couple of times because I wanted him to be sure of what needed to be done.

The first procedure really hurts because the medicine is strong enough to burn away much of the crud and start getting down to the good flesh. No one can endure the treatment without yelling out in pain. Fortunately the pain only lasts a few seconds. When the nurse and the patient see the skin ulcer all healed, there is joy in knowing it was worth it to have gone through the pain. I hardly ever did this procedure without thinking of that verse in Hebrews 12:11, *"Now no chastening seems to be joyful for the present, but painful; nevertheless, afterward it yields the peaceable fruit of righteousness to those who have been trained by it"* (NKJV). The Lord has to discipline His children when we go astray. He allows us to go through difficulties so we will turn to Him.

It was three months later when Pasteur Daboumrou came back with a huge grin on his face and handed me the empty can. "Mademoiselle, the children's skin ulcers are all healed."

I rejoiced with him. This was one of the many times I thought of the women at home in the States who spent hours and hours rolling sheet bandages so we would have them to help others. Someday their loving work will be rewarded.

It was Louvrou's job at our clinic to take care of all the sores, except those needing sterile technique. These were the responsibility of the nurses. Not once did I hear her complain about the odor, not even the day when we had eighty people in the clinic, with a variety of sores that needed bandaging. For years people would pass up the town hospital to come to us. Why? Because most of the time the hospital only had one kind of medicine to put on all kinds of sores, and they had no bandages. Sometimes when I sent a client there for surgery, I had to furnish the dressing, the IVs, and the antibiotics so they could do their job.

Louvrou Veronique took care of the many people that came to the clinic with skin sores.

Itch

"The seven-year itch" isn't just an expression. It's a microscopic mite called scabies. It has nine legs and travels under the skin. As the mite makes its journey, the host person frantically scratches. If they dig at the skin with their nails, the skin breaks open, letting in bacteria, and the area becomes infected. It doesn't do a bit of good to put on the itch salve unless the crud on the skin is first rubbed off. The best way to do that is to wash a corncob and use it as a scraper on the infected skin. This harsh treatment gets through to the mites.

It was a three-day treatment for our patients. They had to take a bath the first day, then put the itch medicine all over their body for three days. They were to change their clothes daily. All of their clothing had to be boiled, and boiling water was to be poured over all their furniture. We would give instructions with the salve so the complete treatment could be done at home. We never had to take a skin scraping to put on a glass slide to make a diagnosis under the microscope. Scabies was easily recognized.

One day a little girl who had the itch so bad she could hardly walk came to us alone. Louvrou took her out back, and using a brush, scraped her infected skin the best she could. After Louvrou applied the salve and Andre gave her an injection of penicillin, she was told to go home and change her dress. With tears streaming down her face from the pain of the scrubbing, she looked up at Louvrou and said, "But I only have this one dress." Louvrou tore up a worn sheet, wrapped part of it around her, and told her to see that her mother boiled the dress before she put it back on the next day. She did get rid of those crawly creatures.

Once I got into an argument with a man who kept saying, "Your itch medicine doesn't work."

"Oh yes, it does," I replied. "You didn't follow the instructions correctly." I could see the infected part hadn't been scrubbed off.

He said, "Oh, I did. The salve just didn't do any good." And so we argued.

Finally I did something I only did once in my life. I said, "Tomorrow you and your family take a thorough bath before you come here, and each of you bring a clean change of clothes." Upon their arrival the next day, I took the family and hid them behind the shower room. Then I told them to strip to their loincloths. With gloves on my hands because the itch is very contagious, I took a brush and scraped all the infected places, being sure to get into every nook and cranny on their bodies. I knew it hurt, but it had to be done. I supervised as they put the salve all over their bodies, but I did it over again on the infected areas. I wanted to kill those microscopic creatures that made life a torment. I remember thinking, *If my supporting people at home could see me now, they would wonder how I spend my time.*

About three months later a man came to the clinic and said, "*Balao.*"

I replied, "*Balao.*"

Then he said, "You don't remember me, do you?" I didn't. He told me he was the "itch man." Then he said, "The itch salve did work, and we are well and can spend our nights sleeping instead of scratching."

That reminds me of Pasteur Zacherie, who came to me once and laughingly said, "Mademoiselle, we can't sleep at night. Our little six-month-old baby just works his legs all night like he is riding a bike. Please, I need some itch salve."

For years I made up the itch salve using ingredients which were hard to obtain. What a day it was when a pharmaceutical company in England made a concentrated salve we could just mix with water.

Burns

We also treated many terrible burns, and always our prayer was, "Please, Lord, don't let it get infected." An infected burn is very difficult to treat and is very painful for the patient.

On one occasion parents brought their little girl to us. She was just a toddler and was badly burned. The burns were healing nicely, but I had to take her to the town hospital because we had to empty our beds for a doctor who was coming to do surgery. Afterward her parents brought her back to us. We were horrified to see the condition of her now-infected burn. We did our best, but the little one died a few days later. Even so, I am thankful to the Lord for the many we were able to help.

A Hunting Expedition

One Sunday afternoon I was called to the clinic to find two men wrapped in dusty, women's wrap-around clothes quietly waiting for me. When they removed the clothing, my first thought was, *Why aren't they crying out with pain?* Then they told me their story.

That morning they had gone out into the woods to go hunting and came upon two wild boars. Before the men could kill the boars, the animals attacked. One of the men was able to climb a tree, but the other fellow didn't get to the tree in time, and he was bitten and gored. The man in the tree felt so badly about his friend that he scrambled down to help. Then he was attacked. They had nineteen bites on their bodies. One had the side of his face badly torn, the palm of one hand half destroyed, and a forearm laid wide open. Some of the flesh was just hanging. They immediately found a ride and traveled the thirty miles to Sibut.

The first thing I did was to start them on the antibiotic ampicillin to try to prevent infection. I kept praying silently over and over again, *Lord, do a miracle; don't let these bites become infected. What chance would their bodies have to fight off infection with so many bites, and all the road dust covering them from the journey into Sibut?* But the chance was good with the Lord on their side, and He answered our prayers. All the wounds healed without any infection. That was one of the greatest miracles that I remember.

Yaws, A Most Disfiguring Disease

There was a disease called yaws that was prevalent in my first two terms. The yaws bacteria (spirochetes) enter the skin and the underlying tissues through abrasions on the skin. Initial symptoms include fever, pain, and itching. This is followed by the appearance of small tumors on the hands, face, legs, and feet, each covered by a yellow crust of dried serum. These tumors may deteriorate to become deep skin ulcers. I did see people that had the deep skin ulcers. For a while I used an experimental drug given to me by a French company. I reported back to them on the results. This worked fairly well, but when we could finally buy penicillin, that did the trick. I marveled at how quickly the ulcers would dry up.

One time I was in a village far down along the river where a three-year-old girl had yaws skin ulcers on her body. My heart ached over her pathetic condition. I took out a syringe and a penicillin vial from my medicine bag and gave her an injection. It was so good to talk with Pastor Tono at the next pastor's conference, for he told me that the little girl's ulcers had all cleared up. He said the people had put me on a pedestal because of the powerful medicine I had. Soon after that the French had a mobile unit that went to every village in the Central African Republic and gave each person a penicillin injection, and thus yaws was eradicated in the entire country.

I never caught any of the skin diseases. When I think of some of the situations I got into with ungloved hands, this was another miracle of God's grace.

Noma Infection

Never will I forget one mother who came to us with a three-year-old boy, Nestor, who had a noma infection. Gangrene had eaten through his nose and into his right jaw. He was very malnourished because he was not able to eat. I had to snip and snip, pulling out the dead, smelly, gangrenous flesh. I kept thinking, *I can't do this*, as I kept snipping away, pulling out a large part of his jaw, the lower part of his right cheek and leaving only the two nostrils of his nose. With large doses of antibiotics and continuous wet, antiseptic dressing, the noma cleared up and he was able to eat. But this left Nestor's appearance very grotesque. When he was almost well, Dr. Brison McGowan was passing through Sibut and remarked that he had never seen anything like it. Subsequently I heard that he later had a similar case at Ippy.

When Nestor and his mother were ready to go home, I thought, *This child is going to live his life in misery when he gets old enough to look into a mirror and face the reality of his appearance and he hears the taunts and teasing of other children.* We had no plastic surgeons in the Central African Republic and no possible way to protect him from the certain rejection of his fellow Africans.

About two weeks later the mother returned with Nestor. He had dysentery and was still skin and bones. We couldn't stop the dysentery, and he died. Somehow my helpers and I felt this was the way the Lord was saving him from a miserable life.

26 - A Reluctant Dentist

Never had it occurred to me that some day I would be extracting teeth, much less that I would be doing fillings. But when I saw the suffering Africans, I felt compelled to do something.

It was Ruth Nephew who first gave me the courage to try learning dentistry when she came to visit me in 1953 at the start of our African Bible conference. Dr. Cullen came from Ippy to do physical exams on all of our pastors, and this included checking their teeth. Since the Africans never had any dental help, a decayed tooth would break off little by little. This would leave the tooth roots that could work up to the gum line. Ruth pulled most of these, but I had the 'privilege' of doing a few.

When I was in Hyden, Kentucky, for my midwifery training, I learned that a missionary couple from the Central African Republic was on furlough just fifteen miles away, taking a missionary dental course. I visited them and thought, *This is interesting.* An idea was forming in the back of my mind. Maybe when I was on my next furlough, I could take that training.

When I arrived in the United States in October 1958, the dental school was in Canada and classes had already started. They had written to me in Africa and said that even if I came late, it was all right. I could attend and learn what I was able. My dear friend Ilene again came from Seattle and met me at O'Hare Airport in Chicago and drove me to Drumheller, Alberta. She stayed overnight and then went back to Seattle. Oh, it was cold in Canada—30 degrees below zero. I had only a spring coat and was miserable, but the pastor's wife took pity on me and loaned me one of her long, heavy, winter coats.

Since I had missed a lot of the teaching, it wasn't surprising that I found the course difficult, especially the theoretical part of it. I spent the evenings practicing drilling and filling on teeth that had already been extracted. It was tedious and not very interesting work, but it had to be done.

I remember well my first assignment on a client. I had to fill an upper tooth, and this could only be done by looking in the dental mirror. I got up enough courage to begin, but when I couldn't get the feel of it, I panicked. I went to my instructor, Nick, and said to him, "I can't do it. I need to start on a filling on the lower jaw, where I can see what I am doing."

He said, "Yes, you can."

I was so emotionally upset I just quit and walked to the back room and sat down. I told Nick, "Nothing can make me go back to do that filling."

I took the situation to the Lord. I knew I was here by His direction and could only do this by His enabling. The promise in 1 John 5:14-15 had always meant a lot to me, and I claimed it that evening in my prayers. "And we can be confident that he will listen to us whenever we ask him for anything in line with his will. And if we know he is listening when we make our requests, we can be sure that he will give us what we ask for" (NLT).

The Lord didn't fail me. The next day I had the inner strength I needed to follow through on Nick's instruction. After that breakthrough I was able to face everything that was still ahead of me in the months left of the course.

When we finished the course, Nick told us how a dental chair could be made of wood and assembled on the field. I immediately ordered one made and also purchased a low-speed dental drill. A couple of women in the Baptist church in Kuna, Idaho, asked their Christian dentist if he had extra

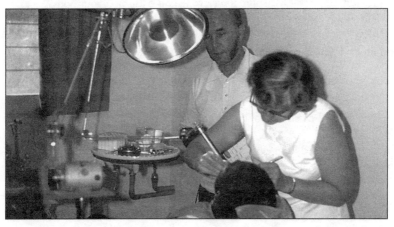

Doctor DeWald instructing Margery in dentistry.

instruments he could donate to a missionary nurse in Africa. It was such a blessing to add his donation to all the cargo I took back to Africa.

During my next furlough Al Undi was working at King's Garden in the Medicine for Missions department. When he heard that I was doing some dentistry, he said, "We have a dental chair at King's Garden that I'll pack up for you to take back." I replied, "But I have a wooden dental chair." He wouldn't take no for an answer and said, "Who wants to sit in a wooden chair when getting their teeth worked on? Don't worry. I'll crate it up for you." And he did. He also found a dental light to give me.

The chair was broken in transit. It was two years before Eugene found time to weld it and put it in place. He also attached the light so I could discard my headlamp! With the field dental case I bought in France on a table nearby, the room now looked a little more like a dental office.

The first person to occupy the dental chair was our oldest pastor, Jouse Wangbi. In the early 1930s he had been put in prison in Grimari several times for preaching the Gospel. On this occasion he was present for a pastors' conference being held at our mission station.

Pastor Jouse told me that one of his teeth was hurting. As I examined his teeth, I saw that the painful tooth needed extracting. The rest of his teeth were very dirty and covered with tartar that stuck in chunks.

After scraping off the tartar, which took more than half an hour, I needed to use the electric drill to clean them. As I pressed my foot on the drill pedal, an electric current passed through my arm and back. Pastor was sitting calmly in the chair not saying a word while the current ran through him. I quickly turned off the electricity. I asked him, "Didn't your body hurt, and didn't you feel something strong going through your body?"

He didn't change his facial expression as he replied, "Yes, my body was getting hot." He wasn't the kind of person to complain. He had confidence in me and that what was happening to him was part of the dental procedure. I was glad that Pastor Wangbi had confidence in me, but not to the extent of letting electricity run through his body, thinking it was part of sitting in a dental chair.

Eugene had recently changed the electrical system at the clinic from 220 volts to 110. I had used a transformer for the drill, but something was wrong. I wasn't able to clean the pastor's teeth, but I did extract the aching tooth. Since Eugene was busy with the other pastors, I waited until the end of the conference before I explained to him what had happened.

I really didn't enjoy doing dentistry, and I couldn't spend much time doing it, but it was so good to be able to help people. Because I had free time on Wednesday evenings, I reserved that time to do fillings. The generator that produced our electricity was always on in the evenings, and I was available to do simple fillings for whoever needed one.

In the quietness of those hours, the Lord gave me many opportunities to talk about Him. My patients listened with their mouths wide open and couldn't talk back. He also helped me lead several people to find the Way of Life. Telling the Gospel story never gets old.

A few years later, when Oumar started working at the clinic, I taught him how to pull teeth. He could give the anesthesia for the upper teeth, but I never taught him how to inject the mandibular nerve in the lower jaw. Why? Because a quarter of the time I couldn't do it right myself.

Knute Orton, one of our missionaries who took the complete course of missionary dentistry, added volumes to his training by working with Christian dentists in the United States. He first worked at Ippy and then in Kaga-Bondoro. Even qualified dentists from other missions would go to him for help. He had a dental building with three dental units in which any dentist would be proud to work. On his furlough he would increase his qualifications by doing further work with dentists back in the States.

Once one of the dentists that he worked with in Michigan came out to help him for six weeks in Africa. For some reason, during the first two weeks Dr. DeWald couldn't go to Kaga-Bondoro to be with Knute in his dental practice. So who should receive two weeks' training but Margery? I felt like a first grader with Dr. DeWald at my side. He had eight people working for

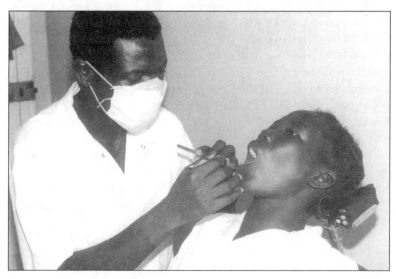

Our African dentist, Jeannot.

him in his dental office in the United States, and here he was now patiently being my assistant. The main thing I appreciated was that he taught me how to use elevators (instruments that lifted the teeth out instead of always pulling them).

He was a very gracious, kind man, and Christ's love radiated in everything he did. He was a soul winner, always telling people how Jesus changed his life and how He could change their lives also. At first his wife didn't plan to go with him to Africa, but she reluctantly consented. It didn't take her long to see the difference the missionaries could make in the lives of the African brethren, both spiritually and physically. She came to love them. Her heart changed so much that after her visit she enthusiastically said to us, "I hope we can come back sometime."

Once when Knute returned from furlough, he brought back a new dental unit. He remarked to me, "There is a place in Newberg, Oregon, that makes dental units for third world countries, and they do everything my big unit does but are much smaller. And the great part of it is, it has the high-speed drill attached and it takes only two quarts of water a day. If I were you, Margery, I'd buy one. I could order it for you for they know me and would give me a discount." I replied, "I can't use the high-speed drill, and I don't have the time or even the desire to learn."

He had a ready answer to that remark. "Find a capable young fellow here and send him up to me for eighteen months, and I will train him." When I heard those words, I wanted to shout a dozen hallelujahs. I did order the unit, and it was in place when Jeannot came back from his training with Knute. What a day that was!

I met Jeannot and his brother when they came from Kaga-Bondoro to attend high school at Sibut. They had pleasing personalities and were faithful in church attendance. They both had good bass voices and were a great asset to the church choir. When Jeannot finished his high school training, I chose him to return to his hometown to learn dentistry under Knute. After his return to Sibut I didn't do any dental work except in an emergency.

Later, when Knute transferred to Bangui to work, he brought some of his equipment to Sibut, and he made our unused delivery/surgery room into a dental office. Before Knute retired, he and his wife Lillian scheduled some time to be in Sibut, so they could teach a course in our Bible School and he could still do the work he so enjoyed doing—dentistry.

The Lord was good to let us have this ministry. The vision the Lord had given me to help years before continues to be a reality today—through Jeannot.

There is much that has been said about AIDS, so I do not have to go into detail. HIV/AIDS first became an important issue for us in Africa by the late '80s, and you know by now that so many Africans are infected and millions of adults have perished because of this horrible disease—leaving thousands upon thousands of orphans. I want to tell you the stories of just five of the people I knew who had the disease.

Lucien

One day while my helpers and I were busy working in the clinic, the superintendent of schools in Sibut came, bringing with him a nice-looking fellow about thirty years old. The superintendent said, "This is my brother, Lucien, from Bangui. He has been ill for several months with diarrhea. He was not helped at the hospital there, so I told him about the mission clinic here. He has come to see what you can do for him."

We put Lucien in a private room in one of our buildings. My head nurse, John, and I examined him thoroughly but could not come up with a diagnosis. A certain medication helped a little, but we were both puzzled.

Lucien had become a Christian just a few weeks before coming to see us, but he didn't have a Bible. We gave him one, and he would read it by the hour. The church he attended before becoming a Christian didn't study the Bible, and their doctrine was different than what he was reading, so he always had some questions to ask when either John or I made rounds. I really enjoyed talking with him.

During this time the six churches in our district had their quarterly youth rally. At these rallies I always had charge of the written Bible contest between the churches. There would be a panel of pastors to answer the youths' questions and to direct the discussion based on the theme. The host church always sent the program and theme to be discussed to the other churches ahead of time. One day Lucien was feeling better, so I took him with me to the youth rally.

Lucien was amazed at all of this. When I was taking him home, he kept remarking how wonderful the rally was and how much the youth knew about the Bible. He thanked me several times for taking him, even though he had been too tired to stay for the whole program.

We were just hearing about this new plague of AIDS that was spreading throughout Africa. At that time there was no lab exam at Sibut to confirm an HIV diagnosis. But after discussing it with John, we came to the conclusion that Lucien had AIDS. Finally I had to tell Lucien that we couldn't do anything further for him. I took him to his brother's home.

When he became very ill and was close to the end, I visited him. We talked a little, and then I prayed. I left with a sorrowful heart. What an end for a fellow who had just graduated from the university and had a wife and four small children. But he had peace in his heart. I was glad that someone had witnessed to him, for I knew he would be with the Lord he had so recently come to know and love.

John from N'dele

In the month of December the hospital in Ippy was always closed for cleaning, accepting only emergencies. I had gone there in December 1991 to help June Stone and Tom Dessossfy. My assignment was to teach Bible, parasitology, and obstetric complications and to help June in their pharmacy depot.

When I arrived, June had three shipments of medicine that she didn't have time to put on the shelves. Before the shelves could be stocked, the prices had to be changed from Dutch guilders into United States dollars and then into francs and marked on the bottles. It was a lot of work, but I enjoyed helping.

On my first day of teaching the workers and nurses at our mission hospital, I immediately noticed a young, emaciated fellow among the faces before me and wondered what he was doing there. He only had a New Testament instead of the complete Bible the others in the class had. I was teaching the Old Testament book of Nehemiah. Nevertheless he listened very intently as I taught. I thought to myself, *I'm going to make his acquaintance when the class is finished.*

Before I could even make an effort to greet him, however, he came up to me and said, "My name is John. The missionary pilot [Doug Golike] flew to N'dele yesterday to pick up our pastor, who is very ill, to bring him here to the hospital. I have been ill for some time, and since there was room in the plane for me, the pilot said I could come along. I liked your class. Some day, I would like to prepare myself to teach the Bible."

N'dele is a remote area in the North. This critically ill pastor of the town church was one of only four pastors in the whole area. John had been in high school in the capitol, Bangui, but had gone home to N'dele because of his illness. For several months an infection on his mouth and throat had refused to heal in spite of medication.

I rejoiced with him in his desire to serve the Lord, yet I was concerned about his illness. June noticed my interest in John and the next day told me that he was HIV positive. My heart sank at the news. At that time the government forbade caregivers to tell a patient that he was HIV positive. The mission hospital staff didn't agree with this policy. We felt that if HIV patients did not know that they had this disease, they would not get ready to meet God and would continue to spread the illness. However, we had to obey the law.

As it turned out, I had no more opportunity to minister to John. During the night the N'dele pastor died. It was a great loss in our eyes, and everyone was saddened. The next day Doug flew the body, the pastor's wife, and John back to N'dele. A couple of months later I received a letter from John saying he was very weak. I knew it wouldn't be long before he, too, would be in the presence of the Lord.

Antoinette and Jonas

I always liked Antoinette, even when she was a little girl. She was a pastor's daughter and had come to know the Lord as a child. She grew up in our girl's youth movement called Lumieres (Lights).

When she came of marriageable age, Jonas, one of the boys in the area, asked her male relatives for her hand in marriage. Jonas professed to be a Christian and had a good job. He had gone to the *Gendarmare* (the country's police academy in Bangui), so he was considered a good match.

After their marriage Jonas was sent to work in the town of Ippy, where our mission hospital was. I told our nurse at the hospital there that one of my prize girls from Sibut was now married and living in Ippy.

When I met June later she informed me that Antoinette was very faithful in church and was helping the leader of the Lumieres. But then she told me that Jonas had come to the clinic with a venereal disease. He continued to come for treatment as he became re-infected. He took two other wives, and eventually he contracted HIV.

When I heard this, my heart hurt so for Antoinette. She hadn't realized what kind of man she had married. Jonas was a Christian in name only. Antoinette and Jonas had two boys. When the boys were teenagers, Antoinette became very ill with AIDS. She and her sons came back to Sibut to be with her parents.

Immediately I went to see her. She was just skin and bones. *This can't be dear Antoinette,* I thought, but it was. She was in the last stages of AIDS and had come home to receive tender loving care from her family.

A few weeks later her husband, Jonas, also came back to Sibut, to spend his last days with his stepmother. One morning when I went to the clinic, I was surprised to find Jonas in a hospital bed. He was hoping we could work a miracle so his life would be spared. Both John and I could tell that his days on earth were few.

I sat down by his bed and began to speak with him about the Lord. I read him some verses from the Bible. He had heard much about the Lord as a child, but now he needed to make it applicable to his own life.

He could understand what I was saying, but he was not able to talk. I asked him, "Jonas, do you want to confess your sins and really believe in the Lord for salvation?"

He nodded his head yes. "Jonas, I am going to pray. Since you can't talk, I want you to say in your heart what I say out loud. Will you do this?" Again he nodded. Then I prayed, "Lord, I know I am a sinner. I know Christ died for my sins. I want you to forgive me for my sinful life. I now accept your sacrifice on the cross for my sins."

After the prayer, I asked Jonas, "Did you really pray those words in your heart?" Again he nodded yes. "Then let's thank the Lord for your salvation. You thank Him in your heart."

We really have a God who shows mercy to someone who knows The Way but thinks he can find more joy in the pleasure of this world. Satan loves to deceive people into believing this, and some people are foolish enough to fall for his lies.

After work was over for the day, I went to see Antoinette and told her that Jonas had only a couple of days to live. "Do you want to see him? If you do, I'll take you there," I said. She wanted to go, so I helped her into the truck and we drove the three miles back to the mission station. As we entered the building where Jonas lay, my thoughts went back to earlier days when Antoinette and fifteen other teenage girls had stayed there for a week to learn homemaking. We all had lots of fun. But now the homemaking house was turned into a hospital ward.

Antoinette sat on the bed, leaned over close to Jonas, and said, "Jonas, I forgive you for giving me AIDS." My tears were flowing hard as I left the room. What grace on Antoinette's part! What maturity was manifested in her Christian life! When it came time to meet her Savior, she wouldn't die with bitterness or unforgiveness in her heart. She would be clean and at peace. I went back into the room about fifteen minutes later to take her home. Jonas died the next day.

When someone dies, the Africans build an overhanging grass shelter that connects to their front door. Then they bring out a bed and display the body on it for twenty-four hours before the burial. This was done for Jonas. When it was close to the time for the burial, I went to Antoinette's house and asked her if she had the strength to go and view Jonas' body.

"I am so very weak and tired," she said, "but, yes, I want to go."

When we arrived at Jonas's stepmother's house, I helped Antoinette shuffle slowly to the thatched overhang. Antoinette lay down on the bed beside Jonas' body. She did not have the strength to sit up. Jonas's two other wives were sitting on mats on the ground. Jonas and Antoinette's sons were also in the group gathered around the bed.

Nearly everyone was singing hymns, a custom at Christian burials. The hymn-sing would go on all night long. Close by there is always a box on a table where anyone can put a contribution to help pay for the casket and for the food to feed the many people who come at a time like this. Having other things to attend to, I left and returned a couple of hours later to take Antoinette home just before the casket was nailed shut and the procession to the cemetery began. It wasn't long before Antoinette also passed away. Both lives were lost because Jonas didn't keep his marriage vows.

Lazare

Lazare's funeral was one of the saddest I ever attended. His life was such a blessing to me and to many, and yet it was tragically cut short when he was only twenty-two.

Lazare came to know the Lord at an early age. He lived only a mile from the mission compound and from the church, so he did not have far to go to Bible classes. As a child he was always faithful to attend Florence's children's classes. As he got older, he became a faithful student in my classes. He was a good helper in junior high. In high school he became a leader with the Flambeaux (Torches)—the boys' branch of the youth movement. Lazare was certainly one of my special students.

He went to Bangui, the capital of the Central African Republic, for his last two years of high school, to study subjects that were not taught in our local school. It was difficult there for him. He was often hungry. The aunt he stayed with didn't have good resources to obtain food. Also, he was frequently ill and received many injections at the government hospital.

I am sad to report that at most of the government hospitals the same needle was used over and over again many times without sterilization. The state of medical care was very poor and remains so today. In fact, it may be worse today, as no new government hospitals have been built since the French left in 1960, other than one built by the Chinese.

One day in the mid '80s an agitated Lazare appeared at my door and wanted to talk with me. He told me that he had AIDS. Then he looked me straight in the eye and declared, "Mademoiselle, I have never slept with a woman. I have always kept myself clean. I gave my life to the Lord years ago and vowed to walk with Him, to be a light for Him and to live for His glory. I have kept that vow."

Looking into his earnest face, I said, "I believe you." Receiving medicine with contaminated needles, as he did, can certainly give someone AIDS.

Lazare went back to Bangui to live with his aunt. A year later he was back at my door. Now he was in agony, hurting terribly and unable to sit still for a minute. The hospital in Bangui, the hospital in Sibut, and even our clinic had given up his case and refused to do anything more for him. I had turned over the Sibut clinic to another missionary nurse in 1990, and it was my habit not to interfere in any of the medical issues. But this time I did go to her and asked that she let John, the head nurse, go to Lazare's village and do what he could to relieve some of Lazare's pain. She gladly gave permission. John was anxious to help because of his brotherly love for Lazare and was able to temporarily relieve some of Lazare's pain.

A couple of days later Lazare died. At his funeral many gave wonderful testimonies of Lazare's life. I also told the people what his life had meant to me. How glad I am that some day I will see him again in that land where there is no sorrow, no pain, no death, and no AIDS.

28 - Learning About Rabies

"Ruth, Ruth, don't just sit there. Run, run quickly!"

The rest of us in the class had been sitting in chairs or on stools under the mango trees and had already run for shelter at the cry of the African who was yelling, *"Mbo ti sioni, mbo ti sioni."*

Ruth got up from her stool with a bewildered expression on her face and ran to us, saying, "What's up?" She didn't understand that the African was yelling, "mad dog" in Sango.

After I returned from my first furlough in 1955, I learned that Florence and Marian, the nurse who had taken my place at the clinic, had been coming out to this village to have Bible and reading classes. Marian was now in charge of the clinic at Crampel. I had been coming for a year and enjoying these Sundays of Bible study and reading classes.

Ruth Slocum, who was now with me, was a new missionary learning Sango at Crampel. She came to Sibut to help Ernie and me take care of Madame, who was very ill. I took Ruth with me that Sunday morning to let her get away from the station for a while and see what a village class was like.

The Africans chased away the rabid dog, and we settled down again under the mango trees, which sheltered us from the sun. We had no more than returned to our seats when the mad dog appeared again and the same scenario was repeated. Finally I asked them, "Why don't you just kill the dog? He shouldn't be allowed to roam around like that."

They replied, "We don't know who the dog belongs to, and if we kill it, we might have to pay a fine."

The next Sunday I was informed that someone had killed the dog. I learned to expect the unexpected wherever I taught a class in one of the many villages we served.

On another occasion, Florence and I were sitting on our veranda, enjoying the evening, when we heard tearful howling coming from an old pineapple patch about one hundred yards down the hill, among the avocado trees. I said to Florence, "I wonder what is wrong with that dog?"

She replied, "He does sound like he has lost his last friend." Since it was dark, we didn't go down to investigate and forgot about the dog until the next night, when his howling started up again.

Three days later Florence heard a scratching on her bedroom door. When she opened the door, a pitiful, drooling dog was lying on the cement step. She called me to come and see the very ill dog. We came to the conclusion that this must be the howling dog we had been hearing. I said, "We had better call Eugene to come and shoot the poor thing and put it out of its misery."

The next day Eugene came over and told us he thought the dog had rabies and shot it. Our African guard came to bury it. A rabid animal is either very voracious or very quiet. We were glad that this one had not snapped at us.

Dolly

When I returned to Africa in 1975 after being on furlough, Wilma said to me, "Margery, we saved one of our German Shepherd pups for you. Her name is Dolly, and we thought it would be good for you to have a watchdog." Florence had always had a dog, but now she was retired and at home in Chicago.

"I don't want to bother with a dog," I replied. She didn't argue with me and left the subject alone.

Three days later, at 1 a.m., I was awakened from my sleep to see an African leaning over my bed with a knife in his hand. He said only two words, "Money, money." I didn't argue. I gave him some. The next morning, after the excitement of the night, I told Wilma and Bruce, "I've changed my mind. I do need Dolly."

Judy, a short-termer who had been with me for eleven months, helped me take care of Dolly by bathing and de-ticking her. One day she counted 200 ticks that she had taken off of Dolly. The ticks seemed to thrive on the medicine we put into the bath water to kill them.

In the two years I had Dolly, I became attached to her. Judy and I enjoyed playing ball with her. She became a good watch dog, keeping the visitors at bay until I came out of the house and said, "Good dog, it's okay now." Occasionally she would tempt the Muhr's dog, Chip, to go with her into the brush for a good run. Once an African told me he had seen the dogs eight miles from the mission.

Late one afternoon several months later, I noticed Dolly was listless and wouldn't eat. I don't remember what pills I gave her, but I had to open her mouth and thrust them way down her throat. She didn't resist. Later that evening she was slobbering while trying to eat some leaves off a vine growing up the wall by the outside door. I petted her but didn't bring her into the house for the night as I usually did.

The next morning she wouldn't eat. The thought of rabies did enter my mind, but I dismissed the idea because I had given her the rabies vaccine injections. She was lying on my veranda when I left for work.

About 10 a.m. Bob Bixby, Jr., ran down to the clinic and said, "Dolly is having convulsions on the little path near your house." By the time I arrived back up the hill, she was dead. It was rabies. The Pasteur Institute Laboratory in Bangui confirmed my diagnosis. I learned that the rabies vaccine is only 70 percent effective. I was so glad I did not have a cut on my hand when I gave Dolly those pills. A rabid animal must have bitten her on one of her runs.

The dog that I didn't want had died, and I missed her.

What Was Wrong With Her?

One day a young man, Julien, brought his twelve-year-old sister, Celine, to the clinic with what I thought was a mysterious illness. She was restless, would turn her face away when a family member would try to give her a drink, and she had no fever.

When I saw the French doctor's car going by to go see Madame the next morning, I ran out of the clinic and motioned him to drive into the clinic road. I asked him to see Celine, explaining her symptoms as we made our way to her bed. It didn't take long for him to say; "I don't know what is wrong with her."

Within a week she quietly passed on. Shortly afterwards, as I was pondering over the cause of Celine's death, the diagnosis hit me, but I wanted to be sure. I went the two miles to her home, and I asked the family, "Did a dog bite Celine sometime in the last two months?"

Julien quickly replied, "Yes, about a month ago a dog nipped her leg. We could barely see the teeth marks, so we didn't think it was serious."

I told them I had been thinking Celine died of rabies. I explained one of the main symptoms of rabies was a rejection of water.

If a rabid dog bites a person, the vaccine must be given within ten days. Celine was past that deadline when we first saw her at the clinic. Sadly, nothing could have saved her, even if we had made an earlier diagnosis. We were glad Celine knew the Lord and was now in her heavenly home.

Would She Ever Walk Again?

As I turned into our mission road one day, I saw a woman sitting in front of the first house on the left side of the road. Someone flagged me down. I immediately noticed a blood-soaked sheet-bandage around the woman's foot. I knew somehow she must have been associated with the mission as only our clinic had sheet-bandages. Then I recognized her. It was Sarah, one of our pastor's wives, who lived about thirty miles from Sibut.

As she was sitting in the truck beside me, I asked, "What happened to your foot?"

Her answer sent chills down my spine. "A mad dog came into our front yard while I was cooking, and he chewed on my foot. I couldn't chase him away, but finally someone came with a stick and hit him. Then he left."

At the clinic I unwrapped the bandage. My helpers and I were horrified. The dog truly had mangled her foot. My first thought was, *She will never walk again*, and my second thought was, *I'll have to go to Bangui to buy the rabies vaccine*, as I didn't have any on hand.

I always told my co-workers when I was leaving the station to go any distance at all. When missionary Lee Einfeldt heard my intentions, he said, "Let me go. I have some business to take care of there." How I appreciated the many times my fellow missionaries helped me out in difficult situations.

The next morning in the devotional time I shared with our African nurses, we talked about Sarah. We covenanted among us to ask the Lord for a miracle to heal her foot so she could walk again. The Lord answered our prayers. In the clinic storeroom I always kept several pairs of wooden crutches. After a week Andre, one of my nurses, showed Sarah how to use them. It took two months before we could let her go home, even with the crutches she had learned to use.

As I passed through her village one day the following year, I stopped to say hello. She jumped up from her stool and ran to greet me. When I saw her coming toward my truck with a huge smile on her face, my heart was filled with praise to the Lord, for He had healed her. Our God is a living God that hears and answers prayer!

29 - Doctor's Helping Hands

The missionary nurses in charge of the six Baptist Mid-Missions clinics throughout the Central African Republic were not trained to be doctors, dentists, laboratory technicians, nor pharmacists. At one of our missionary conferences, I told Doctors Rouch and Fisher, who were in our hospital at Ippy, "You teach your knowledge to the Africans, but we nurses need it, too. Couldn't you have a seminar for us?"

They answered, "We have considered it, but we thought it would be impossible to get all of you who have clinics together at one time."

I quickly replied and said, "You try us and see." So I talked to all the nurses at the conference, and they all agreed they could come when a date could be arranged. The date was set for January 14-28, 1958.

From dawn to dusk the doctors taught us nine nurses procedures, treatments, minor surgery, and physical diagnosis. Knute Orton showed us how to do lab work and tooth extractions, while Ruth Carlson, a hospital midwife, taught prenatal exams and the procedure for normal deliveries. Then we did the procedures, including spinal taps—a very necessary procedure because meningitis is prevalent in Africa, and early diagnosis is possible only by spinal fluid exam. We sutured wounds, including incisions in surgery. We did skin grafts to non-healing skin ulcers, anesthetized, and extracted teeth. It was a very profitable and informative time for all of us.

We continued to learn from our Ippy doctors and from books all the time we were in Africa. I remember learning a quick, valuable diagnosis tool from Dr. Charles Rhodes. If an amoebic abscess of the liver is suspected, the examiner just needs to take his fist and hit the bottom of the lower right ribs of the patient. If there is an abscess, the patient will cry out in pain. I did this many times. I even had June Stone use it once on me. It worked!

Over the years there were eight doctors that worked at Ippy. When I knew a doctor would be traveling through Sibut, I would have patients waiting for him or her to examine. They were very good about seeing the patients I had for them. Missionaries frequently found their way to Sibut, for a variety of reasons. Some came to have their vehicle worked on at our garage; others to teach block courses in our Bible School. Some just needed a rest, while others were just passing through.

We always knew we would see Dr. Rhodes, from our Ippy hospital. He seemed to have his truck in our garage more than most people. Bob Vaughn, an excellent mechanic, said, "If Doctor wouldn't drive so fast over these roads, we wouldn't have to spend so much time working on his truck."

I considered his visits a blessing. It was always a profitable time. He was very willing to spend his waiting time examining my patients. It was a great event when our mission stations got radio communication. Then we knew when to expect company, including our doctors.

When Dr. Mary Broeckert came with Dr. Joy Hart, who was in her last three months of medical school, she had warned her, "Be prepared! Margery will have several patients with diverse kinds of serious illnesses ready for us to see." But this time most of the patients I had were women with gynecological problems. Dr. Joy had been debating in her mind what to specialize in after her internship. After seeing many of my patients, she said, "I didn't think there were many female medical problems here in Africa, but now I think I want to specialize in obstetrics and gynecology." She did! She finished her training and was accepted by our mission to return to Africa as a career missionary.

Dr. Brison McGowan was not only a surgeon; he was also an osteopathic doctor. He had great manipulative skills. Noah, one of our Bible School students, complained continuously for months about chest pains. I couldn't find anything wrong and was at wit's end how to help him. Noah certainly helped to deplete my aspirin supply! Blessed was the day when Dr. McGowan came through and Noah was one of the patients on the docket.

At first he was puzzled about Noah. Then he said to me, "I'm going to do a manipulation I don't do very often, but it is worth giving it a try." I watched doctor put Noah in a near fetal-like position. He knew just where to manipulate Noah in what seemed to me a very complicated procedure.

Noah uncurled his body, and exclaimed, "The pain is gone!"

I wanted to jump up and down and shout a dozen hallelujahs, but I just said, "Thank you. Thank you."

Doctor said, "It was a pinched nerve. Sometimes," he went on to say, "doctors have been known to treat it as a heart condition."

My nurse friend, Loie Knight, worked with him for a while at our hospital in Ippy. She learned a lot from him about manipulations, which she wasn't afraid to use. I only learned one from him. It proved to be an invaluable tool in my nursing ministry.

While I was working at the clinic one morning, a family came in pushing the father in a wheelbarrow. John and I listened as he said, "I have had terrible back pain for four months and haven't been able to walk. My family has to push me everywhere."

After I examined him and saw that one of his legs was shorter than the other, I said to John, "I think this is a case for Mademoiselle Knight to do a manipulation.

Loie was living with me at the time, as she had on several different occasions. I needed her advice and help many times, and she was always willing to give me a hand. I sent someone to my house to ask her to come to the clinic. She agreed that a manipulation should be tried and proceeded to do it. The sharp pain was relieved, but the patient still needed help. She told him how to get up, to lie down, and to turn over. Even so, we had to do the manipulation again and again.

We kept him for a couple of weeks, and I'll never forget his thankful smile when he and his wife were leaving as he said to us, "Thank you so much. How good it is that I can go to the bathroom now by myself."

I'm sure you can understand why I enjoyed nursing. There is joy in helping others.

I have a vivid memory of another time when Dr. Brison McGowan's hands were needed. Margo Muhr, a missionary co-worker, was pregnant with her third child. She and her husband, Lynn, had made arrangements to go to Bangui to have the baby in a private clinic. Two weeks before the baby was due, Margo was busy serving a meal to four men when her first symptom of labor started. They sent for me, and I advised them not to take the risk of making the three-hour trip to the capitol. (If they had, the baby would have been born on the way.) I really didn't want the responsibility of delivering the baby, but of course I was willing.

We didn't have the maternity building yet. The labor and delivery room were combined in one room of our seven-room clinic. I wanted to give it a special antiseptic cleaning. Conditions in the field were never as clean as required by Western standards. The car that stopped in front of the clinic interrupted me, and soon Margo appeared in the doorway and said, "I didn't want to be left up there all by myself, so Bob Bixby brought me down in his station wagon." She will always enjoy telling of the mouse that ran across the room, the very room where she was to have her baby! But she knew she was in Africa, not America or Europe!

After a short time of labor, her baby was anxious to make her appearance. Margo was on the delivery table, and I was ready for the delivery. In all this hustle and bustle, I was amazed to hear another car arrive. Who could it be? All the missionaries here were waiting on the veranda.

In a few minutes Dr. McGowan walked in saying, "We just arrived from

Ippy. I saw the clinic all ablaze with lights and cars outside. I knew something serious was going on, so I stopped to see if I was needed."

I immediately replied, "Yes, you can take over. The baby is about to be born. You won't have time to clean up"—African roads are dusty, and one needs a shower after a trip, especially after traveling for six hours—"but wash your hands and put on a gown. I have sterile gloves for you here." So in ten minutes he delivered Margo's third girl, Becky.

Helping Hands in Surgery

Not long after our maternity building was finished, Dr. Rhodes, from our Ippy hospital, approached me and said, "Would you like for me to come some time and do surgery at your clinic? We could use your delivery room."

The offer took me by surprise, and I replied, "That would be great! I am all for it because many of our pastors need hernia surgery, but it has been a long time since I've had anything to do with surgery. I know I have forgotten a lot."

He answered, "We would bring the surgery packs of the needed linens, the spinal anesthesia, and the surgical instruments. June [the missionary nurse from Ippy] would be with me, and she would help you."

So it was settled, and a date was set. The week before the surgery we didn't admit any new hospital patients. As soon as a room was emptied, our extra help gave it a thorough antiseptic cleaning. After all, people with meningitis, tuberculosis, putrid sores, etc., had occupied those beds. I dug into one of my metal barrels to get sheets for the beds and used white shirts that women at home had made into hospital gowns. I didn't have enough for our daily-hospitalized patients, so I saved them for special occasions, and surgery was one of those times. The director of our town hospital had given me permission to take the surgery packs of linens and gowns to them for sterilization. What a relief!

Everything was ready for the arrival of Dr. Rhodes and June. I was a little apprehensive the night before they came, but capable June soon put me at ease. The next morning we were off to a good start.

The news that a doctor was at the mission clinic doing hernia surgeries spread like wildfire. The people at Sibut were excitingly telling others what we were doing. "You know what?" they would say. "The night of the operation the patients stand by their beds, and the next day they are walking. And they get to eat! They take pills only for pain, and they don't seem to have much of it. And can you believe it, they go home in three days and their incisions don't get infected!"

During five visits our mission doctors operated on a total of eighty-five hernia patients at our clinic, and not one of the incisions became infected. For Africa that is a miracle! We were very adamant that sterile techniques be carried out with meticulous detail. It was just the opposite at the town government hospital, where many of their surgery incisions became infected. I remember taking one of our pastors' wives there who needed a caesarean section. When I visited her later in the hospital, she exclaimed with anguish in her voice, "Mademoiselle, the pus is just pouring out of my incision." She lifted up her gown, and no truer words were ever spoken.

To show more clearly how this could be possible, here's an example. Once there was a bad bus accident near Sibut, and the injured were taken to the government hospital. Someone sent word for me to come and help, bringing supplies for the injured. When I arrived at the ward where the injured were, I was amazed (though I shouldn't have been) to see a nurse wearing no gloves and holding a suture forceps in his hand, with a suture dangling down touching the patient's clothing and bed, etc. He was going from patient to patient with the same needle, sewing up the wounds without even cleaning them or putting antiseptic on the areas to be sutured. You can see why we were swamped with people pleading with us to have their surgeries done at our clinic.

The last doctor to operate at our Sibut clinic was Dr. Mary Broeckert. She came to our clinic twice in the 1980's to do surgery. The first time she operated on twenty-three patients in four days, and the second time she did thirty-six in five days.

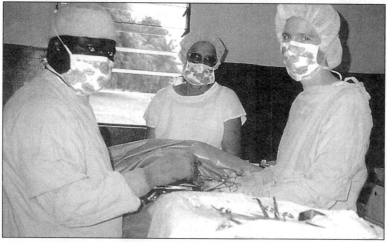

Doctor Mary Broeckert operating with the help of John Saboyambo and Margery at the Sibut clinic.

Dr. Mary was our doctor at the Ippy hospital for two terms. Her husband, Hubert, worked with the churches and the youth. They also home-schooled their five children. She was a dear. It would be difficult to find a more gracious and loving woman.

It was not easy operating in our small, hot delivery room with only a fan going, but she never complained. One afternoon I knew her feet were hurting because she stood first on one foot and then the other. I knelt down while she was operating and massaged her feet. Later Jan Rosenau helped those hurting feet when she found a pair of thongs that just fit Dr. Mary.

In the surgery room, John, my main African helper at that time, would give a spinal anesthesia to the patient. He would then assist Dr. Mary with the surgery. We called June the *floating* nurse. She saw that everything went well in the surgery room and monitored the vital signs of the patient.

What did I do? I just kept the ball rolling by talking to the relatives, seeing that the next scheduled patient received the pre-surgical preparation, checking that the surgery room was ready for the next patient, and being sure the bloody linens were taken to my house to be laundered in our wringer washer. If it were a sunny day, they would then be hung on our outside clotheslines. If it were a rainy day, an African would put the heavy basket filled with wet linens on his head. He would then go to our kitchen, climb the straight metal ladder by using one hand to hold the basket on his head and the other to grab the rungs and this way slowly make his way to the attic to hang the clothes.

I would climb the ladder at 5 a.m. the next day to get the dry linens and throw them down on a sheet spread out on our kitchen floor. Then I would make up the surgery packs. Sometimes Dr. Mary would help me with this task. I would then take them to the town hospital to be sterilized, getting them ready to use the next day.

John would start scheduling the pastors, deacons, and Christian workers months in advance, as soon as we knew a doctor would be coming to operate. Many people pleaded with us to schedule them, but it was impossible to help everyone, though we wanted to.

Once a man appeared at the clinic the second day Dr. Mary was operating. He said, "I've come from Damara [a town about seventy miles from Sibut]. I have had three hernia operations; the right side wasn't successful. It was repaired, but that was a fizzle also. I've heard how good the doctors are who come here, and I have come to be operated on."

He was told, "We only have one doctor and she is here for five days, and our schedule is full."

He wouldn't take no for an answer. He replied, "I'm going to stay on the clinic veranda just in case there will be room."

He stayed there three days before he gave up and left. It was sad, so sad. But what could we do? This was Africa! There are so very few qualified people to help her citizens.

There was a Dr. Potter, an English ophthalmologist from another mission who came to our clinic five different times to see patients and do eye surgery, which included many cataract surgeries. How he loved the game Rook, and he spent evenings playing with his assistant or anyone else who had time. Through this ministry there were several conversions among our eye patients.

There were two unforgettable men whose names appeared on the surgery list, Andre and Yagaza.

On one occasion Andre, a deacon of one of our churches, was scheduled for hernia surgery. He was a leper. His fingers were just stubs. For a handshake, he put out his arm and the other person clasped his wrist. He was last on our day's schedule. By the time we arrived to do his surgery, we had used up all the disposable spinal anesthesia packs. June made up a pack with the last vial of spinal anesthesia, and I sterilized it in a pressure cooker. Since the pack was damp when I took it out, I had to dry it in Wilma's automatic dryer (the only one on the field). Unfortunately the dryer broke the vial.

How was I going to explain to Andre about the broken vial? I tried my best, but he was beside himself. He closed his ears and said, "This happened because you didn't want to operate on me because I am a leper."

"No, no," I exclaimed, "it was an accident. We love you. You are a member of the body of Christ just as we are. We don't see you different from anyone else." My words were to no avail.

My African nurses tried to explain to Andre, but he turned a deaf ear to their attempts too. I was heartbroken. Did he really think missionaries would lie and discriminate like that? And if he did, what was our testimony among the Africans? Finally, I just had to turn away so he wouldn't see the tears forming in my eyes. All of us were sad as he and his family gathered up his things for their walk home.

When I visited Andre's church several weeks later, he came up to greet me with a smile on his face as he put out his arm so I could give him a handshake. He had let the Lord take away the bitterness that had previously engulfed his heart. I was so thankful. That handshake was so meaningful to me.

Andre had to wait several years for his needed operation. When God brought Dr. Mary to us, Andre received what we couldn't give him the day that our last vial broke!

Another time Yagaza, a deacon from another nearby church, was scheduled for surgery. The day Dr. McGowan was scheduled to arrive, Yagaza came to us with a terrible chest cold and a miserable cough.

After my examination I told him, "It looks like we will have to cancel your surgery. The doctor won't operate on you with a cough like that. When you cough after surgery, you will experience more pain, and it could hurt your incision. You stay here until his arrival this evening, and I'll have him examine you. We will do what he says."

Later Dr. McGowan examined him. He told Yagaza the same thing. Yagaza looked up at the doctor with indignation in his voice and replied, "I'm on the surgery schedule. I'm going home to pray about this. I want to be operated on tomorrow. The Lord will answer my prayer."

Low and behold! Yagaza was back at 4 a.m. the next morning, being carried to the clinic by his friends. Nurse John said, "His hernia has strangulated." With the knowledge John had gained at Ippy, he was able to reduce the hernia by putting back the small portion of the intestine that protruded through the abdominal wall.

When Dr. McGowan arrived at 7:30 a.m. to operate, John, with a grin on his face, said to him, "It looks like deacon Yagaza will keep his place on the surgery schedule." When the doctor heard what had happened at the clinic early that morning, he agreed.

Yagaza looked up with a mischievous smile on his face and said, "You see, God answered my prayer." So the capable hands of the doctor operated on Yagaza.

When I left the medical work in 1990, there were no more surgeries, but I was thankful for the physicians who took their time and so willingly helped us by doing hernia, vasectomy, and eye surgeries.

30 - Sometimes Missionaries Become Ill

It is so good of the Lord not to let us know what a day may bring forth. We know He is faithful, and with each day He gives us strength, courage, and faith to carry on. I feel that way as I write about some of the medical experiences I had with my co-workers in Africa.

Carol Rosenau

Several times during my second term I was called to care for the four Rosenau children while they were home during their vacation from the school at Crampel. It seemed that the enemy was coming in with all his helpers by using illness to hinder the work of the Lord from going forth. In a letter to the United States I asked for special prayer regarding the children and myself as I treated them. The people must have prayed, for soon after that there was less illness.

In September 1962, two weeks before Bruce and Wilma were to go on furlough, a language committee member who was staying with them called me in the early hours of the morning. Outside my window he said, "Margery, we need you. Carol is having convulsions." Carol was the twenty-three-month-old second daughter of Bruce and Wilma. I wasn't too frightened when I heard his words, for I had treated many little ones that had convulsions for malaria, and with treatment they came out of them. I said, "I'll be right over, but go downtown and call Dr. Garola, the French doctor."

I gathered together the necessary medications and syringes and took them with me to Bruce's house. Dr. Garola came immediately, and I followed his orders in treating Carol. It was the same as I would have done, but dear Carol didn't come out of her convulsions. They went on for two more hours. We all agreed that we should take her to the Bangui hospital.

Meanwhile the other missionaries on the station and the language committee members were alerted to the crisis. There was much prayer going up before the throne of God on Carol's behalf.

Soon Bruce, Wilma, Carol, and I were in the truck and on our way. A half hour later the convulsions stopped. Carol became very pale and went into a coma. There was nothing more we could do but silently pray as we made the three-hour trip to the capital.

When we arrived at the hospital, there was a French nurse in the corridor, and Bruce quickly put Carol into her arms, whereupon Carol took her last breath. I was amazed at the calmness of her parents. We went to the Bangui mission station and told them what had happened and then took the road home.

We came to the conclusion that Carol died from Paludism falciparum malaria, one of the four types of malaria. This type attacks the brain and can cause death. Carol had been taking choloroquine, a preventive malaria drug. We learned later that choloroquine does not touch this deadly form of the disease.

Carol was the darling of the Sibut station. We used to call her "the language-conference baby," for the committee met often during her short life. A couple of weeks after her death, we were at our Sunday night meeting singing the hymn "Does Jesus Care." The last verse says:

> *Does Jesus care when I've said good-bye*
> *To the dearest on earth to me,*

And my sad heart aches till it nearly breaks
Is it aught to Him? Does he care?
Oh yes, He cares; I know He cares
His heart is touched with my grief;
When the days are weary, the long nights dreary,
I know my Savior cares.

(Words by: Frank E. Graeff)

As we were singing that hymn, Wilma started sobbing, and Bruce put his arm around her. Then tears began flowing down all our cheeks, for our hearts ached for them. None of us could understand why Carol was taken. The hope of the Christian is that some day in heaven we will all be together again. David, the Shepherd King of Israel, said in his grief when one of his babies died, "I will go to him, but he will not return to me" (2 Samuel 12:23).

Madame Rosenau

In 1962, Madame Ina Rosenau returned to Sibut from furlough. After her husband's death in Bangui in 1959, she had taken a long overdue rest in the States. Early in 1963 she became very ill and went into a coma. We called Dr. Garola, the same French doctor that had treated her granddaughter, Carol. He diagnosed her as having had a stroke and encephalitis. Later our two doctors from Ippy came to see her.

In the first twenty-four hours I gave her twenty-three injections. She was completely paralyzed. None of us thought she would recover. In preparation for her death, her son Eugene bought wood to make her casket, and they addressed letters to her supporting churches and her friends at home.

But she lingered on. Dr. Garola came twice a day to see her, and I followed his orders regarding her care. Eugene fixed up the small office room in the large house as a bedroom for her recovery. She took a lot of care, and it took two people to turn her often to prevent bedsores.

Ruth Slocum, a new nurse on the field at the time, was at Crampel learning the Sango language. The Rosenaus sent for her to come and help out with Ina's nursing. She was a terrific help. After a month or so Madame could wiggle one of her toes. That was all Ruth needed to start physical therapy on her. Physical therapy had been nonexistent in my schooling, but Ruth was a recent graduate, and the medical profession had learned the value of it since my day.

Soon Ruth involved all of us in helping her with this. Madame would cry out with pain, but Ruth wouldn't stop. She knew that if it weren't done, Madame would be a hopeless invalid. Her daughter-in-law,

Ernestine, had the brunt of her care.

When Dr. Garola came to see her one day, she was just waking up a bit from her coma. She realized the doctor was French and said her first words, "*Bonjour, Docteur.*"

He gasped and said, "Well, if she can say a few words in three languages again, she'll pull through." And she did.

Many things stand out in my mind regarding her care. One was the tape recorder by her bed. Ernestine would play hymns for her by the hour. When Madame could barely talk, the hymn that she wanted played over and over again was "He the Pearly Gates Will Open." To this day, when I sing that song, my thoughts go back to Madame and her very slow words saying, "Play that song again."

The other thing that stands out is very trivial. One night as I was on duty with her, I heard some terrifying squawks coming from some kind of animal near the piano. I looked behind the piano, and there was a large shrew with a frog in its mouth. The frog knew his life was on the line, and he was hollering for all that could hear to come save him. I was his rescuer. I yelled, and the shrew let go of its prey.

It took eight months before Madame could sit in a chair, and she stayed in Africa until August 1964. Then she had enough strength to travel to the United States. In the ensuing fifteen years of her life she suffered many times with broken bones. On December 24, 1979, she was promoted to glory. What a Christmas present!

Al Undi

My good friends, Al and Olive Undi from Seattle, had gone to the Congo as career missionaries in the 1950s. Al became so ill he had to be evacuated, and they were never able to return. Their hope had been that some day they could go to some mission field again.

Al was a help to me whenever I came home on furlough. He helped me buy my three-quarter-ton truck and hand-made a camper for it. I could count on him to crate up anything I wanted to take to Africa and see to its shipping.

One day in 1967, the Undis arrived in Bangui, having come from helping the Wycliffe mission for a while in New Guinea. While he was there, he put together the camper he had made. He could fix anything, and Olive was his capable assistant. Bob Vaughn, a very capable mechanic, said, "I felt like an apprentice next to Al."

He worked at Sibut for a while, then Ippy asked if he would come up there to help. Then he became ill. The amoeba parasite that had caused his earlier return from the Congo again invaded his body and went into his lungs. He had to be evacuated to Bangui, and Ruth Slocum, an Ippy nurse now, went with him. But this time it was she that needed my help, and I went to help care for Al.

After two weeks of Al being very ill, the doctors said he had to get out of the tropics. It was a sad day for all of us when we bid them good-bye. But their work for missionaries wasn't over. Al recovered from his illness and was always helping missionaries get their baggage ready for shipment to their country of service, and their home was always open to any missionaries and Christian workers that needed a place to stay.

I will never forget one winter day before I left Seattle to drive to Boise, Idaho, when Al was working on my car. He looked at my feet and said, "You do have boots in your car, don't you?"

I replied, "No, I don't."

He didn't hesitate to say, "You are going through the mountains. Please go buy a pair. You never know what can happen on a trip."

I knew he would bug me until I did, and it was the sensible thing to do, so I obeyed. He and his wife felt a real responsibility to look after my needs every time I came home for furlough. It was so heartwarming to know they were always there when I needed them.

Today they live in Arizona and, in spite of Al's almost continuous migraine headaches and Olive's painful arthritic knee, they go to a prison nearby five times weekly. They are Mom and Dad to hundreds of prisoners. Al is praising the Lord his headache disappears when he stands to give a chapel message.

Bob Vaughn

Once in 1982, when we were very shorthanded at Sibut, a very likeable veteran missionary couple, Bob and Vera Vaughn, came from another station to work with us. With Bob's mechanical and teaching abilities and Vera's capability as a teacher, they were more than welcome.

In June of 1983 Bob wasn't feeling well, so I talked to Dr. Rhodes in Ippy over the radio, and he prescribed a medication for me to give to Bob. It didn't help, so I decided to do a blood count. I found an extremely high white count and told Dr. Rhodes my findings. He said Bob had to go to America immediately. They went to Cleveland, Ohio, where our mission doctor was waiting for him. Bob was diagnosed with leukemia.

Bruce and Wilma were on furlough and went to be with Bob and Vera. There is a bond between missionaries that is difficult to explain. Later they had to leave and another missionary couple went to minister to them. Six weeks later Bob died and went to be with the Savior he had served on the mission field since 1945. In his years on this earth, he blessed the Body of Christ to the fullest with his gifts and talents.

Lynn Muhr

I could hardly believe my eyes in September 1983 when I saw Lynn Muhr trying to walk up from his house to the big one. His strength was gone. I immediately did a blood count on him, and when I couldn't or wouldn't believe the results, I did another one. It was the same. Lynn had a very low red cell count and thus his hemoglobin was low. This made him so anemic he hardly had any strength.

I said to myself, "Oh no, not another one." Bob's death was still fresh in all our minds, and though there were different blood cells affected, I knew it was very serious.

After tests and examinations by doctors at our capital, they couldn't find the cause of his anemia, so he and his family returned to the United States.

When they left, I taught three of Lynn's wife Margo's weekly Bible School classes on the book of Luke. It kept me very busy, with my other duties, but I knew many people were praying for me, and for that I was thankful.

Soon after the Muhr's arrival in the United States we received a telegram saying his anemia was caused by a reaction from the preventive drug he had been taking for malaria. Only one person in 80,000 has this reaction. He had a couple of transfusions and was back to his normal self. We were all praising the Lord for his recovery, and soon they returned to us at Sibut. Of course he changed his drug for malaria prevention.

Faye Hull

Tracy and Faye Hull joined us in Sibut as new missionaries after their Sango language study was completed. He became our mechanic for one term. Each station had a place where they could work on their trucks, but Sibut had a large garage where the mechanic kept busy working on vehicles from many different stations.

The Hulls, as many missionaries did, had a gray parrot that entertained people with its talk. We got a kick out of an expression he had learned and repeated often. It was "Faye, it's time to get up." So we learned from the parrot that Faye liked to sleep in.

Two months before they were to go home on their first furlough, Tracy came down with hepatitis, but he gradually regained some of his strength. Then Faye became ill with nausea and pain, and I felt that it was inflammation of her gall bladder. They were to fly out of Bangui on a Tuesday, so on

Saturday I went with them to the capital. She went to a doctor, who also thought it was her gall bladder. With them leaving so soon, he didn't have time to take x-rays, so we went back to the Bangui mission station, and I kept IVs going, hoping that would give her strength to make the trip home.

It was really a testing time for those new missionaries. But with prayer they made it home, and soon Faye was in the capable hands of a doctor in the United States. She has never had her gall bladder removed but must be continually cautious with her diet.

Vera Vaughn

Vera Vaughn came out of retirement and returned to Sibut in May 1991 for a short period to help teach in our Bible School. Even when missionaries retire, their hearts are still in the country where they had served.

On Saturday, May 11, at 5:00 a.m., Vera called my name outside my bedroom window. Her upper lip was quite swollen. I gave her some medication and suggested that she wait a little, then go to Paula Beckman, the other nurse on the station, who was in charge. I had left the medical work when I went home in 1990.

At noon the swelling had gone up into her face, so we asked Margo to contact Dr. Rhodes by the short-wave radio that was kept at her house, but the static made this impossible. Margo suggested she could try to call Dr. Fred, a ham radio operator doctor to whom she sometimes spoke on Saturdays.

We were relieved as his voice came in loud and clear. Margo relayed the emergency situation to him. By this time the swelling was going down to her neck and throat. We had a drug on hand we were about to use when Dr. Fred took over. He put his medical work in the United States in the hands of another doctor, and for three hours we communicated with each other through Margo.

The swelling was threatening to cut off her breathing, and we did not know if we were going to lose her or not. Paula and I felt relieved that we could now use the drug under his direction. The doctor's wife activated her church's prayer chain, and the Sibut students had an emergency prayer meeting on site.

We were thankful that the medicines Dr. Fred ordered were at the clinic and that she passed the crisis, and we were so thankful to the Lord for how He worked everything out. The doctor was home just at the time we needed him, and the airwaves were clear to carry the voices back and forth. Our God is a God of miracles.

I stayed with Vera that night as she began to recover. Two days later she was back teaching in the Bible School.

We all thought Vera had some kind of allergy causing that frightening attack, but later, when she was back in the United States, she had two other attacks. The doctors finally diagnosed the illness as acquired ageo edema, which is very rare. Only one person in one million has it. Now she always carries medicine in her purse, just in case she needs it.

God's Timing

Throughout my years in Africa, I had very little illness, for which I am so thankful. But I had one unforgettable experience I'd like to share.

For a year I had a lower molar tooth that had been aching on and off. Then one week it hurt continually. My furlough was almost due, and I was hoping that I could stand the pain until I went home to the States. I couldn't take time to go to the capital with the clinic going at full speed. Against my better judgment, I was just ready to show my nurse helper, Andre, how to give a mandible injection so he could pull it. But the Lord was merciful and saw my need.

Just then one of our missionaries who did some dentistry, Dick Paulson, who lived about 350 miles from Sibut, arrived unexpectedly with the American Ambassador. The ambassador's plane had made a forced landing close to Dick's house, so Dick had offered to take him in his truck to Bangui. During the trip Dick had a wonderful opportunity to talk to the ambassador about his soul, and I got rid of a tooth. It's a good thing I didn't wait until my furlough to deal with it. The roots were rotten, and one had even disintegrated. This reminded me of God's care for his people in Nahum 1:7: "The Lord is good, a strong hold in the day of trouble; and He knoweth them that trust in him."

31 - Dealing with Death

One Sunday morning at the end of my second term, I had planned to leave with Florence after breakfast, filling the back of our pickup with students and going to different villages for meetings. Early that morning I was awakened by our guard saying a man had just come in from a village about ten miles from Sibut. A would-be mother had been in labor for a long time and was not able to deliver. He asked if I would go out to see her.

I went and found a very complicated case. The baby was breech and had no heartbeat. The house was filled to capacity with men, women, and some children. All were moaning, crying, and carrying on. I understood why.

They thought the mother would soon die, too. With the exception of two women and the husband, I asked everyone else to leave the room. I couldn't find an adequate place to work and think straight with all the commotion.

I knelt on the mother's mat and started to work. It is always harder to deliver a dead baby than a live one, and it being in a breech position made it more difficult. But I was able to bring the legs down, and by working with the mother during her contractions and doing some maneuvers, I was able to deliver the baby, much to my relief.

Many times today, if there is a breech presentation and they can't turn the baby, a Caesarean section is done. I took the mother back with me, for I wanted to give her a penicillin injection. I realized that many women had probably tried to help her, and she was a prime case for a serious infection.

When I returned to the house, it was breakfast time. Afterwards Florence and I took the truck to pick up the students. As they were getting into the back of the truck, a young fellow came running down the hill from the clinic to tell me that a man had just died. I could hardly believe it, for when we passed by there only five minutes earlier he was sitting on the large rock in front of the clinic. His wife was bathing him by throwing cold water on his body. But I thought, *I'd better go back and check.* The report was true. He must have died of a heart attack. I was so glad he was a Christian. I sent word to Florence to go on and take the students while I walked up the hill to get permission from Eugene to use his truck to take the man's body to his village.

When we arrived in the village, the dead man's daughters really carried on, tearing their clothes, throwing ashes on their bodies, and wailing. I

Our pickup truck served many roles—this one being a hearse.

finally quieted the people down and talked quietly to them for a few minutes. The people knew the man was a Christian, and I was glad I could tell them that his spirit had gone to his heavenly home, and that was the hope of the Christian. The big canton chief was there, and I prayed that my words would penetrate his heart, as well as the others'. At the clinic my helpers and I had prayed often for this chief.

It was church time when I returned to the station, and for the first time in ages, I attended the worship service at home.

Treating so many people daily, we were bound to experience some deaths. I usually took the bodies and any family present to the person's home, unless he or she had lived close by, in which case the family used the clinic stretcher to perform this service.

Some families would begin their mourning by wailing and carrying on in the back of the truck. Some even stood up. I was afraid they might fall off and we would have another death in the family, or possibly a lawsuit. I soon learned to tell them before I started the truck motor to sit down quietly on the benches by the body. I remember once with a Muslim family, there was such carrying on that I had to stop the truck twice to warn them to sit down. The second time I said, "If I have to stop again, I will leave the body by the side of the road." They quieted down.

Many times the bereaved would be quiet in their grief, but when I came to the edge of the village, the wailing would start, for the villagers usually knew who it was. Once I was amazed as one woman threw herself on the ground and rolled headfirst over and over in a gymnastic manner. I knew she probably couldn't do it again unless her adrenal glands were triggered.

Most of the Christians grieved very differently than those who had no hope. They would cry, and that was how it should have been. I soon learned that this was a good time to talk to all the people who were gathered around the house and to explain the hope we can have after death. Then I would pray with them.

What saddened me at a time of death was that the children were neglected. The adults were so caught up in their grief, they didn't think of the children. Many times I would see a child with his head leaning on the outside wall of the house, crying his heart out but no one thinking to go and put their arms around him to comfort him in his sorrow. In my classes I would sometimes bring up this subject: "Don't forget the children."

One time after church I went to the classroom where we had our library. Just as I was finishing checking out books, a fellow came in from the main road and asked me to go to the mission crossroad and pick up a very ill woman who had come in by bus. I said I would.

But before I could get my truck, someone else came to say the woman had died under the tree where they were waiting for me. They lived about twenty-five miles out, so I knew I would take them home. I asked Oumar, my nurse helper, to go with me. I also had been teaching him to drive, and this gave him more driving experience.

When we arrived to pick up the body, the only relative with her was a thirteen-year-old daughter, sitting by her mother's body and sobbing her heart out. Of course others in the village were around them, but here was this small girl with such a terrible responsibility. I burned with righteous indignation. *Where was her husband?*

We found out when we arrived at their village; he was at a dance in the next village. He couldn't be bothered with his sick wife. Now this isn't typical of Africans. Most of them were very caring, but under the influence of alcohol and the dance craze, human kindness went out the window. My heart hurt all the more. I was so glad that Oumar was with me. He could deal with the situation better than I could. He sent someone to get the husband.

When the fifteen-year-old son saw his mother's body, he was beside himself in grief, crying, "Mama, mama." The lady had left four children. It was so hard for us to leave them there.

So goes the work of a nurse, or should I say, a hearse driver, in the middle of Africa.

There were many people we could have kept alive if they had only come to us sooner. Some tried African medicine first, and if it didn't work, they would come to our clinic.

There are some African medicinal herbs that do work. Missionary Knute Orton mentioned that a Christian in one of the villages in his area showed him his fenced-in herbal garden in back of his house. He told Knute what some of the herbs were used for. One, he said, was for malaria, and when Knute broke off a small part of the plant and tasted it, it was quinine, a very effective drug for malaria. Unfortunately most herbal treatment is also associated with witchcraft, wearing of charms, sacrifices, etc.

Sometimes they would bring their medicine with them to the clinic. I remember one man who was very ill with pneumonia and had a temperature of 106 degrees. How we worked. He was getting better, eating and sitting up. Then one morning he was in a coma, and the next night he died. We were all stunned. My nurse helpers told me he must have taken some other medicine without our knowledge, but his family denied it. It was so strange.

What hurt my heart a lot was when they had an abscess, and the Africans seemed to have deep ones. Some were treated by putting on a poultice made out of tree bark, dung, and I don't know what else. Sometimes the infection would eat way down into the flesh. A mother had put one on her baby's abdomen, and it ate down to the intestinal cavity. It was only the Lord that saved that little one. Yet one African came in with a child that had gangrene in the jaw that was stopped with a poultice made out of several different herbs put together. It didn't repair the damage that had been done, but kept it from going any deeper.

I was thankful for the Lord's sustaining strength, to keep me going when some of the ill that came to us died. It was always difficult, but we had to continue to take care of the many we could help.

Part Five

Ministries

Pastor Malibissi, from the Galabadja Church, told me when he came for a pastor's conference that he wanted to have a week of Bible classes and related subjects for the officers and deacons of seven churches in his area that were without a pastor.

"Would you come and help me?" he asked. "I have asked Pastor Irimou to come and help teach, and you could bring him."

Pastor Malibissi was in the river area where the graduates of our Bible School were not eager to go. The locale was not easily accessible. Vehicles going in that direction were very few, so it was almost impossible to buy supplies. The area had few government schools, and witchcraft prevailed. The request appealed to me very much, so the date was arranged for us to go. I had a great respect for Pastor Malibissi and appreciated his vision and great burden to have this Bible and leadership conference. If I could use my truck so Pastor Irimou and I could go and help, I wanted to do so.

The week before we were to leave I was very lethargic. I would do my work and go home and collapse on my bed. I didn't hurt anywhere. It was strange. My co-workers knew I wasn't up to par, and they also knew that I was scheduled to go on that trip.

One of them came over and asked me, "Do you think it is wise for you to go so far when you haven't enough strength?"

I knew the natural thing to do was to cancel the trip. But from the core of my being, I knew I had to go. If I didn't, there would be no way for Pastor

Kembi Louis preaching in an African chapel.

Irimou to go either, and Pastor Malibissi would be on his own all day teaching thirty men. There was no way I could get word to him.

As I continued to pray, the Lord revealed to me, *This is from the enemy. He doesn't want this seminar. You are going into his territory.* I told my co-workers I had to go, and the Lord would give me the strength. I told the Lord on Saturday evening, "I can't do it on my own. I'm counting on You and that verse in Philippians 4:13, 'I can do all things through Christ who strengthens me'" (NKJV).

On Saturday evening my helper, Nojo Louis, got most of the things that were needed for a week of village work packed into the back of my truck. Nojo was one of the best house helpers I ever had. He was always more than willing to make my life easier in any way possible. I enjoyed having him around.

At daybreak the next morning, Pastor Irimou and I left for our ninety-mile trip to Galabadja. Because of the rutted road, we didn't take the shorter route. We went to Grimari, then cut off on the road going to the Massengue church, where we were to stop for the morning service. That church hadn't had a missionary visit for twenty years and had been without a pastor for almost the same length of time.

I had been to the Massengue church once before but not for a service. Four years earlier, when Eugene knew I was going to Grimari for girls' camp, he had asked me to move a pastor ten miles from Grimari to this church. After camp I went to the village where the pastor was expecting me. The people loaded his family and belongings into my Chevy truck.

As we were traveling down the road, we came upon a brush fire that was burning on both sides of the narrow road. As I drove through, I was frightened and asked the Lord to help us. Just a few yards ahead there was a bridge. I had to stop before crossing it, as this road was seldom used and there were deep ruts to navigate on the bank entering the bridge. As I stopped, the motor of the truck also stopped. What could we do? The fire was coming right behind us, and we could hear the crackling of the flames. I told Pastor Kandia from Grimari, who was with us, "Let's look under the hood." He found the battery cable had come loose. He quickly attached it, slammed the hood shut, and we ran back to the cab. I slowly inched my way up over the boards, praying the fire wouldn't catch up to us. It didn't. That was one of the scariest experiences I had in Africa, though.

These memories were going through my mind now as Pastor Irimou and I were traveling. I also remembered reading about Pastor Wangbi, who in the 1930s was the first pastor in the whole area. He was still an active pastor. Back then, Grimari was a large village of over 5,000 that was strongly

Catholic, so Wangbi had gone to Massengue instead. He suffered imprisonment several times for Christ's sake, but through these trials, churches were established in the Massengue-Grimari area.

I was exhausted when we arrived at Massengue. Of course the people hadn't been expecting us, but we received a warm welcome, as we always do when we are among believers. Pastor Irimou took a mat out of the back of the truck and laid it under a nearby shade tree, where I rested as he preached.

After the service we were on our way again to Galabadja. I had never seen so many anthills on any road. I was driving like a drunken person the whole way, trying to dodge these uninhabited, foot-high, red dirt anthills. I prayed silently that no damage would be done to the underneath of the truck, as I couldn't avoid hitting some of the hills. The ants in this area build their homes out of the red soil after a rain when the ground is soft. When the soil dries, the mound hardens. Some anthills can be five or more feet high, but not in this area.

It was almost dark when we arrived at Galabadja. Malibissi and his wife, Nicole, and fellows from the churches made us welcome. The Africans quickly unpacked my things, set up my bed, and tied my mosquito net over it. My two folding tables and chair fit into the small room with barely enough space left to turn around, but it didn't bother me; I had stayed there before. At the time I was almost at the end of my strength. I quickly had a bite to eat and went to bed, thanking the Lord we had made it. The next morning my energy had returned, and I was as good as new.

We had a tremendous week. I taught the people how to be disciples of Christ, song leading, and new hymns. Whenever I went to the villages, if I was going to stay awhile, I would teach spiritual life (how to be a disciple).

I especially enjoyed becoming acquainted with Francois, a

Jouse Wangbi, one of our first pastors, graduated from Bible School in the thirties, and passed away in 1992.

school teacher who lived just across the road. He had been saved as a child, but when he became a teacher, he started drinking and walking in the world, as many of them do when they get into a high position. But with Pastor Malibissi's influence, he came back to the Lord. He sat on the front row and was so eager to learn. Thus began a friendship between us that lasted throughout the rest of my time in Africa.

I received this letter, translated below, two months after I went to Galabadja. I thanked the Lord over and over for letting me be a part of that week. It would have been worth it just to meet Francois!

Monsieur NABENA DIMANCHE   *Possel, le 21 Janvier, 87*
   FRANCOIS   *Mademoiselle Margery Benedict*
Teacher at Possel School *a la Mission Baptist, P.B. 6 at Sibut*

Mademoiselle,

I greet you in the name of our Lord Jesus Christ. I have much joy to let you know by this letter. I am no longer at Galabadja with Pasteur Malibissi, but in the town of Possel. I am teaching in their school but I also attend the church here. They have trusted me with the responsibility some-time with the preaching, and they have also voted me in as a deacon. To be able to carry out these duties, I study my Bible a lot. I utilize and put into practice all the counsel that you gave us during the formation of "Christian Workers," and the way to learn Bible verses under the

Francois Nabena copying notes at music camp.

Navigator system.

All the study material that you gave us has helped me in my Bible study. If you have anything else you think would help me, booklets or tracts, and above all, the booklet "THE DAILY BREAD," I would appreciate them so much. You could send them with the Peace Corps teacher, Mademoiselle Cotter Charlotte, when she comes here. I will come some day to see you if God so wills.

My distinguished greetings,
Francois

No matter where the government sent Francois to teach, I would send him Christian literature from France, even when he was promoted to principal of a large school at Dekoa. He maintained his Christian testimony no matter where he was.

A blind man walked twenty miles in his bare feet to attend the seminar in Galabadja. His feet were sore and bleeding from hitting all the debris and rocks along an abandoned old road, which was now only a path. It was a privilege to bandage the feet of this one who was so happy to be there to learn more about the Christ he loved. Many times during the week I thought, *What if we hadn't come?* I thanked the Lord many times for letting us be there. Our churches were the most important ministry of Baptist Mid-Missions in the Central African Republic.

When Ferd and Ina Rosenau came to Sibut in 1921, Ferd spent most of his time evangelizing the many villages along the paths that radiated out of Sibut. Eugene's earliest recollection is going to the foot of the hill with his mother to kiss his daddy good-bye and wave as he set off on his bicycle, followed by two tall Africans pushing a one-wheeled rickshaw with his camping equipment.

In his meetings, people were repenting of their sins and trusting in Christ as their Savior. It didn't take long for him to realize they needed to start a Bible school to train men to be pastors so they could go out and start churches. Some of his equipment carriers were the first students in the school. The missionaries never pastored churches, but they would go out and preach in the churches on Sundays and support the local, indigenous pastors.

Our African Churches

The churches have morning services and Sunday School much like they do here, only longer, since people walk from villages up to five miles away.

The afternoon services are held each week in the larger villages, led by a deacon, with the pastor visiting each Sunday on a rotating basis. Wednesday prayer service followed the same pattern, as well as evening Bible classes. Out of these came new churches because villages five miles away grow to where they need resident pastors. The older pastors and churches help the new ones until they become self-supporting like themselves.

The early villages (and their associated churches) were named after their chief. It was a bit confusing when the village names and thus the church names changed each time a chief died and a new one took his place. In addition, some of the chiefs were anti-God and anti-church, so little by little the churches took on the names of the local geography: creeks, woods, and hills. Some of the names were:

Katakpa	Ironwood
Galafondo	Banana Town
Libi	Marsh
Amou	Pasture
Gbassago	Tall Grass
Wawa	Crossroads
Ngoto	Bat Creek
Ngoukpe	Rocky Creek
Nogloyo	No Healing Creek
Damara	House of Barrenness

Most of the churches had baptismal services at least twice a year and an annual Bible Conference, to which a missionary was always invited to speak. They called upon their founding mission agency for special advice when problems arose. There was an average of around a thousand baptized each year in the forty churches in the Sibut area.

In the early years, before the people were baptized, they had to learn to read. The missionaries and pastors felt that if their conversions were real, they should have a desire to read the Word of God. Otherwise there would have been hundreds more baptized, many who had not repented of their sins and would think baptism was a way to heaven.

The first baptism I remember attending was about fifteen miles out on the Grimari road. There were seventeen baptized, and twelve of them were young people that had come to the Lord in a class that a couple of high school fellows and I had in their village. Words can't describe the joy I had to see them take this important step in their Christian lives.

When the new church was built on the mission station in 1958, they had the first baptistry in the mission. The Saturday before the baptism, the people who were to be baptized had to come and fill the baptistry from a well over a block away. If it were an elderly person, they would send a child to do their water carrying—all on their heads, of course.

I will forever remember one baptism. It started to rain just before Sunday School that morning, and I didn't have very many out for my high school class. I didn't think there would be a church service, for when it pours like it did that morning, the people do not come because very few of them have umbrellas. But, surprisingly, 300 people braved the rain because there was to be a baptismal service.

Just before Pastor Zemio began baptizing, a deacon with a small junior-age boy crying at his side came out of the room on the right side. The deacon called out, "Is there any adult here that came with this child?" There was no answer. Then he continued, "Look at this boy. He doesn't have any clothes to put on after his baptism (we had no baptismal garments). Does anyone have a cloth to lend him to put on after his baptism?" Then a woman from the audience unwrapped the extra piece of cloth that makes up a woman's Sunday outfit from around her waist, went to the front, and gave it to the deacon. He and the child returned happily to the waiting room. Then a deaconess came out from the left side with a little girl at her side and the scenario was repeated. Evidently the children had come to church before the rain started, and their parents, who would have had an extra pair of shorts or dress for them, wouldn't come out in the downpour.

Three of my Sunday School class boys were baptized—two brothers, the

An original African church during the Ndo Kindji Church Conference.

sons of our Sibut mayor, Caine, and a young Christian from the Sibut track team. One woman was so happy that after the service she came to me and said, "Four of my children were baptized." It was a happy day for me too.

Our Sibut church is not noted for its quietness during baptismal Sundays, for many outsiders come and they have many comments to make. At one baptismal, Pastor Zemio stressed very specifically that the people were not to talk. Soon a woman at the end of the bench in front of me started talking rather loudly. I couldn't see her, but I said, "Ssssssssh," and it turned out to be the pastor's wife. I was embarrassed and thought I also should learn when to be quiet.

Many times during the dry season the level of water in the small, dirty streams and rivers would be so low the people would have to dam them up to make them deep enough for baptizing. I very seldom went to baptismal services (that was out of my sphere of ministry), but when I did, my mind would invariably think of the parasite bilharziasis that is so prevalent in the African waters. I was glad the people who were baptized dried themselves quickly before the parasite could have a chance to penetrate their skin.

When Lois, Erma, and I went to Israel in 1977, we also visited Greece. While there we took a bus down to the Adriatic Sea. The water was incredibly blue, clean, and so very beautiful. As I sat on a rock by the sea, tears came into my eyes as I thought of the contaminated water in Africa. I had some rebellious thoughts as I told the Lord, *It isn't fair that some have such beautiful, clean water and others don't.*

Then the Lord so sweetly reminded me, *I'm preparing a clear, crystal river*

A newly constructed African church building after a youth rally.

in heaven, and the African believers will have all eternity to enjoy it. A great peace overwhelmed my soul as I thought again of the heaven that we believers would be going to some day. And all I could do was to lift up my head toward heaven and say, "Thank you, Lord." We believers often need to be reminded of that verse in 2 Corinthians 4:18: "So we don't look at the troubles we can see right now; rather, we look forward to what we have not yet seen. For the troubles we see will soon be over, but the joys to come will last forever" (NLT).

How Can I Help?

During my first term it didn't take me long to get immersed in what I could do to help our pastors at the annual Bible conference. For the first couple of years the clinic staff automatically examined each pastor, especially for parasites. Later they didn't have to be asked; it was routine if they thought it necessary. Before each conference I would put into small plastic bags two or three rolled sheet bandages, some zinc oxide ointment for their sores (which I made up five to ten pounds at a time), and other medications they could use for their families and charged them a minimal price.

At the beginning of each conference I would schedule a time to meet with our pastors separately or sometimes as a group. They would give me a list of the medications they needed, and I would take time to explain the usage and treatment of when and how to use them. This took time but it was a vital part of my ministry to our pastors. I never gave out antibiotics unless my primary nurse helper or I diagnosed an illness where it was needed.

At one conference I told the pastors who lived close by not to come to me with their list, because they could come see me at any time. I needed to use my time with the ones who lived far away. On one occasion a local pastor came with his list along with the others, and I was so busy. Twice he came and insisted I see him now, with the others. I became so exasperated I lost my temper and told him to please leave. I later apologized to him for my harsh words and took care of him. I couldn't understand why he did not want to do what I had requested. I still felt badly when I went home that evening to think I had let my temper get the best of me. I longed for the time when we would be like Christ and our old bodies replaced by new ones. That will be a wonderful day.

One Saturday afternoon I took my load of pastors and families home after a Bible conference. I had arranged to meet with a youth group in a new church. When I arrived, I was so tired I didn't even want to get out of my truck. I knew the Lord doesn't require us to do anything He doesn't give us strength for, so I prayed for strength. It was wonderful how the Lord answered my prayer. I was with the group for two hours; I wasn't tired and sang most of the way home.

In the fall of 1971 there were circumstances at our clinic for three weeks before an eight-day pastor's conference that I never want to repeat. I quote part of a letter I sent home about it the day before Christmas:

> "My child just coughs and coughs. She won't eat any-thing, just cries and moans." Many, many times I've heard mothers come to me with those words recently. We have had about eighty cases of measles the past two weeks, with whooping cough a second runner up. I had some sick, sick babies, but I am so thankful that only one was lost. A little over a month ago I also heard these words, "Mademoiselle, I just cough and cough, and I hurt all over." Yes, a flu epidemic! Talk about running people through the assembly line! We were doing that with patients! And with many patients the flu turned into pneumonia. My penicillin supply ran lower than ever. The time I wasn't treating patients, my helpers were. I was running an ambulance service because some of the people just couldn't walk any distance with a high temperature. At this time we also had a pastor's conference for eight days. The fourth day, Bruce got the flu, and I was teaching three to four hours a day instead of the scheduled two. At the close of the conference, Wilma had a burn accident that could have taken her life. All of us had much to thank the Lord for. He cared enough to give us the strength we needed during that time.

Trials come to all believers. Some the Lord sends to strengthen our faith; some come from the enemy who would bring discouragement to weaken our faith and make us ineffective witnesses for Christ. Other trials come because we live in a world that is not perfect and sickness is a part of life. Some will come, and we will never know why.

Our pastors face many trials, and many times I was involved with their physical problems. One time in my earlier years Pastor Serenganza had moved from a prosperous church to one of the largest villages in our district, where the church was dying. Many people didn't want the Gospel message to be preached, and he had been beaten repeatedly by them. Then Satan attacked the pastor's children through sickness.

One day the pastor and his family arrived at the clinic, and how I wished I had the instant means of communication now available through e-mail or fax to send messages home requesting prayers—but I did send a letter. The pastor's three-year-old girl was desperately ill with cerebral malaria, and I despaired for her life. Their seven-year-old daughter had an acute infection in her right leg, and his wife still lacked strength from delivering their baby five days earlier. My co-workers at the clinic, our student body, and the missionaries also prayed. The Lord did undertake, and it was a happy day when I could make the ninety-mile journey and take them back home. The Lord did bless his ministry, and the church grew in numbers and maturity.

Pastors With An Even Dozen

Pastor Serenganza, Pastor Oualisso, and Pastor Ngaite each had twelve children. Thirty-five of the thirty-six made it to adulthood. This is very unusual for the middle of Africa. But it could have been a different story if there hadn't been a clinic on our mission station. The time we spent with four of their children has never been blotted out of my memory.

Pastor Serenganza lived in Yabalangba (Mala), about ninety miles northeast of Sibut. It was a rainy day when I received a note he had given to a runner to let me know that his two-year old girl, whom I nicknamed Flavoquine (a malaria drug), was dying. He asked me to please come quickly and take her and her mother, Ichange, to our clinic at Sibut. I didn't want to go that far in rainy season because one twenty-five-mile stretch had deep ruts. I knew I had to go though, because a precious life was in the balance.

Phonse, Bruce and Wilma's house helper, offered to go with me. Yabalangba was his hometown, and Serenganza was his former pastor. I was thankful for this because he knew how to change a tire and would be a help to me in many ways. I packed my doctor's bag with everything I could think of that I might need and prepared a suitcase for an overnight stay, and we were on our way.

After going sixty-five miles we turned onto the Dekoa-Grimari Road. It was slow going, not that I was breaking any speed limits on the other road. Once we came to an overflowing creek, and water was everywhere. Phonse immediately waded into it to see how deep it was (it was mid-thigh on him) and because he needed to find the road so he could put two sticks at each side. This would help me know where to drive my truck. We made it.

Upon arrival at Yabalangba that evening, I found a very sick little girl with bronchial pneumonia. I immediately started treatment that continued throughout the night. By mid-morning there was an improvement. Even though she was better, I felt the rough trip to Sibut might give her a setback, so I gave medicine to her parents, so they could continue the treatment at home. Phonse and I made it back to Sibut that night; tired but happy that Flavoquine would live.

On another occasion, Wajourou, wife of Pastor Oualisso, came to me with their small daughter Colleen. She was very dehydrated from diarrhea and vomiting, and so lethargic she could hardly move. I immediately gave her infusions of saline under the skin in different parts of her body. When the tissue swelling would go down, I would repeat the procedure. That way I was able to replace a small amount of the fluids she lost in her illness. It was nip and tuck for hours, but gradually she opened her eyes and whimpered. Never had a whimper pleased me more. I knew then that she would make it. Thus every child of that family grew to be adults. Every time I saw Colleen in her growing-up years, I thanked the Lord for His help in saving this beautiful girl.

Pastor Ngaite was the fastest speaker I ever heard preach. When a missionary could follow his sermon with understanding, they knew Sango well. We all loved this family; they were very special to us. Pastor's mother had tuberculosis. I tried my best to tell the family how contagious it was and how to keep the mother's eating utensils separate and to always boil them after they had been used. But in their culture, it wasn't easy.

One week before our annual conference, Ngaite and his wife, Yassimindi, came in from their home seventy miles out on the Damara road. They brought their five-year old Georgine to me. It only took one glance for me to know she was a very ill child. I diagnosed her with tubercular meningitis.

At that time this illness was difficult to treat and the mortality rate was high, even in the best hospitals. What I did for her, which wasn't much, was in vain. It was the day before our three-day conference. How helpless I felt as I told her dear parents there was nothing more I could do, and she would die soon unless the Lord performed a miracle. How well I remember Pastor's prayer, "Lord, don't take Georgine home to you until after the conference." He knew it would interrupt the conference. The day after conference the Lord answered. It was a sweet home-going, as we were all around her as she passed into the presence of Jesus.

The other eleven children grew to adulthood. One of them, Joel, is now a pastor. Later Ngaite and his wife died in a lightning storm, as they took refuge under a tree. When we were called to the accident, their bodies were badly charred. It was a very traumatic moment for me.

Encouraging Words

It is always exciting at conference time to listen to African testimonies of what the Lord has done for them. He is as precious to them as He is to

Christians in America. One testimony I'll never forget was a fellow saying, "I'm glad my house burned down. I had some non-believing relatives in my house, and they were making life miserable for my family with their drinking and carrying on. It was hard to live a Christian life with them around. I didn't have the nerve to ask them to leave [that is not the African way of doing things], so I prayed that the Lord would work out this problem for me. He did, by burning down my house. I ask you to pray that I might have strength to build another one. As you know, it is hard this season of the year to find four-foot-long dry grass for the roof, for it is still green."

The pastor from the La Kandja church once said, "As you know, there is a soap factory in my town, and the owner of the factory knew that his employees were stealing a lot of soap. So he and a *gendarme* [policeman] went around to the different employees' houses. They found a lot of it, some buried. But they didn't find any among the Christian employees." I was so glad that the Christians were letting their light shine in this way.

Yet another Christian thanked the Lord for having a tree right in his path when he was running pell-mell from a buffalo coming out of the burning grass and starting for him. He climbed a tree and was safe.

One time, after spending a week having children's classes in a distant church, another nurse and I went twenty miles further, so we could spend Saturday night in Pastor Gourna's home. We wanted to attend their Sunday morning service.

On my arrival at their house, Josephine, the pastor's wife gave me a grapefruit. It was one of the most welcome gifts I have ever received. For the previous four days, I had felt like I had a cotton ball in the back of my throat. No matter how much tepid water I drank from my plastic jerry can, I couldn't quench my thirst. But as I ate that grapefruit, it cut the phlegm from my throat, and I felt well again.

That evening Pastor asked me, "Do you have any extra bread I could have so I can serve communion tomorrow? We haven't had communion for months, as bread is not available here."

"Yes," I told him, "I have some. It is hard, but that shouldn't make any difference for communion." He was so grateful, as he accepted the bread.

The next morning the pastor sheepishly came to me again and said, "Please forgive me for asking you again, but last night Ferdinand, my six-year-old son, ate the bread you gave me. Would you give me some more?" Happily I gave him the bread I had left. I knew Ferdinand did what any normal child would do if there were something special to eat in the house.

I'm Going To See Jesus

During the Pastor's Conference at our mission station the next year, we were all amazed as we listened to a testimony from Pastor Gourna. A month before, his seven-year old son, Ferdinand, woke up and told them he had a dream, and God told him that in a week He was going to take him to heaven. They didn't take his words seriously. A couple of days later, however, he very calmly remarked, "I'm going to see Jesus soon." Later, to the astonishment of Pastor Gourna and his wife Josephine, he repeated the phrase, "I'm going to see Jesus," and then he quickly passed on.

The pastor couldn't explain it. The boy wasn't ill, but the family knew Jesus must have wanted Ferdinand in heaven with Him. They missed him so much but knew he was happy there. None of us who listened to these words could explain it either, but we knew that Isaiah 55:8-9 says, "'For my thoughts are not your thoughts, neither are your ways my ways,' declares the Lord. As the heavens are higher than the earth, so are my ways higher than your ways and my thoughts than your thoughts" (NIV).

Some of my happiest times in Africa were with the pastors and their families, helping them "feed the flock."

33 - Training to Be Pastors

It was near midnight when a voice woke me out of a sound sleep. "Mademoiselle! Mademoiselle! Is Mademoiselle there?" I opened the door to a Bible School couple holding their very ill four-year-old girl, Marie. She had been passing pure blood and vomiting.

Earlier I had given the parents medication to give her during the night, and here they were back at my door accompanied by two sympathizing students. I couldn't blame them; they loved their little one. They were worried about her, and I was their only help. Marie had stopped vomiting, but she was still passing blood. The father informed me he had given her, in about four hour's time, almost all of the *yolo* (medication) that I prescribed for the whole night. I was quite upset.

We were all very concerned about Marie. I didn't know anything more I could do. I said, "Let's pray," and right then we had a prayer meeting on my little veranda. I surely didn't want Marie to die. We had lost a student's child the year before, and it was heart rending.

The parents took Marie back home, and two hours later, at 2:00 a.m., I walked down to the village to see how she was doing. The bleeding had almost stopped, and I could see she was better. We rejoiced in a God that answered prayer!

I always became attached to each Bible School student and family while they were with us the four years. I had responsibility for the health care of around 200 people in our student village, which included a lot of children. The students were young, and as Christians, they had none of the diseases that would prevent them from having children.

Our students came from five mission stations. Though every one of our fifteen mission stations held Bible classes, there were only two that had a Bible School like ours at Sibut. The wonderful part was they all spoke the same language, Sango, even though they were from several different tribes. All of these students lived in our mission village at the bottom of the hill during their four years of pastor training.

When I first arrived in Africa in 1952, the student houses were made of mud and grass, requiring continual upkeep and replacement. We needed permanent houses. We were delighted when we could afford to build four duplexes made of cement blocks and aluminum roofing. We continued to pray that we would receive the finances to have all permanent houses.

We mentioned this request in prayer letters sent home, and Glory to God, one of Eugene's supporting churches in Jacksonville, Florida, made this a major project. Each church member had a dime bank they were to fill and refill during the year. At the end of that year the total was $12,000, with another $8,000 added the next year.

The Bible School students made cement blocks during their work hours. With the help of our two African masons and the missionary men, four new houses were built. When the funds came in, more were constructed.

The classes for male students were held from 6:30 a.m. to 11:30 a.m. In

Contrast between temporary Bible School houses and the permanent brick housing.

the afternoons, from 2 p.m. to 5 p.m., the students worked for the mission. This arrangement provided the money they needed to buy a few of their simple necessities of life. For us it provided the needed upkeep for our station. In December, the students made a ten-foot fire path, cutting the tall grass that surrounded our 124-acre mission station. This was to prevent the annual fires from coming up the hill and destroying our homes and fruit trees.

In my earlier years there was only one classroom for the students. The men were taught in the mornings and the women in the afternoons. Because there was no nursery, the mothers held their babies during class. The classroom had only two and a half sides. When the rains came and the wind blew, the water leaked onto the students at their desks, which wasn't very conducive to learning. Something had to be done! We often discussed the need for a new building but never had the finances.

One time, at a monthly missionary business meeting, we gave it more serious thought. We knew the Lord was leading each of us by faith to promise $400 each until enough was received. We prayed to that end, and the Lord honored our faith. The money came in, and under the able supervision of Lee Einfeldt the school was built.

There were four rooms: the nursery, the library-study, the women's classroom, and one for the men. Harold Dark made new desks for the classrooms. A new era had begun! Years later we rejoiced even more when another large building was built and used not only for the men's classes but also for the annual missionary conferences. How true are those two verses in 1 John 5:14-15: "And we can be confident that he will listen to us when-

Preparing a meal in front of the student's houses.

ever we ask him for anything in line with his will. And if we know he is listening when we make our requests, we can be sure that he will give us what we ask for" (NLT).

Our school was growing. We now had around thirty-five families, which caused more of a housing shortage. Later we fixed the back of the old church to make room for one couple. The first to live there was Joel Ngaite, a pastor's son, and his wife and eight children.

The terrain around the place was rocky and hadn't been kept up very well since the church moved to its new location near town. When the family had lived there a week, Joel gave this testimony in prayer meeting: "I have much to thank the Lord for in keeping us safe this week. We killed eight snakes around our new living quarters, and none of us were harmed. The Lord protected us."

The student prayer meetings were on Wednesday at 5:00 p.m., in the children's classroom building. After the singing and a short message from one of the students, they divided up into small groups to pray. The women and children remained on the inside, while the men went outside on the grass. The children from three years through primary age made up one or two groups. There was an adult with them, and often it was one of the missionary women.

Sometimes the smaller ones would put both hands over their faces and mumble a fairly long prayer that only they and God could understand. Many times their prayers would go on and on. I remember one little girl who would always see that the next one prayed by giving her a nudge. If there was a missionary on furlough, we could be certain that we were prayed

Children of the Bible School students enjoying mangos at their 'nursery' break.

for by several of them. When I was the one in their prayer group, I'd think of the words Jesus spoke when He said, *"Let the little children come to me, and do not hinder them"* (Mark 10:14, NIV).

Two of the entry requirements of our Bible School were that the students had to be married and had to have a marriage license. It was difficult for couples in the Central African Republic to obtain a marriage license right away. When a couple wanted to get married, the families on both sides would meet together to discuss what the bride price would be. The grooms family first made a down payment of some material things, such as clothes, cases of soda pop, and money. Then the two were considered married according to the African way and could live together. They continued to pay a certain amount each year until the amount agreed upon was paid. When all the money was paid, the couple could go to the government office and arrange for their license.

Because the annual income was around $100 a year, it was difficult to come up with the payments. Often the bride's family would send for her to come home until the husband "paid up." This would play havoc for students in school and was the reason for the requirement for Bible School students to have a marriage license upon entrance. Many times over the years I made the last payment for some couples that I knew well who wanted to go to school. I considered this money well spent.

All of the students had the same curriculum, no matter what year they entered. There weren't enough teachers to teach a different curriculum for each year. However, when they graduated, they had all four-year subjects, and they had studied all sixty-six of the books of the Bible. Most all the missionaries who lived at Sibut taught in our Bible School, and this ministry was a very important part of our lives.

The women and men had separate classes, though the curriculum was almost the same. The women didn't respond to the lessons with the men around, and they weren't as educated prior to entrance. A few of the women had never gone to school, but some had learned to read and write in their villages. Most of the men had a sixth-grade education. Some now have attained a twelfth-grade level.

I remember John Pierre, a good natured, lovable fellow who lived in the village of Ouiti. He helped me teach when I held Vacation Bible School in his village. When he realized the joy of teaching God's Word and seeing children come to Christ, it really touched his heart. The last evening of Vacation Bible School, as we sat around the fireside, he told me, "I want to enter Bible School."

I asked him, "Does your wife, Melonie, know how to read and write?"

"No," he responded. "She has never gone to school."

I told him, "It is a school requirement that a wife of a student in Bible School know how to read the Bible fluently." The wives had a rigorous Bible School training schedule as well, and they needed to be able to read.

The tears started streaming down his face as he said, "But I want to go now."

"If you really want to go to school, you can teach Melonie to read here. I will send Sango reading lessons to you when I get back, and I can find someone going your way to give them to you."

That satisfied him, for he was in earnest. At the beginning of school two years later there they were, husband and wife, in the new class. Since then they have been in the pastorate several years.

I taught both men and women in our schools. I enjoyed the subjects I taught through the years: Bible, child evangelism, missions, Biblical geography, hygiene, spiritual life, and even music.

Later Polly Strong taught the subjects I had been teaching to the men, except hygiene. She would come up from Bangui and teach block courses. I taught the women and men together in hygiene, and I enjoyed it immensely. There were so many African myths as to why they became ill. One was that when there is a gurgling sound in their stomachs, it's a *gnama*, the universal word for any animal, large or small. For instance, hadn't many seen the twelve-inch roundworm or a fifteen-foot tapeworm expelled from their own or someone else's body? Couldn't they make a noise in their tummies? I saw a great improvement in their thinking, however, as we examined them year after year for parasites, for they had fewer and fewer of them.

I am so glad I taught artificial respiration. I received a letter from Goumba, one of the two students who was now a pastor working near the Sudan border, as translated:

> Pastor Lundongar and I were riding on top of a loaded truck. As the truck was going downhill, it went out of control and turned over near a creek. Lundongar was thrown into the creek, and he received a slight concussion. I wasn't hurt, but when I pulled Lundongar out of the shallow, muddy creek, he wasn't breathing. I got the debris out of his mouth, turned him over on his stomach, and gave him artificial respiration. Praise the Lord, he started breathing! I am thankful for what I was taught when I was in school.

Teaching child evangelism was a challenge and was always interesting to me. Before 1960 very few of the churches had children's Sunday School. The girls met with the women and the boys with the men. It was a great day for us when we published children's lessons that the Africans could use.

Africans are great storytellers. They sit around the fire in the evenings and swap stories. However, when they stood in front of a group of children, most of them would preach a sermon more appropriate for adults. I tried my best to teach them how to tell a Bible story. I would go over the story one of them was assigned to tell the following week, and we would discuss the gestures and the voice changes they could use. The idea got across to some of them.

One of them, a student from Bambari, one day told the story of Namaan, the Syrian general of Bible times who had leprosy. The student gave a very dramatic presentation. I could almost feel the water as Namaan stooped down six times, then felt his disappointment because he still had the disease. At the seventh time, when Namaan discovered his cleansing, we all rejoiced in his healing! Our storyteller had us in the palm of his hand.

I can still remember the astonished expressions on the faces of the students in our missions classes as I was telling them about the life history of David Livingstone. The government schools taught that he was an explorer and doctor, but they never mentioned that he was a great pioneer missionary.

Our class always prayed for missionaries I knew in other countries. This informally added world geography to their studies. When I received letters from my missionary friends, I shared their prayer requests. When I met with

Students in one of the many Bible School classes Margery taught.

former students in later years, they would ask about some of the missionaries they had prayed for.

It was a terrific responsibility to take care of the health of all the students, but God enabled us. During the years I served in this way, I lost two male students. It was heart-rending each time.

The first one was from our Damara church. He had just entered his second year of school and was a very promising student. He had diarrhea and was vomiting. However, we got it stopped. He seemed to be doing well, or so I thought. A couple of mornings later he went into shock and died two hours later. I almost went into shock as well. I couldn't see any reason for this tragedy. I had taken care of many people more ill than he was, and they had recovered. It caused me to realize anew what David said in one of his Psalms: "My times are in Your hand" (Psalm 31:15, NKJV).

The other student, Bagaza, from Grimari, came to the clinic one Sunday morning. My nurse helper on duty didn't see any reason to call me at that time. I always went to the clinic each Sunday evening, though, to check on our hospitalized patients, and when I arrived that evening, Bagaza was on his way to see me. I could see immediately he was in much pain. Upon questioning him, I discerned he probably had an intestinal obstruction and needed to go immediately to Bangui for surgery. I knew the doctor in our government hospital at Sibut was not capable of doing this type of surgery. (Two different times in the last year I had taken patients with bowel obstructions to him. He didn't operate, and they died. He once sent me a notice saying, "Please do not send your serious patients down here to die.")

When I explained to my co-workers, the Muhrs, about Bagaza, they quickly readied themselves and the vehicle and took Bagaza and his wife to Bangui, arriving at the hospital at 10 p.m. There x-rays were taken, and they confirmed the diagnosis of a bowel obstruction. The Muhrs took for granted that the nurses would call a doctor immediately and that he would operate, so they went to the Bangui mission for the night.

The next morning they went to the hospital to check on Bagaza. A nurse informed them he had died at 6 a.m. Lynn asked, "Didn't they operate on him last night?" They hadn't. This was Africa! They brought his wife and Bagaza's body back to Sibut and then sixty miles further to their hometown at Grimari. It was difficult for the believers to understand why Bagaza died when he was training for the Lord's work. We puzzled over the loss, too, but as Isaiah 55:8-9 says, "'For my thoughts are not your thoughts, neither are your ways my ways,' declares the Lord. 'As the heavens are higher than the earth, so are my ways higher than your ways and my thoughts than your thoughts'" (NIV).

One of the students who came to us from Bangui was a blind *gendarme* (policeman), Dieudonne Mebourou. He used to drive a motorcycle in the brigade of the President's entourage when there was an official function.

Once while on duty he was going at a very fast pace when a woman with a load of wood on her head inadvertently stepped out from the curb. She became so scared she dropped her wood in the street and stepped back. Dieudonne dodged her and hit the wood. His motorcycle went out of control, throwing him headlong into the curb with a terrific force. His injuries were so severe he had to be flown to France, where a plate was inserted in his head. As a result of his injuries he became blind.

Upon his return to Bangui he asked the Lord for a Christian, handicapped wife, and he became acquainted with Claire, a paraplegic due to polio. She was the sister of Pastor Malepou, who is now the director of the Sibut Bible School.

Dieudonne and Claire married and came to our Bible School. The missionary men fixed two rooms for them close to our school building. Dieudonne wanted to train to become a chaplain at the *Gendarmare* (police academy). He had learned Braille, so he brought his Bible, which was made up of many books, with him. He had a tape recorder on which he taped all the school lectures. He graduated with the highest grade point average of any student in our school history. This couple was a joy to teach and know.

Graduation day was always a time of joy, yet also a time of sadness. The students put on an excellent program, and the church was always filled to overflowing. It was hard to say good-bye. Most of the graduates would return to their district to pastor a church, and some of them we never saw again. But those in the Sibut area would remain our friends as we continued

The graduating women, class of 1993.

to minister to them and they to us. I thanked the Lord many times for allowing me the privilege of teaching them and being their nurse.

When Pastor Rene Malepou knew he was leaving his church at Grimari to go to a Brethren seminary in the Central African Republic to further his biblical education, he scheduled a three-day seminar for all of his church leaders. He sent word to me that he wanted me to come and teach the book of Ruth, and he was going to teach the life of Moses. I didn't receive the letter until the day before the seminar was to start. I was willing to go, but Ruth was one of the books of the Bible I had never taught, and I was then teaching Exodus (the life of Moses) in the Bible School. When I arrived in Grimari, I explained the situation to Malepou and asked if it would be possible for us to exchange the teaching of the two Bible books. He quickly answered, "No problem. I taught the book of Ruth recently in another church." So I had a blessed time in teaching some on the life of Moses.

As I sat and listened to Malepou teach the book of Ruth, I knew I was sitting under the training of a gifted teacher. I silently thanked the Lord that He had put it into Vernon's and my hearts to finance most of his seminary school years.

Pastor Malepou and his wife Henriette both graduated with honors. He from the seminary and she from a neighboring Bible school, where she was asked to teach even while attending. They came back to Sibut just after I left to come to the States to stay. He is now the director of the Sibut Bible School and president of more than 400 Baptist churches in our association of churches.

It is the prayer of all of the missionaries to be able to train leaders that can take over the ministry of reaching their own people for Christ.

34 - Jeunesse Evangelique Africaine (Evangelical African Youth)

One day in 1961 Raymond Buck, who was then president of the Central African Republic field council, asked me to be the delegate for Baptist Mid-Missions at a conference that five different missions from the Central African Republic and Tchad were having in Bangui. These missions had a burden to start a youth organization that could be used by many of the African nations whose official language was French. Pastor Pakindji, who had a church near Sibut, went with me. African representatives were part of each mission's delegation. Don Hocking, from the Brethren, became our conference president.

This was the first trip of many that African delegates and I made to different mission stations in both countries. In the beginning the meetings were frequent, but later we had them every eighteen months.

The name of the organization was Jeunesse (Youth) Evangelique (Evangelical) Africaine (African) commonly referred to as JEA. There were two different groups under the umbrella of the JEA: the Flambeaux (Torches) for the boys and the Lumieres (Lights) for the girls. Both groups were subdivided into two age groups: the Little Lights (6-11 age group) and the Lights (12-18). The Lumieres and the Flambeaux had their programs and meetings separately, but both were under the umbrella of the same church committee.

We were thankful for Mr. Young from Chicago, who gave us several large donations, which we used for transportation and for printing literature. The Brethren Press did the printing until it went bankrupt under African leadership. Another person for whom we were thankful was a Swiss, French-speaking missionary lady, Marguerite Cruchet, who was loaned for several years to the JEA from another mission. She was a pleasant worker with gifts as a writer and an artist. She used her abilities to put the content agreed upon at our committee meetings into attractive French manuals for our JEA movement. Each mission would then translate the manuals into the language they spoke.

The manuals included four major "steps" for each group. For example, the Lumiere steps were (English Translations): 1) Searchers of the Lights, 2) Friends of the Lights, 3) Guardians of the Lights, and 4) Carriers of the Lights. As a girl would complete the lessons from the first step she would pass to the next step,

It was a terrific responsibility—not only being on the committee and representing Baptist Mid-Missions, but helping to get the JEA started in different locations in our mission. Before I attempted to conduct the first leadership camp at Sibut, I accepted the hospitality of Don and Betty Hocking at their Brethren station of Mbaike, 200 miles from Sibut. I wanted to see how they put the new program into practice. I worked with them for two weeks to help train twenty-five women to become leaders of the Lumieres.

Before we had our first leadership conference at Sibut, I prayed that there would be no serious medical problems at the clinic. Never before (or since) has the sick ward had so few hospitalized patients as there were when conference time came. The Saturday night before the conference we had two baby deliveries, but there were none during the two weeks the conference lasted until four hours after the last class. What an answer to prayer!

Twenty-eight African women came from different Sibut churches for the conference. My female co-workers on the station gave me a hand doing what they could, as they did each year for the conference. Later, Africans helped to teach the classes and then eventually took over.

What did we teach? The main teaching hour, after the Bible lesson, was "How to Teach a Lesson." Each participant had to give a lesson during the conference. Other classes were on the JEA movement, the work of the JEA church committees, learning the Lumiere songs, moving through the different steps outlined in the manual, how to play games, marching, and a practical lesson on a subject each year, such as elementary sewing, laundry, baby care, Bible, first aid, or homemaking. When participants passed their exams on these subjects, they received badges, each with a picture representing the subject material on it.

Marguerite drew the colorful designs for the badges, and they were then made in Switzerland. The Lumieres sewed their badges onto a red band that was worn over the left shoulder and across the body to the right side. The Flambeaux sewed their badges onto their uniform shirts.

At first, when I taught the class for the laundry badge, I began by asking, "Has the color faded from the dress I have on?"

"No," they would answer.

"Have you seen me wear this dress often?"

"Yes."

"How many years have you seen me wear this dress?"

"Many years."

"Now I want to tell you the simple rule for keeping the color in your

Leaders of the JEA camp with their badges.

clothes. Don't dry them in the sun. Always dry them in the shade. The sun can make your clothes look old in a very short time."

As a result I saw a great improvement, as their clothing remained colorful longer than ever before experienced.

Therese, one of my favorite leaders, had led the Lumieres for years in our Sibut town church. She had earned many badges, one of them the first aid badge. In that class I always taught artificial respiration (as it was known then), for helping those who were rescued from drowning.

One day in the rainy season, shortly after a cloudburst, Therese came to see me and excitedly exclaimed, "The water from the cloudburst quickly filled up the deep ditch that ran beside the road in front of my house. A little girl fell in and was being swept away in the current. A man rescued her, but she wasn't breathing. I remembered what you taught, and I did artificial respiration, and she started breathing. Everybody around us was so excited to see her alive!"

Of course I was thrilled over what Therese had done.

When I left Africa for the last time, Therese was at the airport to see me off. I'll always have the memory of her being there. She had been a vital part of my life in Africa. We had worked and prayed together in our youth groups, camps, rallies, and later, in women's ministry. Now in her advancing years, she lived in Bangui near three of her children.

Therese (right), one of Margery's favorite leaders in JEA, listens as a student recites a Bible verse.

The second year we had our Lumieres conference, missionaries came from two other mission stations to learn about the these groups. They were a great help assisting me with the program.

The Baptist Mid-Missions mission station that had the best group of the JEA was at Bangassou, a town 550 miles from Sibut in the Southeast part of the Central African Republic. Most of this was due to Ruth Nephews's organizational ability. Soon the Africans were able to lead the program on their own. Later Ruth went to Bangui for a year to get the JEA organized in their churches.

The Flambeau leaders' conference also met once a year under the direction of our pastors. At first I always had a lot to do, seeing that they had their literature and exams and helping to purchase food. They had some fun times the last day, when I took them to a wooded area a few miles out, where they sang and goofed off while cutting firewood for their campfire.

For a while we thought a fellow named Jeremie would be the overall leader of the JEA in the Sibut district. Jeremie was the youngest of fourteen children. He was in one of the Israeli agriculture schools in the Central African Republic. He had been a drinking, swearing, bad-tempered fellow, but that was all changed because of the witness of a Christian boy in the bunk next to him. He came to know Christ as his Savior. He came to one of the Flambeaux leaders' training conferences and soon proved to be a capable, likeable, and confident leader.

For a couple of years he would go with me when I went out to churches to work with their youth groups, taking a load of responsibility off my shoulders. My parents paid the bride price of $100, so he and his fiancèe could be married. They entered Bible School, and after graduation he became a pastor of a nearby church. I was so disappointed I could have wept. I had expected that Jeremie and his wife would continue to go with me to the churches to check on their JEA groups. Then I had hopes the churches would vote him as the *Surviellant* of the JEA. However, it is not for another to tell a believer what the Lord's will is for his life.

For several years I went out and checked on the twenty-two groups of Lumieres. In a letter I wrote to my friends at home I said:

> Over the holidays I took the truck and camper and vis-
> ited six different Lumiere groups. I took different Bible
> School couples with me in order to train them in working
> with the youth. It would have been easier if I had taken
> the same couple each time, but in the long run this way
> was better. It was hard for them to tell a simple Bible story
> so it would be interesting, but they had to learn. On New
> Years Day, 126 girls from five nearby churches gathered at
> the mission for a large rally.

Not all of our churches had the JEA program, as they couldn't find qualified leaders. Sometimes the churches couldn't get the vision that today's youth are part of the church today and tomorrow, and they didn't want to spend the money it would take to start a group. In a mission of the Tchad area, 90 percent of their pastors came from the Flambeaux.

Sometimes a church would have a good group going and suddenly half of the group would be gone. This was because of the circumcision rites. Although some of the circumcised girls continued in JEA, most were too ashamed to attend anymore. You can read more about this rite in the June 1997 *Reader's Digest* article entitled "Desert Flower," written by an African woman who is now a model in the States.

What a heartache. The older women in our area kept this rite going by telling the girls they wouldn't be desirable to the men if they didn't go through with it, but one of the main reasons the practice continued was that these grandmothers got paid for each girl they circumcised. The girls in a village used to go as a group and have it done at the same time. After the ceremonial rites, the girls would dress up in grass skirts, naked on top, wearing homemade ankle bracelets that rattled as they danced the whole night and throughout the next day. In the seventies President Bokassa outlawed these rites, but they were still done in secret. It had some old devil-spirit worship connected with it, so the African churches forbade the practice. Many a leader would weep when she realized how many of her girls had this done nevertheless.

One year there were more circumcisions than usual among the girls. These rites depleted many of the Lumiere groups. The devil seemed to be letting loose all of his demons in trying to hurt these girls. It was tragic.

One evening we had an overnight fun-time rally on the station for fifty-six girls who didn't go to the rites. Two nights before the rally, Louvrou and I had stayed up all night (off and on) with a woman in difficult labor. Then we had three deliveries in one half-hour that morning, and we were still busy with our regular clinic work. I was so tired when greeting the girls, but the Lord gave me strength, as He promised. I was so grateful one of the missionary women gave the message. The leaders let the girls talk into all hours of the night and on into the next day. They felt that if the girls in the rites could dance all night, our girls should have a wakeful slumber party. My mind had ceased functioning by that time. One baby who was born two days earlier died during the night, the seventh child to expire of twelve for the mother.

One day we had an all-day training session (as we often did) for eighty-six teenage girls, who worked in their Lumiere books and recited to their leaders what they learned. Early in the afternoon I had to spend time at the clinic, as a Christian teenage girl hospitalized there was dying. My heart was heavy as I walked back to the classroom and told the girls she had died. I gave an impromptu talk on living each day for the Lord because we don't know when He may call us. In prayer different girls asked the Lord to be with the girl's family in their loss and asked Him for help so they themselves would walk closer to Him. We had a precious time together.

A Whimpering Child

It was only a two-hour trip on a fairly good road to our Damara church. Years before, the missionary men had supervised the building of this enclosed cement-block church, a memorial to a faithful member of the Ferd Rosenau's home church.

I received a warm welcome from the two pastors and their wives. Pastor Malimado pastored the Damara church and Pastor Ali pastored a church close by. Pastor Ali was also a *Surviellant* of the JEA for the district. I was looking forward to working together with him for the week, a training time for the future leaders of the Lumieres in that area. The youth committee would also take charge of the meals, housing, and sale of literature—a busy schedule. The aluminum roof radiated the heat of the sun, especially in the dry season, and I was grateful it wasn't too scorching hot for us.

The next morning we registered women from eight different churches. I could see one of them was obviously very pregnant. The first class was a devotional message. We had no nursery for the children, and as I was talking, a toddler in the back started fretting. He whimpered throughout the message and almost continuously throughout the whole day. The sounds echoed throughout the building. It was so disturbing, and the poor mother was almost beside herself, not knowing what to do.

The next morning the baby started fretting again just as I was starting the devotional. I stopped suddenly and said, "How many of you believe God answers prayer?" All hands went up. I quoted a couple of verses on prayer and told them, "We are going to pray that the Lord will quiet this child, for we all know he is bothering both the mother and us. Let us pray."

Before I started praying out loud, I quickly said a short silent prayer, "*Lord, you must answer this prayer.*" Then I prayed out loud, "You know about this child, Lord. You know how he is disrupting our class, and it is difficult for us to concentrate. Please, Lord, stop his crying."

Within a minute the child stopped crying. All the women looked at each other in wonderment. For the rest of the week the toddler didn't disturb our class. I'm sure that one answer to prayer did more for the women's faith in our God than any of the morning devotionals.

On Wednesday morning Henriette, the pregnant woman, was absent. She had begun labor during the night, and a couple of the women and the pastor's wife, Helene, had walked with her the half-mile to the hospital, staying with her until the baby was born. I wondered why they didn't call me to take her down in my truck. Maybe they didn't realize that I often used my truck as an ambulance.

After lunch the women and I walked to the hospital to see the new mom and baby. After talking a few minutes, Helene closed the two doors to the maternity ward and said, "Let us pray." So every mother and the caretakers in that ward heard her prayer as she thanked the Lord for this new life. The next morning Henriette was back with the group, and the women gladly took turns holding the new little one.

It was a good week, but there was one problem that became almost universal in our churches. The churches hadn't given the women enough money to pay for their transportation, their food, and their booklets. So the JEA committee took the money out of the literature fund and used it to buy food. The literature fund was to be paid to me, for I brought the literature from the JEA depot in Sibut. I was burdened. How long would it take for all the churches to really take on the responsibility of being on their own? The Bangassou churches could do it. Why couldn't the ones in Sibut do the same?

Twenty years later I spoke at a women's rally in that same area. The leaders were sitting on a side bench near the front. Right after the service one of the leaders came and introduced herself to me. She told me she was one of the leaders at the Lumieres' conference at Damara so many years ago.

I said, "Do you remember that day when we were having our conference there, how the Lord stopped the whimpering of that toddler?"

She replied, "Do I ever! I will remember it all of my life."

I answered, "I will, also."

Please Come and Help Us

Ten years after we had our first inter-mission JEA meeting, I received a letter from a Tchadian missionary, Gerald Fisher, and their churches, asking me to come and help them get the Lumieres started.

It would all have to be in French. Though I could carry on a conversation in French, I did not feel qualified to teach in it all day for two weeks, and I didn't want to close the clinic, so my answer to them was no. Then another letter arrived with the request repeated. This time, after prayer, I replied I would go and try. Now I knew why I had started to read the Bible through in French that year. Also, my high school class was learning the Navigators' verse memory system in French. I had been reviewing those Bible verses that I had learned twenty years earlier in France. When we made up the JEA manuals, we included those verses as their memory work in the manuals.

Doug Rosenau used some of his summer vacation from Dallas Theological Seminary to teach my Bible School classes in Sibut. I closed the clinic, except for injections, and asked our students John Saboyombo and his wife, Georgette, to go with me. Georgette would help me teach, and John would be able to work at the hospital at Koumra, learning whatever he could.

There had been an outbreak of cholera in Tchad, so before we entered the country, we were all required to have the vaccine injection, including Georgette's baby. At the last minute we took the Koumra Hospital head nurse's daughter, Hannah, with us. I didn't think to ask if she had been vaccinated until we neared the border. She hadn't. We knew Hannah could receive a cholera injection at the Koumra hospital, but what were we to do about getting into Tchad? Pray. We surely didn't want to leave a teenage girl stranded at the border.

When we arrived at the Tchadian border and I got out of the car, the guard blurted out, "Mademoiselle Benedict, Mademoiselle Benedict, I am Pastor Ziba's son who was a student in the Sibut Bible School." So we reminisced for a few minutes, then I showed him the four cholera certificates. He barely looked at them before returning them. We then said *balao* and were on our way. We breathed a sigh of relief and gave thanks to the Lord.

That trip was filled with many unforgettable experiences. It took eighteen hours, but it should have taken twelve. We had a four-hour wait at the rain barrier, but the time was not wasted. We didn't know anyone in the village, but we made contact with some Christians. We asked them to come for a songfest, and we had a great time together singing hymns and learning a new one. We also had the opportunity to talk to several unsaved people.

We had a good two weeks, teaching eighteen women from three different mission stations in Tchad. They represented different tribes, and French was their common language. There was also a new missionary there who had just arrived from French language study in France. The Lord brought her to us at just the right time. She was a great help, for she gave the Bible devotional each day.

The trip home was something else! We took a short cut on one eighty-mile section of road. The customs men had said the road "wasn't bad at all." It wasn't for the first forty miles. We could go twenty-five miles an hour. But the last fifty-five miles! Rocks! Gullies! Water holes! We even had to fill a gully at one point before we could cross it. By the time we arrived at Kaga-Bondoro, three hours from Sibut, I was so tense I didn't see how we could make it the rest of the way, but we did! We were so thankful for God's care. And, miracle of miracles, we didn't have a flat tire. The car did have to be fixed two days later, but the Lord saw us home. I was so glad the Lord had given me a shove to go, for it was worth it.

An Annual JEA Meeting

One of our annual inter-mission JEA committee meetings was scheduled for Sarh, Tchad. Don and Betty Teachout, two African pastors, and I made the trip there in my truck. We had to show our passports in thirteen different places during the 400 miles from the Central African Republic border to the city of Sarh, Tchad. As usual it was a time of discussing programs, literature, and other aspects of the JEA movement.

On our way back, when we arrived at the border, we had to wait two hours for the customs official, so I decided to take a walk. During my walk, I met a good-looking young *gendarme* in front of one of the houses.

Without hesitation he put out his hand to greet me with a smile and said, "*Balao*. Where are you from?"

I immediately replied, "I am from Sibut, and the other missionaries are from Bambari. We have been in Sarh, Tchad for a youth conference, and are on our way back."

With an astonished expression on his face, he said, "My name is David, and I'm sure you must know my brother Daniel Lafindema, who is a Bible School student in your school."

Then it was my turn to be astonished. I answered, "Oh yes, I know him well. I'm the nurse there, so I take care of the students' illnesses, and I also teach in the Bible School."

Daniel was from Bangui and was considered different from any student we ever had in that he was considered prosperous because he owned two trucks. We talked about Daniel and the school, and soon we were talking about spiritual things. I do not remember who first brought up the subject.

I was surprised to hear him say, "I am not a believer like my brother. I'm a sinful man, and I am tired of my way of life."

By that time we were sitting under a shade tree by his house. I took my French New Testament and explained to him how his heart could be changed. When I knew he was ready to believe, I took him to where my truck was parked so Don Teachout could talk to him man-to-man. I had never before encountered anyone whom the Holy Spirit had so prepared to believe. Praise the Lord!

As Don was talking with David, I continued my walk and found a soldier who was reading a thick French book of Mao's sayings. I had never before seen one. He had obtained the book when he was on a trip to

China. I had the opportunity to tell him there was a better way of life than Mao's way. He was very interested, but I didn't feel led to press him for a decision. He needed time for the Holy Spirit to make the verses of the New Testament speak to him. He asked me if I would give him my New Testament so he could continue to read it. I was never happier in my life to be giving one away.

When the custom official finally came and we were given permission to continue our journey, David said to me, "Don't forget to tell my brother that I'm a believer now." I was more than happy to relay those most important words.

At each stop along the way, tracts and Gospels of John were given out. We were tired when we arrived home but ever so thankful once more for God's care and for the opportunity of giving out the Good News

In the Central African Republic and Tchad there are over 10,000 youth in the JEA. Our prayer is not for this organization to be a show of how many badges they can have on their uniforms, but rather to have leaders to lead the children and youth to the Lord and teach them to live godly lives for Him.

35 - Vacation Bible Schools

"Mademoiselle, I would like to have Vacation Bible School in two of my churches, but I do not know how to do it. Would you come and show us?"

I had held many Vacation Bible Schools in different churches, but I would go only if the pastor and at least two of his leaders attended. Two or three experienced helpers would always go with me.

I hesitated in answering Pastor Dabourmou, but then I said, "Pastor, you know the last thirty miles of the road going to your area are becoming almost impossible to travel in my low Toyota truck."

"But if you come in dry season, you could make it, really you could. We would be praying for you."

I couldn't resist his fervent pleas, so I replied, "Okay, I'll plan on Christmas vacation, for then we will be two months into the dry season."

He left very pleased, saying as he departed, "Remember now, we'll be praying for you."

For many years I had the joy of spending the week between Christmas and New Years in one or more of our forty churches. We might have a camp for the girls, Vacation Bible School, or a music camp.

I have vivid memories of the trip to Ndengou that December of 1982. It was my second and last trip to our farthest church, which was one hundred miles from Sibut by the Ubangui River, which separated the Central African Republic from Zaire. At that time Pastor Daboumrou had the responsibility of pastoring four churches along the river.

As the month of December rolled around that year, I began to anticipate the privilege of going to Ndengou, remembering Pastor Daboumrou's words, "We'll be praying for you." The week before Christmas was a busy one. Besides the medical work, I had two student parties (one for fifty-five high school students and one for junior-age kids). I also had a waffle dinner for three homesick Peace Corps workers and the missionary Christmas Eve dinner, which is always a festive time.

Early Christmas morning a helper and I finished packing the custom-made camper shell on the back of my pickup. Items packed included a folding camp cot with a mattress, three grass mats (two for my helpers and one for the floor beside my cot), two folding tables, two folding chairs, and two hurricane lanterns, along with three liters of kerosene (kerosene makes a nice hostess gift). There was also a metal barrel filled with my accordion, two soccer balls, tennis balls (for the small kids to kick), four jump ropes, Frisbees, and my Vacation Bible School supplies. Lastly we packed a metal footlocker with my personal things and my doctor's bag, which had been given to me by a doctor's wife in Seattle whose husband had passed away.

It was 9 a.m. when I left my hilltop residence to pick up my helpers, two twenty-year-old high school graduates, Dieudonne and Komesse, and a teenage girl who was going to visit her parents. We spent time in prayer as we began our journey. We knew we needed the Lord's protection as we traveled. After spending most of the day driving through tall grass, dodging rock-like ant hills, going up and down rocky landslides, and dodging gullies, we finally arrived, breathing a sigh of relief. We all said, "*Merci na, Nzapa* [Thank you, Lord]."

Pastor Daboumrou greeted us with a hearty handshake, and his booming voice rang out: "*Balao, balao.* We knew you would make it; we were praying for you." They showed me their small living room, with its uneven mud floor, and said, "This is where you will stay."

It was a little difficult finding an even place for my table and cot, but I made do. His wife, Yasika, had also given us a warm welcome. She was a good hostess and always saw that I had one meal a day and a bucket of warm water to bathe with each evening. For the two other meals I fixed simple things I had brought with me, like homemade granola for breakfast and a sandwich for supper. It was easier for them and for me.

That evening we had our planning session with Dieudonne, Komesse, a couple of older youth from the church, and Pastor Dabourmou. I explained to them how we always started with a picture to color so the kids would come on time. They had never colored before, and they would run pell-mell to get there, to have the time of their lives. For the sake of the two church workers, I showed them what a box of crayons looked like and one of the pictures to be colored, one that went with the lesson of the day—we would be teaching five lessons on Elijah. I cautioned them, "Be sure to watch out for stealing, especially as they trade the crayons among themselves. It is so easy to break one in half and hide it."

I explained that after coloring time we would have singing, scripture memorization, the Bible lesson, recess, and an illustrated biography of John Patan (a Scottish man who in 1858 went as a missionary to a group of South Pacific islands 1200 miles northeast of Australia). Then we would have a count of who was there and how many new kids they had brought with them. The few that could read and write would receive a worksheet on the lesson and the memory verse for the day.

I could see the excitement mounting on their faces as I talked. I continued, "Dieudonne and Komesse will be in charge of most of the activities the first day, so the rest of you can see how things can be done."

The last day of Vacation Bible School was always an exciting and difficult time. We had oral contests about the Bible story and the missionary story, listened to memory verses, and recognized those who had brought the most children. Our prizes were a Bible, New Testament, songbook, and gifts such as marbles, jewelry, calendar pictures, little cars, and used clothing. I

Children who had never colored before ... coloring their first pictures.

brought the small prizes back with me when I returned from furlough, many from children in Vacation Bible School programs that I had participated in. As we were giving away the prizes, I often wished that the people at home could have some of the pleasure we were experiencing when we saw the joy on the faces of the children receiving their prizes.

The six sessions of the first three days passed quickly, and seven children came to know the Lord. The children were fascinated with the biography of John Patan, the first missionary story they had ever heard. They sat quietly as they listened and saw the pictures that portrayed his life.

After we finished our first Vacation Bible School, we packed at daybreak the next morning in order to be on time for the first session in the village of Ndengou, ten miles away. There I stayed in a three-room, thatched-roof guesthouse with a mud floor. I so enjoyed my stay there! Each morning I slipped out to enjoy devotions while sitting on a rock on the riverbank. Across the river in Zaire I could see the tall, stately palm trees with their hard, round, dark orange nuts hanging in clusters from the branches. I could see fisherman who had come out in their canoes early and sometimes a lone young boy having fun in his.

Since the church in that village had burned down three weeks earlier, the Pastor had received permission to have Vacation Bible School in the run-down government school building. It had a cement floor and some broken-down benches, but it was better than the previous church building had been.

Twelve children came to know the Lord at Ndengou, and everyone had such a good time. The children and youth played enthusiastically with everything I had brought. Since we were meeting in a schoolhouse, there

The Bible School children and leaders at Dengou.

was a large playing field for the children to enjoy. Dieudonne and Komesse had such fun showing them how to throw a Frisbee, and once they learned how, it was difficult for them to stop. They not only played at recess but also after the morning session, if they didn't have to go home right away. (The Africans usually don't have a definite time to eat. They fix a meal when food is available and they have time to prepare it.)

Between morning and afternoon sessions, there were people who needed sores bandaged, eye salve applied, or a tooth pulled, or needed to be provided with medicine for babies with malaria, colds, or other ailments. I was glad that Dieudonne's constant attempt to play tunes on my accordion didn't bother me too much. I did ask him, however, to stop during siesta time.

When Saturday evening came, we were all tired, but it was amazing how the Lord gave us strength for the things that needed to be accomplished. We woke up refreshed for Sunday morning, and about 175 of us met for worship under the mango trees. In all the churches the children's Sunday School classes are held under the trees because the chapels only have one large area. When it came time for the offering, the congregation sang hymns. As they sang, people went up front to put their offerings into a small metal can that was on a table, first the women, then the men and children.

After the offering, the deacon gave the announcements, saying, "Now you all know we do not have a church to meet in since ours burned down three weeks ago. You men know what to do. Go down to the river, cut the bamboo poles, and bring them here. We need a lot of them. Women, your job is to cut and bring in the bundles of elephant grass for the roof. Don't delay doing this. You know this is the season for fires, and if you don't bring it in soon, it will be too late. Next Sunday we want to see the materials here that we need for our new chapel."

Bamboo was plentiful along the river. It grew straight and tall there and was ideal for use as the underneath framework of a house or church. It was a pleasure to sit in a church and look up to see these long, even poles overhead. In other places people had to use uneven, knotty poles.

The Ndengou Church hadn't had a missionary visit them in almost twenty years, so I was glad to talk to them during the message time. After the meeting, someone had prepared a meal of chicken with sauce, rice, and bananas for us. Delicious! They really do know how to flavor their chicken-and-sauce dish.

For that afternoon the pastor had arranged for us to go for another service to the village of Mbolobolo, five miles from Ndengou. This church, which had never had a regular pastor, was situated in one of the most picturesque settings I had ever seen in Africa, with palm trees and flowering bushes attractively planted around the chapel. The church was packed inside and out, with 345 people in attendance. Many mothers with babies and toddlers were sitting on their stools outside. There were four chiefs of nearby villages sitting together on the back row. The government made it easy to recognize the chiefs by requiring them to wear a badge denoting their authority. My heart was overflowing as I spoke to them on how great is the God whom we serve.

It was late when my helpers and I got into our truck to leave for Ndengou. As usual, many people asked for rides home. But what can you do when you only have a small, half-ton truck? This is the time when missionaries have to ask the Lord for patience. Many look up pleadingly, saying, "Just me, Mademoiselle, just me." But just me can turn out to be twenty people. I did take a few older people and a couple of mothers with toddlers, and we arrived back at Ndengou at dusk.

Many times during that week I contemplated the trouble we might face on the road going home. *Would we make it? If we didn't, what would happen to us in this out-of-the-way place, where a truck travels these roads only once a month?* But I realized that it was the enemy (Satan) bringing those thoughts to my mind. So I told the Lord all about it. "Father, these thoughts are not of You, and I reject them in the name of Jesus." I again claimed the promises in Philippians 4:6-7. "Don't worry about anything; instead, pray about everything. Tell God what you need, and thank him for all he has done. If you do this, you will experience God's peace, which is far more wonderful than the human mind can understand. His peace will guard your hearts and minds as you live in Christ Jesus" (NLT). And I had peace.

Early the next morning there were many people helping me pack up the truck. It was hard to leave. Precious friendships are made in a short time. I knew I would never see them again, for in a few years' time the road would be impassable. The people crowded around us as we stood by the truck, ready to say good-bye. The kids kept shaking hands with Dieudonne and Komesse until the pastor said, "Let us pray." We all thanked the Lord for letting us come and asked for His protection on our journey home.

The Lord gave us a safe journey that New Year's Day. The petitions, "Remember now, we will be praying for you," were answered. I was exhausted, but just as when returning from similar trips, my heart was overwhelmed with wonderment and the love of God. I thought to myself, *Why should I be so fortunate to have this privilege of going out to people who love Him and those He loves in return?* Truly there is joy in the Lord's service that cannot be described.

In 1993, when my brother, Paul, came to Africa to show *The Jesus Film,* the last thirty miles of the road were impassable for any truck. An African pastor arranged for Paul and his team of three Africans to go by canoe to Ndengou. The canoe was thirty feet long, five feet wide, and capable of hauling two tons. It took five rowers to go the thirty miles, and it was a ten-day journey, stopping two nights each at five churches along the way. Since the people had never seen a film, two nights were necessary for them to grasp the meaning of this wonderful message. It was a trip that Paul and his team will never forget!

Choosing the Right Helpers

I prayed, "Lord, show me which student couple you want me to take to the Poumayasse Church when I go for Vacation Bible School."

The Lord impressed on my mind to take Djibrine and his wife, Louise, who were from N'dele, an area in the northern region of the country. This didn't exactly please me, because he was one of the few students in my years of teaching that always disturbed my class. Nevertheless, I asked them if they would go with me. They said yes, as I knew they would. Coming from far away, they couldn't travel back to their home village during vacation time. This was a chance for them to do something different. They would have a ministry learning how to work with the children. The Lord gave us a great time as we worked together.

We had some serious talks around the campfire in the evenings. One evening I approached them about the subject that had been on my heart. "Djibrine, I don't need to tell you about your behavior in school this last year. Do you think you were being a testimony for the Lord acting that way? You told me your younger brother is entering school next year. Don't you want to be a role model for him?"

He quickly responded, "I do want to change my ways."

The next school year he did. The last day of school the following year he said to me in class in front of the whole student body, which included his younger brother, "Mademoiselle, I've been good this year, haven't I?"

He almost reminded me of a six-year-old as he looked up at me with his hands folded on his desk. I could hardly keep from laughing, but I answered his question with gusto, "You sure have, Djibrine. You sure have." I was so happy I had obeyed the Lord and taken him and his wife with me.

Sixteen Miles a Day - Mala Church

When we went to the Mala church, ninety miles from Sibut, I took two high school graduates with me. One was Dennis Zemio, our station pastor's son. We had Vacation Bible School at two churches. On the last day, Eme, a twelve-year-old boy in our first school, cried when he didn't win a New Testament. I so wanted to give him one, but how could I do that and not give all of the children one? I did not have enough to give one to every child.

We went on to the second school, held at the Komo church, about eight miles from Mala. Imagine our surprise to see Eme sitting with the group of children. He came all three days, for the six sessions, walking the eight miles to and from home. It was dark by the time he arrived back at his village each evening. Oh, how I wanted him to win a New Testament, and he did! He had a grin from ear to ear as he accepted the Testament. In a group of fifty children in our out-station churches, maybe one owned a New Testament.

Another time, on the last day of Vacation Bible School at our Ndokindji church, Marie, a small girl about thirteen years of age, was first in every contest. She won a New Testament and a songbook. I couldn't help but notice that she wore the same ragged dress every day. I was surprised when I discovered that among the few used clothes I had brought with me, there was a dress that would fit her. My heart was filled with thankfulness to the Lord as I realized how He led me to put in "just the right dress." He knew there was a child of His in our church at Ndokindji who needed it. As she looked at the dress, and then up at me with a shy sweet smile on her face, she said, "*Merci, mingui* [thanks very much]."

Harold and Faith Dark, who lived in Bangui during the later years of their missionary career, made our Vacation Bible Schools possible. Faith wrote lessons on some Old Testament characters. She then searched for pictures from children's coloring books to go with the stories she had written. She did an excellent job! Harold had a small printing press in his home and was able to print thousands of the lessons and pictures for us to use.

With the help of the director of our Bible School, we saw that each of our students participated in one or two Vacation Bible Schools, so when they went out as pastors, they would know how to conduct one. The Bible School students went to the nearby churches for an afternoon Vacation Bible School after their morning classes. Several Christian teachers directed one in their area churches. It was always a blessing to see more Christians get involved in nurturing children in their relationship with Jesus.

A Terrific Week

In the rainy season of June 1977 four senior-high school students and I traveled 120 miles from Sibut to conduct Vacation Bible School in three churches. These students had helped me before, and I knew they were capable of directing one on their own.

After traveling several hours, we stopped at the Bozo church, and I introduced the two students who were going to conduct their school to Pastor Moussa. They had their materials plus a mat, soccer ball, jumping rope, and Frisbees. We all had prayer, and then the other two students and I traveled fifteen miles further to the Bobombo church, which didn't have a pastor. After we had prayer there, I left them with the church people who had arrived and I went ten miles further to the large Boban church.

The Boban village was 75 percent Christian. I didn't have any students to help me, so I was counting on the pastor and his son. I was told that fifteen high school students from the village were home from Bangui for their summer vacation. It was very rare to have that many high school students from one village, and they were all eager to help. Part of our planning meeting was deciding who would do what.

We had one session in the afternoon each day for one week. I took this terrific opportunity to have special classes with the high school students morning and evening. I was in my glory. I had brought five Christian books in French with me, and they were all very eager to read them. When I left, I gave the books to the church so they could start a small library.

The Bible story that week was about the Joseph who wore the coat of many colors. The pastor, who had been out of school for many years, taught the lesson on Thursday. I wondered if he had even read the lesson beforehand, for he got the story all mixed up. I was shocked. I glanced over at the high school kids to see what they thought of it. I was thankful that I couldn't tell from the expression on their faces that they knew their pastor was botching the story.

On the third day it rained all morning and was still raining at 2 p.m. In half an hour it would be time to start classes. I really prayed that the rain would stop. At 2:15 it was still pouring.

I can still remember opening the door and standing there looking at the rain pouring down in buckets, praying, "Lord, we are here doing your work. We need an immediate answer. You said in your Word that 'whatever ye shall ask in my name, that will I do' [John 14:13]. So I'm asking this in Your name. Please stop this rain now." Wow! He did! What a miracle!

The kids started running out of their houses and raced for the chapel. When we were all settled in, the rain that the Lord had held back for fifteen minutes again let loose. The kids did not have raincoats or umbrellas, and if they had come during the rain, their clothes would have been soaked. How miserable they would have been.

The wind blew right into the chapel, which was not enclosed. Beside the thatched roof chapel were four cement pillars that were waiting for wood and aluminum for the roof. The Christians had been praying for a permanent chapel. Later my parents, through sacrificial giving, supplied this need.

When the five days ended, I was so happy for the wonderful week the Lord had given us.

On the way back, when I picked up the four high school helpers from their churches, one of them exclaimed right off, "Mademoiselle, the Lord stopped the rain many times, so we could have class."

Another one went on to repeat what a junior-high boy had told him: "It has been an eye-opener for us to see you fellows come to help us. You love the Lord so much and have such knowledge of the Word. I want to be like you."

Dennis said to me, "I never knew I could have so much joy as when that boy spoke those words. It puts a real responsibility on us, doesn't it, to keep our way straight because people are watching us."

So the high school students, as well as the Vacation Bible School kids, grew in the Lord. God's word says just that in Proverbs 11:25: "And he who waters will also be watered himself" (NKJV).

This is a translation of a note I received after I sent three young men to the Koyamba church, twenty-five miles from Sibut, to have Vacation Bible School:

> Thank you for the three young men that you sent here
> to have a VBS. They gave us much joy in how they
> worked with the children and the lessons they taught.
> Therefore, if God keeps Mademoiselle in the year 1984,
> we want her to send them back to us again to have anoth-
> er one. We will give you many thanks. We are asking God
> to always keep Mademoiselle so she can work among us.
> Many greetings in the name of Jesus.
>
> > *Diacre* [Deacon] Mafouta Gabriel
> > and Pasteur Kakobanga Louis

After receiving this note, I realized that they didn't understand that I sent the young men out there to show the church people how to have Vacation Bible School. Then, if they wanted to have one the next year, I would send them the materials and they could do it themselves.

It was an enjoyable time going to the different churches in the years from 1975 to 1983. After that the churches were on their own. Before each summer the pastors who wanted to have Vacation Bible School would send me word and I would make up the packets of materials to help them with their teaching.

Some summers there were eighteen such schools going on among our forty churches. I loved to see the children learn the Bible stories and know the history of some of the pioneer missionaries.

Through the years many young people came to know the Lord. One deacon, Joshua, wrote to me saying that there were fourteen teenagers who came to the Lord the week of their Vacation Bible School.

36 - Bible Classes in Government Schools

"Mademoiselle, will you lend me the picture roll of the birth of Christ?"

Charles, the eighteen-year-old high school student standing before me now, was the son of Andre Komesse. Andre had passed away six years earlier but previously had worked at the clinic with me for fifteen years.

"I have written to the principal of a government school two miles from Sibut, asking him if six of us high school students could take turns having Bible classes in his school. He has now given us permission to do so."

I was thrilled with his request. Of course I gave him the picture roll, so he and the other students could use it in their Bible classes.

When I saw Charles later, I asked, "How are the classes coming along?"

With a huge grin on his face he answered, "Last week we had 105 children from the first to the sixth grades. The teacher stays in the room and helps us keep order."

Two years later I received a letter from Charles, now in Bangui, where he was continuing his schooling. He had another request (I loved the kind of requests he made). Translated it reads:

> When I was in your high school Sunday School class at
> Sibut, you had a Russian New Testament that you gave to the
> Russian high school teacher there. I have a Russian professor
> here, and I have talked to him about Christ. He told me that in
> his country they do not talk about God. Right away I thought
> of that Russian New Testament you had and wondered if you
> had another one. I remember that you had in your library the
> book Marie et Sa Bible [Mary and Her Bible] and that it had
> John 3:16 in it in Russian. I borrowed one like it here, and
> that is the only verse I am able to give to our professor in his
> language. So, if you still have a Russian New Testament, I can
> get it when I come to Sibut next month.

He closed his letter:

> I don't have any more words to say, but I ask you to
> pray for us in our studies, and for us to resist temptation.
> There are lots of ways here to tempt the youth. I greet you
> and Mademoiselle Florence in the name of Jesus.

I was so sorry to have to write to him that I didn't have a Russian New Testament. I was glad he loved the Lord and wasn't afraid to witness to his professor.

In the late '60s we started having Bible classes in the government schools. The law stated each class could have an hour a week in religious education. What an opportunity! Bob Bixby and Loie Knight, missionaries on our mission station, taught a couple of classes each week, as did some of our Bible students and two area pastors. Though French was the language of the school, the classes were taught in Sango.

We used the picture rolls a lot with the school classes. Each roll contained about twenty 23x36-inch pictures. There were three Old Testament rolls and two New Testament ones. I also had twenty-one 14x10-inch picture cards illustrating different stories. The children never got tired of seeing these visual aids. When I left, I gave these items to our Bible School library. My prayer is they are still being used.

One Monday morning the director of the town school took me to my first class. I could hardly believe my eyes when I saw 179 first-graders waiting. Can you imagine one person teaching that many children at one time? About all I was able to teach was John 3:16 and a song with twelve lines.

The following week I was hoping there would be fewer children, but, alas, word must have spread, for I had 201! I took my problem to two other missionaries. Wilma and Florence said they would take the class and divide it into one hundred each. I was so glad I no longer had a Monday-morning class, for I was needed at the clinic on our busiest day.

I did take two other classes, one of eighty third-graders and one of fifty-five fifth-graders. With all of us teaching, we figured we reached 800 schoolchildren a week. It was a wonderful opportunity, but it sure kept me hopping.

One of our problems in this program was that many pastors weren't faithful in their responsibilities for it. The teachers would come to me and say, "The children are waiting in the classroom for their scheduled Bible time class. Where are the teachers?" We truly prayed that the pastors would see the classes as an important ministry, or that someone in their churches would accept this wonderful responsibility.

The greatest need all of us have is faithfulness to our responsibilities. *Dependability is the greatest ability.* Though this is not a Bible quotation, we know that it dwarfs all other qualities when it comes to preparing for leadership.

When I returned from furlough in 1975, all the classes I taught were at 11 a.m. One was in a school near the mission. The classroom building had a thatched roof, typical for most village schools, with a division wall that didn't go to the ceiling. I could plainly hear the other teacher over the partition wall, and I knew that teacher could also hear what I was saying. This hampered me, especially with the singing and teaching of verses, but we made do.

Many children accepted Christ as their Savior, and as a result the churches had an increase of children. The children always marched in from the outside, where they had the Sunday School classes under the trees. There was always a deacon available to see that the benches were filled in an orderly way. If a child came into church late and couldn't see a place to sit, he would go to the middle of a bench and squeeze in. This caused the child on the end to fall off the bench, and he would then have to go to the back behind the adults. This wasn't fair, but it seemed to be a cultural thing. If a child didn't want to be bumped off the bench, it was safest to sit in the middle.

My heart ached for all the churches in our district to seize this opportunity for reaching souls in the schools in their villages. Pastor Doguet was one that truly did. He had four classes a week in the schools, and sixty-eight children became believers. Two had been of the Muslim faith. The father of one of the boys beat his child and said he didn't want him ever to go again to the pastor's class. During Pastor Doguet's time three school teachers were saved, and he had a class especially for them. He really used his gifts of evangelism and teaching. He built that church for 600 people. There were too many for the inside, so people sat on stools outside.

The previous pastor had been asked to leave because he and his wife couldn't control their wayward teenage daughter. When she became pregnant with her second child, he and the deacons of the church said, "Enough!" They knew the Bible passage in I Timothy 3:4 giving the qualifications of a pastor. "He must manage his own family well and see that his children obey him with proper respect" (NIV).

There were eighteen school teachers in the district that were having Bible classes with their own pupils. I look back on those classes as some of the greatest times in my life, and only eternity will reveal their fruit. In the late '80s I had to stop going to the school classes. There were so few missionaries that we no longer had the resources for this ministry. How I longed for the churches to continue it.

37 - Do You Have Something to Read?

"Mademoiselle, could I talk with you sometime?"

The voice behind me spoke as I stood one Saturday morning at a gas station, holding the gasoline hose for the African who was pumping gas into my car. Don't visualize a gas station like those in the United States. Most stations over there have three tanks, one each for gasoline, kerosene, and diesel fuel. When a vehicle pulls up to one of these tanks, the station attendant attaches a two-foot metal handle to the pump. The driver of the vehicle holds the nozzle in the gas tank, and the attendant pumps the fuel through the hose by pushing the handle back and forth.

When I turned around, I saw Jean Louis, the postmaster of Sibut. I told him I had to go through town that afternoon on my way to a girls' meeting and could stop in to see him on my way back.

That evening Yangakola, a student, and I returned to visit with Jean Louis. He had been reading my library books for quite some time, and he started the conversation.

"As you know, I have been reading your books for over a year, and they have really spoken to me. I realize that God has power. Recently I wanted to test God's power. I opened my Bible [given to him by a pastor in another town], and there was a verse saying nothing is impossible with God [Luke 1:37]. I then asked God to take away my desire for smoking, and you know, I haven't smoked since that day."

Jean Louis had an expression of awe on his face while he was saying this. I talked to him about the Lord Jesus, who was all-powerful, and he accepted Christ as his Savior. The Holy Spirit had prepared him. Soon I started him on our Bible correspondence course. Moreover, on Monday I returned and talked with his wife, and she was also saved. Jean Louis and I both rejoiced, as another lost sheep had found its Shepherd.

Books were scarce in the Central African Republic. My heart ached to know a child could go all the way through school and never own or read a book. The children would copy everything from a blackboard into small notebooks and memorize the copied notes. Even if they could afford to buy a textbook, very few were ever available. This sad situation remains today.

I realized this early in my ministry, so I bought many French books, including Christian biographies, Bible storybooks, and books by Billy Graham and other Christian writers. I carried a suitcase of books with me as I went around to the schools for classes. The teachers always enjoyed browsing through my "library," and they could choose which books they wanted to read. I also stopped off at the post office and police station, so the men there could have a choice of books to read.

I even had a library for the high school students. It was very popular. Many books were never returned, and the excuses I heard when students came back empty-handed were lame. The only consolation was that the books would then be stolen from the first stealers and the cycle would go on and on. Books would be read by many people who otherwise would never have had an opportunity to read them.

I also had small libraries in twelve of our churches, and I had books at the clinic office too, to lend to patients or their caregivers. I often wished it could have been more. As it was, the people who came in always said yes when I asked them if they would like a book to read. It was difficult for them to have nothing to do hour after hour, day after day. (I also kept simple puzzles at the clinic, and people would spend hours assembling them.) Several came to the Lord or were strengthened in their faith through this book ministry.

One of the teachers who read books out of my suitcase library was Ngaibou. Two years after he started reading them, we hospitalized his very ill baby at the clinic. I loaned him Jim Vaus's autobiography, which tells how Vaus came out of organized crime and "walked the sawdust trail" to repent in the first of Billy Graham's campaigns.

The Holy Spirit was working in Ngaibou's heart. Whenever I greeted him as I made rounds, he would tell me, "This book is so good." One day I asked him if he had had Jim Vaus's experience of really believing on the Lord and having a changed life. He quickly replied that he had not. I

Government teachers check out books from Margery's "portable library".

promptly got our French Bible, and we went over a lot of verses together. Two days later he believed, and all of my staff rejoiced.

One summer vacation three visiting high school boys came to the clinic. On their third visit I asked them if they would like some books to read. This was just like putting candy before a child; they each took a book. Then they borrowed each other's before returning them to me.

The Lord was speaking to their hearts. When I asked them if they would like to come to the Saturday night meeting for high school kids, two came. (The third one had left town.) Jeremie, who helped me in the Saturday Club, led these two fellows to Christ. What a blessing it was to hear their testimonies the next morning when they came to Sunday School. Surely there is no greater joy than seeing one turn from darkness to the light that is the Lord Jesus.

One day at the clinic a school teacher said to me, "I want to talk with you." My main nurse, John, had been used of the Lord to bring this teacher back into fellowship with Christ. He was weak and almost ill from alcohol withdrawal. He wanted to tell me his story to make sure I would pray for him. Then he asked if I had anything he could read, and I gave him the booklet *The Daily Bread*.

The day I heard that this devotional booklet was published in French, I could have shouted a hundred hallelujahs. *The Daily Bread* is put out by the Radio Bible Class. Each trimester I ordered forty of them from Quebec, Canada. I gave them regularly to thirty people and reserved the other ten for people like the teacher at the clinic who wanted something to read.

Once when I was in Bangui, Lucien, one of my former students who was now a *gendarme*, was riding in the back of a *gendarme* truck. He spotted my white truck with the Red Cross on it and told the driver to stop. He quickly got out, dodging cars to cross the street to wave me down.

He didn't even take time to say hello before he said, "I didn't receive the last booklet of *The Daily Bread*. Do you have one here?"

I could have given out thousands of these booklets, and they would have been read over and over again. There was so much demand from African countries for these booklets that Quebec had to start charging for them. They eventually put a whole year's readings into one book and charged ten United States dollars each. I ordered forty my last two years in Africa.

Three years after I returned to the States for good, I heard that a retired missionary working with international people in Washington, D.C. bought the back issues for half price. When I read this, I made a phone call to Quebec. Glory to God! After talking to them and explaining that I wanted to send the books to Africa, they let me have four years' worth, 800 outdated copies, for $1.00 each, which I gladly had shipped to the Central African Republic. Never was $800 spent more wisely.

Some of our older pastors didn't read French very well, so I picked out forty-three *The Daily Bread* devotionals for inclusion in a booklet we could distribute and translated them into Sango. Clara DeRosset typed them up, and a friend in the United States, Doris Ferguson, had 5,000 booklets printed.

When the rewards are given out in heaven, I'm sure a Frenchman, Pasteur Kries, will receive a big one. Over the span of twenty years he sent me about seventy-five shoeboxes of Christian literature. He bought thousands of tracts and collected outdated Christian pamphlets, booklets, and magazines from others. He knew how many pastors we had and how many students there were in our Bible School. He would put five good tracts for Christian growth or evangelism in an envelope for each one so I could easily distribute them. If there was one tract I felt was especially beneficial, I would ask for more. Once I remember asking him for 2,000 tracts by George Muller on "How to Know the Lord's Will for My Life."

I received many thanks from our Africans for the literature and how much it meant to them. I wish Pasteur Kries could have had the joy of giving out some of the literature and receiving their thanks, but that will have to wait for the trumpet call.

Loie Knight also received some literature from him. When we went home together on furlough in 1989, we stopped off in Mulhouse, in northeastern France, to visit Pasteur Kries and his sweet wife. I'll never forget carrying all our luggage up five flights of steps to get to their flat. Loie had an extra small suitcase filled with papers she intended to translate while at home.

Literature sent from France by Pasteur Kries.

Her arm gave out two flights up, and I ended up carrying the suitcases the rest of the way. Mrs. Kries had recently had heart surgery, and her husband was a little man about five feet tall, so they couldn't be much help to us.

We had a delightful visit. They showed us around their town, their church, and their small garden outside the city. They were so pleased that we would stop by and see them. Loie and I were delighted that we could thank this couple in person for what they were doing for the Lord's work in the Central African Republic.

By the time we had left the Kries family in Mulhouse, crossed the English Channel, and arrived in London by the boat train, I had become too exhausted to carry all of the my luggage. There were no carts available except those reserved for a tourist group. I finally had to put one of my suitcases on the floor and push it along with my foot. Later an Asian man, a member of the tourist group, looked at Loie and me and said, "Take my cart." To this day I think of him as an angel sent to us by the Lord in our desperate need.

When our first automated press arrived at Sibut, it was a marvel in the eyes of the Africans. As one pastor watched the printed pages roll off the press, he looked at Eugene and said, "Monsieur Eugene, did a white man really think of how to make this machine, or did God give it to him in a dream?"

Eugene was our first printer in Sibut. Then there was Bob Owen, followed by Lynn Muhr, who spent twenty years with this ministry. Also, Harold Dark in Bangui did a lot of printing for our station. A large print building was erected down the hill in 1960, and an addition was made in 1980.

Over 100,000 volumes of song books (words only) have been printed at Sibut and in America. Over 50,000 Sango Bibles were printed by the British and Foreign Bible Society and have been sold from our Sibut print shop. During the last twenty years there have been approximately 1,000 Bibles sold every year.

I remember some of the first years after I came to the field, when many times the language committee would meet at Sibut to work on translating the Old Testament into our Sango language. A vital member of the committee was Clara Crumb (later to become Clara DeRosset), who stayed with me. She could type twelve offset stencils without a mistake, and it was almost beyond my imagination how she could be so fast and accurate. Eugene Rosenau wrote this about her:

> For many years Clara mimeographed many of the
> materials used in the Sunday Schools and Bible classes in the
> churches of our country. Her perfection as a typist was
> evident in the printer's copy of the Sango Bible, concordance,

dictionary, and other major works. The Bible Society said of her work on the Sango Bible, "We have never received a more perfect typescript of a Bible." The printer of our Sango concordance said, "If she did that on an old IBM typewriter, she can name her machine and her wage and start working here next week." But Clara worked for her Lord, not for earthly gain nor for applause or praise.

Several Africans worked in the print press building over the years, but Kilas worked there the longest. He was one of the nicest men Africa ever produced. Lynn Muhr, our last foreign printer, left in 1999, but Kilas is still there printing and selling literature. He always greeted everyone with a big smile.

Once when I went in for something, he said, "We had our eighth girl last night."

After he told me her name I asked him in fun, "Can you name all your girls?"

"Sure I can," he responded and proceeded to do so. But he could only remember seven of them.

If Africans could blush, he would have, but I quickly said, "That's all right; we all forget names."

His wife, Marie, was also one of the sweetest women I knew. She worked with the teenage girls in the Lumieres for many years. After I retired, I heard that Kilas and Marie had had a baby boy. I'm sure he is spoiled with so many sisters to wait on him.

Polly Strong is still producing teaching materials and selling the needed French books. This is one area where the missionary is still vitally needed. Yes, Africans learn to read, but how tragic it is that there is so little for them to read. We are thankful that they have the "book of books," the Bible.

38 - My Dreams Come True

In the summer of 1947, when the Lord turned my sights from learning to sew and cook and directed my path to have me spend the summer as a camp counselor instead, I found one of the loves of my life. When I arrived in Africa, it didn't take me long to start dreaming that maybe some day we could have youth camps at Sibut. Ten years after my arrival, when Levi and Andre learned to take more responsibility at the clinic, I felt it was time to make my dream known to my co-workers.

They weren't against the project, but they were not enthusiastic either. They thought it was a large venture and that if it weren't of the Lord, it would fail. They knew I had enough to do with my medical ministry and classes. Camps had never been tried before, either, and they were skeptical about whether or not it was possible to have one with our limited facilities and leaders. I explained that I had prayed a lot about it and felt the Lord was leading me to do this. They reluctantly told me to go ahead.

First I wrote to my friends at home and asked them to pray about all aspects of the new adventure. I knew the project was so big that it would not succeed without a lot of prayer. My faithful church family immediately sent $200 to the mission to help get the project on its feet. That sum paid for one hundred enamel dishes, four large cooking pots, a few serving dishes, and one hundred spoons.

Sibut Boys' Camp

I planned for the first camp to be for teenage boys on our mission station. We could house the boys in the children's class building. Part of the thatched roof had caved in, but Bruce saw to it that the roof was temporarily repaired with some palm branches and grass. He supervised the building of a small outdoor shelter in front that the women could use for a kitchen. Every time I went to the market I bought dried meat, beans, manioc, and whatever else I knew would be needed to feed my young charges for the eight days they would be at camp. I took the responsibility of paying for the food.

I sent word to thirty-eight churches asking them each to send two teenage boys to the eight-day camp. On arrival day sixty-eight tired, dusty, but happy kids came trudging in. I was so naïve. I hadn't realized how far away some of our churches were. Three boys from our farthest church, Ndengou, walked a hundred miles to come, and one of these boys was only eight years old. We couldn't send him back home without his companions, so he joined us to learn more about Jesus and His love for him. Not all brought grass sleeping mats, so after that camp I bought twenty-five mats from the river area where they are made as an investment for the camp the next year.

For someone who was reluctant at first to see a camp ministry started, Bruce really pitched in. He taught, served up food, tried to teach baseball (I tried volleyball), and really directed the camp.

We had prepared to teach four Bible classes a day. The testimonies at the end of camp were rewarding. Many asked three requests for prayer: (1) that they would arrive safely back home, (2) that they would have a more meaningful walk with the Lord, and (3) that they could come back next year.

On the last day of camp Kodon and Kaila, the cooks, remarked, "Have you noticed how the faces of the boys have filled out? They have put on weight." And it was true. Three meals a day made the difference.

We didn't have the boys' camp the next year due to staffing. Bruce and Wilma went home on furlough, and Lee Einfeldt was the only missionary man on the station.

Sibut Girls' Camp

The next year, instead of there being a boys' camp, 148 girls came from nearby churches. The first meal was to be Monday evening. Imagine my surprise when two girls arrived Friday evening. I couldn't send them home after they had walked thirty miles to come for camp. On Saturday I was more astonished to see twenty more girls arrive. I had to send for one of the counselors to come early to be with them.

For the camp meals the girls were asked to bring food to make their sauces. I would furnish manioc for the main meal and rice for their breakfast. (Manioc would have been too heavy for them to carry for so many miles.)

A mother beating the manioc into flour.

Manioc is the starchy root of the tropical plant cassava. These roots can grow two feet long and are thick. The leaves can be cooked with peanut butter to make one of the healthy sauces to eat with manioc. Starch from the cassava root is also the source of tapioca, although the Africans do not use manioc in that way.

There are two species of manioc. The sweet can be eaten raw or boiled. The second kind is more acidic and is eaten for the main meal. It is also poisonous when gathered and must be soaked in water for three days and then put in the sun to dry. After the manioc is dried, the women pound and sift it and then mix it with almost-boiling water. The result is molded into large balls of a size that would be sufficient to feed four to five people.

My home supporters supplied the finances to build two thirty-foot cement slabs in the middle of our student village for the drying of manioc. In the larger villages someone would have a large manioc-grinding machine and people would pay to have their manioc ground, thus saving hours of labor.

Sadly this starchy root has no vitamins, but it does fill stomachs. The Africans don't feel they have eaten enough unless they have their part of a ball of manioc.

On Monday night, when I inspected their food, the girls who came early said, "We have already eaten our food." I was thankful to have bought forty pounds of dried buffalo meat to supplement their diet.

We had the same two volunteer cooks that had served in the boys' camp. From experience the year before, they had learned what it means to have a schedule, and we could count on them to have the meals on time. The girls were divided into teams, and each team had chores to do. One day I was surprised to see one of them on KP duty eating the burned rice she had scraped out of the bottom of a large pot; I had thought the girls couldn't eat another mouthful.

My five inexperienced counselors eagerly took on their challenge. Each one had thirty girls to supervise, counsel, train, and help to just have fun. The counselors and their girls were housed in the children's classroom, which had one large classroom in the center with two more classrooms off either side. There was no door on any of the rooms.

That first night will always be remembered. The girls had a heyday, or I

Girls at a youth meeting with a finished ball of manioc and a sauce of greens and peanut butter.

should say a *heynight*. The counselors couldn't control them, and neither could I. I stayed until 2 a.m., when I thought they were asleep. When I left the building, I was so tired that I felt I couldn't even drag myself up the steepest part of the hill. I didn't remember ever being so tired and sat down on the bottom step to tell the Lord all about it.

He reminded me of a verse I had learned: "But they that wait upon the Lord shall renew their strength; they shall mount up with wings as eagles; they shall run, and not be weary; and they shall walk, and not faint" (Isaiah 40:31).

I told the Lord, "I know I can't climb those steps in my own strength. I'm relying on you." I can't say I then raced up those steps, but I did manage to climb them, rest a little, and go a block further to my house.

So many times I have been grateful for verses I memorized. In numerous circumstances the Lord brought the right verse to mind for the situation at hand.

Two missionary women from the station did the teaching for this camp, and Florence was the main speaker. I also spoke some in the evenings. It was sad that only twenty-eight of the girls knew the right side up on a book. Twelve of them who did were from a village eight miles from the mission, where a high school boy and I went once a week to teach reading to the children and youth.

During the week of camp seven girls came to know the Lord. I learned that girls are more hesitant than boys are to stand and tell what the Lord has done for them. The week was also a training period for us, as well as the girls. One thing I really learned was to have more counselors at a camp. Sometimes that was difficult in camps at the villages, for I couldn't be there ahead of time to organize them. In spite of our failures, however, the Lord blessed that week. How wonderful to know that He takes our insufficiencies and uses us anyway.

Over the years we had several girls' camps at Sibut, but I especially remember one weekend camp. It was the rainy season, and the girls were to sleep in the children's classroom building, which was not yet enclosed with windows. The night before camp was to open, there was a strong wind and it rained hard. I asked my co-workers to join me in prayer that the weather would cooperate for this special weekend. During the two days the seventy girls were there, not a drop of rain fell; the sun shone both days, and the nights were calm. The night after the girls left, the temperature dropped to seventy degrees. For Africa, that is cold. My heart was again overwhelmed at our mighty God, who could look down on just one tiny space of the universe that He had created and give seventy of his children two comfortable nights.

Yabalangba Camp

A week after the girls' camp at Sibut, Florence and I, with our two cooks, went out to the large village of Yabalangba, ninety miles from Sibut.

It was a good thing that Florence was an excellent Bible teacher. The depth of Bible knowledge among those forty-five girls was appalling. There was only one of them who owned a New Testament, and only eight could read. We heard that the government was going to start bush schools, and we rejoiced to hear it. Within a couple of years schools were started in many of the larger bush villages.

The girls slept in back of the open church, so they hung blankets to have some privacy. Florence and I slept in the pastor's house. There was a rooster that was very faithful in crowing each morning at 3 a.m., and some pigeons were cooing the whole night. In the daytime the birds flew back and forth over us and perched on the walls beside us. We knew things like that were just a part of village life.

The difficult part for me living in a pastor's house was hearing the almost continuous French rock music played on the battery powered transistor radios. With the exception of short wave transmissions, there was only the one government station to listen to. This broadcast was used as the only means of communication between some of the remote villages. The Africans would send a paid announcement of a death or conference to the station, and the announcer would broadcast the information between music selections, which were played for hours. The Africans wanted to hear any news that pertained to them—which could be announced at any time—so they became accustomed to the rock-and-roll type of music.

Pastor Sereganza had a gun, and though he hadn't killed a buffalo in two years, the Lord enabled him to shoot one, so the girls had sufficient food to eat.

Florence and I had become good friends with the pastor and his wife eight months earlier. A wounded buffalo had gored him, and a co-worker went out to his village and brought him back to our clinic. His wife proved to be a joy to have around. Fortunately, the pastor's wounds didn't become infected, so he was able to return home after one month.

Florence went with me when I took them home so we could have classes that weekend and could worship with the 500 people in the church. When our truck pulled into their village, people came running and shouting. My heart was filled with thankfulness to God to see their happiness in welcoming home their pastor and his wife.

Happily, there was no incident like that with the buffalo, and we had a good camp week.

Yongo Camp

The most difficult camp that Florence and I had was in April 1964. It seemed like the devil was working overtime to ruin our time together. The girls would not cooperate, I had three snakebites to take care of, and I helped a Sunday School teacher in the difficult delivery of her baby among the trees down by the river.

My medical ministry followed me wherever I went. It could be snakebites, horrible skin ulcers due to lack of medical care or knowledge of elementary hygiene, teeth that needed to be pulled, or any number of other health issues.

All these distractions were heaped upon us during this camp.

Grimari Camp

The town of Grimari, sixty miles east of Sibut, had a large population. There were two churches in the town. Florence enjoyed going there occasionally and spending two weeks conducting children's and women's classes. The larger church had a brick building that was dedicated during my first term.

It was in this building that Florence and I had girls' camp, with girls coming from four different churches. One group of six came from a church thirty miles away. They were well behaved, had nice clothes, and learned quickly. What a pleasure it was to work with them.

Five of them dedicated their lives to the Lord that week. This caused jealousy among the girls from the host church, however, and two girls got into a fight. It all happened so fast that I didn't know what was going on. I

Margery doing field work in the outlying villages and settlements.

had gone to see about the food and help dish it up when I heard the noise. By the time I arrived, the blouse of one of the girls in the well-behaved group was almost torn off. So where the Lord is working, the enemy can come in quickly. I had to send the one girl home when she refused to ask forgiveness for her actions. (She finally did when camp was over.) Peace was restored, and the leaders and I prayed that it would be a lesson to all about jealousy, having a temper, and the need to ask for forgiveness.

The temperature that week was the hottest we had experienced thus far. We returned home that Sunday afternoon and drank a nice, refreshing glass of cold water.

Doboro Camp

Florence and I borrowed a tent to go to the village of Doboro since they didn't have a place for us to stay. The heat inside the tent was almost unbearable, and outside the tent the little sweat flies tormented us. If you killed one, their stinky odor only attracted others. With the Lord's help we were able to endure it.

We didn't know that the creek where Doboro residents got their water had dried up. It would take the girls three hours to get water from another stream. If I had known the water situation beforehand, I would have made arrangements to have the camp in a neighboring church. We knew that we couldn't have a camp if most of the girls would be spending their hours carrying large basins of water on their heads. The solution was to empty our two metal barrels and haul water in them with my pickup.

The girls vied to be one of the five that I took with me each trip; they thought it was a treat to ride in a vehicle. They would be able to take a quick bath in the stream where there was sufficient water, as well as just have a fun time together. They couldn't understand that the weight of two barrels of water plus the weight of more than five girls might overload the truck. I can still picture the face of one of the girls as she looked up at me and said, "Isn't the Lord able to see that the truck doesn't break down?" Everywhere we went it was comforting to know that the Africans always prayed that the Lord would take care of our truck.

Mala Camp

It was another stifling hot week of camp in the distant church of Mala, ninety miles from Sibut. I really knew it was hot when the girls didn't want to kick a soccer ball or even jump rope.

There was a full moon that week, and one of the girls became mentally deranged. The word for moon in French is *lune,* and when the moon is full, it can affect a few people mentally. Her family came and locked her up in a house. I was told that each time there was a full moon, they had to confine her. I thought maybe I could help, but little did I know my incapability. When they took me to her, she didn't know me and was shouting and pacing to and fro. I left the house with a saddened heart. I realized then where the word lunatic came from.

We went on with the camp, and the Lord helped us in spite of the heat. When I returned to Sibut, one of the first questions asked was "Did you know how hot it was last week?"

"No," I replied, "but I know it was hot."

The quick reply to that was, "It was 138 degrees!"

In our camps during the spring of 1964, we reached about 300 teenage girls. Soon it was time for my furlough. Just before time to leave, I wrote home, "I don't really feel like meeting a lot of people." Life would be so different in America. All I wanted to do was put my feet in a cool stream of water. I spent much of that summer being a missionary speaker and a nurse and sometimes counselor at different camps. I loved it. I didn't have the responsibility for the whole camp, and the ministry of seeing lives changed in a camp environment never grows old.

Sibut High-School Camp

For years I had wanted to reach out to the high school boys with a camp program. Our other boys camps were not well attended by the boys who were going to high school. My dream came to pass in June 1973. Bob Bixby came to Sibut as a new missionary, with a burden to work with youth. I felt that he would be the ideal one to direct a high school camp for boys.

Bob and I got our heads together and started planning. I said I would finance it and see to the meals. We put up a second basketball backboard, (something we had wanted for six years). We invited a missionary from another station to help teach and an African pastor from Bambari for the main speaker. For counselors we used our mature Bible School students and two of our pastors.

When the day of the camp finally arrived, we had fifty-two boys, the right number for the space we had to house them. It was one of the greatest joys of my life to see the arrival of Biro and David. They were in their last year of high school in Bangui, equivalent to the first year of college in the United States. I had sent word for them to try to come if they could. Two years previously they had been my assistants in the high school club we held on Saturday mornings. They were a great help to me.

We had a good week, but there were problems with the two pastor counselors. They didn't enter into the spirit of the camp; they kept to themselves, came to meals late, and didn't come to the classes. But the Lord undertook, and the kids pitched in and took over in their dorms.

One of the assignments for the boys was to memorize as many verses from the book of James as they could. Six of the campers memorized all five chapters. Several learned one to four chapters. I was astounded; I don't know how they did it. For a fellow that had been in Africa less than a year, Bob Bixby did a great job of directing the camp. Seven students were saved, and several dedicated their lives to the Lord. It was a precious time.

At the close of camp some of the fellows told us what the camp had meant to them.

From Patrice: "This camp has made me very happy because it has given me the opportunity to study and to understand the Bible. Had I not participated in it, I would have missed one of the best times of my life. This week I accepted Jesus Christ as my Savior, and it has made me very happy. I have been so blessed and strengthened through studying the book of James and by the preaching of Pastor Pepe. I enjoyed the different games, especially basketball. I am so thankful to the Lord because he gave me the courage to come to this camp and to be fed from the Word of God."

From Silvan: "I had been at the crossroads in my life: the world was calling me, and Jesus was calling me to keep on the narrow road. But at this camp I determined to follow Jesus."

After camp was over, Silvan came to me and said, "Mademoiselle, do you have a Bible I could borrow until I go on vacation? I learned at camp we should pray and study the Bible every day, and I want to start doing that."

After camp ... too tired to put away all the equipment.

244   *I'd do it again ...*

His words thrilled me, and I told him I would lend him a Bible from the clinic.

Two days later he came to the clinic and said, "My throat hurts." I examined his throat, then took his temperature, which was 104 degrees. I knew he had tonsillitis. I hospitalized him at the clinic for a week. It was an enjoyable time for me to take care of him. I came to know him better and appreciated his new love for the Lord.

The third testimony was from Biro, whom I knew well and who came back to Sibut for the camp. I asked him frankly to tell me what the camp had meant to him and what he would suggest if we were to have another one.

"With all my heart I want to thank our good God that he put it in Mr. Bixby's and your hearts to organize a camp like this—a camp where we could better know Jesus, who died for us. Next time it would be good if we had a session on marriage, and to have a film on the life of Christ, and a class on how to reinforce our convictions that the Bible is the Word of God, so we can tell others."

In the 1970s the African churches took responsibility for both boys' and girls' camps. At that time the camps became associated with their youth program, the Juenesse Evangelique Africaine.

39 - My Beloved High Schoolers

One day in the late sixties, as I was returning from Sunday-morning church service and was passing the clinic building, I noticed a couple on the veranda waving to me. The woman had a two-year-old girl in her arms. As I got out of my truck, I could see at a glance that the little one didn't have long to live.

The father explained the situation. The child had been hospitalized at the government hospital, and the parents could see she was getting worse by the minute. In desperation they came to me. I told them they should return to the hospital, as the staff there wouldn't appreciate my taking over one of their patients. Oh, how the parents pleaded with me in words and with anguished concern on their faces! I relented. I also told them that if the little one were to live, it would only be the Lord who could help save her.

First of all I prayed, asking God for wisdom in taking care of little Odette. I needed His help desperately. I then went to work. First, teaspoon by teaspoon I slowly gave her electrolyte fluids. I did this myself, not trusting the parents to do it. I stayed with her until I saw a very slow improvement. Odette did live, and the parents were profuse in saying thank-you. Of course my heart was grateful to the Lord, on whose help I had relied. Shortly after that the family moved away.

When I started teaching high school students, we had four girls among sixty boys. But each year there were a few more girls, as more of them entered high school. One of the girls I had the privilege to teach was Odette. Her family had moved back to Sibut. She let me know right away that her parents told her how the Lord gave her the miracle of life that Sunday afternoon so long ago. She was a very pretty girl and loved being one of the few girls among so many fellows.

When the government started the high school at Sibut, Bruce and Wilma had classes on Saturday mornings with students in our town classroom. Wilma was musically talented and taught music, and Bruce gave the message. They had a good ministry.

When they went home on furlough, I took over the class with a great feeling of inadequacy, or as the expression goes, "with fear and trembling." But I took to heart Joshua 1:9: "Have I not commanded you? Be strong and courageous! Do not be terrified; do not be discouraged, for the Lord your God will be with you wherever you go" (NIV). That was just the verse I needed!

I found that the Brethren had an excellent program, prepared for high school students by a French Swiss missionary, so I used their program. The leaders would come to my house during the week, and we would talk over the subject and how to summarize the topic in a message. There were lessons on doctrine and character-building, each with six questions and Bible references on the theme. Glory to God! It worked.

I really got to know the leaders, Biro, David, Daniel, Noel, and Fezan. I

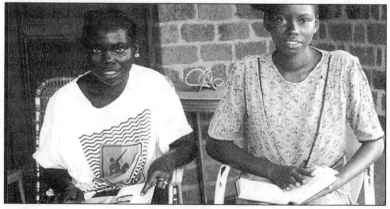

Books are scarce in Central African Republic. Odette and friend enjoy this opportunity to read.

want to tell you about their lives.

Biro was a pastor's son from Kaga-Bondoro (Crampel) and was the president of the Sibut high school student body. I was proud seeing him march in front of their Independence Day parade. After graduation from the only university in the country, he became a tax accountant for the government. It hurt to see him walk away from the Lord, but later he repented and became active in a Bangui church.

Daniel first became a rural public health nurse and then retrained as an x-ray technician in Bangui. He and his wife had a home Bible class, which increased to 400 people. They were building a church as the funds came in. It was hard saying good-bye to him when I left Africa for the last time.

Noel worked in our print shop for years, and later he started a stamp business on his own in Bangui. Fezan became a youth leader in the main Sibut church. I'll tell about David a little later.

Every three months I had a party for the high school gang, a new concept for them. It was held in the mission's children's classroom from 3 p.m. to 9 p.m. Months before our first party, I ordered soccer balls from the States and different table games to add to those I already had. As the time of the party neared, I was praying that the packages would arrive in time for it. They arrived the Saturday before—a definite answer to prayer. The mail service was more reliable in those days.

Before that first party, I spent time with some of the kids, teaching them how to play Chinese checkers, Probe, Memory, and an assortment of other games. Years before, in a teen-age boys' class, I had each of the fellows make a checkerboard. I could never play with them, for the people of that country had their own rules, which differ from international ones.

Here is the schedule we usually followed:

3:00-4:00 - outdoor sports - soccer - basketball
4:00-5:30 - table games
5:30-6:30 - indoor group games
6:30-7:00 - Bible quizzes, with prizes and testimonies
7:30-8:30 - singing and message
8:30-9:00 - before departure, a hearty meal

For a while, Jeremie, our youth leader, was my main helper at these parties. He could direct them like a pro.

I will never forget when once, while they were playing table games, I walked by a group and asked them, "How is it going?" (They were playing Probe, a word game in which they had to find out the word that the others had.) They answered, "Not so hot." I learned that out of the four players, three had selected words in three different languages, English, French, and Sango. I can still hear myself say, "You guys should first decide which language you are going to use."

The boys had to be taught to finish their table games and put them away before going to another group that looked more interesting.

When it was time for the message, I often had a pastor or another missionary give it. One year, though, I left the closing program completely to the five enthusiastic high school leaders. They planned it to the minute. There was no time for any recreation, just a brief break. There were three messages, plus five planned by the leaders and several voluntary testimonies.

I'll never forget the testimonies as long as I live, as it was one of the most precious hours of my life. I sat there silently praising Him: "Thank you, Lord. Thank you." This is what I wanted to see in their lives. They were no longer babes but had grown into mature Christians. They told of their love for the Lord, how He had answered their prayers, and how much the Word of God had meant to them that year. David told how many times he was hungry and prayed for something to eat, and how the Lord laid it on Christians to ask him to come eat with them. Biro and David were from Kaga-Bondoro, a town that didn't have a high school. They had come to Sibut and rented a small house in order to attend school. Many times money was too scarce to buy food. At the end of the year I had a dinner in my home for the five leaders and Florence and two missionary couples. I wanted the missionaries to know the group I had been working with that year.

I loved my high school Sunday School class of forty to sixty teenagers who met in the women's classroom at the Bible School. The Africans moved the church off the mission property to be closer to town, and it was near the high school. I wasn't looking forward to having my class under a tree about a block away, but thankfully, the principal of the high school gave us permission to use one of the school classrooms.

Our class was always learning the Navigator Topical Memory System in French. I was very grateful for a women's group in the States that made us one hundred packets of these ninety-six memory verses on cards.

One year, fifty-one of the students did a Bible correspondence course for young believers. It kept me busy grading them, but it was well worth it to see them get into the Word. The Sunday I gave out the first lesson, three of the boys were at my door at 3 p.m., saying, "We did the first lesson, and we want the second one."

Sometimes I taught a book study. I especially enjoyed teaching Genesis and Daniel. When I get to heaven, I'm looking forward to talking with Joseph and Daniel. I want to tell them how much I appreciated their close walk with the Lord, so I could use their lives as examples of how God can keep people pure and honest in difficult circumstances.

One Sunday morning three years later, I was surprised and excited to see David, one of the former leaders in our Bible club, walk into our classroom. I stopped my class early and asked him if he would tell us what was happening in his life. My heart was so warmed to hear him tell how the Lord had been with him in his university years in Bangui and how he had been helping in a Bible class with high school students.

Then he went on, "In a week I am going overseas somewhere to go to medical school. When an outside government furnishes the scholarships for your schooling, you don't have much of a choice, although I did refuse one offer to go to Russia." Imagine, a week before departure he still didn't know where he was going to spend the next six years of his life! After church we spent two hours talking and had a time of prayer, asking the Lord to lead in his life.

David was sent to medical school in Barash, Iraq. The Central African Republic ambassador to Iraq was a Christian, and David spent his vacation times with him and his family. They had some sweet Christian fellowship together. When the ambassador was recalled, David was left alone for several years, without any Christian fellowship. In one letter he informed me that early Sunday mornings he took his Sango hymnal and sang some songs, prayed, and listened to a message in French on the Trans-World Christian

Biro Philippe and David Dofora, two university fellows that came up from Bangui to our High School Camp.

Radio. Blessed are those radio stations that preach the Word of God to those who are in isolated places. I kept in correspondence with him all the time he was in Iraq. My mother and I sent him books and tapes to encourage him. A Christian school teacher in Kuna, Idaho, became his pen pal, possible because David's schooling was in English.

David received his medical degree in Iraq and then came back to the Central African Republic. It was great to see him again. He had never faltered in his testimony, although many had tried to convert him to Islam. Throughout the years he had many different medical ministries, some taking him to Japan, the United States, and France.

Over the years the Lord gave me the privilege of leading many high school kids to the Lord, at the clinic, in classes, and some who were brought to my house by their Christian classmates. We never had to have a discussion explaining why the Bible is the Word of God. They never doubted. But as I used the Bible, which is the Word of God, the Lord made it like a two-edged sword to do the convicting work of the Holy Spirit to change their lives. I never met a student who believed in evolution. The evolution theory had as much influence on them as water rolling off a duck's back.

When I returned from furlough in 1985, the Lord didn't lead me to teach the class again. A Christian grade school teacher was teaching it, and that is the way it should be.

I don't know why I was blessed to have had this ministry for fifteen years, but I never cease to praise the Lord for those years. The verse the Lord gave me at the beginning was true: "Have I not commanded you? Be strong and courageous. Do not be terrified; do not be discouraged, for the Lord your God will be with you wherever you go" (Joshua 1:9, NIV). Praise His Holy Name!

40 - Maturing in the Faith

"And the things you have heard me say in the presence of many witnesses entrust to reliable men who will also be qualified to teach others."

2 TIMOTHY 2:2, NIV

This verse comes to mind when I think of Joseph. Joseph was a teenager saved at my home when he came with a friend who wanted something to read. I have never seen a new convert so eager to get into the Word.

After three Bible studies with him, I felt it would be better if an African took over the discipleship, so he could become acquainted with other Christians. I asked Pierre, a young man from my disciple class, to do this. He went right over to where Joseph lived and found him teaching five fellows the way of salvation and that there isn't a purgatory. On Saturday morning Joseph brought those five fellows to join him in the Bible study with Pierre.

Pierre was able to lead all five of them to the Lord! How thrilled Pierre was to tell me about them when I saw him later that afternoon at a youth rally. I rejoiced with him.

An Amazing Contest

I don't remember if it was the pastors or the young people themselves who in 1987 wanted to start a youth rally for the six churches in our district. They asked me to take part in it, but I told them I didn't want to become involved. I had enough to do, and they were capable of doing it on their own. Later though, I reconsidered. For my part, I wanted to start a Bible contest among the youth between the churches. So I did.

I was thrilled with these youth meetings. They were held every two months, rotating between the six churches in our area. The furthest church (Nguereko) was twenty-two miles away. When it was their turn to have the rally, the others walked the twenty-two miles to be there. Each meeting included preaching, a debate on assigned topics, and special music from each group. There was always good food, cooked by the youth committee of the host church.

The most exciting part on the program was the Bible quiz. At each rally I revealed the Bible chapters that I would quiz them on during the next rally. At each gathering I gave a written test of forty questions to each team. What a contest! One time two groups missed only a half point in forty questions on the book of Judges. Another time three groups were tied, getting only three questions wrong on the last eleven chapters of the Gospel of John. I quickly prepared three more questions to break the tie, and the winning church won by just a half point. The winning church took home the flag, and their voices rang out in victory, singing as they marched back to their villages. I learned that the church that won the most contests held a Bible study twice weekly to study the required passages. The boys worked hard for their victories.

Only one time did I give out exams to every individual, rather than each team. When the quiz was over, I asked the fellow that won, who had missed only a half point, "How could you answer so many questions correctly?"

He replied, "I sit on a stool and put my Bible, notebook, and lamp on the seat of a chair and study for two hours every night." It was no wonder he won a new Bible for first place.

Pastors in other districts saw the results of the rallies in the Sibut churches and started their own. I was so thankful our mission had a photocopier to use for preparing multiple copies. Throughout the years I made up questions on all the story parts of the Old Testament, the four Gospels, Acts, and some of the epistles. It was well worth the time spent in making up the exams and correcting them, for this was one way to help the youth study the Word of God. "Thy Word is a lamp unto my feet, and a light unto my path" (Psalms 119:105).

Enthusiastic Agriculture Students

Once in 1971, while I was having a youth meeting at the Grimari church, I noticed a group of older teenage boys in attendance. Afterward I talked with them, and they told me, "We are from the agriculture school that is five kilometers out of Grimari." It is the only agriculture school of its kind in the Central African Republic.

I found out there were many Christians among the eighty students who attended. The next morning I went to the school, and a couple of the fellows took me to meet the director. The students told me beforehand he was a backslidden Christian, but he told me he had no objection if the students wanted to start a Bible club. I later returned to Grimari with the French lessons that we used in our high school club at Sibut.

I helped the fellows organize their Bible club. I longed to have Christian young people grounded in the Word. I prayed the Lord would mean so much to them that they wouldn't fall when they came into leadership positions and temptation to sin came their way.

I also asked the director, "If I sent some books to start a library here, would there be a place where you could keep them?"

He replied, "No problem, that can be arranged." So they had their Bible club and their library.

Fruit That Remained

At Sibut there was a group of young men in their late teens and early twenties that I felt were ready for a deeper study of the Word. Some of them were Flambeau leaders, choir directors, or older boys in high school, and some I knew were free and foot-loose. When I returned from furlough in 1985, I started a class for these young men on the mission station at 6:00 p.m. on Friday nights. I had the joy of helping until two weeks before I left

Africa the last time. I called them my "disciple class."

They learned two Bible verses a week, and in class they recited them to each other. Then as a group we would review them and others they had previously learned. It was no problem getting them to master the verses. One young man, Darlen, learned the sixty verses both in Sango and French.

Most of the time we also did book studies, and each week at home they would outline or summarize a chapter. Then in class we would discuss their homework and how the Word could be applied to their lives. I saw real growth in their lives.

Once, after we finished studying the book of Philippians, one of the fellows, Eme, remarked, "Why don't you give us an exam on the book?" I groaned to myself and thought, *That would be one more thing to do.* Outwardly I said, "Okay, if that is what you want. I'll give you an oral exam next Friday."

Then Daniel spoke up. "But we would rather have a written one." This was something different, students asking for an exam! The next week I gave them their written exam, and Eme and Daniel received the two highest scores.

One time we were studying the book of Daniel. When I was teaching the second chapter, I wanted to draw the image that King Nebuchadnezzar saw in his dream, but I have absolutely no artistic ability. Then I said, "Can any of you come up and draw the image?"

Everyone spontaneously called out, "Didier!" Didier didn't need to be persuaded. He quickly rose from his seat and came up and in no time at all

Drawing Kassai Didier did of Margery in one of her classes. Artist is shown bottom right of drawing, just above his signature.

drew a fantastic image. I was so amazed at his ability. I hadn't had a clue he was so artistic, and I complimented him on his drawing. He was so touched by my appreciation of his talent that in two weeks he presented me with two drawings on typewriter paper. One was of me teaching up front, with the red skirt and the white blouse, shoes, and socks, just like I always wore. In back of me was the blackboard with the image of Nebuchadnezzar's dream, divided into the four different empires the image represented. The other picture was of the students sitting at their desks in various poses and me in one of the aisles pointing to something on the students' Bibles.

When Lynn Muhr saw the drawings, he hired Didier to draw pictures to go with the Bible verses on the calendars the press printed each year for the country. For two years they had printed the calendars without pictures, but now Lynn had found an artist.

About six months before I went home in 1994, four boys who were in my Friday class came to me and said, "We have formed an evangelistic team and have been doing house-to-house evangelism in the area. Now we want to go out to different areas and reach souls." They asked me to consider using my truck as a bus to take them.

Part of the youth evangelistic team singing in the evening after an afternoon of witnessing.

I rejoiced to hear what they were doing, and I was glad to help them. Once we had an overnighter. I took them twenty miles out on the Grimari road. The seven of them witnessed all afternoon, and ten people believed.

In the evening we stayed at John Saboyambo's parents' home. John was my head nurse. It was a large brick house with a cement floor, a rarity in that area. The young men spent the evening singing, with two of them playing accordions and a guitar. I just sat there like an old mother hen, rejoicing in the dedicated lives of these young people. On Sunday morning, they taught the Sunday School classes, led the singing, and presented vocal and instrumental music, followed by one of them preaching.

One Sunday morning the group and I were scheduled to go out in another direction. I went to my truck only to notice one of the tires was flat. Much to my dismay, I found the two spare tires were also flat. That year I had more flat tires than all of my years in Africa put together. I talked to our mechanic, Doug Murtoff, and explained my tire dilemma and that I needed to pick up eight young people in twenty minutes. Bless his heart! He came to the rescue and quickly fixed two of the tires.

I treasured those few trips taken with the young people. I was so happy they had the desire to reach others. It was difficult to put into words what the disciple group meant to me. If it was my turn on Fridays to have guests for the evening meal, the other missionary ladies knew they had to skip me. This was our arrangement, because they knew I didn't want to miss this class.

Several of these boys went on to Bible School and are now in the ministry. I was so thankful that Timothy Tikouzou, one of my former "boys" who now worked at the American embassy in Bangui, sent me money to help some of the boys who wanted to go into the ministry by providing the last payment for their wives.

The last meeting I attended with the youth of the six churches was for my farewell. It was held at the large Sibut Center church a week before I left. I gave my farewell talk to the 350 young people gathered there, and I could hardly keep the tears back as they ended the meeting by singing "God Be with You 'Til We Meet Again."

I thanked the Lord many times for the privilege of working with the African youth. My prayer for them as I left is paraphrased from I Corinthians 15:58: "Finally, my beloved *young people*, be ye steadfast, unmovable, always abounding in the work of the Lord, forasmuch as ye know that your labor is not in vain in the Lord" [*Italics mine*].

41 - Music, God's Gift

"But, Mademoiselle, did you pray about it?"

Two weeks before, the young people of the mission church had asked me to start a choir. This was 1986 and the Bangui churches all had choirs, so the young people at Sibut also wanted one.

Of course I wanted them to have a choir, but when they asked me to start one, I said, "It isn't possible! I have never sung in a choir in my life, because

I don't have the voice to do so." I thought that was the end of it.

They came back two weeks later and said, "When are you going to start the choir?"

"I told you, I am not able to do so." Many times the Lord brought to my mind I Thessalonians 5:24, "Faithful is he that calleth you, who also will do it," but I felt even the Lord couldn't help me on this request. It was beyond my limits.

Then the spokesman for the young people looked me squarely in the face and asked, "Have you prayed about it?"

No, I hadn't, for I knew it was impossible for me. Or so I thought.

I had two years of piano lessons as a child and more lessons while attending Simpson Bible Institute. I bought my first accordion when I was at Simpson and used it when I went on a service assignment for the school at the King County Jail in Seattle, Washington. When I graduated I gave the used accordion to my sister, Esther, when she went to Mexico as a missionary. I bought a new one in New York City when I was leaving for my first term as a missionary in Africa. In my second term I helped Francois, a teacher, learn to play. From that time on, whenever I was on furlough, I looked for good used accordions in pawnshops, second-hand stores, and homes of people who had them just sitting idle. I would take these back to Africa with me.

Once when I was with my friends, Edith and Bob Olsen in Spokane, they took me to see the beautiful scenery in Coeur d'Alene, Idaho.

I suddenly yelled, "Stop!"

Bob slammed on the brakes and anxiously asked, "What is the matter?"

I replied, "We just passed a pawn shop."

He looked puzzled. "Did you want to go into the store?"

"Please," I replied. "I want to see if they have any used accordions."

So Bob and I went in. My heart leaped when the owner told us he had one available for $50. It was a small, complete 124 bass.

I tried it out and quickly said, "I will buy it." Then I realized I didn't have my checkbook with me.

Bob eagerly replied, "I have my checkbook" and paid for it. When I was going to repay him, he refused to take my money, saying he was thrilled to pay for an accordion which would one day be played in some African church.

Over time I took back about twenty accordions. What joy my beloved African people found in playing and listening to a musical instrument. As a result, one term in Africa I spent Monday afternoons giving accordion lessons. Thankfully, someone had put lesson books in one of the accordion cases.

Before a church could buy an accordion (which I sold for a very nominal price), they had to send someone to Sibut to learn how to play it. I was proud as a peacock one Sunday morning when four young people from the mission church played a special number for the morning service.

Because I could play the accordion, the youth thought I would be able to direct the choir. After their second request I went home and prayed, "Lord, is this something I should try, and if so, how?"

I felt a little like Moses when he kept giving God excuses why he shouldn't be the one to lead the children of Israel out of Egypt back to Canaan.

God finally asked him, "What is that in your hand?"

"A staff," he replied.

God then showed Moses how he could use that staff in the work He had chosen him to do.

The Lord directed my hand to a melodica I owned. A melodica is an instrument four inches wide, having a keyboard of one and a half octaves. It is played by holding it straight in front of your body and blowing into the mouthpiece. The melodica became my "Moses rod."

Approximately twenty boys and girls came for the first choir practice. I would play the parts of tenor, bass, and alto on the melodica. I would then teach the soprano part by voice. I was thrilled how quickly they learned their parts. I kept thinking, *It is going to work! It is going to work!*

About a month later, the young people from two other churches, one a

Music camp helpers: Eme Emanuel with the melodica and Ferdinard Pakindji teaching notes at the black board.

mile south and the other a mile north of our small town of 15,000, came to me and asked, "When are you going to help us have a choir?"

I replied, "I do not have the time."

But they kept pleading with me. We talked and finally agreed that both churches would meet one afternoon a week in a class building we have in the middle of town. I picked three youth from the mission church choir to go with me to our town building. They would teach the alto, tenor, and bass, and I would teach the soprano.

My last term, requests came in for me to have music camps in the different areas. I wasn't doing medical work the last four years in Sibut but was teaching full-time in the Bible School. Again I doubted that it could be done, but we made a start during school vacation.

Several years earlier Wilma Rosenau had taught music to some of our high school students. Ferdinand, now a senior in our Bible School, had been one of her students. He had a gift for music and learned well. I took him and Aime, one of my best choir members and an accordion player, with me to the river district to have our first music camp. I thought that if it flopped, not many people around the mission would know about it, since we were holding it so far away. Pride, pride, pride.

We had twelve students. Some of them walked forty-five miles to attend. We had classes for seven hours a day, beginning at 7 a.m. I started the classes rolling with a discipling Bible study. We had three classes in music theory, one hour in choir, one about music in the church, and one spent in learning new hymns. We used two booklets that other missionaries had translated into Sango for the music theory time. At the end of the week I was encouraged, realizing that it was worthwhile.

During my last term in Africa we had several music camps in the Sibut district. We always closed the camp on Friday night with a mini-concert for the church people. We featured the students singing hymns in harmony, accompanied by a melodica, an accordion, and a small battery-run keyboard. It wasn't much, but the Lord used it to give joy to His own. I am so glad that the Lord can take weak things and weak people and use them for His glory in unexpected ways!

One day, as I was playing the hymn "There is Coming a Day" on the piano, I thought, *This song has such meaningful words, as well as a catchy tune. I wish the words were in Sango.*

The Lord seemed to say, Why don't you translate it?

I thought, to myself, *That is impossible,* but I couldn't get the idea out of my mind. I finally sat down with the hymnbook, and I surprised myself by translating four verses of the song. I ran up the hill to Jan and Vernon's house and into their kitchen, where they had just finished their evening meal.

Excitedly I said, "Look what the Lord let me do!" Then I sang the song to them.

Thankfully they encouraged me by commenting favorably on it. Of course, the verses had to be gone over by the language and music committees and changed several times, but it was a start. During the remaining time I was in Africa, the Lord enabled me to put Sango words to about forty hymns. I have thanked the Lord many times for helping me.

On two occasions grateful Africans expressed their thanks for the songs. It meant much to me. The first time was when thirty pastors gathered for a leadership conference at Sibut. I taught them "Until Then," a song that I especially liked. Several months later, when I was in Bangui, one of their pastors who had been at the conference remarked to me, "Thank you for teaching us that song 'Until Then.' I sing it every day as a prayer while I go places on my bike. I do want to be faithful until the day He calls me home."

I agreed with him. "That is my prayer also."

The second occasion concerned Bruce Rosenau. He went to be with the Lord in October of 1990. He died in Bangui, where he had worked for the last years of his life. Vernon, his nephew, brought his body back to Sibut so he could be buried in our small graveyard. Bruce's wife stayed with me that night, and we talked for hours. She remarked, "For the last two weeks Bruce often sang 'I'll Fly Away' as he went about his work."

Interrupting her, I said, "Recently I've written words to that song in Sango, and three church choirs in the area have learned it. Would you like them to sing it at the funeral tomorrow?"

Her eyes lit up, and she replied, "Oh, could they? That would be wonderful."

"I'll ask Vernon if it will be okay. If he agrees, I'll arrange for the choirs to come early tomorrow, and they can practice it together."

And so it was. The following are two verses and the chorus of the song in Sango and in English.

I'll Fly Away (Sango)
> *Mbeni la fini ti mbi aoue,*
> *Fade mbi goue,*
> *Ti douti na kodro ndjoni koue,*
> *Fade mbi goue.*

> Choeur:
> *Fade mbi goue, O ita,*
> *Fade mbi goue.*

Ti douti na kodro ndjoni koue,
Fade mbi goue.

Mbeni la Jesue A yeke ga,
Fade Mbi goue.
Fade mbi te Lo na ya mbinda
Fade mbi goue.

I'll Fly Away (English)
Some glad morning when this life is o'er,
I'll fly away.
To a home on God's celestial shore,
I'll fly away.

Chorus:
I'll fly away, O glory,
I'll fly away.
When I die, hallelujah, by and by,
I'll fly away.

Just a few more weary days and then,
I'll fly away.
To a land where joys shall never end,
I'll fly away

— *Albert E. Brumley*

Over two thousand people came to remember this servant of Christ who had spent most of his years in the Central African Republic. The choir sang "I'll Fly Away" in Sango, symbolizing that, in a moment, he had been transported from earth to his heavenly home. It could be said of Bruce what the apostle Paul had written in Philippians 1:21: "For to me, to live is Christ and to die is gain" (NIV).

Years ago our mission produced a song book which contained 250 songs, but only the words. Thousands were printed and distributed. Polly Strong, one of our talented missionaries, worked many hours on a music typewriter to add the music notes to these songs, making possible a complete hymnal. The first printing was of 1,000 copies. That version of our hymnal is now out of print. Jonathan Teachout redid it on a computer, and a new hymnal was printed in 1999.

Over the years, I discovered that hundreds of Africans could sing by memory all of the verses of many hymns. Sometimes they would say at the end of their testimonies, "This hymn expresses what is in my heart." Yes, music is a universal language. It was a universal language when hundreds of delegates from all over Africa met in Egypt for an agriculture conference.

One of my best friends, Hilaire, was the delegate from the Central African Republic. When he returned, he told me about his trip. His face lit up with joy as he shared one of his experiences: "We found out that many of us were Christians, so on Sunday we met together for a worship service. The speaking was in English, but what were we to do about the singing? Very few of us knew any English hymn words. We decided we would sing one we all knew in our own language. We chose "Since Jesus Came into My Heart." I'll never forget that day as our voices were raised in praise to God, as we bonded together as members of the body of Christ."

The Africans in the Central African Republic have many of their own songs. My hope and prayer is that someday a committee will collect the best of these songs. Then a qualified person could put notes to them, and we could have another hymnbook. Let us all remember Psalms 100:1-2: "Make a joyful noise unto the Lord, all ye lands. Serve the Lord with gladness: come before his presence with singing."

Part Six

Unforgettable People

One of the requirements for being accepted by a mission board is to have a physical examination. In addition, a missionary must have one each time he or she goes home on furlough. I chose Dr. Burg for my physician.

I became acquainted with him when I worked at Seattle's Maynard Hospital during my time at Simpson Bible Institute. He was a kind, considerate, Jewish doctor in his forties, an internist and diagnostician. When I attended Simpson, I was the school nurse for two years, and when a student needed a doctor, I always suggested Dr. Burg.

During my second furlough I updated my nursing procedures by working at Maynard Hospital for a few months. I also scheduled a complete physical with Dr. Burg. After my physical exam he asked me about my work in Africa. I explained how I was responsible for a clinic with 200 patients a day. I didn't tell him that occasionally that number reached over 300.

He seemed very interested and asked me many questions. Then I said to him, "I have medical books that I often study for help, but I have no idea how to diagnose heart problems or what to do for them." He spent the next forty-five minutes giving me a lecture on that subject. Of course, it was just the rudiments, but it was a great help.

While he was talking, my thoughts went to the people who were waiting for their appointments. How kind of him to take time to help me! I left there knowing Dr. Burg was not only my physician but also my friend.

One afternoon while working at Maynard Hospital, caring for one of Dr. Burg's patients, he walked into the room. He greeted his patient, then he saw me standing at the bedside. He came over and put his arm on my shoulder, and said to his patient, "Do you know anything about the nurse who is taking care of you?" He then told her about my work in Africa. I felt so proud!

Soon after I returned to Africa, I was reading an interesting article in a Christian magazine that told about the conversion of a physician. Immediately I thought, *This would be a good article for Dr. Burg to read. It would be so wonderful if he would come to know Christ as his Messiah.* I cut it out and put it in my file box, intending to send it to him with a letter giving my testimony. But I just left it there, thinking *I'll do it later.*

A few months afterward I received a letter from Ilene (who knew Dr. Burg well, as she was the head lab technician at Maynard Hospital), informing me that Dr. Burg had died of a heart attack. I was shocked, heart-broken, and ashamed. I knew I had failed my Lord and Dr. Burg. Months ago it had been God's appointed time for me to send Dr. Burg that article, so he could learn about salvation in Christ, but I had disobeyed the Lord's leading.

Later I came to the conclusion that I had wanted to keep his good opinion of me and didn't want him to think of me as a "religious fanatic." I asked myself plainly, *was I ashamed of the gospel of Christ when it involved an influential person?*

Then I thought about another time when I was not ashamed and let the Holy Spirit lead me. One day before going to work at the hospital, I had asked the Lord to direct me to someone to whom I could witness. (I often prayed that prayer.)

Upon receiving the report from the day nurse, she ended up telling the other nurse and me, "There is a patient in the last room down the south hall who is one of Seattle's important judges. He doesn't have a good disposition and snaps at us nurses. Don't go into his room until he puts on his light or it's necessary to give him his medication or his evening care."

Imagine my disappointment when the other nurse on my shift assigned me the south hall. It was late in the evening before I was ready to take care of the judge. I was hesitant to go into his room. I didn't want to get snapped at. But of course I went in, and to my surprise he gave me a warm "Good evening."

The Holy Spirit seemed to tell me, *This is the one you are to witness to.*

I immediately thought, *Oh no, Lord, I can't talk to him.* But as I was giving him a back rub (the nurses did that in those days), it came naturally for me to say, "Judge, you have judged many people in your lifetime. Have you ever thought about going before the Judge of all men?"

He turned his head around and looked at me with an astonished expression and said, "I have, many times."

I spent about fifteen minutes talking with him about how he could meet God, not as his judge but as the redeemer of his soul. He didn't accept Christ that evening, but the seed was sown, and I prayed that someday it would be harvested.

As I was remembering the judge, my thoughts again turned to Dr. Burg. If I had obeyed the Lord and had sent him that article, He would have given me the words to write. But now it was too late, too late!

In Acts, chapter 8, it was God's appointed time to send Philip on the Gaza Road to meet a caravan with an important Ethiopian man in his chariot. God told Philip to go, and he obeyed. The Ethiopian man was returning to his country from Jerusalem and hadn't accomplished one of his objectives. He wanted to learn about God. Philip met the man, and he found that the Ethiopian was reading Isaiah 53.

When Philip joined him in his chariot, the Ethiopian asked Philip, "Tell me, please, who is the prophet talking about, himself or someone else?"

Philip explained he was talking about Jesus, the Messiah. When the man understood, he believed and was baptized. Philip had obeyed the appointed time that God called him to go on the desert road, and the result was that the Ethiopian "went on his way rejoicing."

My earnest prayer is, *Oh, Lord, help me not to be afraid of what people might think when you prompt me to share the Gospel with someone. Let me live with eternity's values in view.*

43 - An African Hannah

One advantage of staying in Sibut for all the years I was in Africa is that I could follow the lives of many dear people with whom the Lord graced my life. One of those people was a woman named Martine from the village of Kouchingou, about twenty miles from Sibut.

I first became acquainted with this village in 1955, after returning from my first furlough. At that time it was called Kouchingou, after its chief. Now the village is called Amou, after the creek that runs by it. It used to be that village names changed every time a chief died and a new one took his place.

While I was on furlough, Florence my co-worker, and Marian, the nurse who filled in for me, used our truck to go to Chief Kouchingou's village each

Martine with her beautiful baby girl.

Sunday morning to conduct Bible reading classes. After I returned from furlough, Florence and I went instead. I learned the joy of teaching people to read through Florence's enthusiasm. At that time the only person in Kouchingou that could read was Francois, the twenty-five-year-old son of the chief.

Martine was Francois' first wife. Since Martine was unable to give Francois any children after several years of marriage, he took a second wife. The second wife conceived and bore a child. Martine was very unhappy; she desperately wanted a child of her own.

One Sunday, as I was about to leave the village to return to Sibut, Martine asked to speak with me privately. We sat in the shade by the side of her mud-brick, thatched-roof house. She wanted to know if I could help her become pregnant. The Lord quickly reminded me of Hannah's story in 1 Samuel. Hannah didn't have any children, and she prayed for a son. She promised the Lord that if He gave her a son, she would give the son back to Him. The Lord answered Hannah's prayer, and she bore a son and named him Samuel. Hannah didn't forget her promise to God. When Samuel was weaned, she took him to the tabernacle at Shiloh and presented him to the priest.

Hannah could have reneged on her promise to the Lord. I can just imagine the joy of having a child of her own to nourish and care for. But Hannah put her promise to the Lord first, and God rewarded her by giving her other children.

I read Hannah's story to Martine, who still couldn't read well, even though she attended our reading classes under the trees. Her eyes shone as she listened to the story. I said, "Let's ask the Lord to do for you what He did for Hannah."

So we both prayed, asking by faith that the Lord would answer our prayers for a child. As I look back, I wonder how I had the faith to pray like that. The only answer is that the Lord gave me faith at that moment.

Many Sundays later Martine came to me with shining eyes to tell me that she was pregnant. How my heart rejoiced with her! Months later she had a beautiful baby girl.

In a couple of years I began to teach a high school class in town on Sundays and quit going out to the village. I lost track of Martine. Years later I heard that she had died.

One morning in the early '80s, I was making my usual early morning rounds in the clinic wards, checking on my patients. I entered a four-bed room, and in one of the beds was a young woman with a sick baby.

Before I could ask any questions of my patients, the young woman spoke up and said, "Do you remember a woman named Martine, from Kouchingou's village?"

"Of course I do," I said. "How could I forget that wonderful answer to prayer?"

Smiling broadly, she said, "I am the baby my mother had in answer to prayer."

I gave her a hug and rejoiced with her.

The last time I saw Martine's daughter was during my last term in Africa. I went out to Amou village to speak at an area women's meeting, and she was there. In the years since those reading classes in the 1950s, a church had sprung up in Amou, and they now had their own pastor. Many of the people in the village were Christians.

We cannot understand why the Lord gives faith at times to pray for certain things. But it was His will to answer this prayer, and He gave us the faith to pray. I like 1 John 5:14-15: "And we can be confident that he will listen to us whenever we ask him for anything in line with his will. And if we know he is listening when we make our requests, we can be sure that he will give us what we ask for" (NLT).

44 - Chief Sai

For several years during my second term, before we had churches in the area, twice a week I would take Bible School students out to the villages so they could learn to preach and reach the people for Christ. I let them off two by two at the villages, to which they had been assigned for teaching the Bible lesson.

Usually I went to the village of Chief Sai with a student named Djibrine. Djibrine was from N'dele, a remote area in the north of our country. How well I remember the first time he went with me to the village. He was petrified as he stood to give his Bible lesson and spoke all of three minutes.

For the meeting in Sai's village there were a couple of small logs where the smaller children would sit and two back-less wooden benches for the older ones. The women usually brought their own small, more comfortable stools to sit on.

I remember there was a naked, lame boy about three years old who always sat on the first log. We could count on him to give us one of his big smiles. Once when we went to the village, he was clothed in a new loincloth, a leftover piece of material from a shirt or dress that had been made. Oh, was he proud of his first piece of clothing. During the meeting he stood up about three times and turned around and then sat down. A model couldn't have done it better. I didn't rebuke him; it was a wonderful day for him.

Chief Sai would never come to the meetings but sat nearby in his chair in front of his house. There he would listen to the singing and preaching. He never believed, though many in his village had become believers.

One day I was alone when I drove into the village. It was immediately apparent that something was wrong because everyone was gathered around the chief's house and all their faces were downcast. Of course, as soon as I got out of my pickup, I asked what was wrong. They told me that Chief Sai had a strangulated hernia.

I strode into the chief's house and told him that I would take him to the government hospital in Sibut, where he could be operated on. With a strangulated hernia, if it can't be reduced, surgery is the only cure, and the Africans know this.

Imagine my great surprise when Chief Sai refused my offer. I returned home with a heavy heart. I knew he wasn't a Christian, and I also knew that death in two days would be the result if his hernia were not repaired.

The next day I made a special trip out to the village to see the chief, hoping I could persuade him to go to the government hospital. They had made a small grass hut for Chief Sai a few yards away from his house. He was lying on a mat inside. I knelt down beside him to talk with him. Again he refused to let me take him to the hospital. By this time tears were streaming down my face. What a useless way to die!

I then spoke to him about his soul and his need to accept Christ as his Savior. He again refused God's special gift of eternal life through Christ. I was sobbing, and the chief laid his hand on my arm and said, "Don't cry, Mademoiselle, don't cry."

I left with a broken heart. As I drove the eight miles back home, I prayed for him and for wisdom for me. My helpers at the clinic had been praying, too.

The next morning, the third day, I went to our African pastor Sesse and explained the situation to him. He readily agreed to go with me to see Chief Sai once more.

We got out of the pickup, greeted the crowd of people there, and walked to the hut. When we got close, I knew that the chief had only hours to live, for the smell of death was potent. I again knelt by his side and explained that I had brought our Sibut pastor to talk with him about his soul.

Sai now knew there was no turning back about the medical decision he had made, but through the prayers of many, as the pastor talked with him, his heart became ready to receive Christ as his Savior. The Lord said to the thief on the cross that believed, "Today you will be with me in paradise" (Luke 23:43, NIV). I had joy in my heart to know with assurance that this would be true of Chief Sai also. The next day I returned to the village and spoke at the Chief's funeral.

Several weeks later someone explained to me the reason Sai didn't want to go to Sibut to have surgery. He thought that in his helpless state in the back of the pickup a witch or someone would pronounce a curse on him and his family, and that the evil spirits would carry it out.

I never did really understand all the witchcraft that was part of the African culture. Many critics of missions say we shouldn't change the culture of the people to whom we preach. In some ways I agree, but in many others I do not. How wonderful it is to hear the testimonies of the redeemed, proclaiming how the coming of the gospel has changed their lives and freed them from fear. Instead of fear, they experience love, joy, peace, forgiveness, and the hope of the inheritance waiting for them in heaven. Glory, what a day it will be when our Savior we will see!

45 - God's Plans

One evening I was alone in the delivery room with Pauline and her pastor husband, Philip Yamete. They had traveled about seventy miles to our hospital for the delivery of their second child. Sometimes it gets a little boring waiting for a baby to be born, and it was that way that evening.

To liven things up a little, I kept making small talk in the delivery room, saying things like "Come on, David, we want to know what you look like" and "Come on, David, the Lord has work for you to do. Don't you know your mother is tired?"

When the baby boy was finally born, we rejoiced that everything had gone well, and they named him David. Seventeen months later Pauline died as a result of complications during the delivery of her third child, chronicled earlier in this book.

Later, David's father took another wife to help him raise the two children. When David was nine, he believed in the Lord Jesus Christ for his salvation and was baptized some months later.

Years later, the now grown-up David appeared at my door asking if he could work in the clinic. I had a full staff then and said that I couldn't use him. So he talked to Bob Owen, the director of the print shop, and found work there.

David worked in the print shop for six years. It was at that time that the Lord began to change the direction of David's life. Here is a translated excerpt from David's testimony:

> I looked around the Central African Republic field and saw that many of the new missionaries coming to work with Baptist Mid-Missions in the C.A.R. were children of missionaries. But why was it that so few of the African pastors' children entered into the service of the Lord? But I didn't do anything about it myself until one evening in Mademoiselle Benedict's Friday night class. We were studying 1 Timothy chapter three (concerning the qualifications for pastors and deacons). "Here is a trustworthy saying: if anyone sets his heart on being an overseer, he desires a noble task" (1 Timothy 3:1, NIV). Those verses really touched my heart. I returned home after class, and I knew I had to make a decision to yield to the Lord or not. Before I went to bed that evening, I told my wife that the Lord was calling me to become a pastor and that I wanted to enter Bible School. My wife Claudia agreed with me.

We have a policy that if the husband enters Bible School, his wife must enter also. They must both be surrendered to the Lord's will and work as a team. Five years later, on a hot November afternoon, David received his diploma and Claudia received her certificate.

The graduation service was always held on the first Sunday in November. There was great anticipation of the event and much preparation to make it a special time. The church was packed with over a thousand people, and those who couldn't find room inside stood outside.

After the service at the church, we missionaries would host a "high tea" for the graduates and for their pastors and teachers back at the mission station. The missionaries presented the graduates with gifts that would be useful in their future ministries. It was a fun time as the Africans ate foods that they normally did not have: cakes, cookies, sandwiches, and punch. Usually there was food left over, and we gave it to the graduates to take home to their children and guests.

As David was leaving the hilltop with his hands full of goodies, he came to me and said, "Mademoiselle, remember before I was born? My father told me what you said in the delivery room. You kept saying, 'David, the

Lord has work for you to do.' Well, here I am now—ready to go do what you wished before I was born."

I was surprised at his words. I had nearly forgotten the incident that day so long ago. The Lord had turned my idle words spoken to make the time go faster into a prophetic utterance. I was filled with the awe of it all. I was so happy for David.

The Katakpa church—about forty miles out on the Dekoa Road—had already called David to be their pastor, so it wasn't long before my co-worker, Lynn Muhr, came down with his truck to take their belongings and five children to their new home in Katakpa. David and Claudia had a good send-off as the people in the mission village gathered around to bid them goodbye. The Katakpa Christians knew they were coming, and upon arrival of the truck, the people lined up on both sides of the road to give them a great welcome. The church parsonage was all cleaned and ready for them.

The main deacon of the church, Joshua Demagaza, has always been a good friend of mine. In 1964 he was in the first leadership training in Sibut for the boys' movement—the Flambeaux. He became an excellent leader.

He also took charge of the annual Vacation Bible School in his church and was conscientious in sending me the report for the week. I still have the report where he wrote that fourteen young people had believed in Christ as Savior that week. Over the years, if the church was without a pastor or if the pastor was absent, Joshua would be the one to give the message.

At the Katakpa church, David had a good group of young people to teach. David often sent word requesting literature for them. After three years of pastoring, the Lord put it in David's heart to start an elementary Bible school. Up to this time, the ones who wanted to enter the Sibut

Pastor David Yamete and wife Claudia at the dedication of a new Elementary Bible School.

Bible School had to go to Bambari, a mission station east of Sibut, for two years of preparatory study.

Formerly many of the wives could scarcely read and write, so the elementary school prepared them for the advanced school. It was also a training time for the husbands to see if they were earnest about serving the Lord. David wanted a school like that in our area, so he presented the project to the missionaries and pastors. The project was approved.

The government gave the land for the school near the town of Dekoa. The future students went there and built their own houses. The believers in the nearby churches came to help clear the land and to help build David's house and the small building that was to be the Bible School classroom. Many days the youth of the Katakpa church walked the eight miles to help with this project.

In July 1994 the place was ready for the dedication service. The seven couples who were to be the first class, the youth who had worked so hard in the construction, a choir, the church members and leaders, and the missionaries from the Sibut station were all there. We were all praising the Lord for this new project led by Pastor David Yamete and his wife Claudia!

At the end of the dedication the missionaries were served a delicious chicken and rice dinner and the Africans enjoyed a good dinner of goat and manioc. The chickens had been a gift of the young people from his church.

As of the writing of this book, David is scheduled to attend a seminary in the neighboring country of Cameroon. His longtime dream is coming true. Meanwhile he and the other pastors in the district are training future workers for the Lord. I am so glad that the Lord truly did have a work for David to do!

46 - Everyone Loved Kaila

Kaila was from one of the many Sara tribes in the Tchad. Like Louvrou, she was stationed with her soldier husband at Sibut. Although they left Sibut for a while, she returned after her husband died. She and Louvrou lived together for years, known as the "Widows of the Sibut Mission Station."

Kaila had two ministries at Sibut. She helped Florence in the children's classes, and she continued to work with the children after Florence's death. She also helped me for a while in the maternity work.

I shall never forget the day she appeared early one morning at my door. She had been at the clinic, watching her own daughter, Laporo, who was in labor. She said, "There is something wrong with my daughter. Would you come down and check on her?"

"Of course," I replied. After examining Laporo, I told Kaila, "She has a fast pulse, and her abdominal girth is larger than it should be. I think she has a premature separation of the placenta and needs to have surgery."

I went back up the hill, got my truck, and took Kaila and her daughter to the town hospital. I explained to the French doctor why I thought she needed a caesarean. I left her to go back to the mission, confident that all would be well. After all, didn't I leave her in a doctor's hands?

At 6 p.m. that evening I took my evening supper out to the front veranda where I could sit and put my tired feet up on the wall. Suddenly I heard the death wail of many people on the main road. Immediately I thought, *That can't be for Laporo,* for she lived in the village just before the turnoff into our mission.

I left my supper and hurriedly drove the quarter of a mile down to her village, to see if it was she who had died. Yes, it was Laporo. The doctor hadn't done a thing for her all day. He decided at 5:30 p.m. to operate, but before he could start, she died on the operating table. I was heart broken. To say I was upset didn't exactly describe how I felt. All I could think of was, *Why, oh, why didn't the doctor operate? Even if he had just graduated from medical school, obstetrics was in his curriculum.*

Kaila took over raising Laporo's four children, who were still at home, because Laporo's husband had a drinking problem and wasn't very responsible. With this added responsibility, Kaila was no longer able to help me with

Kaila next to a banana tree.

the maternity work, but she was very faithful in her work with the children's classes. She would be the first to open the doors of the class building. If the floor was dirty, she swept it. If it had rained during the night (there were no windows in the building at that time), she would sweep the water out the door.

The children loved Kaila, as all of us did. They called both her and Louvrou *Ata*, which means "grandmother." *Ata* Kaila helped teach the children aged three and up to memorize Bible passages. Even after Florence died, Kaila remained faithful.

She was one of the first to receive the completed Sango Bible when it arrived from the British and Foreign Bible Society, a gift from Ernestine. I can still picture her as she held it in her arms and, with her face lifted toward heaven, kept saying, "Thank you, Jesus; thank you, Jesus."

At Easter Kaila taught the children the last few verses of the resurrection chapter of 1 Corinthians, chapter 15. They were to recite it at our Easter morning service.

Three days before Easter, Kaila was brought to the clinic unconscious from a stroke, only the second such case we had had in our medical work. Putting her in one of our three private rooms, with her youngest grand-daughter, Celine, weeping beside her, I sorrowfully explained to the people who gathered around what a stroke was.

Two days later, without regaining consciousness, Kaila went to be with the Lord. Her funeral was one that will stay in my memory. Many people were there. At the burial site, with the casket on logs over the open grave, "her children" stood on the mound of dirt from the grave and lifted their voices in unison as they recited in Sango, without a mistake, the verses in 1 Corinthians that Kaila had just taught them. Here is part of it from The *Living Bible*:

> I tell you this, my brothers: an earthly body made of flesh and blood cannot get into God's kingdom. These perishable bodies of ours are not the right kind to live forever. But I am telling you this strange and wonderful secret: we shall not all die, but we shall all be given new bodies! It will all happen in a moment, in the twinkling of an eye, when the last trumpet is blown. For there will be a trumpet blast from the sky and all the Christians who have died will suddenly become alive, with new bodies that will never, never die; and then we who are still alive shall suddenly have new bodies too. For our earthly

bodies, the ones we have now that can die, must be transformed into heavenly bodies that cannot perish but will live forever.

When this happens, then at last this Scripture will come true—"Death is swallowed up in victory." O death, where then your victory? Where then your sting? For—sin—the sting that causes death—will all be gone; and the law, which reveals our sins, will no longer be our judge. How we thank God for all of this! It is he who makes us victorious through Jesus Christ our Lord!

The hope of the resurrection was never more real to me than on that day the children were reciting their verses around her casket. I could almost hear the trumpet blast and see Jesus appearing in the sky and Kaila and other saints being raised in their new bodies. I was also remembering what Christ said to Martha in John 11:25, "I am the resurrection and the life. He who believes in me will live, even though he dies; and whoever lives and believes in me will never die. Do you believe this" (NIV)?

One little girl, with tearful eyes, looked up at me and said, "When we get hurt, who is going to wipe away our tears with *Ata* Kaila gone?"

I knelt and put my arm around this little one. "We are all going to miss our beloved Kaila," I replied.

On Easter Sunday morning, before a congregation of over 800 people, the children's voices rang out again as they repeated their resurrection verses. They ended with "O death, where is thy sting? O grave, where is thy victory? ...But thanks be to God, who giveth us the victory through our Lord Jesus Christ" (1 Corinthians 15:55, 57).

With those promises, we know we will see Kaila some day.

47 - A Woman Named Anne

Christians hear or read about many prayer requests. It would be impossible to pray for all of them. We do know the Lord impresses upon our hearts certain things or people for whom we should pray. It was that way with Anne Firisiuk.

One day I was browsing through a pamphlet and saw the headline, "Russian woman used for experiments." She had been put in prison because of her faith in Christ. Later they transferred her to a psychiatric hospital where the prisoners were used as guinea pigs in experiments using new, unproven drugs. I knew immediately that she should be put on my prayer list.

The Lord really put a burden on my heart for her. Wasn't she one of us—part of the body of Christ, my sister in the Lord? Anne, whom I had never met, became very dear to me. I not only prayed for her, but I asked some of my African friends to remember her in prayer, even though it was difficult trying to explain to them what it meant to be used as a "guinea pig."

I vividly recollect a time about two years later when I prayed something like this: "Lord, I know you are great and loving and there is nothing too hard for You. You know my concern for Anne. You know all about her and what she is suffering. I know it would take a miracle for me to find out how she is doing. There is no way I can find out but through You. But somehow, would You please let me know?"

Shortly after that prayer, I received three shoeboxes of French Christian literature from Pasteur Kries of France for the pastors and Christian leaders in our churches. In one of the boxes was a small publication from Open Doors. The main theme of the pamphlet was giving the names of persecuted Christians in different parts of the world and their circumstances. As I was looking through this material, my eyes focused on the only picture of a person in it, and I read "Anne Firisiuk of Russia has been set free."

I can't begin to describe the emotions I felt at that time! I just looked up to the Lord and started praising and thanking him for this miraculous answer to prayer. The Lord was so very near, so precious. He seemed to say to me, "You see, I do care." I could hardly wait to go to two of my classes and tell them, "Anne is free, Anne is free!" They rejoiced with me, and there was a real bond between us as we thanked the Lord for answered prayer.

There are several reasons why we love the Lord and Psalm 116:1-2 expresses my thoughts: "I love the Lord, for he heard my voice; he heard me cry for mercy. Because he turned his ear to me, I will call on him as long as I live" (NIV).

48 - My Jewish Friend

When Helene Bagasse came to the clinic, she usually had one or more of her six children with her. One morning, however, she came alone, and I could see she was very troubled.

She came directly to me and asked, "Could I talk with you privately?"

"Of course," I replied, and we went into my office.

"I don't know what to do," she said. "I need someone to talk to and to pray with me."

I had a feeling it was something to do with her husband. It was. We talked a while and then went down on our knees and talked to the Lord about her needs.

Helene was a small, attractive, Jewish-French lady who had married a tall, handsome African man while he was a student in France. After he received his master's degree in education, he made arrangements to take his wife back to Africa with him.

The government school system sent Mr. Bagasse to the large town of Mobaye, where he became the high school principal. Eventually he started drinking, making life unbearable for his wife and children.

Once when the children were ill, Helene went to the clinic at Elim, a Swiss mission a few miles out of Mobaye. There she found help for the children and also for her soul. She came to know Jesus as her Messiah. After Helene's conversion, the missionary nurse had a Bible study with her, and Helene became a mature woman of faith.

A few years later her husband was transferred to his hometown of Sibut, to be the high school principal. They bought a house in town next to our two-room class building. We became acquainted when she brought her children to our clinic. I really came to know her as a friend when she brought her children to my Tuesday afternoon classes. I especially enjoyed her oldest child Sylvia, a beautiful, graceful, fourteen-year-old girl who had come to a sweet faith in the Lord.

I had a small lending library of French children's books and was kept busy

Helene and her husband Bagasse, after his conversion.

before classes checking them in and out. Right away Helene said, "I could help with that." She was terrific. While we worked with the books, Sylvia handed out the many children's puzzles. These kept the kids occupied until class started. I almost think a few of those children could have been nominated for the *Guinness Book of Records* for the number of times they put the same puzzle together. They never seemed to tire of doing this, because they didn't have anything like that to do at home.

Helene shared experiences with me that she and her children suffered when her husband became drunk or brought another woman into the house. My heart ached for Helene, and I was amazed at her sincere love for the Lord that manifested itself in her daily life. It showed in her knowledge of the scriptures and in the way she helped her children come into the faith and become partners with her in praying for their father's salvation. Her faith in the Lord was unmovable, not like the waves tossed on troubled seas. She told me many times, "The Lord is going to save my husband."

But she suffered a lot, and I was glad to be a prayer partner with her. We poured our hearts out to the Lord, who sees the afflictions of the righteous. She also attended the women's Bible classes that Ernie had on Thursdays and made friends with many of the African women. In class she requested the women to pray for her husband. And they would reply, "We are praying." They weren't the only ones who assured her. At this time I was teaching the high school Sunday School class. All the students knew that their principal was a heavy drinker, so I asked them to pray that he would become a believer. I know many of them did.

Mr. Bagasse's brother Kaien was the mayor of Sibut. Outwardly he never showed any interest in spiritual things, although three of his wives were faithful in going to classes. He had a number of wives (four to six) and thirty-five children that we took care of at the clinic. Four of his teenage boys were in my Sunday School class, and we were praying for two others to come to know Christ, and they later did. I had the rare privilege of having six teenage boys from this one family in class at the same time.

After about four years at Sibut, Helene's husband was made principal of the high school in Bambari, the second largest town in the country, located one hundred miles east of Sibut. After they moved, I missed Helene, but I didn't forget to pray for the family. When the president of our country, Andre Kolingba, made a visit to Bambari, the town committee chose beautiful Sylvia to present a bouquet of flowers to him at the town flagpole.

Two years later the Bagasses came to visit me, and I didn't have to be told that Mr. Bagasse was a new man in Christ. He had such a radiant and peaceful expression on his face. As they sat in my living room, he related to me the story of his "born again" experience. The Holy Spirit made him so miserable in his sinful ways that he knew Christ was the only answer. It was great to see the delightful expression on Helene's face as she watched her husband talk about the change Christ had made in his life and with his family. My heart was overflowing with thankfulness to the Lord. Helene's faith in our Lord had accomplished much.

They had more good news for me. Helene said, "My husband has been appointed the Central African Republic's ambassador to France. We are going to leave right away and we wanted you to know."

The next day was Sunday, and the couple attended church. It was a day of rejoicing, and there was a parade of people shaking their hands in welcome.

That was one of the happiest days of my life. I knew many of us were thinking, *Glory to God, He has answered prayer.*

Soon after their arrival in France, Helene's husband bought an accordion for the Sibut Church.

One morning in 1987, a sophisticated, dressed-up Helene came to the clinic to say hello. I felt so unkempt next to her, especially when she asked me with a worried expression on her face, "Have you been ill?"

She was the same sweet Helene I formerly knew as she said, "All our family goes to a wonderful church in Paris now. We are so happy in our Christian life." She also mentioned she was working as a secretary at a television station there.

Two years later Mr. Bagasse came back to see his brother and to check on their property. When he left Sibut, he gave me their Paris address and telephone number, saying, "Please come to see us when you travel to Paris on your way home. We would be so glad to welcome you."

I never did, but I now realize I should at least have given them a telephone call, when passing through France.

When I hear someone ask for prayer for an unsaved spouse, I often think of the Bagasse family. What God did for that family, He can do for others. He does not play favorites. "He is patient with you, not wanting anyone to perish, but everyone to come to repentance" (2 Peter 3:9, NIV).

As that song by Stuart Hamblen says, "It is no secret what God can do."

49 - Lovely Claire Mafouta

My! Eight-year-old Claire looked terrific marching proudly in front of the grade school Independence Day parade. She had the personality that made her a natural to lead this important event.

My co-worker Florence had made her a dress with the colors of the Central African Republic flag—blue, white, green, yellow, and red.

I had known Claire's family since the time I arrived in Africa, for they lived only about a quarter of a mile from the Sibut station. Her mother, Gbenou, became one of the leaders of our girls' movement, the Lumieres. I remember the evening when Louvrou and I delivered Gbenou's twins at the clinic. One of the twins died during the night. I could never understand why the child had died. It had appeared healthy at birth. Claire was the surviving twin. Claire and her brothers and sisters were all faithful in Florence's children's classes. They all came to know Christ as Savior. Later Claire and her two younger sisters were faithful members of my teenage girls' class.

Each time I came back from furlough, I brought back good used clothing. My co-workers did the same. I always enjoyed having something to give to someone in need. Once I gave Claire a lovely white pleated skirt. It was a perfect fit, with the hem coming to her knees. Imagine my dismay to find that she had cut it off to make a very short miniskirt, the style of the sixties! It doesn't take long for styles from France to reach Africa.

Claire was good friends with Cheryl Owen, the oldest daughter of our missionary printer Bob Owen and his wife Georgia. After Cheryl graduated from our high school in Bangui, she stayed in Africa with her parents for another year. I liked Cheryl and wanted to do something special for her. I was scheduled to do Vacation Bible School in one of our smaller churches, so I asked Cheryl and Claire to come with me and be my helpers.

We went to Possel, a town about sixty miles out of Sibut, on the river that

Claire Mafouta

divides the Central African Republic from Zaire. Claire and Cheryl, along with some of the young people from the church, were good helpers. We had about forty children that week. It was the rainy season, so every time we got into my truck camper, we had to take time to scrape off the horrible clay stuck to our shoes. I was so glad we didn't have that kind of soil on our Sibut hilltop.

Later, for fun, a couple of the believers in Possel took us canoeing on the river, which is home to the largest crocodiles in the world. As long as we kept our fingers out of the water, we didn't have to worry about them. Once when I was getting out of a canoe after a delightful ride, my foot slipped. I fell on the edge of the canoe. It was very painful. I realized later I must have cracked a couple of ribs, but it was better than having a crocodile get me.

Sometime later Sibut ran out of kerosene, a necessity for the hurricane lamps used by the Africans. Claire and her fiancèe were trying to mix gasoline and diesel fuel to make a mixture that would burn in a lamp. Some unthinking person came up to them with a lighted lamp to see what they were doing, and there was an explosion!

I was enjoying my Sunday afternoon siesta when someone called to me. The teenage boy at my door blurted out his tragic message: "Claire Mafouta has been badly burned. Come quickly." As I dashed to my truck and sped down to the clinic, I hoped and prayed that he was exaggerating. However, one look at the charred body confirmed my worst fears. Lovely, vivacious Claire was unrecognizable, burned on 70 percent of her body.

One of our pastor's sons, Philippe, had helped carry Claire to the clinic. Since I had no helpers on hand, I asked him to assist me. I was so thankful there was a large reserve basin of sterilized Vaseline gauze ready for such an emergency. I donned surgical gloves and a mask and went to work. It was a horrible two hours. I had to fight to keep my emotions under control as I began to carefully remove the charred skin and bandage her body. Philippe did a terrific job as my assistant. He was tender to Claire, and he quickly understood the different things I asked him to do. But Claire went into shock. Her veins collapsed, and I couldn't insert an IV line to give her needed fluids and medication.

When we had finished, I went to see Claire's family, who were anxiously waiting on the veranda. I tried to be calm as I spoke. "Claire's body is badly burned. We will put her in a private room out back, but outside of a miracle from the Lord, it is impossible for her to live. I could take her to the hospital in Bangui, but I know it would be useless, and the three-hour journey would be very painful for her. What do you want me to do?"

"We would like her to remain here," her parents immediately replied.

About noon the next day, Claire went into the presence of the Lord. I'm glad that Claire was prepared for eternity.

We never know what tomorrow will bring. In my medical practice I have had babies, children, youth, young adults, and seniors leave this world. Death is no respecter of age. Each of us needs to be prepared for whenever that time comes. In Mark 8:36 it says, "What good is it for a man to gain the whole world, yet forfeit his soul" (NIV)?

50 - Memories of Muslims

In my medical ministry in Africa I had many contacts with Muslims. We called them Arabs because of their long, flowing, white robes, though most of them were African, from two northern tribes in Nigeria. They came to our towns for business and to spread their religion.

I have to admit that at the clinic many of the Arab men frequently tried my patience. Each day before the clinic opened, someone from my staff would give a short evangelistic message to the people waiting on the veranda to be seen. The Arab men would come late in the morning, so that they wouldn't have to hear the Word of God proclaimed. They would then come directly into the consultation room, expecting us to take care of them immediately. Sometimes I had to be very firm and tell them two or three times to please go back outside and wait their turn. The Arab women, on the other hand, were very cooperative, and we enjoyed taking care of them.

One day, as I was in my truck, going to my Thursday afternoon class at our mission downtown, I noticed about seven Muslims kneeling on mats, reciting their prayers. (They do this five times a day.) The Lord convicted my heart about their need for salvation. My heart ached, for I knew that they had no personal relationship with their god, Allah, and I prayed, *Lord, please let me have the privilege of seeing at least one Muslim come to You during my time in Africa.*

Waggie

Not long after that, in 1977, my good friend from Seattle, Erma Swanson Sowers, came to Africa with a friend for a ten-day visit. She had plans to go on to Israel and arranged for me to go with her as her guest.

We took the Russian airline, *Aeroflot,* from the Central African Republic north to Egypt and stayed there three days. Imagine our surprise when the British Airways travel agent informed us that we could not go directly to Israel from Cairo, because there were no diplomatic relations between the two countries at that time. They advised us to go to the Mediterranean island of Cyprus first, and then proceed on to Israel. We had to contact four airlines but at last found a plane that could take us there.

Our plane was not crowded, and when I saw a young African man about twenty-four years of age sitting by himself, I took the seat next to him. We immediately started to talk, and I asked, "Why are you going to Cyprus?"

"I am a sailor on Greek merchant ships," he replied. "The ship I was on was wrecked in the Mediterranean Sea, and fourteen drowned. I was injured and hospitalized in Egypt. I lost my passport and other things and will have to go to Cyprus to try to get a new one."

"Where do you live in Africa?" I asked after he said his name was Waggie.

"In West Africa," he replied.

"Are there Christian missionaries there?" I asked.

"Oh no, in our area we are all Muslims," Waggie said.

"Then you don't know anything about Christ, do you?" I said, continuing my questioning.

"Oh, yes I do," he countered. "When I decided to become a sailor, I went to Perugia, Italy, to learn Greek, for I wanted to be employed by a Greek shipping company. While I was there, I became friends with a Nigerian who was a follower of Christ. He used to talk to me about Jesus. A few times I went with him to a Bible study taught by an American missionary, and this missionary gave me a Bible. I had it with me on board the ship, but I lost it."

By this time I was very interested in Waggie, and the conversation flowed. "Do you believe that Jesus Christ is the Son of God?" I asked.

"Yes, I do, " he replied.

"Do you believe that, as God, He died on the cross to pay the penalty for your sins and the sins of the world?"

"Yes, " he said.

"Do you believe that after three days He rose from the dead?" I asked with surprise.

"Yes."

"Do you believe that after forty days He returned to heaven and is coming again someday to take the followers of Christ back to heaven?" I asked.

"Yes, I do."

Again I was amazed. I then asked my final question: "Then why is it that you haven't become a follower of Jesus?"

"You do not understand," the young man declared. "I was raised a Muslim. If I became a follower of Christ, I could never go back to my village and visit my family again. They would be required to arrange somehow to have me killed."

"I have heard of this happening," I said to him, "but I have never met one who spoke of it to me personally. But if you ever want to become a follower of Christ, you can do it wherever you are—in your room aboard ship, on the ship's deck, or anywhere you happen to be. You know your eternal destiny rests on that great decision."

At that moment the stewardess came with our meal, though it was only an hour's flight. After we had eaten and the stewardess had cleared away our trays, Waggie tapped my left shoulder and said, "I want to believe in Christ right now." So we bowed our heads and prayed, and he became a new man in Christ.

After that there was no more time to talk, for the plane was landing. We walked together from the plane to the airport. As long as I live, I will never forget the words he said to me: "I have such peace in my heart!"

We couldn't go through customs in the same place because he had papers to show the official in another part of the building. When we said goodbye, I felt like I had lost my child, my friend, and I knew I would never see him again until we meet in heaven.

After twenty-five years I have never forgotten Waggie. I often pray, "Lord, somehow let him encounter other Christians, to share his testimony and grow in the knowledge of God."

Often when I think of him, I think of those verses in I Corinthians: "What, after all, is Apollos? And what is Paul? Only servants, through whom you came to believe—as the Lord has assigned to each his task. I planted the seed, Apollos watered it, but God made it grow. So neither he who plants nor he who waters is anything, but only God, who makes things grow. The man who plants and the man who waters have one purpose, and each will be rewarded according to his own labor. For we are God's fellow workers" (3:5-9, NIV).

This is exactly what happened with Waggie. His Nigerian friend told him of Christ which planted the seed, the missionary at Perugia watered the seed in his Bible studies, I reaped the harvest on the airplane, but God was the one who made it grow.

I had a similar experience on one of my furloughs:

Once, when I missed my flight out of Las Vegas for Los Angeles and was rescheduled for a flight three hours later, I said to the Lord, "You must have a reason for this delay in my plans. I'm trusting you."

The next plane had many empty seats, so I was surprised when a young fellow about thirty years old boarded the plane after I did and sat next to me. He was an Australian scientist who had come to the United States for an important conference.

After talking about general things for awhile, our conversation turned to spiritual topics, and he remarked, "You talk just like my best friend from high school talks now. Something happened to him that changed him since we left school."

My Australian traveling companion didn't accept Christ there and then, but I have thanked the Lord many times for letting me water the seed that his high school friend had sown in his heart. I often pray, "Lord, send someone to him that will reap the harvest that has already been sown and watered." I know in my heart why the Lord had me miss my flight.

Ibrahim

Forty-year-old Ibrahim was a tall, personable, handsome Arab man who came to our clinic. He owned two large trucks that he used to travel to Chad, the country to the north of the Central African Republic—or even further away to Nigeria—to buy merchandise to sell to the small store owners in Sibut.

Ibrahim had a chauffeur whose name was Benjamin. Benjamin's wife was hospitalized at our clinic, and while she was with us, she became a follower of Christ. We gave Benjamin a French Bible, which he would often read when his wife was with us. A few years later he came to my house, and we had a long talk on the veranda about Christianity. He was very close to becoming a Christian, but I think he was afraid of losing his job if he was converted. He always had a smile when we met.

One day Benjamin came to my rescue when I had a flat tire in downtown Sibut. He was right there when it happened and said, "Mademoiselle, I'll change that tire for you." And in no time it was done.

Soon after this, Ibrahim came to the clinic in his spotless long white robe. He informed me that he and Benjamin were leaving the next day to go to Chad on a buying trip. I asked him if he would buy several bolts of cloth for me while he was there.

Without hesitation he replied, "I would be glad to. What would you like?"

From the start of our youth movement in 1964, I had been responsible for the supply depot, which included cloth for their uniforms. I considered myself fortunate to be able to put in a large order with Ibrahim.

When he returned, he delivered my order to the print shop, where the supply depot was. "I'm so thankful for your doing this for me," I said as I paid him.

With a nice smile he replied, "Anytime you want me to do something for you, just let me know."

During the last few years I was in Africa, there was some bandit activity in different areas. The bandits would stop buses or cars with their guns and rob everyone. At first this activity was only prevalent in the northern part of our country because the bandits were from Sudan and Chad. Later, bandits were operating all over the country. We were very saddened to hear once that they had killed an American who had come out to Africa to visit his Lutheran missionary friend.

Even my brother Paul came upon them when he was in the Central African Republic during my last year on the field. Paul traveled on the roads most of the time, going from church to church and showing *The Jesus Film*. He used my truck and always had an African team of three with him. Once, on a much-traveled road to the capital, Paul came around a sharp curve and was forced to slam on the brakes to avoid several large rocks scattered across the road. My brother got out of the truck and began to toss the rocks off the road. The Africans uncharacteristically remained in the vehicle.

After finishing the job, he climbed back into the truck and said, "Why didn't you fellows come and give me a hand?" Only then did he notice the concern in their eyes.

"Monsieur, did you not see that there are bandits with guns hiding in the tall grass beside the road?"

I often wondered whether the Lord used the signs *Dispensaire De Sibut* and the large red cross painted on both sides of my truck to prevent the bandits from robbing my brother.

In 1994, when I came home from the Central African Republic for the last time, I learned that one of the main leaders of the bandits had been arrested. To my amazement and shock, it was Ibrahim from Sibut. I was reminded of Jeremiah 17:9: "The heart is deceitful above all things, and desperately wicked; who can know it?" Man can't. But God can.

Amadou of the Mbororo Tribes

The Mbororo tribes are nomadic cattle people who practice the Islamic faith. Sometimes we would see them traveling on the roads, carrying their bows and quivers of arrows and leading a couple of burros or herding their African cattle. The burros carry their owners' meager earthly belongings and often a mother with a child. Many times the tribesmen would shun the roads and follow the trails leading through the bush country or the jungles. They camped out in the open, but if they found good grazing land, they built a small, temporary, grass hut. They were pleased if they could camp for a while near a town, because then they would have the opportunity to sell some of their cattle.

Since they seldom mingled with any other African tribes, very few of them spoke the trade language, Sango, which we used in the medical work. At first only a few of them came to the clinic, but as the word spread among them about us and the loving care they received from my staff, more began to come. We always had to put the Mbororo patients in a private room because other Africans did not want to associate with them.

I remember the first Mbororo woman who came with a sick baby. We had to hospitalize them. The mother was a beautiful, graceful woman, but at first it was difficult to be around her. Most African women use some kind of oil or ointment on their bodies. This woman used butter, and after a couple of days it became rancid.

One day a twenty-five-year-old Mbororo fellow and his sick father came to us from a village about 400 miles northeast of Sibut. The father had eye surgery, and Amadou, his son, took good care of him for the three weeks that they were with us.

Several months later we were surprised to see them again. This time we diagnosed the father with tuberculosis, which necessitated a four-month stay. Amadou knew a little Sango, and after associating with my staff, he soon became more fluent in speaking and understanding the language. All of my staff took a special interest in the young man and his father, especially Kembi Louis.

Kembi would spend a lot of time with Amadou, teaching him Sango and simply explaining the Gospel message over and over. Many times Amadou heard the word of Christ preached at the clinic, and all of the staff witnessed to him repeatedly. Praise to the Lord, he believed.

Student helper Philippe bidding good-bye to Amadou.

When the time came to say goodbye, we gathered around them and prayed. Amadou's parting words were, "Who will tell me more about Jesus when I leave here?" His words saddened us as we were thinking the same thing. Their roving way of life would make this difficult.

51 - Visitors From Near and Far

E very mission station has its share of visitors. Sibut station was one of the busiest, for it was at a three-directional crossroads. Everyone from Bangui has to come and go through Sibut, especially when taking children to the missionary school at Crampel.

There are no hotels along the way, so each missionary home has a guestroom (or rooms). Travelers in Central African Republic depended upon these guestrooms since there are no other accommodations available. It was always good to see those who came by—not only from our mission but those strangers passing through as well.

Carol and Rita

One group of people whose visits we enjoyed was the Peace Corp volunteers. The first two volunteers at Sibut, Carol and Rita, were delightful girls. Carol taught math and Rita taught science in the high school. The volunteers have only two months of French study before they begin teaching. It always amazed me how they could teach with such limited language study.

Carol and Rita were both Christians, and they came up to our mission every Sunday night for a meal and our evening service. On Christmas Eve all of us, Carol and Rita included, went to Bangui for a Christmas-carol sing and program that the Bangui missionaries had for us. We were a sleepy bunch when we came back home at 2:00 a.m.

I had a Bible study with Carol. I still treasure the letter she wrote to me after she returned home in which she thanked me for my help to her spiritually while she was in Africa.

There were others I had studies with. For instance, Kathy who had gone to church all of her life. She owned a Bible but had never studied it. In our time together she realized she had never been *born again*, but when she understood God's plan of salvation, she made that commitment to Christ.

Heide

In the earlier days we never knew when a Peace Corps volunteer would be stopping by. Late one Good Friday evening, I opened the dining room door in answer to a knock. There stood a tall, dark-haired lady with a disarrayed, dusty appearance.

She said with a loud voice, "I'm Heide, and I'm with the Peace Corps at Bambari. I've just come back from a trip to Bamingui-Bangoran Park near N'dele. My, did I see the animals! I hitchhiked back with an Arab truck driver. He let me off downtown, and I walked out here."

I immediately invited her in. Since I was about to eat supper, I asked her to join me. During the meal she told me about her trip to the park and seeing all the different kinds of animals. I could share her enthusiasm, for I had been there in 1954.

Then she casually mentioned, "If I were home tonight, I would be celebrating the Passover with my family." I knew then she was Jewish.

I asked her, "Have you ever read in the Bible how the Passover started?"

"No," she replied.

"Would you like to?"

"Yes, I think I would."

"Okay, while you take your shower, I'll open a Bible to the book of Exodus, where Moses tells the Israelites how to get ready to depart from Egypt, and I'll put it on your bedside table."

The next morning at breakfast she said, "I became so interested in reading about Moses, I kept reading for a long time."

"Would you like to keep the Bible?"

"Yes, I would."

She thanked me many times as she prepared to leave and find a way back to Bambari. That was the last time I saw her. She did come back to Sibut once, but I was on a road trip and was so disappointed at not being able to see her.

Shortly after that, it was furlough time. One evening I went with my parents to their church for a presentation by the group called "Jews for Jesus." After the presentation the audience was asked, "How many of you people are praying for someone Jewish?" Very few hands went up in that crowded church. I couldn't even raise mine.

Then came the challenge to us all: "How many of you will start praying for at least one Jewish person you know to come to know Christ?" I immediately thought of Heide. My hand went up. I have prayed for Heide for many years. I don't know where she is, but the Lord does. I so want to see her in heaven and hear her say, "Thank you for that Bible you gave to me."

The Right Cassette Tape

Late one Easter afternoon, Marty Murtoff came to my house and said, "John, a Peace Corps fellow from Mbres [forty miles from Kaga-Bondoro] has arrived with his father to spend the night at our house. We knew John at Kaga-Bondoro when we were studying Sango there. I thought I would let you know, since you're having the evening meal and meeting at your house tonight."

I answered, "No problem. I have enough food prepared."

Then she remarked, "Oh, I forgot to tell you, they are Jewish, and his father is an orthopedic surgeon."

After she left, I prayed, *Lord, you know about this situation, and I need just the right tape to play for our evening meeting tonight. Please help me choose the one that will speak to their hearts.* I had a treasure box of many tapes by Chuck Swindoll and John McArthur that a friend, Polly Gwinn, had given to me. I found two Easter messages by Swindoll and chose the tape called "Proofs of the Resurrection."

John and his father came over to my house a little before the evening meal. It was interesting to talk with the doctor and hear his impressions about Africa and the government medical facility at Mbres.

I can still remember one sentence he uttered: "I wouldn't take off a toenail in that room."

I wanted to say, *If that room was all you had, you would, and you would even do a C-section there.*

The taped message that Swindoll preached that night was powerful. He gave so many proofs from the scriptures and history that proved Christ did rise from the dead.

After the service the doctor remarked, "He gave a very convincing evidence of Jesus' resurrection."

I quickly thanked the Lord for helping me choose that tape. I don't know where the surgeon lives, but once in a while I still pray, *Lord, may He find his rest and peace in Jesus, his Messiah.*

The Shy American

One day Margo saw me passing her house and called out to me to come and meet some Peace Corps workers: Mary, who lived at Sibut, and two other volunteers who had come to visit her. One was a very shy Asian-American named Michael. When meeting another American in the middle of Africa, one of the first questions asked is "Where are you from?" As I was sitting close to Michael, I asked that question.

He answered, "Out west."

"Where out west?"

"Oregon."

Now I was really becoming interested, so I continued, "Where in Oregon?"

"The southeast part."

I had never met anyone who was so short in answering questions. "But where in the southeast part?" I was interested because I had attended my last two years of high school in southeastern Oregon.

"It's a little town you've never heard of."

I answered, "Try me."

"Nyssa."

"Nyssa!" I exclaimed as I put out my hand to clasp his. "I am from there also. I graduated from Nyssa High School in 1942."

All his shyness disappeared, his face brightened up, and we had a wonderful talk like long-lost friends. How good it is when living far away to meet someone who knows about your hometown.

The Russians Came

Since Russians were teaching in many of our Central African Republic high schools in the '70s, a Russian couple came to teach in our high school. He taught science, and she taught math. The students at Sibut had many arguments with him when he taught evolution as a fact. Many told him about our Creator, the God who made the world and man, but he wasn't interested.

I made friends with the Russian couple and once took them to Kaga-Bondoro for dental work. I invited them to our station's Christmas Eve celebration at my house. I was fortunate to have a Russian New Testament with Psalms that I bought in Switzerland, which I gave to them as a gift. I also gave them Billy Graham's book, *Peace with God*, in French and prayed that they would read it and the words would speak to their hearts.

These two people had grown up in Russia with little access to information about God. I could not let the opportunity pass. As it says in Romans 10:16-17, "But not everyone welcomes the Good News...Yet faith comes from listening to this message of good news—the Good News about Christ" (NLT).

The Wanderer

Late one afternoon a very attractive blonde lady about thirty years of age appeared at my door. She spoke perfect English with a delightful accent.

"My name is Elizabeth, and I'm traveling through Africa. May I stay with you tonight?"

She wore shorts and sandals and had a small knapsack on her back. I was horrified at the thought of her traveling through Africa with only a knapsack, without drinking water or food. I invited her in, gave her a cold drink of water, showed her the guestroom, and prepared her shower. She wasn't talkative and seemed very aloof. I took her up to another household for the evening meal, for they had guests from another mission, the Rickmans, and it was their turn to provide the meal for all guests.

When Elizabeth returned to my house, she went to her room, stayed there a while, and then joined me on the veranda. She still didn't carry on much of a conversation. I didn't even find out what nationality she was.

The next morning we had breakfast, and she prepared to go. I noticed her sandals again and said, "I have a new pair of tennis shoes. Would you like to have them?"

Her eyes lit up, and she smiled and said, "Yes, please."

They were a perfect fit. I walked with her to the end of the path, where she gave me a casual good-bye. She walked several yards down the path and then turned around and came back.

Much to my amazement she threw her arms around me, gave me a hug, and said, "Thank you, thank you very much."

Four months later the Rickman family (who was visiting the same night as Elizabeth had been) was our guest again. They were on their way to Crampel to pick up their two children from school for their summer vacation. Lois said, "Remember the lady who was with you the same night we were here?"

"How could I forget her?" I replied. "She was so unusual."

Lois continued, "One of the Christians in our district told me about her. She was in a small village when she became very ill with dysentery. The Africans didn't know what to do, but they put her in a wheelbarrow and took her to a small first aid place, which didn't have any medication, and she died there. Of course they had to bury her the next day. They found her passport. She was Austrian, so the authorities sent the passport to her home."

I felt bad when I heard this news. I could imagine loving parents in faraway Austria wondering and praying for a long-lost daughter. How it must have grieved them to know she died among strangers and was buried in an unmarked grave in the middle of Africa.

She was different from any visitor I ever had.

A Pastor and His Son

The first American visitors I remember coming to Sibut directly from the

States were Pastor Sandgren and his son, Leo. Ferd Rosenau was a member of Pastor Sandgren's church in Austin, Minnesota, which was Ferd's main supporting church.

Pastor Sandgren and Leo came out to go hunting, for there were a lot of animals in the earlier days. I don't remember what they killed, but I do remember the Africans had a good feed. The main thing I remember about him is his remarks about how well the missionaries ate. He did not understand that he was getting the "visitor treatment," and that we did not eat like this on a daily basis.

When they left, I took them to Bangui in my newly arrived pickup. In Bangui, Pastor Sandgren became very ill with malaria. We knew he realized then that missionary work in Africa wasn't all a bed of roses.

It was part of the Lord's plan that the Sandgren's made that trip to Sibut. As Leo sat on the veranda of the house that overlooked the Sibut student village, the Lord spoke to his heart, saying, *I want you to come back here as a missionary*. He and his family did. Leo and Gloria were a delightful couple and a blessing at Crampel, where they worked for years.

Many a young person who came out for a short visit later returned as a career missionary.

Paul and Ruth's Visit

How wonderful it was to have someone from my own family, my brother Paul and his wife Ruth, come out for a three-week visit and see the place where I spent so many years of my life.

They arrived one stormy night in July of 1987. Their plane attempted to land in the downpour three times before it succeeded. It was a relieved group of passengers who walked into the terminal, not to mention the relief of those of us waiting.

Poor Paul. Since I wasn't seeing too well at night, I asked him to drive us to the Bangui mission station. He was game, driving down the muddy dirt road when it was difficult for anyone to see much, with the rain still pelting us in torrents. We finally arrived on pavement and continued safely on to the mission.

At the time Paul and Ruth came, there were two couples and two single ladies, Loie Knight and I, on the Sibut station. One of Ernie's sisters had also come to visit.

Loie had come to live with me, so she could help with our teaching ministry, and she was always more than willing to help me make a diagnosis on a patient when I asked her. I also appreciated it that she took over the main responsibility for the cooking. It was a comfort having her around.

Ruth's main observation during her three-week stay was that everyone was so busy that no one had much time to spend with visitors. If they did find time to visit, it was in the evening after a day's work, and they were nearly exhausted. However, we did have time to play games some evenings. Paul spent most of his time repairing things and working in the garage with Doug Murtoff.

One of the most memorable evenings of my life was when Paul, Ruth, and I sat on the veranda for almost an hour watching nature's fireworks as lightning flashed continually across the sky. I never saw anything like it.

I hated to see them leave, because they were a delight to have around. I never dreamed that some day they would be coming back on a short-term mission trip.

An Eighty-four-year-old Friend

Neva Prindle, the mother of Eric Elmer of Bambari, visited me often. She first came to Bambari in 1982 to help take care of her two teenage grand-daughters, Christy and Vicky, and help school them when their mother, Cheryl, was busy teaching the Africans. Neva didn't have any family back home, so she stayed in Africa for three terms (twelve years).

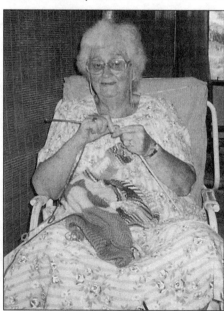

Margery's eighty-four-year-old friend, Neva Prindle.

Neva's hands were never idle; she was always knitting. She could knit a sweater in a day, and she knitted a sweater for every missionary man, woman, and child on the field. Then she knitted for some Africans. She made anything that could be knitted and all without patterns.

She loved to come and visit me, and I enjoyed having her. We had such good fellowship together, sharing Bible verses, thoughts, and prayers. In addition she loved to play *Scrabble*. When Loie came back with the game *Upwords*, it quickly replaced *Scrabble*. Ernie used to join us. We enjoyed it because we were about equal in our ability to play the game.

Neva was always asking how she could help me. She asked that question one day in December 1993 as she sat at the dining room table writing her Christmas letter.

I told her, "You can write a letter for me." She didn't think I was serious, but I said half-jesting, "I had a short-termer here once, Judy, and she wrote three letters for me." So Neva wrote:

> I am staying with Margery B. for a few days. She is so busy I cannot see how she will ever get a Christmas letter written. It is impossible for you to realize how much God is using her in His service. Besides her teaching in our Sibut Bible School, she has Bible classes in which all Africans are welcome. And her door is always besieged. She hardly has a moment to herself. Then there is the entertaining and feeding of other missionaries. Margery now has a VCR she bought from a Christian Embassy couple, and different groups come in to view the many Christian French ones that she has, plus some entertaining animal videos.
>
> Someone gave Margery some John McArthur tapes, which she generously lends to other missionaries. A good Christmas message is in 1 John. It brings JOY to the Christian heart. McArthur says the Gospel of John was written to the unsaved that they might believe in the Lord Jesus Christ (John 20-21).
>
> John the apostle also wrote the three epistles, later in our Bible, to Christians. There are three things man desires more than anything: 1. Happiness, 2. A clear conscience, 3. Security. 1 John gives the Christians all three joys at this Christmas season.
>
> 1. We can have Happiness when we believe in the Lord Jesus, and he answers prayer. 1 John 1:4; 3:22-23.
> 2. Our Conscience is clear when our sins are forgiven. 1 John 1:9; 2:12.
> 3. We have Security in the assurance that when we trust in the Lord Jesus; we will go to heaven. 1 John 5:22, 13; 3:14
>
> May you know these three joys at this Christmas season.

Many do not know of the following report from the U.S. government: "For an American to live in CAR, cost of living is over twice as much as living in Washington D.C." Tourists tell us that in CAR things are much more expensive than any other African country. To post a letter costs $1.00. I feel sorry for the Africans. They are very poor and can live only on what they grow as there are no factories in which to work in this country."

An Enjoyable Short-term Nurse

During my years in Africa, three short-term nurses came to visit and work at the clinic. Judy Stanton stayed the longest. She would have made a good career missionary, but her heart was with David, a young lifeguard she met at a Bible camp where she was the nurse. I enjoyed her help in the clinic, our Bible studies together, de-ticking our dog, Dolly, and her writing ability. She wrote several letters home for me when I was too tired or couldn't think of anything to write. Here are two of those letters.

Judy Stanton getting medications ready to give to hospitalized patients.

March, 1982

Hello, this is not Margery writing. I am a short-termer who has been out here helping with the dispensary work for about eight months. We are both on letter-writing sprees, and she gave me permission to cook up a little epistle on her behalf. But little does she know that she gave up all editing rights! Now...what would you like to know?

We are in Bangui for a few days— officially on vacation. The dispensary is partially closed for a couple of weeks while the workers take their vacations. We had classes with the two newest helpers through Wednesday morning and left for Bangui after Margery's Bible School class on Thursday morning. Two fellows came along with us to visit relatives and to see the "big city." In the villages along the way, the people have stands in their yards with various things for sale. We saw all kinds of fruits, firewood, woven baskets, mats, and DEAD MONKEYS. Dieudonne wanted to stop and buy one, but he didn't find one he thought he could afford. We weren't too disappointed. Somehow the thought of a dead monkey and any accompanying microscopic creatures on it directly behind us...just didn't appeal.

The first week of April Margery spent at another station, Bambari. They had sponsored a camp for Lumiere leaders and wanted Margery to oversee it. The Lumieres are the girls' group (and the Flambeaux the boys), similar to our Awana Clubs in the churches at home. She had a busy week, and I had a disastrous one! I couldn't find half the medicines we needed, we ran out of dog food (you can't buy it here), the refrigerator burned up its wick, the instant pudding I fixed for company was NOT instant, and one of our measles babies died. I was ready for her to come back home!

Just after she returned, we had another adventure. We were both in the kitchen one morning when all of a sudden a green mamba snake came slithering out from behind the wood stove. In case the word mamba doesn't strike terror in your heart, let me hasten to assure you it is a most poisonous variety! We both yelled "snake' as it made its exit under the door. Aren't you glad we have a Heavenly Father who takes care of us?

September, 1982

What is Margery up to? Do you REALLY want to know? I know she won't tell you this, so I will. One morning she and Bruce (Rosenau) took the dogs down to the clinic to chase pigs! Can you imagine? They run loose and are a big problem. It was pure bedlam—dogs barking, Bruce shouting, pigs squealing, and half a hundred kids (more or less) following the chase!

Of course she also does a few more serious "missionary-minded" things. It is not unusual for me to get up in the morning and find a note telling me that she left anywhere from 3:30 a.m. to 5:00 a.m. to pick up a sick person or to take a patient and family home. In fact, that happened just this morning.

We are in the rainy season now, and that poses traveling difficulties. Since the roads are dirt, it really tears them up to have big trucks traveling over them right after a rain. All the towns put up rain barriers and traffic stops until six hours after the rain ends. That red cross on Margery's truck does wonders, though. It gets her through barriers where others would have to wait. It worked fine for her this morning. On her return to Sibut she picked up a man walking the 100 miles from the capitol to get his birth certificate, so he could enter police training. By the time she let him out in Sibut, he was a newborn Christian.

All our pastors have been coming in for VBS materials —another project of Margery's. She prepared packets of materials including everything from teachers' booklets to crayons to small prizes for 20 different churches. No less than half a dozen pastors wanted her to conduct their VBS herself! Pray especially for one being held the first week of September about 100 miles from here. Margery will be at that one.

Leah, one of the oldest believers in the area, died a couple of weeks ago. Her mother was a witch doctor when the missionaries first arrived here. Leah had cataracts and was nearly blind. Every day she would come to the clinic for eye medicine. We couldn't seem to explain to her that no medicine could restore her sight. We told her she would have to wait until she got to heaven to get some new eyes. Well, now she has them!

Please continue to pray for the clinic and Bible School. There are still some ten churches in our Sibut area without pastors. The pastors who are busy in the work need prayer as well, like Pastor Irimou who is at the clinic now. He is quite depressed with various problems he is up against.

P.S. Our pastor's wife, Aoua, was with Leah the last day of her illness. As Leah became very restless, Aoua leaned over her and said, "Leah, why don't you just put yourself now in the arms of Jesus and let Him take you to your heavenly home?" Leah whispered back, "I will," closed her eyes, and breathed her last.

Part Seven

Unforgettable Experiences

God has not promised skies always blue
Flower strewn pathways all our lives through.
God had not promised sun without rain,
Joy without sorrow, peace without pain.
But God has promised strength for the day,
Rest for the laborer, light on the way;
Grace for the trial, help from above,
Unfailing sympathy, undying love.

—Annie Johnson Flint

Discouragement comes into the life of anyone who is human. Missionaries are not exempt. How thankful I am, as I look over my life, that when discouragement came, the Lord undertook for me. I never once thought about quitting. That was never an option. I'm sure my friends at home were praying for me when difficult times came, just as I am sure that the Lord led me to His promises in the Word that carried me through. Praise His Name!

I recall the discouragement I felt one evening when, for the first time in my life that I can remember, I lost my temper. It was early in my second term, and I had taken six Bible School students out on the Bambari road for village classes. At that time the first church on that road was twenty miles from the mission. The insurance on our vehicle limited us to eight passengers and a driver. If we took more than that and had an accident, our insurance would be void.

At my last stop on the return trip to pick up students, there were three other people waiting beside the road—a sick woman, her caretaker, and a teenage boy. I told the teenager, "I can't take you. I have my insurance quota." I know he was thinking there was enough room for him, and he argued with me. Twice I started my truck. Both times I noticed in my rear view mirror that the teenager was getting into the truck. The second time I got out of the truck and went back to tell him to get out. He wouldn't. Finally I said, "I will stand here until you do!" After a few minutes he reluctantly got out.

At the mission village I let the students out and went up the hill to the clinic to leave the ill lady and her caretaker. Imagine my astonishment when I saw the teenager also getting out. I quickly marched to the back, and as he put his leg over the tailgate, I gave him a good swat on his bottom. I stood there, shocked at what I had done.

To make matters worse, one hundred yards away I saw Pastor Sesse coming towards us. I immediately thought, *Did he see what I just did?* Needless to say, I was ashamed to realize I had lost my temper and disgraced my testimony. I was usually an easy-going person. Because of this, I apparently thought I was immune to losing my temper. How wrong I was.

That night the old hymn "What A Friend We Have in Jesus" came to mind and I remembered the well-known words, "Take it to the Lord in prayer."

Later I found myself losing patience when the sick ward patients or their caretakers threw their trash nearby. Then the Lord always reminded me of Romans 12:8, which lists some of the gifts of the Spirit. The last part of that verse speaks of one who "showeth mercy, with cheerfulness." I will always thank the Lord for giving me that verse at the many times I needed it. Isn't that like God's Word? It is living and always sufficient. What a comfort to know that God is speaking to us through it.

Another time the Lord spoke to me so sweetly about patience. As our patient load increased up to 150 people a day, we started work at 6:00 a.m. and I found myself getting irritated. This really bothered me; I so wanted to show the love of Christ to others under any circumstances. I wrote home asking my friends to pray that I might have more patience, not patients.

Right after that, I read this version of part of I Corinthians 13 somewhere. It struck me enough that I included it in a letter I wrote home.

> *Love suffereth long; it drives away all impatience.*
> *Love is kind; it leaves no room for unkindness.*
> *Love envieth not; all jealousy is banished.*
> *Love does not behave itself unseemly; folly goes.*
> *Seeketh not its own; selfishness will be unknown.*
> *It is not easily provoked; anger will not be seen.*
> *Taketh no account of evil; no brooding over so called wrongs.*
> *Beareth all things; complainings will vanish.*
> *Believeth all things; mistrust will not destroy fellowship.*
> *Hopeth all things; despair and anxiety go.*
> *THE GREATEST OF THESE IS LOVE.*

I prayed that that kind of love would be manifested in my life so it would glorify my Savior.

It was always a hard and discouraging time when my house or medical help quit, died, or had to be dismissed. I couldn't continually dwell on the past, thinking of all the hours I spent teaching them. That attitude would lead to depression, so I prayed for strength to go forward. God can erase from our minds discouraging times experienced in our past.

It was like that as I was reading letters I had sent home, especially one from 1976:

> I was in a pitying mood last week. Everything seemed to go wrong, and I couldn't write to anyone. We have had so many ill people, and there never seemed to be a let up. We almost hit the 500 mark, and never did we have less than 300. I got so tired. I was tired of seeing sick people. I was tired of not having water come out of the pipes (water was pumped up to barrels in back and then flowed down into the clinic). I was tired of wondering when a roof would be put on the new building as I had to turn away sick ones needing hospitalization because all our beds were full. I was tired of people saying, "Would you come and get this sick person, he is very sick and can't walk," etc. I worried why I didn't keep Cheryl Owen (a missionary's daughter) on antibiotics for more than ten days for an infection, as she had a relapse. Because of this, I hoped her parents and siblings wouldn't have to cancel their week in Europe on their way to the States for furlough.

As I re-read that letter I thought, *I'm glad I don't have to go through that week again.* Isn't it good of the Lord not to let us know beforehand what a day or a week may bring? He gives us grace as each day comes.

When I left the Central African Republic in 1990 for furlough, I turned my medical ministry over to Alice, a nurse who had been a short-termer at Ippy but had now returned as a career missionary. I wanted to spend my last term teaching in a Bible school and take advantage of the many opportunities that were always available with the youth and adults. I knew it would be difficult for Alice to have me back in Sibut when my furlough ended, and I knew some of the Africans wouldn't understand why I wanted to be free of the medical responsibility. I considered that it might be best if I transferred to another mission station for my last term.

While I was praying, asking the Lord to show me where He wanted me to go, I received a telegram from Vernon, asking me to return to Sibut and teach the women in the Sibut Bible School. In my heart I was glad that I could end my African missionary career at the Sibut station, where I had started.

Alice was living in the single ladies' house, where I had lived for so many years. Since she preferred to live alone, I moved my things into the Muhr's house, as they were in the United States on furlough. Soon it seemed that Satan was attacking me from every angle. I couldn't sleep well on a waterbed, and all three beds in the house were that kind. The waves that were generated when I changed sleeping positions made me a little dizzy. I solved this difficulty by putting a three-quarter-size mattress on top of the water mattress.

Then, the first time it was my turn to have the whole station over for our Sunday evening meal and meeting, everything went wrong. The carrot cake flopped, and I had to make another one. When I opened up the small freezer door for my meat, there was a horrible, repulsive, rotten smell.

Satan kept after me with thoughts like, *See, you are sixty-five years old now. You shouldn't have come back. You can't be useful now; your work is finished.*

I realized it was the enemy. I asked the Lord to give me something from the Word. I needed something I could cling to. He gave me Psalm 71. It tells about the Lord keeping us in our youth and not forsaking us when we become gray (my hair was now partly gray) and how our lips will shout for joy when we praise him. What an answer to prayer! I put my hands up in the air and shouted and praised and thanked the Lord. A great peace engulfed my soul.

My last term in Sibut was great. One of the best. Not that there weren't difficulties (like having to move five times), but I knew without a shadow of a doubt that daily my Lord was strengthening and directing my path.

53 - Obeying The Holy Spirit

One Sunday morning at the Sibut Church, after the choir sang, I felt the Spirit telling me to go to the clinic and have a meeting with the hospitalized patients. I walked out of church (I felt strange doing it because everyone could see me) and went to the clinic. There I presented a Bible lesson and then asked if there were any among them that were not believers. There were two. One of them was an old, gray-haired man who wanted to believe. The other was a man who said he wanted to believe, but later on when he got well.

I asked him, "How do you know you are going to get well?" Now that wasn't the right thing to say to a patient.

At that moment I heard the closing song at church and left the clinic. I needed to return to the church to have the library books available for check-out. But first I spoke to Yakete, one of the medical staff, and asked him to go over to the clinic and talk to the two men who had expressed an interest in the Lord. Yakete went to the clinic, and both men accepted Christ as their Savior.

Monday night, when I went to the clinic to do some dentistry, I first checked on the in-patients. The man who at first wanted to wait until he was better to accept the Lord was now irrational. Later that night he died. After his death people kept telling me what a wicked life he had led. It shook me as I realized again how I needed to be so in touch with the Spirit to heed His leading. I thought back many times, *What if I hadn't gone to the clinic during church?*

Another time I had a similar experience. One evening as I was at home reading, I felt I should go down to the clinic and check on my patients. As I greeted all the people in the sick ward, everyone seemed okay. I was puzzled. *Why was I here?*

Then I thought, *I'll just gather the people together and give them a talk about Jesus.* I went to get our Sango Bible and asked one of the family caretakers to go to the clinic veranda and bring another bench to the back. They usually did that anyway because some of the caretakers slept on them.

One man was too ill to come out of his room, so we had our little service with about fifteen people in front of his door so he could hear. I talked to them for about twenty minutes, and then we had a discussion on what a Christian was. I found out the man on the bed wasn't one, but he was willing to repent after our talk. I was so happy.

About midnight I was called back to the clinic because the man who was too ill to sit outside had suddenly taken a turn for the worse. By the time I got there, he had died. Now I knew why there was an urgency earlier to talk to the group.

The apostle Peter said for us to always be ready to give an answer for the hope that is within us (1 Peter 3:15).

54 - The Devil Wants Me in Hell

In 1947, during my second year at Simpson Bible Institute in Seattle, I told a partial untruth to one of my teachers. I must have wanted to make myself look good in the eyes of my teacher. It bothered me some, but not to the extent that I did anything about it.

Shortly after that a fellow student, Carlo Feriante, came to me and said, "Margery, last Saturday night at our street meeting downtown, I met a girl named Lorraine Johnson. She stayed in the back of the group but listened intently to our testimonies and the message. Afterwards she wanted to talk to one of us. I asked her if she knew the Lord. She told me that for several nights she has been roaming the streets, because she's afraid to go home. Each night she has the same dream. She said she is so frightened she doesn't want to go to bed. She dreams she is dying and the devil is there to take her into hell. She said in the dream she struggles and yells for help so the devil will go away and leave her alone. Then just when she is about to arrive in hell, she wakes up. "

While Carlo was relating the story to me, I kept thinking, *Oh, how horrible, how horrible.* I asked Carlo, "Were you able to help her?"

"No," he replied dejectedly. "I talked to her about the Lord—how she could believe in Him and He could take away her fear. But somehow she just couldn't comprehend the plan of salvation. I asked her to come to the school this Friday night for our mission meeting. She said she would. I'd feel better if a girl would take over. That's why I came to you. Would you talk to her?"

"Sure, Carlo, I'd be glad to," I said.

"Then I'll introduce her to you," he replied.

I prayed much for Lorraine that week and asked the Lord to give me wisdom as to what I should say to her. I kept thinking about that terrible dream she had been experiencing. I knew the Lord could give her peace. I also knew the devil wouldn't give her up easily. Ephesians 6 tells us that we are in a spiritual battle. I kept praying that she would keep her promise and come to campus Friday evening.

And she came! In fact, she came early, so we had time to get acquainted before the meeting.

Afterward I took Lorraine to my room, and we had a long discussion. I explained the plan of salvation, as Carlo had done the week before. I emphasized the love, joy, and peace that could be hers by becoming a Christian if she would repent of her sins and look to Jesus to save her. I stressed how wonderful heaven is and that she wouldn't have to worry about going to hell. I told her the Lord Jesus had taken the penalty for her sins when He died on the cross and rose again. If she became a child of God, the devil would have no right to her. Then I asked her if she wanted to make the decision to let Christ into her life and to let Him change her heart.

She thought for a little while and then shook her head. "Not tonight," she said.

I was devastated! I knew that if she said yes, she could have the peace Christ gives to those who believe. She did promise to go with me to the evening service on Sunday.

That weekend I thought and prayed much about Lorraine. *Why hadn't she accepted Christ as her Savior when she seemed to understand the plan of salvation?* As I prayed, the Spirit reminded me of two verses I had learned. One was Proverbs 28:13: "*He who conceals his sins does not prosper, but whoever confesses and renounces them finds mercy*" (NIV). The other was Psalm 66:18: "If I regard iniquity in my heart, the Lord will not hear me."

The Lord reminded me of what I considered a white lie that I had written on my exam paper. *Lord,* I prayed, *You aren't hearing me now because of that small sin?* I knew that the Lord was asking me to confess the sin of that paper. And yet I balked. How humiliating it would be to admit it. I argued with the Lord, *Besides, it's already the weekend, and my teacher is not at school. It's not that big a deal.* All this was to no avail. I just didn't have peace.

I knew the Lord could save Lorraine without me. Yet I was the one that she had confided in, and I didn't want to fail her. Finally it came to me: *Was I letting my pride get in the way of someone coming to know Christ? Wasn't a soul worth more than the whole world? Oh, Lord, forgive me. It is a sin,* I prayed.

Early Sunday morning, a little after 8:00 a.m., I telephoned my teacher and confessed what I had done and asked for his forgiveness. He readily forgave me.

That evening, after the service, Lorraine was ready to become a follower of Christ. God was free to answer my prayer because the constraint of sin had been removed. That night Lorraine trusted Christ as her Savior and she became a new creature in Him!

There are many verses in the Bible about Christians being holy. I especially like 1 Peter 1:15: "But as he which hath called you is holy, so be ye holy in all manner of conversation." I've learned that I can't be holy in my own strength. But as I live in the Spirit, walk in the Spirit, and let Christ live out His life in me, He is always there to help. No, I won't ever be perfect until that day when I stand in His presence. Then I will be forever holy. But until that time, I have that wonderful promise in 1 John 1:9: "If we confess our sins, he is faithful and just to forgive us our sins, and to cleanse us from all unrighteousness."

During the years, I have used the illustration of Lorraine and myself many times. If we as Christians want the Lord to use us to bear fruit for His glory, and if we want to live the happy and peaceful life He wants us to have, then we need to have a heart that is cleansed from sin.

I kept track of Lorraine for a while, and then we lost contact, but I know that one day Carlo and I will be greeting her in heaven.

55 - Presidential Visits

Since Sibut is only one hundred miles from the capital city of Bangui and at the end of one of the three paved roads in our country, we had frequent visits from the country's presidents. When they came, an entourage of prominent government officials and security guards always accompanied them. Since there isn't much to see in our town, the Sibut officials often took them to visit the Catholic mission and our mission. When that happened, our African workers spent many days making our 124 acres look like a small park.

The first president to visit Sibut was David Dacko, who became our leader after the nation's first president, Barthemy Boganda, was killed in a plane crash. The clinic was included in the tour the president and his dignitaries took of the mission. I was so proud as we went from room to room showing them our new building. They said some nice things about it, and that made me glad, for a lot of effort had gone into the building to make it serviceable and to make it look presentable.

Under President Dacko's administration, Israel sent agricultural experts to the Central African Republic. One of their training schools was at Sibut, and we enjoyed becoming acquainted with the Israelis. Our best friends among them were a couple from Nazareth. She was a Spanish Jew who had gone to Israel from Argentina, and he was an Arabic Jew originally from Morocco. The two had become acquainted at an Israeli kibbutz and later married and moved to Nazareth.

Once in 1967, during the Six-day War in Israel, the couple came to Bruce and Wilma's home for the evening meal, to which I was also invited. As we listened to the news in English, they became excited and didn't want to miss a single word. The husband went into one bedroom and listened to the news in Arabic, and the wife went to another room to hear the broadcast in Spanish.

Almost simultaneously they came out jumping, twirling, clapping, and yelling, "Jerusalem is ours! Jerusalem is ours!"

What an evening it was as we rejoiced in their happiness. That evening will be forever imprinted in my mind. Sadly, after President Bokassa came to power, he expelled the teams of expert agriculturists.

We were sorrowful when in 1966 General John Bokassa overthrew his cousin, David Dacko, in a coup to become the new president. I recall the time he came to Sibut for an official visit on Independence Day, December 2. Besides getting the mission station spruced up for his visit, we spent hours making small triangular flags of green, yellow, white, blue, and red, the colors of the national flag. We strung them everywhere.

Every Independence Day celebration included the erection of a temporary viewing stand on the road through town to give the important town people and visitors the best view of the parade of school children that marched through town. There was always a large turnout for the annual parade, and the street was lined with people. We were always invited to sit in the viewing stand, along with the Catholic missionaries.

After the parade, the mayor of our town, who couldn't read, had a high school boy read a welcome to our president. He didn't read it well. Sadly, the speech consisted of complaints against the government for not doing this or that at Sibut, as well as suggestions as to what should be done. I think everyone was shocked! Even if the words were true, that was an inappropriate way to greet a president. I'm sure the prefect, the head government official of Sibut, hadn't read the speech beforehand.

My seat to the left in the row behind the president offered me a better view of his facial expressions than I might have wanted. He got angrier by the minute. I wasn't surprised when the boy finished his speech and President Bokassa stood and delivered a scathing impromptu talk in response. His prepared speech was not delivered, and he was so furious he didn't stay for the day's activities. He and his entourage immediately returned to Bangui.

Church women marching in Independence Day Parade.

When we returned to our mission station and saw the beautifully decorated grounds, along with all the refreshments for the tea prepared in the president's honor, the common thought on everyone's mind was, *at least we can enjoy it all.*

We were all disappointed to hear that Bokassa also expelled the Taiwanese Aid people. They had been doing a terrific job of teaching agriculture to our citizens. President Bokassa wanted the Communist Chinese to come to the Central African Republic, but the Chinese would not come as long as the Taiwanese were there.

One of the Taiwanese projects was the building of a large pineapple-canning factory. By the time the Taiwanese were expelled, the fields of pineapple were almost ripe, ready to be picked and canned, but the cannery never became a reality.

The Chinese built a beautiful hospital in Bangui, which they never occupied. A medical group later used the hospital as a clinic.

The lust for power really went to President Bokassa's head. He got the harebrained idea that he wanted to be crowned emperor. Money was collected from everyone in the country, including the foreigners, to pay for his throne and the crown, which were to be covered with jewels.

On December 4, 1977, the "crowning day," with all its pomp, was held at the large Notre Dame Catholic cathedral in Bangui. This ceremony was ridiculed by many newspapers around the globe (and, secretly, by most of the nation's citizens). The main American news media also gave their thoughts on the subject. The gist was that a very egotistical leader was exploiting one of the poorest countries in the world. Emperor Bokassa even went so far as to rename our country (for a little over a year) as the Central Africa Empire.

To remember his birthday in 1977, he let all prisoners, except for the political prisoners, go free. What chaos! The freed inmates went on a stealing spree and stole things everywhere. Our mission station was not exempt. All of Polly's books in her book room, the forty metal chairs from the Bible School building, etc., were taken. Yes, the people knew the president had a birthday, but what an awful way to remember it.

Bokassa had his soldiers kill dozens of students when they went on strike because they couldn't afford to buy uniforms made by his wife's clothing factory for the Independence Day parade. The people burned the factory to the ground—the only factory in the country.

The French finally said, "Enough!" In 1979 Bokassa was ousted and put under house arrest in a luxurious house until his death in 1996. The French temporarily restored his cousin, David Dacko, to office.

Soon after his return to power, President Dacko went to the larger cities to speak, attempting to bring healing to his nation. When he came to Sibut, his vice president, three of his cabinet ministers, the Bangui band, soldiers, and many security officials were with him. Because our mission church was the largest building in town, seating 1,000 people, the officials brought the president there to deliver his main speech.

He almost preached a sermon, and we had no doubt that he knew the Lord. We had heard earlier about his faith from our missionaries at Kembe, Dick and Irene Paulson, who were personal friends of his.

After the closing prayer I slipped out quickly to get to the clinic before President Dacko and his entourage arrived. I had Oumar greet him first and introduce the other helpers.

When Oumar started to introduce me, the president quickly interrupted and said, "You don't need to tell me about Mademoiselle Benedict. She has been here at the clinic since 1952."

I then took him and his entourage through the clinic. This time it didn't look as nice as it had for President Dackko's previous visit nearly twenty years earlier, for it had seen a lot of usage. Then we went outside to see the new maternity building. At the door he stopped and, with a grin on his face, said, "Are you sure no one is in there?"

Then we had to wait as the eight cars in the president's line-up started going the wrong direction to visit the print shop. As the security guards were untangling the cars, I had a chance to talk more with President Dacko and his group. One of the men close to me hadn't said anything, so I asked him, "And who are you?"

He smiled and replied, "I am the vice president."

Then the minister of health said to me, "If you ever need anything, come and see me." I appreciated his gesture, but I never needed to take him up on his offer.

One of the other ministers told the group, "A lot of people come here for help. They like the treatment they receive."

I looked at him and asked, "How do you know about the mission clinic?"

With a twinkle in his eye, he answered, "Oh, I've heard. Word gets around."

I knew many people from the capitol came to our clinic for help, but I was still surprised at his remark.

After the group toured the print shop, they went to Bruce and Wilma's house for high tea, a special mode of afternoon tea for dignitaries, and I joined them there. Every one was so gracious. At 8 p.m. we went downtown to the prefect's house and enjoyed a special dinner with all the high government officials.

After Bokassa's downfall, Dacko asked the Chinese to leave and the

Taiwanese were invited back. The irony of it all was that this time there was no agricultural team.

In 1981 President Dacko stepped aside due to ill health. We were so thankful for his willingness to lead our country even for two years. We knew he had come to the country again "for such a time as this."

Soon after his resignation, Vernon, who was in President Dacko's second term, went into a Bangui store to buy chicken feed. A man approached him that he didn't recognize.

The man said, "You are a Rosenau from Sibut aren't you? I am David Dacko."

General Kolingba became president in 1981. There were two interesting events during his term of leadership. First, he ordered enough Sango Bibles to give one to each village chief in the entire country. The second event occurred on February 20, 1982, when he and many of his ministers came to Sibut. During that visit he bestowed the *Chevalier de la Medaille de la Reconnaissance Centrafricaine* on Bruce Rosenau and me. (Recipient of the highest order of the Central African Medal of Recognition.) These medals were in acknowledgment of our service to the people of the Central African Republic. That afternoon he and his entourage came up to the mission as other presidents had done in the past.

Margery receiving *Chevalier de la Medaille de la Reconnaissance Centrafricaine* medal from President Kolingba.

During the time I served in Central African Republic, we were fortunate to have government leaders who were sympathetic to our missionary ministry. We always encouraged the Christians to pray for those in leadership. How true are the words in Psalm 33:12: "Blessed is the nation whose God is the Lord."

A furlough was scheduled after each four-year term in Africa, and I always looked forward to it. Twice I flew home by a varied route so I could see different countries. Three times I visited my sister, Esther, her husband, Ricardo, and their four children in Mexico.

They were helping raise three Indian girls at the time, one from the Oaxaca region of Mexico and two from the Mexican state of Mexico. The two situations were similar. Their mothers had died and their fathers were drunkards and not capable of taking responsibility for their care. Through a series of circumstances, the girls were brought to Esther and Ricardo. They, with the help of Leaora Shultz, an elderly missionary, took responsibility for the girls' care and education for many years.

The first time I visited them in Mexico, the girls' little, wrinkled, old grandmother from Mexico state brought me a gift of three cacti. Esther told me later this was a poor person's gift and it was all she had. I knew the older woman wanted to honor Esther for what she had done for her granddaughters by doing something nice for me. I felt honored.

Esther and her husband have now been in Mexico over forty-six years, mostly living near the city of Puebla. The Lord has used them to start many churches by training young Christian men for the ministry.

I also visited my school teacher sister, Judy, three times in Jacksonville, Florida. On my first visit, in 1969, I went to church with her on my first Sunday back in the States. As I sat with her—and 5,000 others—during the two-and-a-half-hour service, my heart was filled to overflowing. We listened to the choirs sing and enjoyed the four other special musical numbers. The orchestra was playing and the beautiful organ was sending out its majestic sounds. We heard testimonies from newly saved people and saw the beautiful, precious baptismal service. Then we heard a terrific, Spirit-filled, convicting message on the name of Jesus.

One of the special musical numbers was a medley of songs a man had put together about the name of Jesus. I never heard more beautiful, meaningful singing. When the singer sat down, the pastor remarked, "I don't think an angel from heaven could sing better."

I agreed. I leaned over toward Judy and said in a low whisper, "Are we in heaven?" I surely felt we must be.

Which Language Today?

When missionaries are asked to speak back in the States, it is sometimes difficult to remember English words. While in Africa, we mostly spoke

Sango, sometimes French, and English only when speaking with another missionary. I once flew the polar route from London to Seattle via Anchorage, Alaska. In Anchorage I was with Vi Able, my friend from Baptist Mid-Missions. The pastor asked me to speak for five minutes between Sunday School and church.

About a minute into my talk, I couldn't think of the word I needed to say. I stood there feeling so stupid. Right away a male voice rang out from the back of the auditorium saying, "Say it in Sango."

"*Fouti*," I called back.

"Spoiled," he replied.

I could hardly wait until the service was over to learn who in Alaska could possibly know Sango. He was the son of the Metzlers, one of the first missionary couples who were on the field just a brief time after I arrived. His father was one of the language committee members who greeted me upon my arrival in Africa.

Her African Sister

Being away from the States for four years at a time, there were always changes, large and small, that had taken place by the time I returned. One evening, my sister Judy took me to a fast food restaurant. I had never been in one before.

We enjoyed our meal, and as we were leaving, Judy said, "You go first."

I saw that she picked up her tray, so I did the same. I turned around and asked, "What do I do with all of this?" pointing to my tray.

"Put it in the bin over there."

"Do I put in everything?"

"Yes, everything." So I proceeded to put in everything, including the tray.

"Margery, you don't put the tray in!"

"But you told me everything," I responded. I started to reach into the bin to pull it out.

"Don't bother about it now, let's go." She wanted to get her African sister out of there before I did anything more to embarrass her.

Another time I had just flown from Africa into Boise, Idaho, to stay with my family. Jack, a man from one of the churches, helped me buy a good used car. That night I drove out of a side street onto one of the main streets. In my rear view mirror I noticed a car behind me with its red lights flashing. I thought, *I wonder what that means? Could it be a police car? Maybe I'd better stop.* So I did. Sure enough, a policeman appeared at my car window and said, "May I see your driver's license?" I gave it to him. As he was looking at it I asked, "Did I do something wrong?"

"Yes, you just threw your lighted cigarette out of your car window."

"I did what?" I exclaimed. "I don't smoke!" He must have believed me. One can't miss a cigarette smell if a person has been smoking. At least I learned that a car with flashing lights behind you meant stop!

In Seattle, Washington, I was answering questions from a girl at a blood bank just before I was to give blood for my upcoming surgery.

"Are you married?"

"No."

"Do you have any children?"

"I told you, I'm not married."

She had a surprised look on her face as she replied, "That doesn't make any difference these days; times have changed."

I quickly answered, "But God and his laws don't change."

This time she had an astonished expression on her face as if she had never thought about God's laws. Then she replied, "You know, you may be right," and went on with her questioning.

As the blood from my vein was filling the plastic container, I thought, *How good it was to know a God who doesn't change, One who keeps the many promises written in His Word.* I also wondered if the morals of people in the United States had become so bad that people no longer knew right from wrong. As I continued to come home on furloughs, my eyes were opened more and more, and I realized that the United States was also a mission field.

Speaking At Churches

When my parents were alive, I made Boise my headquarters and stayed with them. After they died, I stayed with the Watsons, who lived in Nampa, Idaho. Each time I came home, another church was added to my support team. I usually did not ask to speak at a church unless they were one of my supporting churches. Soon word got around that I was a missionary, and other churches and missionary groups asked me to share my African experiences with them.

During my first presentations I talked while showing slides about my ministry. I soon learned I was talking longer and longer with each presentation. I remedied that by preparing a tape to go with the slide presentation and asked for questions after the presentation.

On my first two furloughs home, I showed slides of some of the horrible sores and burns we took care of in our clinic. After seeing the expressions on some faces in the audiences, I stopped doing this. I just showed a line of about thirty people with their legs or arms bandaged with sheet-strip bandages.

I wanted the women to see how their hard work in rolling so many bandages was paying off. The women from my supporting churches would cut worn sheets into strips two to four inches wide, sewing the ends together until they had enough for a roll about three inches in diameter. I would collect these rolled bandages each time I returned on furlough.

When I returned to the United States for the last time, I traveled to each of my supporting churches to give them the final update on my African work. Over the years we had been advised to generally keep our presentations to about twenty minutes. My last presentation was a "mission no-no" since it lasted forty-four minutes. I hadn't planned it that way, but there was so much to say. Before I showed the slides, I told the congregations, "I've been in Africa forty-four years. This talk represents one minute for each year." They laughed, and they were also prepared.

Friends' Helping Hands

Each time I returned to the field, I took back three fifty-gallon metal drums of sheet bandages. I went to a bakery in Boise and bought empty lard drums and cleaned them up. I packed the bandages one-by-one, so tightly that when I finished, there wasn't room to poke my finger. One furlough I sure appreciated my brothers Steve and Phil for packing two of these drums for me.

People were so good to me. I don't know why I was so privileged and blessed to have so many friends wanting to help me in any way they could. Many church missionary groups made things for me to take back. There were baby layettes, rolled bandages, handmade dresses for my African helpers' wives (and sometimes my cotton dresses and uniforms), hand-drawn designs on embroidery cloth, and much more. The children would collect crayons, small cars, and toys to be used in Vacation Bible Schools.

I don't remember the name of the town in Iowa where Florence knew Mildred, a Christian woman living in a retirement home. Mildred encouraged many of the women living there to sew for me. The buzzing of their machines must have gone on for hours at a time as they made hundreds of baby layettes, simple little dresses, panties, and shorts for children up to four years of age. I often wished I could have visited them to thank them personally.

I can't mention everyone who did things for me, but I want to pay tribute to the small First Baptist Church in Kuna, Idaho. Their group of dedicated women, under the leadership of Verbel Watson, always helped beyond the call of duty. Each time I was home, the women canned barrels of food. At different times the variety included chili, stew, plums, peaches, apricots, prunes, pears, applesauce, and Bing cherries.

Once we even had chicken! We bought sixty chickens at twenty-five cents each and had a chicken party at the Watson farm. Albert Watson and a school teacher, Lois Dustman, slaughtered the chickens, and the rest of us plucked and cut them up. It was a long, fun, stinky day. That evening, Albert put the cut-up chicken into his new livestock-watering trough and filled it with cold water. The next day we took the chicken to a cannery in Boise. There, we cooked and de-boned the chicken then put it into forty-five cans, ready for the canning company to seal the lids and do the final processing.

All the food the women prepared for me was done in one of the canneries in the Treasure Valley of Idaho. The food was a great help to us when we had company, and we also looked forward to eating some of that delicious fruit from Idaho.

In Boise and Seattle I packed most of the things I took back to Africa into metal barrels. On one furlough a man made a large crate that we packed in Nampa, Idaho. It was filled with items from a retired Christian doctor's office. I was told I could take anything I wanted from his office. I was in my glory as I took examination lamps, chrome chairs, and many other things I could use in our clinic. The crate and three barrels were shipped to Seattle, and Al Undi put them on a boat going to Douala, a seaport in the Cameroon.

Unfortunately, someone made a horrible mistake and unloaded them in Accra, Ghana. Two years later I received the three barrels but not the crate. Although some things had been stolen, I had fortunately packed a large pressure cooker underneath the bandages, so I had it for canning and also for

On Margery's 3rd furlough in 1964, Tabernacle Baptist Church gave her a shower.

sterilizing medical items. I often wondered where that crate of medical equipment went and hoped some clinic in Ghana was making good use of it.

Faithful Supporters

Most of my support came from the West Coast of the United States: Idaho, Washington, Oregon, and California. Approximately twelve churches and fifteen individual supporters provided my financial needs. My favorite month to visit my friends and supporters in California was December. The warmer weather was kinder to me, who had spent most of my life in the tropics!

During the '50s and '60s, I spent some of my furlough time working in hospitals in Boise and Seattle. I really enjoyed this. I wanted to keep up on new treatments and procedures, and I enjoyed the care of patients without having the full responsibility of the diagnosis and treatment of their diseases.

Most of my summers were spent in Bible camps in the Northwest as a nurse, speaker, and sometimes counselor. It was so good to be in the cool mountains again and have a ministry with children and young people. Sometimes I was busy in Vacation Bible Schools. I will never forget the one in Kuna, Idaho, where the kids collected enough money to purchase the equivalent of one tire for my new three-quarter-ton truck I was taking back to Africa.

When I arrived home in 1979, I knew I needed to buy a new half-ton truck with a double cab and a bed long enough to hold a stretcher. This seemed almost impossible to find, but many people were praying about it. My brother Phil called around to several cities, but there were none available.

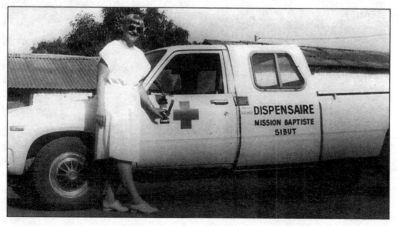

Our 'new' half-ton truck.

Then he received a call from a Toyota dealer in Salt Lake City saying they had located a truck in Denver. If I wanted it, they could put it on a flatbed train car and send it to Salt Lake City, I said, "Yes!" I knew our prayers were being answered.

I rode a bus to Salt Lake City and the dealer met me at the bus depot to take me to a very busy Toyota dealership office. I made out a check for $7,000 and drove my new, white truck back to Boise.

I was thankful to Paul Smith, who painted a large red cross and the words *Dispensaire De Sibut* on both sides of the truck. I also appreciated very much the women's Berean missionary group in Nampa, Idaho, who had a camper shell specially made to fit the truck bed. Later, two of my brothers, Steve and Phil, packed it for me and drove it to Twin Falls, Idaho. Once there, students from Bob Jones University drove it back to Greenville, S.C., where Eugene Rosenau did some work on it. Then he shipped it out in a container from Charleston, S.C.

My, C'est Bizarre

Many thoughts were traveling through my mind as I was getting older, and it was becoming more tiring to climb our Sibut hill from the clinic to my home. With gasoline costing $4.00 a gallon, I didn't use my truck unless it was necessary. I was longing for some kind of small vehicle, but I didn't know what. I knew a moped wouldn't do, for in the rainy season our road up the hill became full of ruts. The moped would not have been able to make it all the way to the top, even though the men spent many hours every dry season repairing the road.

During my third furlough I visited a wonderful Christian family in Connell, Washington. I had graduated with Keith Herrman, the salutatorian of our class at Nyssa High School. He had married Anna Bauman, and they had come to this sagebrush country in southeastern Washington. With the harnessing of the Columbia River, this area opened up to farmers, and Keith and Anna were one of the first couples to come. They were on my route from Boise to Seattle, and each furlough I would visit them two or three times. I knew I was always welcome.

Keith was an excellent farmer, always trying new and different things, and Anna was an unusual lady. She always asked many questions about all phases of my ministry, and she and Keith would involve their three children, Paul, Robin, and Heidi in our discussions. All of the children, of course, were very involved in the farm. When Paul was a senior in high school, he won the Future Farmers of America's National Championship for Vegetable and Fruit Production. I looked forward to visiting the Herrmans every furlough and often in my retirement.

On furlough in 1979, while making my first visit to their home, I saw four weird-looking, three-wheeled vehicles with large tires, made for dirt roads like those on their farm. I asked a few questions about the vehicles but didn't say much at that time. I went on to Spokane to visit the Longs, a couple who supported me, and they had two of these "three-wheelers." They used them for joy riding on the trails in their woods. Dorothy Long persuaded me to try one, and off we went for a pleasant ride. What fun! I was hooked.

Months later, during my second visit to the Herrmans, I asked some serious questions about those three-wheeled Honda motorcycles. The children were still in high school, and after church that Sunday night, Paul, the oldest, came to me and said, "Margery, if you really want one, my sisters and I will buy one for you."

I said, "Thank you, I don't think so."

I can't imagine why I didn't take him up on the offer then and there. It only took me two weeks back in Africa walking up that hill, sometimes several times a day, to write Paul and say, "I'll take you up on your proposal."

The children paid for the motorcycle, along with many spare parts. They had everything crated and then shipped to Eugene in Greenville, South Carolina, where he shipped it on to me.

I rode the Honda daily down to the clinic and to the main road, often picking up an ill person at the mission crossroads. Once my passenger was a woman with a 105-degree temperature. She leaned on my back while trying

The 'weird-looking' three-wheeler so practical for the mission.

to keep her arms around my waist as we bounced up the rocky road to the clinic. I also rode it to the town market, church, and when I went visiting. People who hadn't seen it before were always amazed. One African teacher who came often to the clinic summarized their thoughts in one expression, "*My, c'est bizarre.*"

My Honda started a trend among the missionaries. Knute Orton from Kaga-Bondoro (Crampel) would sometimes ride his Honda forty miles out to the villages to preach in their churches. Three missionaries on Sibut station bought them, but by that time "four-wheelers" were available. Sam and Bill, sons of Vernon and Jan, had a lot of fun with theirs and also ran many errands downhill for their parents. These motorcycles were the greatest helpers we could have had on a mission station. Thank you, Paul, Robin, and Heidi for sending out that first one.

Two Months In Switzerland

After my furlough in 1974, I went to Emmaus Bible College, near Vevy, Switzerland, for two months so I could brush up on my French. It was a very profitable and enjoyable time that I will never forget. I was grateful that I didn't have a car. I liked to walk with other students the two miles to church in a small village, passing by the flowering fields up the hill. My dormitory window overlooked the Alps and Lake Geneva. Although I met students from sixteen countries, my favorites were from Finland, Switzerland, Spain, and France. I also had more time to spend with the Lord and to have wonderful hikes. I visited Geneva and a large cheese factory with a Swiss friend from the Central African Republic and also served as a co-counselor for a dorm full of nurses in a weekend Bible camp.

A Puzzled Policeman

Every missionary could tell tales about their travels and how the Lord helped them through some difficult times, but some of the tales were just simply humorous. When Bruce and Wilma came back from their first furlough, he told us a tale in such a way that it sent us into peals of laughter.

The first thing they did upon arriving in the United States was to visit friends in Michigan and buy a car. As they left their friend's place in their newly purchased used car, they came to a complicated intersection on one of Detroit's busiest streets. Bruce became confused and made a faux pas. Wouldn't you know it, a policeman saw him and told him to pull over to the side of the street.

He said, "May I see your driver's license?" Bruce showed it to him.

"I see you have an International license. Where did you get it?"

"Paris, France."

"What is your address?"

"I don't have any here in the United States."

The policeman looked puzzled and said, "What do you mean, 'you don't have any'?"

"I don't know where we will live."

"What was your last address?"

"Box 6, Sibut, French Equatorial Africa."

"How long have you been in the United States?"

"Two days. We have just come from Africa."

The bewildered policeman patted the equally bewildered Bruce on the shoulder as he said, "You may go, lad, but please be careful."

One Sunday evening, after I spoke in a church in Bremerton, Washington, I went to my hostess's home for the night. Margie Miles was a very pleasant widow twenty years older than I was. There was an instant rapport between us. We both shared the same name and birthday. After we talked a while, she showed me the guestroom and said, "Have a good night."

It was half an hour before I folded the bedspread and blanket back to go to bed. I was surprised when I saw there were no sheets on the bed. By this time I knew my hostess would be in bed. I debated for a few moments whether I should call her or not, but I decided to sleep on the mattress pad and slept well.

The next morning I made up the bed and didn't say a word about the missing sheets. She fed me a good breakfast, and soon I was on my way back to Seattle.

Ten years later I was in Bremerton, and Margie was again my hostess. I had forgotten about the sheet episode. That evening we had a delightful conversation, and when it was bedtime, she said, "Once I had a guest here, and I forgot to put sheets on the bed, and my guest didn't say a word."

I quickly spoke up and said, "Oh, I remember now, I was once in a home, and my hostess forgot..." Then we both started laughing as it dawned on us at the same time who that hostess and guest were.

Once I was in a round-robin conference across Puget Sound from Seattle. That was a conference where several missionaries participated, and each evening they went to a different church. One of the churches was on Bainbridge Island. I realized as I was coming to town that I didn't have the name or address of the place where I was to have dinner that evening. I called the church and the pastor's house. No answer. I knew one couple who lived on the Island, a former member of my Seattle church, but I couldn't think of their name. I drove into the parking lot of a supermarket. I put my head down on the steering wheel and prayed, asking the Lord to give me some guidance about what I should do.

As I lifted my head, who should be coming out of the supermarket but Mrs. Haines, the wife of the one couple I knew. I greeted her and told her I was speaking at her church that evening and I didn't know where I was supposed to go for dinner.

She told me the president of the missionary women's group had been behind her in the checkout line. This lady gave me the name of the couple with whom I was to be and the directions to get to their home. Back in the car, I again bowed my head and thanked the Lord for a quick answer to prayer.

Always A Nurse

I have to admit that one of the things I looked forward to on furlough was being free of the responsibility of the clinic, especially the night calls, but one furlough I wondered. I stopped on the way home to see Bruce and Wilma Rosenau in Greenville, South Carolina. A local couple, the Morgans, had returned from Bangui to Greenville three days earlier. They had been there to visit their daughter, Bonnie Bixby, and her family, who were missionaries in Bangui.

During the night I heard someone calling to me in Sango, "*Mademoiselle, a yeke?*" I knew I was not in Africa and wondered who was calling. Then I realized it was Bruce. I grabbed my robe and quickly went downstairs. Bruce said, "Mrs. Morgan has a temperature of 103, and her husband wants to know what to do for her."

I knew she probably had malaria. They still had the medicine for malaria that they took with them to Africa, so I told him how to administer it to his wife. After I went back upstairs, the thought passed through my mind, *Do I have the right to prescribe medicine in the United States?* I didn't let it bother me very long and soon went back to sleep. The response to a telephone call to them the next morning made me feel better, for she was on the road to recovery.

My Parents' Home-Going

In April 1979 my furlough was only a month away when I received word from my brother Phil that my father was seriously ill. Dad had been in the hospital but was now home, and mother was taking care of him. Phil knew Mother was quite exhausted, so he asked me if I could come home early to help her. As soon as I could, I arranged my work, so I could leave. Dad's illness was diverticulitis, a condition that inflamed his intestinal tract. Several times previously he had been operated on for this illness.

As soon as I landed in Boston, I phoned home and was relieved to hear Mother say Dad was much better. When I arrived home, I was able to help some, and I even took Dad for a couple of rides. Though he was very weak, we had some good times together. About a month after I arrived home, his illness came back with a vengeance. Four days later he died in the Veteran's Hospital in Boise. Seven of his eight children were able to be there with mother for the funeral. The Lord was gracious to let me have that one month with him.

Three months later I took Mother to the cemetery to see Dad's grave. After she looked at the grave for a few minutes, she said, "I'm not coming again. He isn't there. He is with Jesus."

After visiting my California supporters in the latter part of December and into the New Year, I stopped to see my nephew and his family in Auburn, California. There I received a telephone call from my brother Steve saying Mother had had a stroke and was in a coma at a Boise hospital. I quickly took the bus back to Boise.

After three days of unconsciousness, she too was promoted to glory. We sorrowed but "not as those who have no hope." I was glad for her. When Dad died, she mentioned many times that her life on earth was finished, and she wanted to go.

Mom and Dad had a loving relationship most of their married life, and they were both dedicated Christians and dearly loved the Lord. Both of them felt that they failed the Lord in their lifetime. But when I think of how their children are walking with the Lord, I know their lives were not a failure.

Micah 6:8 says, "What does the Lord require of you? To act justly and to love mercy and to walk humbly with your God" (NIV). These requirements my parents could meet without going to a foreign mission field. In their senior years they spent many hours daily studying the Bible and praying together. Material things didn't mean much to them. When they were able to have extra money, they didn't buy anything more than the necessary things for themselves but gave instead to the Lord's work.

Once when I came home on furlough, I saw Mother was still using her old Maytag wringer washing machine on their old back porch. I knew it was time she had a modern washer and dryer, so the family bought her one. When she saw them, she exclaimed, "Why spend money on me? I don't need it." But she came to appreciate not having to handle the clothes outside in winter and to see them stiff from the cold, freezing temperatures.

I am glad to say that Christ had first place in their lives, and I thanked the Lord for His mercy in allowing me to be there when it was time for their home going.

In all the nine furloughs, what I appreciated the most was when people said, "I'm praying for you." I knew that my ministry in Africa was of God. Knowing I had emotional, physical, and spiritual support at home and on the field helped me through many adventures with God. How thankful I was to the Lord for His care over me as I traveled so many miles. Although I always enjoyed my furloughs with friends and family, I always eagerly anticipated going back to my "African home."

57 - Testimonies

When Africans gather around the fireside in the evening or gather in someone's *piotte* (a round, open room with a thatched roof) on a rainy day, they love to talk about their experiences. It is the same when Christians talk at a conference or a retreat. They are excited to relate to others what Christ has done in their lives. Here are just a few translated samples of testimonies I heard when I was part of their audiences.

Your Curse Has No Power

Wajourou, a pastor's wife, gave her testimony at a conference in the late 1950s, when leopards were still prevalent in the Central African Republic.

She was the only one of her family who had come out of heathenism into a relationship with the Lord. She had been praying for her family's salvation for years. Her father had died without Christ, and her mother was a witch and very steeped in her profession.

One day Wajourou received a letter from her mother, Ouibena, who lived at Ippy. She had repented of her sins and now knew Christ. Even though Wajourou had prayed much for her mother's conversion, she was amazed when she received word of her change of heart. Wasn't Ouibena a witch, and wasn't it hard for witches to come out from the influence of Satan and his demons, under whom they are held captive? Wajourou could hardly wait until she got enough money to make the round trip to Ippy, to see her mother and to learn if it was really true.

It was. Ouibena was a changed woman and now had a peace that she had never before known. Wajourou also learned the rest of the story. After her mother had burned all her witchcraft paraphernalia and left that way of life, the witch doctor that showed Ouibena all the tricks of the trade was very upset. He put a curse on her and said she would soon die.

Ouibena told him, "You have no control over me now. My God has set me free, and He is stronger than any witchcraft and the magic that goes with it." He was furious.

Shortly after his outburst a leopard came and took his small child. When Ouibena went over to his house to offer words of comfort, he cursed her and told her to leave him. Two days later the leopard returned, and this time it clawed the man, leaving him with some nasty wounds. His family took him to the mission hospital at Ippy.

As the caring staff tended to the wounds on his body, they also testified to him of the One who could heal his soul from sin. By now the Holy Spirit had prepared his heart to receive the message, and he repented of his sins.

Wajourou's face lit up with joy as she related the story to us. As she finished, ohs and ahs came from the lips of her hearers. As I looked at the audience, I could see by the expressions on their faces that they were enjoying her testimony as much as I was.

As she finished, I thought of Genesis 18:14: *"Is there anything too hard for the Lord?"* No, there isn't. God said that to Sarah when He told her she would have a son in her old age, and He kept that promise also.

Overwhelming Love

A Lumiere leader gave this testimony at one of their conferences:

> My elderly grandfather was a very sinful man. My
> grandmother was a believer, loved by many, and attended
> the Baptist church in their village. She prayed much for
> her husband's salvation, but he refused, saying, "Her
> mission isn't any good." He was hot tempered, didn't
> like people to come visit him, and cursed all the time,
> especially those of his wife's church.
>
> When my grandmother died, the people brought food
> and money to help defray the funeral expenses. The day
> after the burial the believers still brought food and
> firewood to my grandfather's house. During the following

days, they kept this up and tried to help in any way they could. Grandfather often showed his contempt by gathering dirt and trash and throwing it in their church. But this did not deter the Christians from helping him with good deeds and their prayers.

Finally their love overwhelmed him. He was convicted of his sins and repented. He asked the believers to forgive him for his evil ways. How the believers rejoiced to see their prayers answered.

He didn't live long after that, and the believers again showed their love by helping at his funeral.

Jesus honored the Christians for not returning evil for evil, for putting into practice that verse He told the people in the Sermon on the Mount in Luke 6:35: "But love your enemies, do good to them, and lend to them without expecting to get anything back. Then your reward will be great" [NIV].

We All Have A Chance

The pastor of the Yabalangba Church gave this testimony:

Deacon Kadia of Yabalangba owned a gun. He was a good hunter and obtained much meat for his family and friends.

One day the witch doctor, Bagaza, ordered Kadia to bring meat to him and his family. The deacon refused. Bagaza was jealous of Kadia and became very angry. In his anger he worked his witchcraft on Kadia and told him that the next time he went hunting a buffalo would kill him.

One day, when their meat was gone, Kadia went hunting and was gored by a buffalo, receiving some terrible wounds. He and the village Christians prayed that somehow he would get transportation to the nearest medical center, in the city of Dekoa. God answered their prayer, for soon a truck came through their remote village (which was a rarity) and took him to Dekoa. There Kadia was taken care of, and a month later he came back to his village.

When Bagaza saw him walking around, he marveled. Was the God of these Christians stronger than the power given to him by Satan? The next Sunday he went to church with the deacon, and after the service the pastor asked him to have a meal with them. The people were surprised. Why would they give food to a fellow who had tried his best to kill one of their deacons? They came to realize the pastor was putting into practice the love of Christ, to love their enemies. But Bagaza never went back to church. He chose to continue in his old way.

Everyone has to make a decision to accept the Jesus way or to stay on the path of darkness.

A Persevering Joseph

This testimony was given at an African Bible Conference by the pastor of the Grimari Church:

> Mbafara was a witch doctor, and he was more powerful than anyone else in the large town of Grimari. Many feared him, for he had caused many people to die when he worked his witchcraft on them. But there was a believer named Joseph who lived close to him and told him many times about Jesus. Mbafara didn't want to hear about God, and he kept telling Joseph to shut up. But Joseph was concerned about Mbafara's soul and kept witnessing.
>
> Finally Mbafara had had enough. He decided to work his medicine on Joseph, so he would die. He killed a chicken, sprinkled the blood on his witchcraft paraphernalia, and prayed to his spirit demon to kill Joseph.
>
> Days went by and Joseph was still alive. This was a first for Mbafara. He came to the conclusion that the God, Jesus, was more powerful than the demons. He came to church to hear the Word of God, and later he believed. He was a Christian for two and a half years before he passed away in 1959.

As I heard this testimony, my thoughts turned toward the faithfulness of Joseph. *How many Christians who are rebuffed as much as he was for talking about Jesus would keep it up?* But Joseph didn't give up and was rewarded with seeing his former enemy know the peace and joy that only comes through Jesus.

Inspiring Testimonies

The following are translated selections of testimonies that I heard during different meetings and conferences in Africa. It was so encouraging to see the people expressing their day to day stories of God's love and protection.

One of the believers in our church became very ill following the birth of her baby. Her abdomen began to swell enormously. She waddled like a duck. We marveled how she could still be alive and have such an enormous abdomen. The people tried three times to get a truck driver to take her into a medical center, but when the drivers saw her, they refused. What if she would die in their truck; wouldn't they get the blame? Even the head administrator refused.

The family came to me and said, "You try and stop a truck; a driver wouldn't refuse a pastor."

I tried, but it was the same story.

The Christians had been praying for her, but she remained the same. Finally I called the deacons of the church together and invited any other Christians who wanted to come to a special prayer service at her house.

In three days she expelled a large tumor. She continued to drain for three more days, until her abdomen became flat. Today she is alive, and one would never realize that she had been at the point of death. Everyone in the village knows that God performed a miracle, and we are thanking the Lord for a prayer-answering God.

All of you know I have been building my house and it isn't quite finished. One morning I woke up and saw a torn place on my roof. I immediately thought a leopard had jumped onto the roof and tried its best to enter my house. I called my neighbors and showed them the place. They agreed it must have been a leopard. One of them told me something I already knew, "The Lord undertook for you last night." Today I'm thankful to the Lord for

His protection over my family and me.

One night I had a dream that someone said I would die at 7:00 a.m. the next morning. When I didn't, I became so scared that I would die, I came back to the Lord. I'm glad I had this bad dream, for it is better to walk with the Lord and have peace in your heart.

I was coming back from a funeral with two of my friends. Then one of them whispered to me as he pointed his finger to a place up ahead beside the path, "There is an animal in those bushes." I threw my spear at the place. Right away a woman came out from where she was working in the grass holding the spear in her hand. We were all so frightened. We had a short time of prayer, thanking the Lord that the spear missed its mark.

In the time of my childhood, to see a campfire like this meant that we were giving some offerings to *Gakola* [a spirit god], and out of fear we would dance all night, trying to please him. Since the missionaries came with the message of salvation, I'm no longer under the bondage that my parents knew, for I have Christ. Praise the Lord!

Praise the Lord, I belong to Jesus. My parents dedicated me to *Gakola* when I was a baby, because they only knew darkness. But now I know Christ, and I have peace within. I am no longer full of fears as were my forefathers.

My relatives tied me to a stick for days, and then chased me into the woods when I refused to dance to *Gakola*. They didn't know any better, for they had never heard of Jesus. Praise the Lord, He allowed me to hear the Gospel and be saved.

Part Eight

To God Be The Glory

A Trip to Ippy

In the latter part of January 1977, I made plans to go to our hospital at Ippy to help teach for a week. I had closed the clinic for that time, and I took Rene, my youngest aid-helper, with me.

When I stopped at our mission station at Bambari, Azene, an Ippy pastor, asked me to take him and his bike back to Ippy. I gladly consented, for I hadn't seen him since he graduated from our Bible School. About a half-hour before arriving at Ippy, I saw that my oil gauge was very low and realized it hadn't been checked for a long time. Azene remarked that there was a leper colony under the direction of two Catholic sisters about six miles down a small road nearby. He volunteered to ride his bike there to see if he could buy a couple of liters of oil from them.

There were mango trees along the road, and I parked my truck under their large, spreading branches. I prayed that the Lord would send someone from the village for us to talk with.

As I sat in a chair under the tree, two teenage boys came over to say hello and to ask what the trouble was. I told them, and soon turned the conversation to their spiritual condition. They didn't know the Lord, but they were interested. After Rene and I talked with them for a while, they were born into the Lord's family.

An old man sitting nearby had been listening to us and had become interested. Although he was of a different faith, he had no concept of knowing for certain that one can be ready for eternity and had never heard that someday Christ was coming back. So we spent time with him and were delighted when he too came to know Christ.

Pastor Azene soon came back with the oil, and we were on our way again. After a few miles I asked him, "You are so quiet. Tell me, have you had any answers to prayer lately?"

He said, "Why, Mademoiselle, you taking me in your truck right now is an answer to prayer. I rode my bike seventy miles to Bambari, and while there I became ill with amoeba. It left me so weak I knew I couldn't ride my bike back, so I asked the Lord to send someone along to take me back." Then he went on and on, telling me what the Lord had done for him just in that week.

The time passed quickly. I was delighted to see one of the Lord's chosen ones so happy in Christ. I realized anew that if Christians would talk more about the Lord instead of so many trivial things, it would benefit us in our spiritual growth.

Mr. Young

Mr. Young, from Chicago, came to the Central African Republic on two different occasions to provide money for projects that would help the Africans. He was a large, kindly man with a boisterous voice. During his first visit to Sibut, he gave us money for the installation of electricity to our student village, construction of our town class building, and an adobe model house for me to use for homemaking instruction with the teenage girls. The Brethren mission also profited from his generosity.

During his second visit, in 1973, Florence and I invited him for a meal. Right after we started eating, I blurted out, "You don't know how good it is for the students to have electric lights in the village. That is one of the best projects you have ever funded."

Right away he said to me, "I see you have a three-quarter-ton truck. Don't you find it awkward going up and down the hill with it?"

I had an answer to that question. "I didn't realize that a three-quarter-ton truck would be so different from the one-half-ton that I previously had. I don't use this truck to go up and down the hill to the clinic. I walk unless there is an emergency. But it is used a lot in hauling sand and rock for our building projects here on the station and in the building of our out-station churches."

He quickly replied, "What you need is a small car. Would you like one?"

I was shocked. I never thought I would have anything but a truck. That was what we all had. When I could get my breath, I said, "Yes, it would be so handy and save a lot of gasoline." (Gasoline was $4.00 a gallon.)

He didn't take long to respond. "The French have a small car called *Deux*

Margery's *Deus Chevaux* (what a friend called 'a sardine can') on a bad road.

Chevaux [two horses], and they have them in Bangui. I will arrange for you to receive the money to buy one. I have looked over your clinic and ward building, and you need to expand. There will be money for more rooms in the ward building, putting an extra room on the clinic, elongating the veranda around the corner to the new room, and adding a shower room, an open kitchen, and a three-room building for your maternity work."

I was so overwhelmed all I could do was keep saying, "Thank you." He had done his homework, for he had looked over the medical unit thoroughly.

It took almost three years for these projects to be completed. What a joy it was to have the new building. After a few years, when I quit the maternity work, the delivery room was used for an operating room when our doctors came to do surgery. The four-bed ward was always used for hospitalized patients.

Many years earlier, in 1954, when I hired several teenagers to cut the four-foot-tall grass and remove some large stones from around our small clinic building, I never dreamed that someday the Medical Center would cover so much of the same area. To God be the glory!

It was fun running around in the *Deux Chevaux*. When my dear Seattle friends, the Undis, came out to work with us for a time, he nicknamed the car "Margery's Sardine Can." After three years it was giving me a lot of trouble, so Eugene and Ernie persuaded me to buy another small car, a Renault 4, which could be bought in Bangui. I took their advice and got a lot of use out of it for five years.

I will never forget one experience with the Renault. It wasn't built to be a hearse, but one time it was necessary to use it for that purpose. We found a board two feet wide and long enough to place diagonally from the front passenger seat across to the left side of the rear seat. The body was put on the board, and a relative squeezed sideways into the front seat beside the board to hold the body steady when we went over rough roads. Another relative was in the back right seat, also trying to stabilize the board. The family didn't complain. They were so thankful I would use my car for them at such a sad time in their life.

A Long Wait

During the third week of January 1984, I had some good news. Loie Knight was moving from her station at Kaga-Bondoro to live with me. She planned to work with Eugene Rosenau preparing materials in the Sango language. We had always been good friends, and I was looking forward to her expertise in cooking, helping me with difficult cases at the clinic, playing *Scrabble*, and just having good companionship together.

Then there was some bad news. That same week I drove a pastor's wife to the capitol for a chest x-ray, which unhappily proved positive for tuberculosis. I never dreamed that would be the last long trip I would take in my Toyota truck during the next two years.

Two days later, as I was sitting at my desk at the clinic, Nicholas, the young fellow who worked for me in my house, came in breathless and agitated. He burst out, "Mademoiselle, a strong wind just blew your truck off the hilltop!"

I asked him to explain it to me again but more slowly, and he did. I had heard him correctly. The wind had blown the truck over the back retaining wall into the only large tree in the area. I went up immediately and looked down over the embankment. There was my once-beautiful truck with the front end bashed into the tree. I was too stunned to shed tears.

Vernon mentioned that in the States it would be considered a total loss. But not in Africa! The men took another truck and went through the student village to go around the hill to get to my truck and tow it to our mission garage. A few months later we towed it to a repair garage in Bangui, and once there it sat for seventeen months.

That evening the Bible verse I reviewed in my French memory pack was Isaiah 41:10: "Fear thou not; for I am with thee: be not dismayed; for I am thy God: I will strengthen thee; yea, I will help thee; yea, I will uphold thee with the right hand of my righteousness." Wasn't it good of the Lord to give me that verse just when I needed it?

Eugene Rosenau, who was in the States at that time, and my brother Steve, in New York, helped purchase a hood, radiator, and the many other parts that were needed to repair my truck.

The due date for the parts to arrive—June 1985—came and went. They were lost somewhere. Finally, four months later, after many phone calls by the three Rosenau men in South Carolina, France, and the Central African Republic, the parts were found. Some company had inadvertently picked them up in Bangui and put them in their warehouse. The shipment number was almost identical to that on a shipment they were expecting.

Bruce Rosenau, who now worked at the Bangui station, found the parts at that warehouse and took them back to the mission. The next day he took them to the Bangui garage where my truck was parked. The mechanic apologized and said they were now too busy to work on my truck.

During the next several months I don't know what I would have done without my three-wheel Honda. I was so grateful to the three Herrman teenagers who made this wonderful gift to me in 1979. I used it going up and down the hill between my house and the clinic, going to the town market, to my Thursday afternoon women's class, to church, and even sometimes going to the main road to pick up patients, who would sit behind me and put their arms around my waist. When I needed a truck, I used one of the two others that belonged to families at the mission.

Actually, I was only without my truck for a year. During the second year I was home on furlough.

In December 1985, when the mechanics finished repairing my truck, they tried to start it and discovered there was no starter. Someone working there had stolen it, along with the back seats. To cover their theft they said to Lynn Muhr, "There was no paper signed when the truck was brought in saying that there was a starter in it!"

By the end of January 1986 another two months had passed before the starter arrived. Eugene Rosenau, who lived in South Carolina, sent one to us, and it was finally installed. But the garage mechanics couldn't keep the truck running. Vernon, an excellent mechanic, had to go to Bangui to take a couple from Sibut to the airport. He stopped at the garage and made the necessary repairs. You can use your imagination to know how glad I was to finally get my truck again after being without it so long. God is great to have gifted my co-workers with such mechanical abilities.

A Seeking Soul

I had never met Theophile until he came to the clinic with another patient. He was around twenty years old. He stood quietly by as we took care of his friend. I don't know why I should have remembered him when he came back to the clinic several months later with another friend, but it was of the Lord. This time he was wearing a long white robe. I was curious, so I asked him, "Why are you wearing the long robe now and you weren't when you were here several months ago?"

He replied, "Before I was going to another group of religious people, but I couldn't find satisfaction in their teachings, so now I'm trying the Islam faith."

I knew that Theophile was an earnest seeker wanting to know the truth, so I asked him, "Has anyone ever taken the Bible, the Word of God, and explained the way of salvation to you; how to have eternal life and to know for sure you are going to heaven?"

"No, they haven't."

"Would you like for someone to? I don't want to force you, but if you really want to know, you can, and we will help you."

He quickly answered, "Yes, please, I would like to know."

This was a very busy morning, with many people to take care of. I silently prayed, *Lord, show me now who can minister to this seeking soul.* I knew it would take time, for he was so mixed up. Then I thought of Rene Malepou, an outstanding student in our Bible School who was working on his bike in our garage. I took a Bible and walked with Theophile to the garage.

Rene agreed to talk with him, answer his questions, and point him to Jesus, the giver of eternal life.

Theophile did believe, and I started him on the *Young Believer's Bible Workbook*. He seemed to always be at my door with a finished lesson, wanting the next one. Finally I gave him three at one time. He completed the thirteen-lesson course in two weeks, when it usually took three months. God is good to let us see these new believers in Christ, who have such an insatiable desire to know the Word of God.

59 - Medical Variety

During the '80s our patient load decreased considerably. We averaged around 150 patients daily. Nevertheless, we didn't lack for a variety of illnesses. John Saboyombo was such a help to me when he returned to Sibut to help me in my "old age." Recently, as I was reading the letters I had written home during those days, this one amazed me.

> We never lack for different kinds of illnesses here, especially lately. A few we have treated include a sixteen-year-old girl coughing up blood due to tuberculosis, a young mother dying with leukemia, a two-year-old struggling to overcome encephalitis, a teenage boy's foot sloughing away from the bite of a poisonous snake, and a pastor's wife smiling in spite of her cancer. Of course there are the ordinary sicknesses, such as colds, lots of pneumonia, venereal diseases, parasites, sores, etc.
>
> So many come to us for help. Our prayer is that they will find help not only for their physical bodies but their souls as well. A high school boy came for dental work last week and went away with Christ in his heart.
>
> Sometimes we also have a ministry in counseling our Christians. One of these was a woman who didn't want to sleep in the same room where the leukemia woman passed away. She said, "There is an evil spirit in that room. He attacked my child last night. Please put me in a different room!"

God Heals

We had a very sick little five-year-old girl, Elizabeth, who had been at the clinic for several weeks. I couldn't make a clear diagnosis. When the African doctor came from the town hospital to visit me, I asked him to examine her, but he was no help. One of the mission nurses came through Sibut during this time, and she couldn't help either. Oh, for a modern hospital, with x-ray machines, a modern lab, doctors, etc., but I had to face reality. I was in Africa.

But we had the Lord. I did the best I could and thought she was getting better, but she had four hemorrhages and became weak and anemic. I had the father bring her into the clinic consultation room. Two of my nurse helpers, Yakete and Oumar, were with me. As the father was sitting in a chair hugging his little girl, I explained to him that we could do nothing more. Only prayer could save her.

We knelt around the father and child, and the three of us asked the Lord for her healing. That night she only had one last small hemorrhage. How we rejoiced. But we rejoiced even more two days later when Elizabeth sat on a stool asking for some rice to eat. I kept her for a couple more weeks, fortifying her little body with vitamins, milk, and iron. Then the family took her home, and she returned for follow-up care.

As I have mentioned before, I don't understand why God sometimes does a miracle in healing, as He did for Elizabeth, and not for others. He is God. He is sovereign.

I think of Joni Eareckson Tada, who became a quadriplegic in July 1967 when at the age of seventeen she dove into Chesapeake Bay and broke her neck. The first book she wrote about her affliction was *Joni*, telling the story of her accident and her subsequent struggle to accept her handicap. As a result of that first book, Joni received thousands of letters from hurting people all over the world. From those letters came a sense of responsibility to respond, inspiring her to write her second of many books, *A Step Further*.

People had convinced Joni that if she had enough faith, she would be healed. She went with friends and ordained ministers and elders to a church especially to pray for her healing, and she had the faith that He would do it. We know the Lord does many healing miracles, but to some Christians, like Joni, he says, "not now."

Someday He will say to each of us, "It is time to come to your heavenly home." We can all look forward to that home where there is no suffering, no hunger, no pain, and no sorrow. And to think, it is going to be that way forever and ever.

A Medication Not Given

I was quickly attracted to sixteen-year-old Pokalima, lying before me on the examination table. There was something beautiful about her smile, and her eyes reflected a loving spirit. Her mother was by her side, looking anxiously at me. Pokalima was covered with an African cloth; the kind each African woman wears and that has so many uses.

With a smell coming to my nostrils, I already had a good idea what part of her problem was, but I asked her mother, "What is the matter with her?"

She answered, "She has been paralyzed from her waist down for many years."

I don't remember what the mother told me had caused the paralysis, but it was probably polio.

Her mother continued, "She has sores on her back and buttocks, and she desperately needs help."

We tenderly turned her over onto her stomach. My first reaction was, *Oh Lord, this is too much. How can she stand it?* She had bedsores all over her back and some on her buttocks that had penetrated to the bone. Her sores were caused not only from lying on her back but also from urine, for she had lost bladder control.

The first thing I did was put in a retention catheter to collect her urine. Then I started cleaning and cutting the dead flesh from her wounds. It took a couple of hours. I was thinking, *I will use up so many dressings if she stays here very long. What shall I do?* Immediately my spirit was rebuked for thinking such thoughts, for the Lord is able to supply.

It took several weeks for her wounds to almost heal. Pokalima never complained, and we all learned to love her beautiful spirit. Her hardships must have taught her humility and deep gratitude. We found her meek and quickly flashing smile an inspiration.

One day I talked over her situation with my helpers, Andre and Louvrou. If she went home, could we teach her parents how to take care of her so her sores wouldn't reappear? Could her parents learn how to use sterile techniques to change her catheter?

Andre said, "Mademoiselle, there is no way they can do that in a village."

We knew we couldn't keep her, for her parents needed to go back to their village to start their gardens. I went home that evening, and poured my heart out to the Lord about Pokalima. We had prayed for her many times and were so thankful for the Lord's healing power. But now we needed His guidance.

One morning, two days later, Andre and I made rounds of our hospitalized patients. Immediately when we entered Pokalima's private room, her parents said to us, "She can't open her mouth to talk or eat."

Upon examination I saw it was true. I looked at Andre and said,

"Tetanus." But he already knew. Quickly I asked Andre, "Did she receive a tetanus injection when she arrived?"

We examined her chart, and there was no injection given. All I could think of was, *How could we have overlooked that when we gave her so much special attention?* She was so helpless lying on her bed; I felt horrible. Surely this sweetheart didn't need this added to her other problems.

Two days later she died and was with the Lord. As I was praying, the Lord seemed to say, *This was the answer to your prayers.* God in His mercy took her to a home where "No eye has seen, no ear has heard, no mind has conceived what God has prepared for those who love him" (I Corinthians 2:9, NIV).

My Medicine Bag

In the earlier days, before a church was built on the south side of Sibut, I took six Bible School students to three different villages each week to have Bible classes while I went to another village further on. When traveling I always took my medicine (doctor's) bag with me as one would take a tool chest.

One day, when I came back to pick up the students, one of them, Oumar, said, "Mademoiselle, there is an ill woman in a house across the road. A relative asked me to ask you to come see her on your way back."

I grabbed my medicine bag from the front seat, and Oumar took it from me as we walked across the road to see her. She was in back of the house, and Oumar preceded me. As I came to the side of the house, the most horrible smell penetrated my nostrils. I was glad Oumar was in front of me, for I started to gag. I couldn't stop. I never remembered having done that before when I had an undesirable task to perform. I quickly retreated to the front of the house, for I was ashamed to let the people hear or see me.

Breathing deeply a moment or two, I gathered my breath and again started back. The same thing happened, so back I went to the front of the house. This was unbearable, what could I do?

I could pray. "Lord, you know I have an unpleasant task ahead of me, and in my own strength, I can't do it. Please help me." It was one of those prayers the Lord couldn't answer later; it had to be now. Many times He had answered emergency prayers for me, and I trusted Him to do it again.

As I rounded the house I kept walking calmly toward the people sitting under a shade tree. I didn't have to be told who was the sick one among them. My nose led the way, and flies were swarming all around her. On her left shoulder, beside her neck, a putrid green gangrene pus was seeping out of a hole that the people had tried to plug with the ground bark of a tree.

I was astounded when I opened my bag. I hadn't replaced the gloves that I usually had in the bag. So with ungloved hands I used a tongue blade to scrape off the bark and then used leaves to receive the drainage that flowed out as I pressed the sides of the hole. I put all these on an old ragged piece of cloth that was given to us.

When most of the pus was on the cloth, I switched to using torn-off foot-long sheet bandages. While I was doing this, the patient just sat quietly on her stool, not saying a word.

When I had cleaned out the finger-wide hole, I put on several compresses and bandaged it with part of a roll of sheet bandages. Oumar was a good helper who later became a nurse. I gave the relatives enough sulfa pills (before the days of other antibiotics) for two days and told her I wanted to see her at the clinic on Saturday.

I never saw her again. I assumed that once the gangrene pus was out, the wound had healed.

Dentistry on the Spot

One time, as I was passing the village of Wawa, a man ran to the side of the road to flag me down. I stopped. I couldn't stop all the time at different villages where there was a pastor, but the Africans had an uncanny way of knowing where I was going and the time I would be returning. The man said that there was a woman suffering much with a toothache. I was dismayed. For some reason, I don't remember why, I hadn't brought my medicine bag with me for this trip. But I said I would look at it. The tooth needed to be extracted. I hated to leave her suffering. Then an idea came into my mind. I went to my tool chest, got a pair of pliers, and gave them to someone standing by and told them to wash them well with soap and water.

When they were returned to me, I sat the woman down in a chair with someone holding her head and pulled the tooth. The Africans didn't think anything abnormal in this procedure, but I sure did! They had confidence in what I was doing. This was a first for me.

60 - Well of Faith

In March 1993, at the start of our Bible School year, I was distressed when I saw some of my students' wives nodding off in class. I knew why they were sleepy. Some of them had risen at 2:30 a.m. in order to get water for their families. The mission well three blocks from our Bible School village was dry because it was the end of the dry season. This meant that the women had to walk over a half a mile to the community well and then back, balancing their heavy water basins on their heads. They had to go very early because people lined up to get water long before daybreak. Too many people were dependent on this one well that had been drilled as an aid project by another country.

Most of the surface water in the Central African Republic is not drinkable, and much of it is not even fit to wash in. It is contaminated by a parasite called bilharziasis that wreaks havoc with the body.

This aid project was really a wonderful thing. A community that was in need of a well simply had to raise $100 for a fund that would replace parts that might break on the foot pedal that is used to draw up the water. The drilling company came to our mission in 1990, but there was not enough water where they drilled, and the project was abandoned. They promised to come back and drill again, but these were just empty promises. Every time missionary Lynn Muhr went to their headquarters in the capital city, they said they would return sometime. But two years had passed, and we were desperate.

The first week of school my heart was heavy for the plight of our women. It was work enough for them to get their families washed, clothed, and fed before coming to class at 7:30 without the additional burden of walking so far and so early for water. So I cast this problem on the Lord. He reminded me of Ephesians 3:20: *"Now glory be to God! By his mighty power at work within us, he is able to accomplish infinitely more than we would ever dare to ask or hope"* (NLT).

I reviewed in my mind other verses concerning faith. Hebrews 11:1 says, *"What is faith? It is the confident assurance that what we hope for is going to happen. It is the evidence of things we cannot yet see"* (NLT). We were all hoping for a well, and faith was being sure that we would get it.

Then the Spirit reminded me of 1 John 5:14-15: *"And we can be confident that he will listen to us whenever we ask him for anything in line with his will. And if we know he is listening when we make our requests, we can be sure that he will give us what we ask for"* (NLT).

I prayed, *Lord, I know that it is Your will for the students to be here, for You have called them, the husbands with their wives, to come here and go to school so that someday they can serve you as pastors. And since we know that it is Your will, we have the right to ask you for a miracle to meet our need for a well.*

Two years before, I had taught the book of Nehemiah to the students and staff of our hospital at Ippy. And that evening, as I was praying, the Lord reminded me of Nehemiah 1. The prophet was praying about the news he had heard from his brother, who had just come from Jerusalem.

The people of Israel were in great affliction and reproach. The walls of Jerusalem were broken down, and its gates had been burned. Nehemiah prayed about the situation and reminded God of His promises to the people of Israel in Deuteronomy 28:63-29:15. In these verses the Lord told His people that if they sinned, they would be scattered to other nations as punishment, but if they turned back to the Lord and repented, He would gather them to their homeland.

I was getting more and more excited as I read all of this. My heart was pounding. *If Nehemiah could remind God of His promises, and the Lord listened to Nehemiah, then we could do the same thing!* We would ask the Lord for a well, using the promises of the verses that He had given me.

The next morning I could hardly wait for my first class. I started out by asking, "How many of you believe that God answers prayer?" Of course everyone's hand went up. So I gave them an easy assignment for the next day: "I want all of you to come to class with a verse on either faith or prayer." I didn't elaborate further but proceeded to teach a lesson from Ephesians.

The next day everyone shared the verses they had found. I shared the verses from Nehemiah 1. Then I explained the motive behind the assignment. "Would you believe with me that by faith we can ask the Lord for a well?" I challenged. "Come, leave your desks and join hands with me in a circle around the room, and let's pray."

After many of the African women prayed, I asked them to start thanking

The well of faith.

the Lord for the well that He was going to give us. We could sense the presence of the Lord around us as we prayed. Then we broke forth into singing and praising the Lord with thanksgiving. It was a precious time!

Two weeks later, on a Friday evening, Margo Muhr burst into the room where I was getting ready to teach. With excitement in her voice, she asked, "Margery, do you know a family named Gwinn?"

"Of course, I do, " I replied. " They are a couple that have supported me for over forty years—ever since I left the States for my first term in Africa in 1950."

"Well, word has come through that $6,000 has come in from them for a well!" she exclaimed.

I had previously written a letter home to ask my friends to pray that God might provide a well. Hallelujah, the Lord had supplied the money for the well! But where in the middle of Africa could we find a well-drilling outfit?

But God had it figured out! Shortly after, we heard that a well-digging outfit from a Swedish mission located 600 miles away was right then in our town digging a well for the Catholic mission, just two miles from where we stood! What a miracle! Six hundred miles may not seem like much in the United States, but coming over the rough, pot-holed roads of the Central African Republic is quite a different thing!

Lynn Muhr immediately went to the Catholic mission to talk the well-digging crew into coming to our mission to dig a well for us. Three days later the truck with the crew and equipment arrived at our mission village. Our African mission houses are built in a half-circle, with a small acreage in front of them. The crew picked a spot in the center of the village and started drilling. Everyone was so excited, praying that they would strike water.

They did! What a celebration! The women let loose and danced like the Biblical King David did before the Lord. I wish we could have had a video of that scene. I didn't even have my slide camera with me to catch their jubilation. But their joy is imprinted on my mind forever.

The next day I asked the women for their testimonies. One woman declared, "We didn't ask the Lord to put the well in the middle of our village, but He did! It is like that verse we learned in Ephesians 3:20; He did above what we asked Him to do."

I could hardly keep back the tears as I realized they saw the Bible as a living book.

The rejoicing in Africa traveled back around the globe to the Gwinns, who were thrilled that their money had arrived at just the right time. I made a cassette tape of our experience and sent it to them. They shared the tape with the foreman of their orchard in Mattawa, Washington, because the money they had given had come from the sale of the apples grown there. So you see, we are all co-workers together in the service of Christ.

61 - Paul and *The Jesus Film*

In the fall of 1993, malaria and amoebic liver abscesses were trying to get the best of me. I ended up requesting our mission plane, and Doug Golike flew me to Ippy to be treated by Dr. Mary. After her treatment she advised me to go to the United States to have my liver checked. I was feeling tired but otherwise okay, but I thought I should go. I had never before left in the middle of a term to go to the States because of illness. I wrote to my brother Paul and his wife Ruth in Bellingham, Washington, asking them to make an appointment with a doctor there who knew tropical medicine.

I always liked going to Bellingham, a beautiful town eighty miles north of Seattle, situated among lakes and mountains, and where two of my brothers and their families lived.

My brother John met me at Sea-Tac Airport near Seattle where he lives. After a couple of days visiting with him and his wife Doris, they took me to the apartment of my good friend, eighty-six-year-old Erma Swanson Sowers. Her walk was now slower, and it was getting more difficult for her to climb the forty-two steps to her apartment.

The day before I left Seattle for Bellingham, Erma was reading an article about *The Jesus Film* in a Campus Crusade magazine. I knew about the film, which told the life of Christ based on the Gospel of Luke. My good friends Boyd and Kathy Griffith, who worked with Campus Crusade, had sent me three videos of the film which I had left in Africa, one each in English, French, and Sango. At that time the film had been translated into 290 languages. (By the year 2002 the number of languages reached 723.) When I was in Africa, Boyd wrote to ask me to consider getting the four-reel movie version to show in our part of the country. I wrote back, "There is no way I could take it around and show it to the churches. I only have two years left before retiring, and I am teaching full time."

I started to read the article Erma had been reading, but I didn't have time to finish it, so I asked if I could take it with me to Bellingham. However, I was not the only one who read it; my brother Paul did, too.

After he read the article, I was surprised to hear him say, "This is something I would like to do; go to Central African Republic and show this film."

"But how could you?" I replied. "You are still teaching at Ferndale High, and it costs $4,000 for the film and all the equipment to show it."

He answered, "I guess I'm just dreaming." But the thought persisted. Later he remarked, "Maybe I could take an early retirement." He kept mulling the idea over in his mind and began to pray. God had His plans.

I left Bellingham with a clean bill of health. I was so thankful to the Lord and to those who had been praying for me.

It was necessary to go to Boise for a few meetings. On the way I stopped for a night to see my good friends the Herrmans. Robin, one of their daughters, lived close by and came to see me, bringing along her friend Patti. As we talked, Robin casually mentioned, "Margery, what would you like to take back to Africa with you this time, a four-wheeler?"

"Oh no, Robin! I will be coming home for good in a couple of years, and I am still using the three-wheeler." I didn't tell her that it was temporarily waiting to be fixed.

"Well, what would you like to take back?" she asked again.

"The Jesus film," I blurted out.

"*The Jesus Film*. What's that?" So I explained the influence the film was having all over the world.

"Where would you buy one?"

"I have a friend who works with the making of the film in Orlando, Florida."

She promptly replied, "Let's call him."

Paul Benedict and team members setting up the equipment to show *"The Jesus Film"* in an outlying village.

He said he would sell it to us for $3,600. Robin ordered and paid for it, and her friend Patti paid for the generator. It was to be sent to the Seattle home of Jean and Darrell Hayes, my friends since 1946, who would help me send it on to the Central African Republic.

I was a little stunned as I left there the next morning. The enemy put thoughts in my mind. *What if Paul and Ruth weren't really serious about going to Africa?* But as I prayed, I knew this was the Lord's doing. God was putting his plan into place.

The second night of my stay in Idaho I received a telephone call from Paul. He said, "I was just out walking the streets praying about whether Ruth and I should go to Africa."

I quickly answered, "You had better go. The film and equipment have been purchased."

"What?" he exclaimed. "It has been bought?" I told him about the details, and that settled it for Paul and Ruth. He would take early retirement, and they would meet me in Africa.

I had been in the States two months, and it was time to leave. We went to the Seattle airport earlier than usual. Darrell had been wise enough to call the airline supervisor the day before to explain about the extra baggage I would be taking. The supervisor said we should arrive early and it would be $110 for each piece weighing seventy pounds or less.

At the ticket counter I paid $1,100 for the ten extra pieces, which included five pieces of *The Jesus Film* equipment. What a relief to see it all going down the conveyor belt, even the long orange bag containing the ten-foot legs for the screen. The regulation for the baggage length was eight feet, but the supervisor said he would let it go through.

I had asked Erma not to come to the airport. I thought it would be too much for her. But she insisted; the Porters, mutual friends of ours, brought her down. As we were waiting in the airport, Darrell was looking out the window.

He called to us, saying, "Look, there goes the equipment for *The Jesus Film*," and we watched it being loaded on the plane.

I could hardly speak. I was thinking, *This is the Lord's plan being carried out. He had me come home for medical reasons and a rest. But the real reason was to take back the equipment that was now being loaded onto the plane.* I silently thanked him for working everything out so this film could be shown in the Central African Republic.

The only problem I had with my precious baggage was in Paris. The officials questioned if I owned all the extra baggage I had in my name. The receipts of payment satisfied them, and the film and equipment made it safely to

Africa. Once there, I didn't have to pay any customs. This was another answer to many prayers.

In September, I drove to Bangui to get Paul and Ruth who had just arrived from the States. He told me right away that my truck needed to have some work done on it. (I learned later that it had been running on two cylinders.) Paul said he would have been afraid to drive it from the Bangui mission station to the nearby airport, much less the hundred miles from Sibut to Bangui.

At the time, Vernon was the only man on the Sibut station. He had much to do. Besides working on the vehicles of missionaries traveling through, he was also the main teacher of the men's classes in the Bible School. I just didn't have the heart to ask him to work on my truck as well. Instead, I took advantage of my mechanically inclined brother and told Paul about all the flat tires that I had been having the past year, more than all of my time in Africa put together.

Paul immediately replied, "I'll check on that." He later found out the repeated flat tires were caused by road grit inside the tires.

Paul spent the first couple of weeks learning to run the film equipment, dust-proofing the truck camper shell, and digging in my barrel of truck parts for spark plugs, wires, ignition parts, etc., to get my truck in running order. He also got the three-wheel Honda motorcycle running again. Meanwhile I found an old trunk that closed tightly and was just the right size for the film and equipment.

Ruth started teaching Vernon and Jan's sons in their studies, as Jan was so busy it was difficult for her to consistently keep the boys' school schedule.

Paul cleaning one of the four reels, which he did after each showing.

Julie, their high school daughter, was very disciplined to keep her study hours every day, doing her correspondence studies.

Vernon and I picked Paul's film travel team of three men from our student body to accompany him on his trips: Doro, the team leader, Pierre, and Francois. Paul, being a French teacher for many years, had no problem communicating with them, as these men also knew French well. They also helped him learn some Sango.

In each village the team set up the equipment every night and worked with the pastor and his deacons in dealing with the people who came to the front afterwards. They came to believe and to ask questions, and many Christians repented of their wayward life. Pastors reported their churches were filled after the showing of the film.

At first Paul showed the film only in the churches around Sibut and in the surrounding area so his team could return home at night, since the students had school the next morning. Later, when school was out, they made overnight trips.

The churches couldn't accommodate all the people who came, so the film was always shown outside. The screen was approximately six feet by eight feet, placed on ten-foot poles, and it could be seen from both sides. The first film showing was in the courtyard of our center church, with about 12,000 attending, the most in all the places the film was shown.

Prayer was an essential part of the preparation of any film showing. The night of the showing at the second church, it threatened rain. Ruth and I both stayed home and prayed that it wouldn't rain. At the church the lightning flashed across the sky, followed by thunder. Then it started raining across the road from the church but not on the church side, where a crowd of over 400 people was viewing the film. Soon, on the church side a full moon came out in all of its glory.

Paul knew it was as if the Lord was saying to him, *See, I can control the weather, and as I am helping you now, I will be with you in the coming months of showing the story of my life on earth.* A great indescribable peace filled his soul, as he knew the benediction of the Lord was on this ministry. In all the months of showing the film, only once were they rained out.

In November the annual missionary conference was held at Sibut. Paul stayed to help Vernon get the station ready for thirty extra people. He ran errands, repaired water pipes, water heaters, and fans, and did whatever needed to be done. After three weeks on the station fixing things and attending our conference, he was ready to go on the road again, on a ten-day trip up the Oubangui River, on the border between Zaire and the Central African Republic.

Doro, the team leader, would have to deal with the Africans who always wanted to pile in the truck to go here and there. I warned Paul this would be one of the greatest problems that he would have on his trips.

For the trip Ruth made some granola and packed some rice for him to take. All the other food he would eat with the Africans. Sometimes the team wasn't fed until almost noon, so Paul appreciated having the granola. He always took his own drinking water because of the impurity of the sources of most of the African water.

To start the river trip, there were fifteen miles of pot-holed pavement and forty-five miles on a rutted dirt road. The grass and vegetation had grown up in the middle of the road and on both sides, as the fires hadn't burned it off. The grass whipped the sides of the truck as it slowly made its way along at twenty miles an hour. When they arrived at Joukou, they had to cross a river on a very primitive ferry. It had cables attached to tree trunks, and that kept the ferry from floating down the river. When it docked, they put up incline boards so the vehicles could get on or off. An African always stood on the ferry directing the driver so he wouldn't drive off the boards.

After getting off the ferry, there were still a few miles to go to the large Oubangui River, where six men were waiting with a canoe thirty feet long and four-and-a-half feet wide. The canoe could hold about 3,000 pounds, and the men were its rowers. This began one of the most memorable trips that Paul and his team experienced.

Paul sat in a bamboo chair in the canoe, always immensely enjoying the chanting and singing of the rowers. On this ten-day trip they stopped off at five different churches along the river. Paul always showed the film twice in

Crossing the river on an African ferry.

each place for two reasons. First, most villagers had never seen electric lights, let alone a film on a large screen. Second, it took viewing the film two times for them to understand what was really going on. Then those who had attended the first night reached out to others who had come the second evening. The smallest number of people seeing the film in any one place was around 350.

There were fetishes beside some of the paths from the river to the villages. The river tribes were more steeped in witchcraft than most Africans, and many of them believed that these objects, usually made of bones, feathers, stones, etc. had magical protective powers—similar to idols. But after the showing of the film, there were many professions of faith. At 6:30 the next morning, the team members showed Paul a group of people who were burning their fetishes on a small fire. They began trusting Christ to keep them, instead of the demonology of witchcraft.

On this trip Paul and his team ate every kind of meat imaginable: hedgehog, snake, hippo, buffalo, rat, deer, monkey, and lots of fish and chicken. Paul agreed with me that the African women could make the chicken sauce tastier than any chicken dish we ever tasted. In the mornings, after spending time reading the Bible and praying, Paul would spend two hours cleaning from the four film reels the bugs that the light of the projector had attracted the night before.

One Sunday morning at Dengou, the largest church on the river, Pastor Timothy asked Doro to preach. Although Paul didn't understand the Sango message, he appreciated the manner of his preaching and how he kept the attention of the children as well as the grown-ups. Paul videotaped the service. What I appreciated most when I saw the video of the service was the enjoyment on their faces as they sang in harmony the song "When the Saints Go Marching In." I realized once more that though the Africans don't have much of this world's goods, they have the hope that when Jesus comes back for His saints, they will be among them. This fills my heart with great joy.

Paul was on this trip during Christmas season, and he became a little depressed as he thought of the Christmas celebration he could be enjoying with Ruth and the ones back at Sibut. He took a walk and committed this problem to the Lord, and God gave him peace. Paul realized anew the privilege of being out in the middle of Africa doing what the Lord had called him to do.

As the people watched the film, they had many different reactions. Many were in tears and even sobbed as they viewed the crucifixion, but people clapped with happiness as Christ appeared after His resurrection.

We were always glad to see Paul when he came back from his trips. I never heard him complain about anything he experienced, like having to drink tepid water, or sometimes having fifty gnats buzzing around his head during the daytime. His team always took care of him, and he them. He would unwind by riding my three-wheeler and following the African paths many miles out to some of their gardens. Between trips he also spent time repairing the Toyota. The African roads and the climate are real enemies to vehicles.

Even animals were road hazards. Sometimes one of the team would say at the end of a trip, "This was a six-chicken trip." Chickens ran free in the African villages. Occasionally one would meet its demise when a vehicle would visit its village.

Our Sibut district had fifty churches, and Paul showed the film in each of them except the three on the Mala Road. The road was so bad that Pastor Ambroise, who lived on it, remarked, "A couple of the holes are so large the truck could just fall in."

When the Bible School started in March, Paul had a new team: Nestor, a fellow who had just graduated, and Darlan, a young man who had been in my youth classes and now was in my Friday night disciple class. Both of these two mature men gave Paul great joy in the way they lived together and dealt with the people who came for salvation or spiritual help.

Also in March, Ruth returned home to the States. Their daughter, Heather, was going to have her third baby, and Ruth wanted to be there to help her.

Paul and his team also visited churches at other mission stations. In Bambari, the second largest city in the nation, there is a large Muslim population. The mayor of the Muslim quarter had a VCR, and several times he borrowed *The Jesus Film* video from Eric Elmer, one of the missionaries at their station. When Paul went to Bambari to show the film there, Eric visited the small office of the Campus Crusade for Christ. They told him they had the four reels of *The Jesus Film* in Fulani, the language of these Muslims, but had never had the equipment to show it. Eric went to the mayor and told him that *The Jesus Film* was available in Fulani and could be shown in his quarter. The mayor readily gave permission for Paul and Eric to show it.

As the film was being shown, Paul thought it odd to hear another language being spoken other than Sango. There were three miracles the Lord performed for this unusual occasion. The first was that the Campus Crusade had such a film, the second was that the Muslim mayor would agree that all his people could view the film, and the third was that there were several who came to the Lord that night. Eric and the team members dealt with them, showing more clearly the salvation that is in Christ.

After showing the film in several churches in Bambari, Paul went to Ippy. Paul really appreciated the interest and help Jim Johnson gave them. He not only arranged all the meetings in the area churches but also went with Paul to the churches.

In the courtyard of the main church, many people came forward after seeing the film. The African pastor rose up and started to preach to the crowd, using the microphone. He just kept preaching on and on. Jim and the team wanted to deal with the people that came for spiritual help, but they couldn't. So little by little Paul turned down the sound system until it became quiet. Now they could deal with the many people who wanted their help.

On another trip they drove several miles on a very rough road, and when they came to a hill, the road was impassable. It was so treacherous that Paul let out all the people who were with him. He precariously drove down into the canyon and up on the other side of the hill and around boulders. The people held their breath and prayed that the truck wouldn't tip over. As the truck reached the other side, everyone breathed a sigh of relief and gave thanks to God and climbed back in.

In one of the larger villages where they showed the film, an influential Muslim came. As is the African custom, any important people always sat next to Paul, so the Muslim received the seat of honor. During the showing of the film, he sobbed and sobbed, with tears streaming down his face. Later, still crying, he asked to go to Ippy with Paul. As he sat next to Paul, it was evident the Spirit was working in his heart.

Paul tells his story better than I could. He writes of some of his experiences:

> In the last few weeks of my stay in CAR my team, Nestor and Darlan, and I headed off to Kaga-Bondoro (Crampel) to show the film at four or five churches in the area. In earlier times it was a thriving mission station with several missionaries, but now there were none. Once there was even a missionary dental clinic that took care of much of the community dental needs. Most of the buildings were given to the national church, with just a building or two remaining for visiting missionaries.
>
> As was the custom, Margery arranged ahead of time the dates for the showing of the film everywhere, so the churches could prepare for our arrival. The church leaders would then let the people in the villages know we were coming.
>
> In Kaga-Bondoro she entrusted a deacon named

Timothy in the main church to set the dates and to make all the arrangements. For some reason or other, he failed to do this. We arrived at our first church early on Sunday afternoon, introduced ourselves, got acquainted with the pastor, and located the best place to set up the screen. They were polite to us but seemed a little confused. It soon became apparent that they had no knowledge of the fact that we were coming. They wanted us to return at a later date, and that was arranged.

There was nothing to do but go on into Kaga-Bondoro and see where the mix-up was. Timothy had made no appointments in any of the churches. When we arrived at the main church, the minister there wanted us to show the film in his church to some of his Bible School students.

Unfortunately, as sometimes happens to us all, both the pastor and Timothy had an exaggerated sense of their importance. They wanted to control what we did in the area. The pastors of the other churches were somewhat intimidated and didn't feel free to work with their own people when we were with the main church pastor. So my team and I got our heads together and asked many of the Bible School students to go along with us so there wouldn't be room for the other two. The students got real experience in personal evangelism and the other church pastors were free to help their own people.

By the way, we made all advance notices to the area churches ourselves. The main pastor was so unhappy about it that he refused to house my helpers and to feed the team, so they moved in with me. I shared what Margery and my wife, Ruth, had made for me, and we also went down to the local market to buy our own provisions. We had a little kerosene stove and one or two small pans for heating food. It really became an enjoyable experience for us. We knew the Lord could and would provide. I even contemplated buying a pound or two of roasted termites and would have if we had a reliable way of re-cooking them. I always needed to be careful of contaminated food, and heating it was one good way of destroying whatever needed to be destroyed.

On the road from Kaga-Bondoro, north towards Chad, in a village about ten miles out, we set up the equipment in the courtyard of the church that bordered the road. As always, we made sure that the church leaders and the team would be ready to deal with the seekers. All was going well, even to the very end, and then something very unusual and almost frightening happened. As the invitation was given on the screen, there was a mass of people running away from the outskirts of the yard. At first I thought that I never before had seen people so eager to come forward for spiritual counseling. It wasn't so here either. Along the road there came a small band of Fulani, a nomad-type people, with their cattle. Remember, it was dark, and these people with their cattle are sometimes feared. The cattle can be somewhat described as one would describe a Texas longhorn, only bigger. The length of their horns is massive. The animals can also become aggressive. Well, the Fulani had stopped to see the film. Those people already watching turned around to see these fearsome animals right behind them. They made a mad dash for the church building on the far side of the courtyard, stumbling over electrical cords, ropes, and other equipment. We never found out if there were any conversions that night, for at that point the film showing was effectively over.

There was another village and church about six miles west of Kaga-Bondoro where we were scheduled to show the film. Impassable roads were almost the common occurrence on these trips. This road was even more treacherous. Once in a while I have returned to the mission with a muffler or tailpipe broken off, without brakes, or damaged shock absorbers, so I didn't want this to happen here. We were too far away to make effective repairs. After consultation and guidance from above, we were on our way. Skirting ravine-type ruts and large jutting rocks that could rip an oil pan open or do major damage to the chassis made the journey longer than it needed to be, but we arrived.

That evening was the only time in all the film showings that we got rained out. About fifteen minutes into the showing a torrential rain opened up. We had almost no time to shut the generator down and to grab the projector and put it away. The rest of the equipment had to stay where it was until we could venture out again to retrieve it. I asked Nestor and Darlan to dismiss the crowd of about 2,000 because now the ground was too wet and there was a real danger of electrical shock.

The crowd would not disperse. Those who could get inside the church did so, and the others just stood around expecting us to do something. I moved from one side of the church to the other, and the crowd followed again. I then asked Nestor and Darlan if they could preach or something, I didn't know what.

Both of them gathered as many children as they could around them and began to tell them Bible stories. In the meantime I was able to retrieve the screen, cords, and ropes and put them away. It was about time to go back to Kaga-Bondoro, for the weather was threatening again. As we were ready to depart, both the men told what the Lord had done that evening. There were over forty conversions of just the children alone. It was worth being rained out!

On the way back the rain was kept in check for most of the few miles, but then it came down hard again. It was difficult to see more than a few yards in front of the vehicle. Suddenly there was a man in front of us, waving frantically for us to stop. We knew that it could be dangerous to stop for someone in an isolated area like that, for bandits had been known to frequent those parts, but we had no choice but to stop.

The man was desperate to get his wife to the hospital in Kaga-Bondoro. We moved our messy equipment aside to place her in the back. She couldn't even sit up. We didn't find out if she ever recovered or not.

The next day we said our good-byes and returned to Sibut to clean up, put everything back in order, and go to our next assignment.

One evening in a village along the Bogangolo Road, an arterial of the main road to Bangui, after the film showing, counseling, and wrapping things up for the night, we sat around a small table for our evening meal. It was about 9:30 p.m. This was typical. We were in the midst of discussing our American culture and their culture. They know there is a great technological gap between the two. Of all things, they began to discuss how much the Americans cared for them. Of course they invited me to participate. We discussed such things as whether or not the Americans should give more money for various African endeavors. One part of the discussion dealt with whether or not the missionaries should provide more transportation for them. Getting around is hard for them, and sometimes laborious, so it was not unreasonable for them to think that the missionaries should be more generous in sharing their vehicles.

Of course they have very little concept of the tremendous cost of vehicle upkeep. As an example, I had to replace a universal joint on the pickup. It took over a day just to modify a clip for the part. By the time I replaced the universal joint, the cost was over $200 U.S.

Well, as we were finishing up our meal and conversation, a young man came to talk to the pastor's wife and others around the table. I knew it was serious by the way they spoke. Finally, as I finished eating, they told me there was a serious accident down the road. They wanted me to come and help with the injured and to transport them to a clinic. But they didn't want to bother me until I had finished eating. That was one of the few times I really got upset with them, for I could have arrived at the scene much earlier. I quickly cleared out the pickup to make room for those that might need help.

Down the road a very large truck carrying sacked *gozo*, a type of manioc, had slammed into a tree that had fallen across the road. It was dark, and the tree had fallen just in the middle of a curve in the road, so the driver had no time to stop or avoid the tree. As on most trucks, people hitch rides on them, sitting on top of the load or hanging on it in any way they can.

As I came upon the scene, there were about seven or eight bodies strewn about. I was to transport them to a small clinic back beyond the village and church to another village, where we had been the day before. I positioned the pickup the best I could to get the injured inside the back as well as the front. I could hardly stand it as they picked them up to place them inside. At home we have ambulances and medical personnel trained to assist the injured. They had to pick them up by their arms and legs and toss them in. There was a woman among the injured. As they were picking her up, I said, "She goes in front, and be careful." I had to enforce that, for they thought she was getting preferential treatment.

After we arrived at Bogangolo, we had to wake up those who tended the clinic. I had no idea as to their qualifications, but the treatment must have been better than nothing.

It was way into the night before I got back to the church to get ready to retire. Sometimes I wonder if that was a good enough demonstration that Americans cared for them. I also thought of Margery spending most of her life there pointing them to Christ, healing them, and bandaging their wounds.

On June 6 Paul had the last showing of the film in our mission village. He was to show it on the Saturday before, but he had an intestinal upset and couldn't do it. I thought maybe he could have contacted amoeba having lived so much in the villages, but I checked him out and was so thankful that was not the case.

I can't say I got lonely on the mission field. But when Paul left, I really felt a void and missed him a lot. Only eternity will reveal the real results of the thousands of people seeing *The Jesus Film* and understanding better why Christ left heaven's glory and came into the world.

62 - Homeward Bound

As I was nearing my sixty-ninth birthday, I felt that in one year my ministry in Africa should be winding down. For some time my left knee had been hurting (later at home in Seattle I was to receive a new one). I had peace that I should leave the next fall.

As I was meditating on what my life would be like back in the States, the Lord gave me this verse in Isaiah: "And the Lord shall guide you continually, and satisfy thy soul in drought, and make fat thy bones: and thou shalt be like a watered garden, and like a spring of water, whose waters fail not" (58:11).

Soon after that it was time for our annual missionary conference, and a couple from the home office, the Leigh Adamses, came to speak to us. When Carol Adams met with the missionary women, she gave each of us a card with a scripture verse on it, and she wanted each of us to read it aloud. Imagine my surprise when my verse was the same one the Lord had given to me earlier. I knew without a doubt, the Lord would guide me into some ministry at home and I could still water others with the Word of God.

On my way home from Africa in September 1994, one of the people I visited was Judy Stanton Cagle, the nurse who had spent almost a year with me twelve years earlier and the one whose letters you have read in this book. Upon my arrival at the airport in Pensacola, Florida, she and her husband were holding up a large banner on which was written these words: "*Welcome Home to America.*"

After two delightful days with her and her family, Judy and her son Adam and I left early for the airport. There she interviewed me like a reporter. Out of that interview she wrote a letter to my 600 friends who received my quarterly letters, describing far better than I ever could my departure from Africa.

> So you REALLY want to know what Margery Benedict has been up to? Twelve whole years have gone by since we last saw each other. She wrote me before arriving, "Be prepared for an old, gray-haired lady." Well, that got me worried! You mean we might not recognize each other? Hurriedly I wrote back, "Be prepared for a fat, middle-aged lady!"
>
> Well, the plane was on time and off walked Margery, looking very much the same as I remembered her. Why, I think she still wears the same dress size! And nobody else in the entire waiting area recognized that here was a VETERAN of 44 years of service finally arriving "home."
>
> When was the last time you used a *Boggle* game to witness to someone? Personally, I can't remember. I do it so often. JUST KIDDING! But I'm getting ahead of myself. I want to let you in on a few of the "good-byes" that Margery experienced. Good-byes are never easy anyway. It's especially hard for the Africans to understand. *"Mo nde mo yeke na ngangou!"* Literally: "You still have

strength!" Loosely translated: "You're not bedridden. Why on earth are you leaving?" One of the pastors: "Why can't you stay until you die?" But mission policy does foresee a need to come apart and rest.

The first get-together was in the Center Church of Sibut. Nearly 400 young people and their leaders gathered to bid their farewells. Some had walked from as far away as thirty miles! Eight years earlier Margery taught accordion to one young man who now led a combined EIGHT choirs in singing "God Be with You 'Til We Meet Again." (Look out! I'm going to cry onto the computer!) And, if you were wondering what to serve Margery when you invite her to your home, here's the menu: rice and chicken, manioc and greens.

On Friday nights Margery taught a discipleship class, attended by twenty-six young men and one brave young lady. Here she was presented with a picture of herself, with the outline of the country. In the country was a scroll printed with these words in English: "We are very thankful to God for the great work Miss BENEDICT has done for the young people and believers of the CENTRAL AFRICAN REPUBLIC. God keep her and

Eight church choirs singing "God Be with You 'Til We Meet Again" JEA Farewell for Margery.

give her strength!" Underneath the map was written, "Good-bye Miss BENEDICT. God be with you!!" The picture was outlined with a colored flowered wreath, drawn by one of her students, Kassi Didier.

The next good-bye was by far the LOUDEST one. Margery called it the "sobbing party." Women from various churches who attended her Ladies' Class downtown all gathered at the class building. Numerous gifts were presented. And, if you were wondering what to purchase as a gift for Margery, here's what she has already received: a chicken, tomatoes, onions, peanuts, and 4000 francs (about $10). The chicken, with its legs tied, was squawking and flapping all around on the floor. Finally someone stuffed it in its basket to shut it up! The leader of this farewell was Mme. Saboyombo. Sometime back John Saboyombo asked Margery for some advice. He wanted to get married, and he showed her the two names he was considering. To his surprise, Margery suggested a third girl. Today, after twenty-four years of happy marriage, his wife Georgette was there to thank her once again and say "good-bye."

Oh yes! There were fellow missionaries to see her off! Colleagues from four different stations gathered at Sibut to fellowship and to wish her the very best. Across the room hung a banner reading, "Faithful is He that calleth you, who also will do it" (I Thessalonians 5:24). I saw a video of that gathering. And by the way, there were some interesting stories passed around! What fond memories they must have! But have you ever wondered what happens when the NURSE herself is down with malaria? Who gives HER the shots? Ask Margo Muhr! And then Margery was presented with a beautiful gold chain necklace. I mean REAL gold, not just the color gold!

But there's more to come. In between all the people knocking on her door to see if she was leaving *biani* [for really], there was the task of getting rid of her things. UGH! Margery told me that at one point she had twenty-seven garbage bags surrounding her. 'You had THAT much JUNK?' I asked her. No. Twenty-seven was the number of families attending Bible School at Sibut.

She was busy organizing stuff for the students—clothing, books, pens, pencils, sewing supplies, etc.

She also had a smart dog. Her German Shepherd, Bingo, knew something was up! When it came her turn to leave for Ippy to keep another missionary nurse safe, Margery had to lead her down the hill and then hand her over to nurse June. Did you know it's hard to say good-bye to more than just people?

On to Bangui! Oops, I did forget one thing. It happened to be "stink bug season" at Sibut. So, even when Margery was done with all the packing, one poor African helper had to complete the FINAL task— sweeping up all the STINKBUGS! (Sure, it's been twelve whole years, but I will never forget those stinkbugs as long as I live!)

Now on to Bangui, where there was one more of those farewell get-togethers! Some years ago, a sixteen-year old came to work for Margery in the dispensary as a "clean-up boy." Now a pastor in Bangui, he invited her to his home to

Margery's last day in Sibut with the missionaries at the station. From left, standing: Alice Peterson, Lynn Muhr and daughter Jennifer Muhr, Vernon Rosenau and son Samuel. Sitting left: Margo Muhr, Margery, Jan Rosenau with son Billy Rosenau in front.

say good-bye. Eleven pastors and twelve young people came there to see her for the last time this side of the rapture.

And that just about wraps it up. Oh yes, you're still wondering about the *Boggle* game. Well, somewhere in the air between Paris and Washington, D.C., Margery found a novel way to witness to an Irish girl. You know— play a simple little game, get a conversation started, steer it in the right direction. Don't know why I never thought of it myself!

Just to get back to the American way of doing things, Margery missed her scheduled flight into Charleston. She made it in on the next flight and spent a week visiting her sister in Jacksonville before stopping to see us on her way to see another sister in Mexico. She hasn't yet learned about that "coming apart to REST!" We took her back to the airport all too soon after picking her up there. As my son watched the plane take off he said, "Look Mommy! It goes up dwust like a dwet!" " Well, why wouldn't it?" I answered him. "IT IS a dwet...I mean JET!"

Thank you, Margery, for including us. I was indeed honored for my husband and my three children to meet the missionary I worked with for a short time over twelve years ago!

(Signed) Judy Stanton (Cagle)

In Seattle there was a four-room, furnished co-op apartment with a picture window view of the Puget Sound and the Olympic Mountains waiting for me. My friend of fifty years, Erma Swanson Sowers, had willed it to me when she died in February 1993. Jean Hayes had cleaned and prepared the apartment and helped to introduce me again to life in the United States.

How true are the words of Jesus, "Seek ye first the kingdom of God, and his righteousness; and all these things shall be added unto you" (Matthew 6:33). Isn't it great that we have such an awesome God who keeps his promises? If I were young again and knew what my life would be like in Africa, and the Lord called me, I would certainly go and *DO IT AGAIN!*

I t was always the goal of our mission to train the Africans we served so that they would be able to take over the work when we missionaries left. I was privileged to see some of this occur in my lifetime. As of the printing of this book, only eleven missionaries from Baptist Mid-Missions are still in Central African Republic. The missionaries role today is one of support and encouragement for the national church. Missionaries are still teaching in the schools, maintaining the critical literature program, and helping with the maintenance of the infrastructure of ministry but they are not in the leadership roles. Nationals supply the leadership and initiative for the daily ministry.

The Bible School in Sibut is now under the direction of Pastor Rene Malepou, and he is also the president of the association of 430 churches planted by pastors trained in the several Bible Schools. The medical work in Sibut is now in the capable hands of John Saboyambo. The clinic in Bangassou and the hospital in Ippy are also continuing under African management. The thirteen mission stations once started by Baptist Mid-Missions now provide Bible classes through the Africans who have assumed those responsibilities. The Jeunesse Evangelique Africaine youth corps and the summer youth camps continue to reach thousands of children through their African leadership.

For myself, retirement from the mission field did not mean retirement from ministry. The Pacific Northwest part of the United States is the most un-churched area of our country. Less than 10 percent of the people attend

Pastor Rene Malepou and Mme Henriette Malepou.

a church of any kind. Many people attending churches in my neighborhood area of Capital Hill in Seattle, Washington are deluded into thinking that because God is love (which He is), everyone will be with Him in eternity. My Bible says something quite different. The mission field is all around me.

I still attend the church that originally sent me out on the mission field all those years ago, Tabernacle Baptist, though they moved their facilities out of my neighborhood due to expansion restrictions. I am privileged to be a deaconess there and to serve as the missions secretary. I have the joy of reading all of the emails and letters from missionaries supported by our church who are serving all over the world, then providing a summary report to the congregation. I am glad for this opportunity to stay in touch with so many different missionaries.

Recently a new church has been started within walking distance of my apartment. It is called Via Crucis (The Way of the Cross). I sometimes go there to be a part of their congregation. I am encouraged to see a Bible preaching church in my neighborhood.

For the last six years I have been working with the Union Gospel Mission here in Seattle. This large mission has one of their facilities within walking distance of my home and so I have been privileged to work in their prison and senior ministries.

I have "met" many prisoners by correcting Bible correspondence courses, originally from inmates all over the United States and most recently only here in Washington State. For a time I ministered to the women of the King County Jail and saw what terrible things drug abuse can do to your life.

Doing this work has also opened the door for me to make regular visits to Monroe State Correctional Center, where I help with worship services. This means I get to meet some of the inmates face to face, not only grade their correspondence work. What is more, I get to play the Christian hymns I love so much—those piano lessons so many years ago have proved valuable.

Once a week I teach a Bible Study for seniors—a new experience for me —and I am fortunate to visit those seniors who are unable to leave their hospitals and nursing homes.

As I write this, I am planning to move from Seattle to Lynden, Washington, (just six miles from the Canadian border), where I can live near two of my brothers and their families. I do not know what awaits me there, but just like every other phase of my life, the Lord will guide my path.

One advantage of living alone now, and not having a rigid schedule, is that I can spend more time in Bible study and prayer. The title of a song written by Bill Gaither expresses my thoughts. "The Longer I Serve Him the Sweeter He Grows."

The mission I served with, Baptist Mid-Missions, today is literally covering the globe with the Gospel of Jesus Christ. Comprised of 1100 missionaries working in 51 foreign countries and North America supported by a church constituency of 8000 strong. Ministry opportunities are many and varied. Some of the current ministry opportunities are: church planting, camping, literacy ministry, Bible translation, missionary aviation, theological education, field business administration, missionary kid education, medical missions and media ministries. New opportunities are constantly being launched in the cause of global outreach for Jesus Christ. For more information contact:

Baptist Mid-Missions
P.O. Box 308011
7749 Webster Road
Cleveland, Ohio 44130-8011
Email: info@bmm.org
Web: www.bmm.org